# Computer

# Music

# in

# Computer Music in C

Phil Winsor & Gene DeLisa

FIRST EDITION/SECOND PRINTING

© 1991 by **Phil Winsor and Gene DeLisa**.
Published by **Windcrest Books**, an imprint of TAB BOOKS.
TAB BOOKS is a division of McGraw-Hill, Inc.
The name "Windcrest" is a registered trademark of TAB BOOKS.

**Library of Congress Cataloging-in-Publication Data**

Winsor, Phil, 1938 –
    Computer music in C / by Phil Winsor and Gene DeLisa.
      p.    cm.
    Includes index.
    ISBN 0-8306-3637-4 (pbk.)
    1. Computer sound processing.   2. C (Computer program language)
I. DeLisa, Gene.  II. Title.
MT723.W56  1990
780'.285'5133—dc20                    90-39710
                                        CIP
                                       MN

TAB BOOKS offers software for sale. For information and a catalog, please contact TAB Software Department, Blue Ridge Summit, PA 17294-0850.

Questions regarding the content of this book should be addressed to:

**Reader Inquiry Branch**
**TAB BOOKS**
**Blue Ridge Summit, PA 17294-0850**

Acquisitions Editor: Ron Powers
Technical Editor: David M. Harter
Production: Katherine G. Brown

# Contents

# *Preface*

This book is intended to be an ever-growing collection of procedures and functions that serve either synthetic or analytic compositional goals. It is hoped that this volume will expand over time, reflecting contributions of compositional algorithms by composers active in the area of experimental music.

For the first edition, we have selected routines organized into six groups that are of importance to computer-assisted composition. Before delving into the subroutines piecemeal, it is suggested that the reader become acquainted with the nature and scope of the algorithms by examining the descriptions in the Program Guide.

Because this book is a reference work, detailed applications and musical examples have been omitted. Our objective is to present a wide selection of useful algorithms in a relatively small space, leaving detailed discussion of specific musical contexts to a future volume on algorithmic composition.

The software was developed on an IBM PC-AT using Borland's Turbo C programming language. The functions have been kept as trim as possible to illuminate their structure. Driver programs have been included to obviate the need for input data test statements that would pad program code considerably and diminish clarity. (Remember that, in interactive use, the functions will require additional statements to make them user-proof.)

# Introduction

This book contains programs and C functions grouped in six broad categories: Utilities, series and motive operations, probability distribution functions, sorting and searching, sound/text composition, and general composition (including MIDI adaptation procedures). Keep in mind that the presentation of an algorithm in a particular category simply reflects its garb. A process contained in a string-handling function, for example, might be equally useful in manipulating integers; specifics of coding, however, limit its immediate application to ASCII text characters.

Each function, or function group, is preceded by a page of preliminary remarks explaining the purpose, pointing out usage considerations, and offering programming ideas. A complete program and function group listing follows, along with program execution printout.

The structure of this book mirrors its intended use: as a modular library of procedures and functions available for immediate use. Therefore, although it might be desirable to read the book cover-to-cover, it is not necessary. The "Program guide" at the front of the book offers an overview and is intended to serve those who wish to scan the library for specific procedures and functions.

Most of the main programs and functions are "hardwired" to allow their presentation in stripped-down form. Therefore, anyone wishing to modify the programs for interactive use should add functions to accept user input, code to test viability of data entered from the terminal, and prompts to guide the program user. Arrays should also be redimensioned to accommodate variable-size output requests.

## TURBO C

All programs in this text were developed and written using Borland's Turbo C programming language. Most or all of them should run in other C language environments with little or no alteration.

# INTRODUCTION TO C LANGUAGE FUNDAMENTALS

This quick introduction to the C language is not designed to teach the C language, but rather to enable composers to read the algorithms in this book. There are several million (or so it seems) introductory C texts on the market; I refer you to them for a more complete introduction. Actually, the compiler manuals are usually the best source.

The functions in this book have been developed with several compilers in different environments. On NTSU's Vaxen under UNIX and VMS, and on IBM PCs using Turbo C version 1.5 and Microsoft C version 5.0, we have tried to make the code as portable as possible and, have included code for some functions that are not included in many compilers (fpower( ) for example) to increase portability. If such functions are included in the compiler's library, please substitute them.

## Functions

C is a highly structured language. Everything is accomplished by separate functions. A *function* is simply several lines of code that do one thing. There is one special function called "main" that calls every other function. The classic example C program:

```
main( )
{
    printf("Good morning, world?");
}
```

The parentheses after the word "main" tell the compiler that "main" is a function. The opening and closing braces signal the beginning and end of the function. In this example, main( ) calls another function named printf( ). Within the parentheses, arguments are passed to the function. There are no arguments to main( ), but printf( ) is given a string of characters.

You can see what main( ) does because the code is in front of you, but where is printf( )? Usually the programmer needs to define everything in the program. In the case of common functions like printf( ), function definitions are located in files outside of the user's own program. All the programmer must do is tell the c compiler where they are. There are different ways of including files. One way is to start the program with include statements, as follows:

```
#include <stdio.h>
```

This statement tells the computer that it needs to find the file named stdio.h and insert it into the present program at the current line. The second way is to compile functions into object code and then link the object modules together. In this case, the compilation of the user's program will take less time, but the link time will be greater. It is common to have each function of large programs kept in a separate file. The program might be named Main.c. Another file might be Pitchconvert.c. Depending on the programming environment, there might be programs that will help in program maintenance. One such program is called Make. Make keeps track of which functions are needed by the program, and updates the files when changes are made.

The elements of a function definition are:

1. function declaration
2. parameter declarations
3. variable declarations
4. statements or function calls
5. comments

## Function declaration

The *function declaration* specifies the name of the function and the data type of its return value. For example:

```
int test( )
```

This is a declaration of a function named "test" which returns an integer value. To many compilers, the return type is assumed to be integer if not specified.

## Parameter declarations

Parameters are variables that are passed to a function from another function. The data types of these variables must be declared.

```
int test2(junk, array)
int junk;
float array[ ];
```

Here function test2( ) is passed two parameters, "junk" and "array." The names of the parameters are given within the function's parentheses followed by the declaration of their data types: an integer variable and an array of floating point numbers. This format is the most common and portable. Newer compilers support a format similar to Pascal where the data type declarations are contained within the parentheses, as follows:

```
int test(int junk, float array[ ])
```

## Variable declarations

The data types of local variables must then be declared. Local variables are used only within the function, and their values are lost when the program exits the function.

```
int test( )
{
int j;
char c;
} /* end of function */
```

The local variables are declared after the opening brace.

## Statements

A *statement* consists of variables, constants, keywords and operators. Keywords are part of the definition of the C language. There are only 28 keywords (fewer or greater depending on the age of your compiler) in C. Keywords and operators are listed below. Statements are terminated by a semicolon.

```
j = 128;
```

This is an assignment statement. The variable "j" is assigned the value 128 with the assignment operator "=."

```
for (j = 0; j < 10; j+ +)
    puts ("Vaffanculo!");
```

The statement is a loop that prints a character string ten times. The loop consists of the keyword "for," an assignment of the loop's starting value (j = 0), the condition being tested (j < 10), and an increment statement (j+ +). This "for" statement is read:

> begin with j set to zero;
> if j is less than 10,
> increment j and
> execute the following line.

The library function puts( ) is called 10 times, each time with the same parameter.

## Comments

*Comments* are enclosed by a slash-star star-slash pair. For example:

```
/* this is a comment */
```

Comments are ignored by the compiler. They should be used frequently to document source code. Comments are also useful in program development. Statements that are being tested can be "commented out" and thus will be ignored by the compiler.

C keywords:

| | |
|---|---|
| auto | if |
| break | int |
| case | long |
| char | register |
| continue | return |
| default | short |
| do | sizeof |
| double | static |
| else | struct |
| entry | switch |
| extern | typedef |
| float | union |
| for | unsigned |
| goto | while |

## Variables and data types

Before a variable can be used, its data type must be declared. The *data type* of a variable represents how it is to be stored in memory.

| C data types | Description |
|---|---|
| int | integer |
| float | floating point |
| double | double precision floating point |
| char | character |
| FILE * | pointer to file |
| int * | pointer to integer |
| char * | pointer to character |
| float * | pointer to float |
| double * | pointer to double |
| enum | enumerated data type |
| struct | structure |
| void | |
| volatile | |
| auto | |

Data type modifiers:

extern
far
near
huge
short
long
register
signed
unsigned
static

The following program uses an integer variable:

```
main( )
{
    int j;
    for (j = 0; j < 10; j+ +)
        printf("What's up, Jack? ");
}
```

In this example, we have used a loop to print the message 10 times. The "for" statement is read "set j to zero, then while j is less than 10 execute the next statement and increment j." Within the "for" statement there are several operators used. The = and the < operators are the same as in arithmetic. The + + operator increments the variable by one. It is necessary to make certain that a value is assigned to a compatible data type (assignment of an integer to a variable of type int, for example).

Operators:

| | |
|---|---|
| + + | increment |
| – – | decrement |
| ~ | bitwise not |
| ^ | bitwise exclusive or XOR |
| ¦ | bitwise or |
| < < | bitwise shift left |
| > > | bitwise shift right |
| ! | logical not |
| && | logical and |
| ¦ ¦ | logical or |
| & | address of |
| / | division |
| + | addition |
| – | subtraction |
| = = | equal to |
| != | inequality |
| < | less than |
| > | greater than |

| | |
|---|---|
| < = | less than or equal to |
| > = | greater than or equal to |
| ? : | conditional |
| = | assignment |
| operator = | compound assignment |
| , | expression evaluation |
| % | modulus |
| . | structure member. structure.member |
| -> | structure member. structure->member same as (*structure).member (the structure is a pointer) |

When a function is used to calculate a value that is returned, the function must specify which data type is returned. The default type is integer. For example:

```
main()
{
    float value;
    float calculate();
    value = calculate();
} /* end of main function */
/*===============================*/
float calculate()
{
    float a = 2.2
    int b = 5;
    return (a * b);
} /* end of function */
/*===============================*/
```

Here we declare the return value of calculate( ) to be of type float (which matches the data type of value).

## Pointers

A *pointer* is a variable that holds the memory address of another variable. Pointers are necessary when using large data structures such as files. To illustrate:

```
main()
{
 int j;
 int *jp;

 j = 2;      /* j is assigned the value 2 */
 jp = &j;    /* jp is assigned the address of j */

 printf("The value of j is %d which is  stored at  location %u",
        j,jp);
 *jp = 10;      /* 10 is stored at the address contained in jp */
                /* this is the same as: j = 10;      */
 printf("The value  of j  is %d which is stored at location %u",
        j,jp);
} /* end of main function */
```

In this example, "j" is declared to be of type "int" and "jp" of type pointer to "int." "j" is assigned an integer value (2) and "jp" is assigned the address of j. Another common use of pointers is character strings. There are two ways that a string may be declared: as a character array and as a pointer to type char.

```
char string[10];
char *string2;
```

Here "string" is declared to be an array of ten characters; "string2" is declared as a pointer. It is usually necessary to allocate memory for the pointer with the following statement:

```
string = (char *) malloc (80)
```

## Example program

```c
/* comments are enclosed by star-slash combinations */
#include <stdio.h>   /* preprocessor statements;  stdio.h is
                         not in  the current directory */
#include "array.c"   /* array.c is in the current directory */
#define MAXDATA 500
int junk;            /* global variable declaration */

/* function prototype */
void TestFunction(int datarray[], int size);

main()               /* start of main function */
{
   register int j;         /* local variable declarations */
   int *jp;
   int datarray[MAXDATA], num;
   char string[10];
   char ch;

   for(j = 0; j < 10; j++)    /* loop with several  statements */
       {
        printf("Enter a number "); /* function call */
        scanf("%d", &num);          /* the  address of num is passed
                                       to scanf() */
        datarray[j] = num;       /* assign the  value  of  num  to
                                    datarray */
       }                         /* end loop */
   TestFunction(datarray, 10);    /* function call */
} /* end of main function */
/*====================================*/
void TestFunction(datarray, size)  /* definition of function */
int datarray[], size;  /* types of parameters passed to
                          function */

{ /* body of function */
 register int j;    /* local variable definition */

 for(j = 0; j < size; j++)    /* loop through  array */
     datarray[j] += 2;        /* add 2 to each element    */
} /* end of function */
/*====================================*/
```

# *Program Guide*

## Chapter 2: Utilities

## Chapter 3: Series and motive operations

## Chapter 4: Probability distribution functions

## Chapter 5: Sorting and searching

# Chapter 6: Sound/Text composition

# Chapter 7: General composition

# 1
# *Music intelligence and MIDI*

What is "music intelligence," and how can it benefit the musician? This question is the first to come from musicians, and non-musicians, when they are told that the computer has assumed as important a role in music as it has in other disciplines. The answer to how music intelligence can benefit the musician is: the computer is suited to the performance of a wide range of tasks, and will perform those tasks just as readily for musicians as it does for scientists. In the process, it can exhibit characteristics of (human) intelligence.

To precisely define music intelligence is as difficult as to precisely define artificial intelligence, because the complex mixture of skills and talents that comprise human intelligence is not well understood. Through introspection and careful observation, superficial, logical and cognitive functions can be identified—such as the ability to store, recall, compare, model, extrapolate, and parse various data structures—but the workings of the most powerful wellspring of creative activity, the subconscious intelligence, remains elusive and largely uncharted. Until a deeper comprehension of the breadth of human intellectual activity and the dynamics of its component processes is achieved, a temporary definition must suffice:

> Music intelligence is research into methods of making the computer more cognizant of and powerful over the manipulation and organization of musical materials, structures, and systems.

## Uses of music intelligence

Although the immediate goals and rewards of computer applications in the arts might seem less important for society than for science, the methods and procedures of data processing will serve the creative artist at

1

play as unquestioningly as they serve the biochemist in search of a cure for cancer or the material scientist at work on the purification of microprocessor chips.

What can the computer contribute to the musical arts, born of the human soul? Is it really possible to treat music as something that can be quantified, tested, and systematically codified in the same way that you would develop and study a computer-simulated model of a new space craft?

Although it might be argued that the act of creating a spiritually moving piece of music remains a mystery (Esthetics, the philosophy of artistic value systems, is still not able to adequately explain how and why an art object comes to be considered beautiful), care must be taken not to transpose this view to other, more accessible dimensions of musical structure.

Leaving aside the *act* of creation, almost every domain in music is susceptible to computational methods. The question to ask is not "Is it possible to apply the computer to problem-solving in music?," but rather "How can computers be applied in a meaningful way, and what is the best frame of reference for its application?"

## Conceptual overview

Computer music in general can be divided into two primary categories: sound production methods (commercial synthesizers) and music composition methods. When computer music began, as explained in a later chapter, both sound production and compositional processes were carried out in a single environment—the mainframe computer. However, over several decades these areas became distinct through the advent of viable realtime, microprocessor-based music performance devices. Today, the personal computer often fills the role of composer/performer while the synthesizer acts as the instrument of performance, in the same way that people have traditionally played acoustic instruments. It is likely that, as technology advances, there will be a reunification of these separate functions within a single piece of hardware. On a small scale, it already exists in the form of built-in sequencing capability found in some synthesizers. These devices allow the performer to play a musical passage that will be retained in the instrument's memory, and which can be recalled for execution at a later time. This internal sequencer acts as a performance command center, issuing instructions about when to play specific notes, how loudly to play them, and how long to continue them.

## Music research applications

Investigators in each musical subdiscipline are devising ways to enlist the computer's help in solving musical problems. Some of the major research areas are:

1. Algorithmic and Automated Composition
2. Music Theory Expert Systems

3. Computer-Aided Instruction
4. Musicology
5. Performance
6. Psychoacoustic Phenomena (Cognition)
7. Physics of Sound
8. Architectural Acoustics
9. Performance Environment Simulation
10. Ecological (sonic environment) Acoustics
11. Esthetic Perception Theory
12. General System Theory, Information Theory
13. Intermedia Explorations (multidisciplinary events comprised of multiple information media, such as choreography, video, film, laser imagery, light sculpture, and music)

I will now discuss several of these fields in greater detail.

## Composition

Composition heads the list of Music Research Areas, because the "putting-together" (modeling, simulation, designing) of musical structures provides solutions to problems encountered in the remaining music research areas. These areas are heavily model-oriented. Research situations normally require the formulation of a strategy or paradigm (conceptual frame of reference) before there is work for the computer to perform, and in music the composer has traditionally filled this role.

Some of the important research categories are:

1. Algorithmic composition: application of data transformation procedures to sound structures.
2. Automated music: study of self-determining, self-controlling music composition systems based on algorithms which favor a particular musical style.
3. Experimental music systems and structures: General system theory, stochastic music and information theory.
4. Studies in the internal structure of musical sound: Music tone color research aided by direct synthesis techniques.

**Algorithmic composition**   Music composition can be defined as the process of selecting from a finite set of elements (pitches, rhythms, tone-colors, etc.) certain possibilities over others for presentation as a work of art.

In music composition, as in computer science, algorithms are detailed instructions for the successful execution of a particular series of tasks. One simple example is to create a melodic line by programming the computer to apply certain criteria in the selection of tones from a pitch scale. Instructions for this algorithm can be written in pseudocode as:

1. Select at random a note from the seven tones of the C-Major pitch scale.

2. Search the program rule-base (list) for criteria to test the viability of selected tones.
3. Apply the rule to the candidate melody note.
4. If the note passes the test, add it to the list of accepted melody notes; advance notelist counter; Goto 1.
5. If the note fails the rule test, Goto 1.

Whether aware of it or not, composers have always used algorithms to create (select) music, but in the past they had to rely entirely on the power of their internal personal computer (brain) for the execution of various procedures. As a consequence, many potentially fruitful structural and organizational models lay dormant in the minds of composers because of the inordinate amount of human time and effort required for their realization.

**Symbiosis**  Beginning about 1950, composers began to employ their computers as a tireless assistant in the fleshing out of musical structures. Of these, two composer/experimenters—Lejaren A. Hiller in the United States and Iannis Xenakis in France—independently contributed many important precedents to computer music composition. They are generally considered by the professional music community to be the fathers of algorithmic composition by computer. As a consequence of their work, it quickly became apparent that, not only could the computer precisely and unerringly generate complex musical textures, but it was also an unforeseen source of inspiration. Through speculative experiment, and the simulation of novel contexts, composers discovered a virtually unlimited means of expanding their aural imagination. A symbiolic relationship quickly developed between man and machine.

At present, the all-important compositional function cannot be provided by microprocessor-based synthesizers. Perhaps in the future, manufacturers will market devices containing algorithmic composition software. But for now the personal computer—serving as host to one programming language or another (BASIC, FORTRAN, C, or PASCAL)—is the environment increasingly used by contemporary composers for the creation of music scores.

# Music theory

The primary research focus of Music Theory is the description of musical systems as exhibited by the works of composers from various periods in the history of music. Stylistic models are analyzed and resynthesized as a test of theoretical systems.

Music theory's practical side relates to its position at the core of the academic musical curriculum. Its central goal is to impart a deeper understanding of music interpretation by teaching students to compose examples modeled after ancient musical forms. Due to the widespread reliance on core theory courses, interest in the related area of computer-assisted instruction has grown rapidly since 1975.

Some music theory research areas are:

1. Formulation of descriptive theoretical systems.
2. Development of analytical tools for the validation of theoretical hypotheses.
3. Design of expert systems for the simulation of significant musical styles of ancient historical periods: Palestrina, Bach, etc.
4. Analytic/synthetic expert systems.

## Computer-aided instruction

Researchers in each of the primary musical areas are interested in the application of the computer to teaching situations. As instructional systems continue to develop, more time will become available for classroom teachers to deal with problems more worthy of their time than the routine preparation of testing and training exercises. The most intense efforts to prepare effective computerized teaching materials are to be found in the area of Music Theory, but teachers of the performance of traditional musical instruments might soon be able to benefit from software that analyzes and diagnoses particular problems that a performer might have with regard to tone production and quality.

## Musicology

Musicology can be thought of as the archaeology of music. It is the broadest of all musical subdisciplines, encompassing aspects of each of the others. It deals with the discovery and study of musical information having a bearing on contemporary understanding of ancient musical styles, of performance practices, and of their relationship to the culture of a particular epoch.

Some current research areas are:

1. Comparative study usage (related to area (3) of music theory research—expert systems).
2. Research in cross-referencing and indexing of salient stylistic features (database).
3. Comparative study of linguistic/musical structural models.

## Psychoacoustic phenomenology

The composer, as well as the theorist, is concerned with matters arising from the characteristics of human perception. Not only are people perceptually constrained by the physical limitations of their perception systems, but also the relationship between external stimuli and the interpretations placed on them by the brain requires much more research before scientific knowledge about cognitive processes can be considered adequate. For instance, the roles played by long- and short-term memory in the human's perception of esthetic events is of great interest to composers and music theorists alike. At present, all artists rely upon an intuitive comprehension of the dynamics of perception—a risky situation at best. Undoubtedly, future discoveries in this area will enhance the composer's ability to predict the effects of musical structures on the listener, thereby eliminating a great deal of guesswork in the projection of musical patterns and forms.

## Performance environment simulation

Until recently, the acoustics of enclosed music performance spaces were solely the province of architectural acousticians—professionals who study the characteristics of various shapes and sizes of rooms, as well as the attributes of diverse building materials—to arrive at concert hall designs that will satisfy the musical ear with respect to acoustic presence, clarity, and a host of other qualities. Until recently, musicians served primarily as consultants to these acousticians, lending their ears to help evaluate room characteristics such as sound dispersion, attenuation, resonance, image placement, reverberation decay time, and so on.

Over the past few years, the role of the musician in determining acoustical properties of performance spaces has expanded dramatically, due to the development of sophisticated digital devices for the simulation of a broad range of room types. The application of sound reinforcement, imaging, and aural location theory to sonic environment configuration has produced a state-of-the-art in which the virtual size, shape, and acoustical characteristics of diverse performance environments can be simulated regardless of the physical characteristics of the host enclosure.

A number of companies have been formed to promulgate this new technology; foremost among them is the Good Sound Foundation of Woodside, California, which specializes in the installation of digital acoustic alteration systems in pre-existent structures. Founded and operated by musicians (the president is a composer), Good Sound believes that musicians themselves are the best qualified experts to determine optimum acoustics for the performance of various musical styles and media.

In the past, concert halls have been designed with the objective of accommodating soloists, chamber ensembles, and full orchestras. To achieve this goal, compromises were made which rendered an ideal acoustical setting nearly impossible for any specific medium. At most, one could hope that the acoustics would not be disastrous for all types of musical events. The day is now at hand when the musician can "tune" the performance space to suit the qualities of the music to be performed—from a warm, intimate atmosphere amenable to a solo piano recital, to the dryer acoustical environment required for some types of orchestral music. In fact, it is conceivable to digitally reconfigure a performance space between concert pieces in order to support the musical intentions of the composers.

## Ecological (sonic environment) acoustics

At first glance this research area might seem to be remote from the interests of musicians, because it deals with levels, types, and severity of sound pollution. However, musicians are likely to be more sensitive to hazardous noise environments than nonmusicians, giving them the motivation to use their discriminatory talents for abatement research.

There is a second side to the ecology of sound: if some sound environments produce negative effects on the human being, what are the characteristics of environments that generate a sense of well-being, reduced stress, and increased productivity? This area is probably most attractive to the composer/musician, because he has spent a good deal of time increasing his sensitivity to the characteristics of sound in general, and to positive sonic environments in particular.

## Information theory and esthetic perception

This area was born around 1955 through the work of Abraham Moles. Dr. Moles' classic, "Information Theory and Esthetic Perception" (1966, University of Illinois Press, Urbana) laid the groundwork for a fresh approach to theoretical work in the field of esthetics by bringing to bear on artistic objects the analytic methods normally associated with mathematics—probability theory and integral calculus. It can be said that information theory (relative to musical esthetics) deals with the quantification, and categorization of time-related transformation processes, and with the autocorrelation of constituent layers of musical experiences. A theoretical distinction is drawn between information flow across a perceptual channel as a materially quantifiable phenomenon and the meaning of the messages carried by the information medium. To understand this concept, consider the traditional dot-dash signals that make up the international morse code alphabet. To an observer unskilled in deciphering coded messages, the patterns transmitted are nothing more than raw information containing a high degree of repetition (redundancy); but, to the trained telegrapher, the quantitative information flow is loaded with meaning, carried by a set of symbolic conventions agreed upon in advance by sender and receiver for the transmission of intelligible ideas.

## Practical applications of research outcomes

Pure research eventually spawns many useful products and devices for the carrying out of routine tasks in everyday life. The music industry has been the beneficiary of an uncommonly large number of these gifts over the past decade.

The most notable catalyst to musical productivity was developed during the 1970s by Dr. John Chowning, a Stanford University Computer Music Researcher. His theoretical work in the area of FM (frequency modulation) sound synthesis techniques gave rise to a generation of powerful digital sound generating devices produced by a number of MIDI synthesizer manufacturers, such as the Yamaha Company's TX81-Z and New England Digital Corporation's Synclavier II.

Polyphonic (many-voiced), multitimbral (multiple tone-color), synthesizers have revolutionized every dimension of commercial music production because they can convincingly emulate the sound qualities of traditional acoustic instruments such as the violin, clarinet, or trumpet. Indeed, when listening to music broadcast by radio and television, it is frequently difficult even for the trained musician to discover whether the music springs from a natural or synthetic source.

The crafts of orchestration and arranging have been especially well served by technology in recent years. In pre-MIDI days, arrangers and orchestrators usually experienced a large time gap between the conception and realization of music designed for a television or movie production. This condition could be hazardous, especially if the arranger's future employment depended on the production director's immediate approval of a particular musical sequence. Understandably, arrangers were not inclined to take risks; they relied heavily on hackneyed techniques which were certain to work reliably, if not interestingly, in a particular dramatic context, leading to a shopworn handbook of musical cliches called "stock arrangements."

The invention of the MIDI-interfaced synthesizer configuration has eliminated the delay between conception and manifestation to the extent that today it is possible for the arranger/orchestrator to explore more challenging musical ideas without chancing a loss of livelihood). All experiments can be performed and evaluated quickly in the privacy of the arranger's studio, away from the critical ear of the producer.

**Classroom environment**  One important fringe benefit of the rapid evolution of digital music-handling software and hardware since 1982 (the birth of MIDI) is the ease with which musical examples and training materials can be presented. Formerly, courses such as harmony, counterpart, and orchestration relied upon the teacher's ability to perform materials at the piano keyboard, while they gave instructions to the students to imagine one example or another as performed by various instrumental or vocal ensembles. Today, the same illustrations are experienced and manipulated effortlessly by digital equipment and software designed for teaching. Every subject in the music curriculum has been affected by this technology.

## Future research and development

Although it is impossible to foresee with certainty the direction research will take in the coming years, products will undoubtedly be developed in the following areas:

1. Music notation optical scanning devices, along with software to

interpret various notation systems and automatically perform music scores on MIDI synthesizers.

2. Devices and software to digitally sample music improvised by various acoustic instrument ensembles and convert it to music notation.

3. Complex sound synthesis devices, built-into personal computers.

4. Automatic composition software geared to the needs of the entertainment industry (programs that will instantly compose music in a variety of styles).

## ROLE OF *MIDI*

MIDI, Musical Instrument Digital Interface, was originally devised to allow synthesizers to transmit data to each other. During the late 1970s, popular musicians approached instrument manufacturers to find a way to eliminate the need for the elaborate configuration of keyboards (usually of different makes) that had to be transported from concert to concert to ensure maximum variety in the orchestration of various songs. Each synthesizer typically produced a characteristic sound quality, and the insatiable ear of the rock musician demanded an array of equipment that filled the stage with rows of keyboards. To play them all, the performer constantly moved from position to position as each new sound quality was needed.

In 1982, the needs of commercial musicians were answered in the form of MIDI protocol—a communications standard that designers agreed to follow when developing future synthesizers. By accepting the MIDI standard, a manufacturer could be assured that his device would be able to send and receive musical data from synthesizers made by other manufacturers.

The performing musician was finally able to produce a musical passage on one keyboard and hear it simultaneously played on several other MIDI synthesizers; they were responding to the transmitted musical data, played at the master keyboard, recorded as digital command information (what key was pressed, how long it was held down, etc.), and passed on to the slave devices.

Shortly after MIDI emerged, it was extended to include the personal computer as the controlling link in the chain connecting one synthesizer to another. Software was quickly written to record, store, edit, and play back lengthy musical passages (called *sequences*, or *notelists*) on command, opening a dimension of musical texture previously out of reach to the individual performer: the ability to behave as an entire ensemble from a single keyboard. Countermelodies and harmonizations could be prepared in advance and stored in disk files until needed during the performance of a particular piece, thereby releasing the musician from the task of remembering which keyboard to reach for to get the appropriate sound quality.

Around 1985, software designers began to provide programs that would convert ASCII data files, generated as the output of compositional algorithms and coded in a programming language such as C or Pascal, to sequence files performable by synthesizers. Although initially of more interest to researchers and composers affiliated with universities, this resource is rapidly growing in popularity among commercial musicians, and will certainly become the stimulus for a wave of Automatic Composition software for the popular music market.

## THE *MIDI* COMMUNICATIONS INTERFACE:
## Music representation within the computer

Present music notation is a synthesis of logical, symbolic, and graphic (also called *iconic*) elements—a hybrid system that has evolved over hundreds of years and which requires considerable practice to master. Although it allows people to communicate their musical thoughts to one another reasonably well, it is of no use in communicating with computers unless it is converted to machine language.

Because the computer is actually only a complex network of many on/off switches—whose positions are symbolically represented as either low or high, 0 or 1—a method must be devised to meaningfully translate musical information into patterns of binary state switches. This process requires many considerations, but it is convenient to think of it on two different planes: the conceptual and the practical.

## Conceptual perspective

The computer is indifferent to your mental processes. It is not concerned at all with your logical patterns and methods of conceptualizing musical data. You look upon musical styles and systems from many viewpoints; you classify, organize, and group musical events in ways that reflect your physical, psychological and intellectual biases. Therefore, the issue of musical structure and its comprehension by human beings is "precomputational." And, although critically important to effective application of the machine to algorithmic composition, it is an isolated step in the interaction between man and the switching network. Moreover, the method of music conceptualization is usually bound to the orientation of the computer user.

A great deal of research has been done relative to effective systematization of the conceptual framework for the symbolic representation of music. Many different perspectives have emerged in an attempt to accurately model within the computer the salient features of identifiable musical styles and systems. Two important modeling categories are symbolic and procedural approaches.

## Symbolic (grammatical) representation

This perspective considers musical systems to be representative of specific musical "languages," or systems in which the music score contains symbols (signs) that conform to a particular style or grammar. The grammar is defined by the rhetoric it employs—that is by the hierarchically determined, interrelated sets of principles that govern the choices of specific values on the horizontal (melodic) and vertical (harmonic) planes from moment to moment in a sample composition. Often, large databases must be employed to hold the musical style that will be consulted for making a style example. This (linguistic) approach to a musical system is currently of great interest to artificial intelligence researchers in the areas of music theory and musicology—and to a lesser extent, to composers who wish to design Expert Systems to analyze and project further extensions of their personal composing styles.

**Theory versus composition**  The theorist and musicologist see musical structures differently from the composer. While the composer's primary concern is to make music, the analyst's primary concern is with finding the rules that describe a piece of music. One example of this divergence of viewpoint can be found in the "outside-time" notion of a musical system as implemented during the so-called common practice period (roughly 1650–1900). Functional tonality dominated musical structure to an extent that it was virtually impossible to consider alternatives. The analytical, declarative method which evolved to characterize the important relationships of forms and event-structures during this period illustrated the role of symbolic notation in the identification and communication of patterns within familiar musical systems. When you refer to the musical syntax, grammar, or rhetoric of musical examples from functional tonality, you rely almost totally on the symbolic notation of tertian chordal structures and their connective relationships on the immediate level, local level and on a deeper, global (Schenkerian) structural level. The well-worn chord symbol sequence:

I - IV - ii - V - iii - vi - IV - V - I

is immediately converted by the trained musician into a mentally audible harmonic progression. This system of classification is essential to theorists or musicologists who wish to devise expert systems for the analysis and recreation of musical styles from the common practice period, because it provides the macroscopic "handles" to facilitate database encoding of salient stylistic features on a much higher level than statistical data-recording techniques. (Because the music was not constructed from a probabilistic frame of reference, it is pointless to expect a meaningful description of the relationships between musical processes to come from a statistical measurement.) In short, the analytical method must provide insight to the hierarchically organized, context-dependent, natural language oriented textures of traditional music.

## Procedural (formative) representation

In contrast to the *symbolic* (grammatical) approach to musical event-structuring, the *procedural* (formative) approach treats the computer as an extension of the composer's mental workshop. It does the composer's bidding in the application of complex processes to musical event-streams, and generally allows the composer to speedily accomplish goals that might consume a lifetime if performed by hand. This approach toward the computer relies only to a small degree on the computer's "knowledge" of what it is the composer is doing; it simply obeys the master's prescriptions which, incidentally, may involve some analytical operations, but which are generally not aimed either at increasing the computer's awareness of what it is doing, or at teaching it to be an expert in producing one particular musical style or another.

Although the symbolic representation of music must unquestionably play a great role in the design of computer programs for use by theorists and musicologists, composers often use the computer more flexibly by separating the symbolic, conceptual stage from the iconic, generative phase of musical construction. Rather than become committed to a single-focus, style-dependent program for making music, composers often want a specific musical system embodied by the encoded processes to exist outside of the computer. The composer might also wish to subdivide the compositional process into separate procedures.

The intuitive outlook of the composer requires an inherently different application of the computer from that of other musical sub-disciplines.

One consequence of the procedural approach to music representation is that control over, and responsibility for, the final result remains with the composer. The computer digests and processes data that is low-level and primarily iconic in nature, then slavishly generates and outputs data that stands for music. Here, the machine simply acts as a "black-box" that performs the composer's list of procedures according to parameters controlled (often interactively) by data entered at program start-up. Figure 1-1 provides a symbolic view of this process.

# PRACTICAL PERSPECTIVE

Quite apart from the particular musical notation systems, the instantiation of particular system states must be accomplished pragmatically. This can be eased by isolating and classifying the most significant musical elements, which are referred to as parameters.

I. Composer provides low-level input data governing musical parameter ranges for pitch, rhythm, volume, timbre (instrument choice).

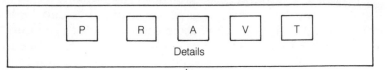

II. Composer provides middle-level input data governing relationships between constituent musical parameters.

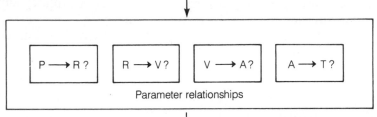

III. Composer provides high-level input data governing relationships between layers of the musical texture.

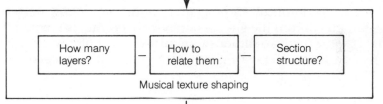

IV. Composer provides input data governing format of output data (music score).

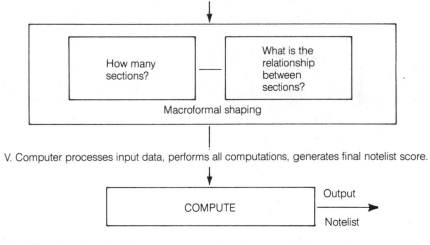

V. Computer processes input data, performs all computations, generates final notelist score.

**1-1** This is a flow chart of the process of creating computer music.

# Encoding of musical data

**Musical parameters** Composers use the term *parameter* to refer to any quantifiable dimension of a musical structure that can be isolated and scaled according to a range of discrete values (such as the integer set, 1 to n). The lower level parameters are similar to what have been called "the elements of music" for centuries: pitch, rhythm, articulation, dynamics, and tone color. Often, these low-level parameters are unified in some way, so that they can be stored as a group, called a *vector*. It is said that a vector contains the key to an aggregate of "attribute/variables" which totally defines the important characteristics of one note-event. For example, a hypothetical event vector containing data for five parameters can be thought of as follows:

NOTE-EVENT #1

| PITCH | DURATION | VOLUME | ARTICULATION | TIMBRE |
|-------|----------|--------|--------------|--------|
| C#3 | Eighth | fff | Staccato | Flute |

In computer terms, a vector is a multidimensional array used to store the specific values (states) of every musical variable associated with each note-event. The total collection of array addresses along an imaginary line 1 to n, which contain the succession of note-events, is termed the *Notelist*. Figure 1-2 shows a two-dimensional array that holds values for the pitch and rhythm parameters of a notelist (sequence of pitches) of *order* (length) ten.

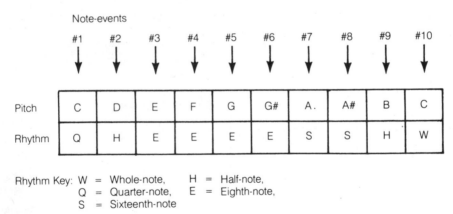

Note-events

| | #1 | #2 | #3 | #4 | #5 | #6 | #7 | #8 | #9 | #10 |
|---|----|----|----|----|----|----|----|----|----|-----|
| Pitch | C | D | E | F | G | G# | A. | A# | B | C |
| Rhythm | Q | H | E | E | E | E | S | S | H | W |

Rhythm Key: W = Whole-note,  H = Half-note,
Q = Quarter-note,  E = Eighth-note,
S = Sixteenth-note

**1-2** A two-dimensional array of a notelist.

In the same manner, parameters at levels higher than the note-event level can also be captured and subjected to interpretation as a scalar range of values. For instance, one identifiable, higher-level parameter of music from the Western contemporary period is Texture Density. It is sometimes used by composers to regulate the number and type of instruments that will participate at any given moment in the performance of a musical score.

In the case of MIDI-system applications when musical data is output from software designed for compositional use, it will most likely be iconic rather than symbolic in form, and will consist of a list of musical data scaled according to the value range of the parameter which it is destined to control.

The final "score"—the output list—will assume a format suitable to the targeted performance device, human or electronic. One commonly used format, sometimes referred to as a list of event vectors, is the notelist format: a first-to-last, time-sequenced succession of note-event attributes. Within this method, each note-event is viewed as a point in time that contains all the necessary information to determine the values of a confluence of musical parameters. As mentioned above, in practical terms the event vector can be visualized as a location (address) in computer memory which contains a list of specific scalar values for each of the significant attributes of a given note-event.

In reality, computer output destined for a device such as a MIDI sound synthesizer, would probably only contain numbers corresponding to the above alphanumeric characters. Therefore, the representation of the preceding NOTE-EVENT #1 inside the computer would take the form:

61   8   127   .50   18

While musicians might think it odd to call a list of event vectors a "music score," the notelist is as specific in every way as the traditional notation; moreover, its format is better suited to performance by digital devices. Admittedly, from a human perspective, the format is difficult to read and discourages analysis of the data primarily because of the one-dimensionality of the score configuration. Figure 1-3 illustrates the notelist concept.

The immediate problem for the person trying to decipher the notelist format is the disentanglement of musical parts. Two distinct voices have been encoded in the example: the first assigned to channel one, the second to channel two. Because the pattern of alternation is regular, we soon discover that the intended effect is one of musical hocketing, and that the voices merely alternate in playing a single melodic line. By contrast, this feature would require little effort to discover in a conventionally notated score. Moreover, harmonic and melodic interval relationships expressed in notelist format are virtually impenetrable.

One solution to the problems caused by the difference between human and computer music representation is software that can convert notelist format to traditional music graphics. It is now possible to compose complex musical events with composition programs and receive parallel digital and music graphic representations. The reverse of this process will undoubtedly soon be available in the form of music notation optical scanners, allowing automatic digital encoding and synthesizer performance of printed music.

NOTELIST KEY:    Field 1 – Note start time in computer clock ticks; 192 ticks = 1/4 note.
                 Field 2 – MIDI pitch number on a scale of 0-127; Middle C = 60.
                 Field 3 – Volume (loudness) on a scale of 0-127; mf dynamic = 64.
                 Field 4 – Duration (in Clock Ticks) of note;
                 Field 5 – Specific instrument (part) that the note is assigned to.

(Line numbers and headings have been provided for reference only)

| Event Number | S.T. | P | V | D | T |
|---|---|---|---|---|---|
| 1 | 200 | 60 | 68 | 40 | 1 |
| 2 | 248 | 65 | 120 | 40 | 1 |
| 3 | 296 | 62 | 120 | 40 | 2 |
| 4 | 344 | 68 | 68 | 40 | 2 |
| 5 | 392 | 64 | 120 | 40 | 1 |
| 6 | 440 | 71 | 120 | 40 | 1 |
| 7 | 488 | 69 | 120 | 40 | 2 |
| 8 | 536 | 70 | 68 | 40 | 2 |
| 9 | 584 | 61 | 120 | 40 | 1 |
| 10 | 632 | 63 | 120 | 40 | 1 |
| 11 | 680 | 67 | 120 | 40 | 2 |
| 12 | 728 | 66 | 68 | 40 | 2 |
| 13 | 776 | 66 | 120 | 40 | 1 |
| 14 | 968 | 60 | 68 | 40 | 1 |
| 15 | 1016 | 71 | 68 | 40 | 2 |
| 16 | 1064 | 65 | 68 | 40 | 2 |
| 17 | 1112 | 68 | 120 | 40 | 1 |
| 18 | 1160 | 64 | 120 | 40 | 1 |
| 29 | 1208 | 62 | 120 | 40 | 2 |
| 30 | 1256 | 63 | 120 | 40 | 2 |
| 31 | 1304 | 70 | 120 | 40 | 1 |
| 32 | 1352 | 67 | 68 | 40 | 1 |
| 33 | 1400 | 69 | 120 | 40 | 2 |
| 34 | 1448 | 61 | 120 | 40 | 2 |
| 35 | 1496 | 66 | 120 | 40 | 1 |
| 36 | 1544 | 66 | 0 | 40 | 1 |
| 37 | 1736 | 60 | 68 | 40 | 2 |
| 38 | 1784 | 67 | 120 | 40 | 2 |
| 39 | 1832 | 65 | 120 | 40 | 1 |

**1-3**  The notelist concept.

The importance of the new notation and music printing capabilities is not immediately obvious. You are accustomed to music notation that is the result of music conceived for people who are limited in their ability to reproduce complex rhythmic and sonic structures. By contrast, music that is the result of data manipulation and processing within the computer (such as that produced by a computer program that generates extremely complex rhythmic patterns) is often not humanly possible to perform. A human pianist has almost laughable physical limitations from the computer's point of view. Not only is the number of notes limited by the number of fingers on the hand, but the fact that those fingers are close together means that the musical textures must be simple. On an 88-key instrument, the computer is the equivalent of a human performer having 88 fingers on a single hand that is as wide as the keyboard and of unlimited flexibility. Of course, quantity does not directly translate into quality, so the burden still rests on the composer to discover imaginative musical textures that fully use this new potential.

One question that arises is: Because music notation exists primarily to convey the composer's intentions to a human performer, why does computer music notation need to be translated into traditional music notation at all? The best answer is so that people can absorb and analyse the music by eye, as people have been accustomed to doing over the years. Other forms of notation, such as totally graphic representations, will probably supplant much of our symbolic notational features. But, for the time being, it still serves well in a number of areas.

## *MIDI* IMPLEMENTATION OF MUSIC SCORES

The marketplace recently has been flooded with books and magazines discussing the details of MIDI sequencing software for standard recording and playback of musical data entered at the synthesizer keyboard. For this reason, and because the focus of this text is on algorithmic composition by computer, only a brief examination of the more general aspects of MIDI communications is included in this chapter. For more detailed information, you may consult any one of the excellent books on the subject published by computer manufacturers.

The discussion that follows is intended to provide the necessary background material to prepare you for algorithmic composition using MIDI synthesizers in conjunction with ASCII-to-MIDI notelist conversion programs supplied by manufacturers of sequencer software (such as the TOP-M.EXE conversion program sold by Systems Design Associates of Dallas, Texas, U.S.A. for use with their Promidi Studio System MIDI Interface Card).

The orientation of this text is toward the composition of music scores that are transmitted to the synthesizer for performance *after* all compositional tasks are completed. If you wish to "bit-fiddle" and pump bytes through the MIDI interface in a real-time control context, then you will have to learn more about the fine points of addressing the MIDI Interface Unit designed for your particular computer. The use of C programming language is recommended for this application, because it is easier to link the Main Routine with a few routines written in Assembly Language. At this writing, the most detailed book on the subject is:

*C Programming for MIDI*, by Jim Conger, 1988
(ISBN   0-934375-86-0)
M & T Publishing Company, Redwood City, California.

## *MIDI* FUNDAMENTALS

MIDI—Musical Instrument Digital Interface—was developed around 1982 to provide a method for musical instruments to communicate with one another. Because digital technology had evolved to the point where most music synthesizers relied heavily on microprocessors (computers), and because many different special- and general-purpose synthesizers were being produced by manufacturers to fill the needs of commercial and popular musicians, it became critically important to invent some means of communication between the various computers in use during any given musical performance.

After some initial, independent attempts by individuals to customize their equipment to this end, an appeal was made to the synthesizer manufacturers to establish and standardize a protocol (operating methodology) for computer music communications that could be followed by all manufacturers in the design of various pieces of equipment. By so doing, many makes and types of instruments could be employed in a performance set up with no communication problems between them.

In 1983, Japanese manufacturers introduced the first MIDI keyboard synthesizers to the marketplace. Since that time, many improvements have been made and the evolution toward complete standardization is well under way. The MIDI file specification of 1988, submitted to the MIDI Manufacturer's Association is a thoroughly documented and detailed statement of software and hardware standards for the implementation of MIDI communications between digital synthesizers, and a more recent link in the chain: The personal computer.

The introduction of the microcomputer in the music-making process greatly expanded the potential for dealing with a stream of sound events, because of the computer's ability to digest and apply external software. In the early days of digital synthesizers, most of the software was contained inside the synthesizer for sequencing pitches and storing patch data; in short, the software was dedicated primarily to the instrument where it resides, and was not of general utility. The advent of the stand-alone personal computer revolutionized the compositional and performance power of digital equipment, leading to the present condition of the hybrid computer music system comprised of two subsystems: The composing/recording/conducting end (the micro) and the performance end (the synthesizer).

## *MIDI* HARDWARE CONFIGURATIONS

**Realtime system**    Figure 1-4 illustrates one of many possible methods of connecting the personal computer with standard MIDI-ready commercial synthesizers: The "daisy-chain." MIDI synthesizers have three primary communications ports which allow them to (1) send MIDI data as source, (2) receive MIDI data as a host, and (3) relay MIDI data to other MIDI synthesizes. This configuration of equipment allows the selective use of part, or all, of a single data stream by one or many synthesizers. For instance, Synthesizer #1 in FIG. 1-4 could be programmed only to respond to certain

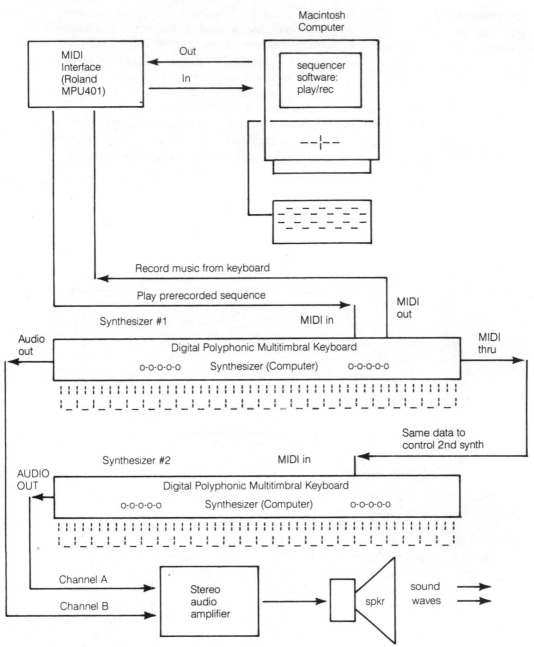

**1-4** One way of interfacing PCs and MIDI synthesizers.

messages traveling down the MIDI cable connecting computer with keyboards; Synthesizer #2 could be set to respond to the remaining MIDI signals. This is possible because the data that enters the first synthesizer is sent on to the second synthesizer unaltered. It is NOT "used-up" or altered in any way as it passes through the immediate host keyboard.

**Performance software** One primary function filled by the personal computer is as host for various commercially available software packages designed to serve as digital information recorders, sound (patch) librarians, and score editing environments. The availability of microcomputers with large quantities of memory has made it possible to play musical passages, called *sequences*, at the synthesizer keyboard, record them in computer memory, store them on computer diskettes, and recall them for future performance. This is the most common use in the popular and commercial music industry. Figure 1-5 illustrates the relationship between the traditional composer, the commercial software packages, and the keyboard synthesizer.

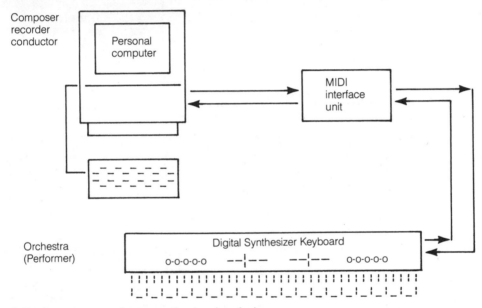

**1-5** A composer-software-synthesizer interfacing.

**Composition software** Since MIDI came into existence during the early 1980s, algorithmic composition has grown in popularity among creative artists in both academic and popular environments. Although several composition software packages are commercially available, the most powerful applications require individual planning, design, and tailoring of programs written in BASIC, PASCAL, C, or FORTRAN.

Although algorithms can be used to shape and send data in realtime from a computer program to a synthesizer, algorithmic composition procedures normally entail complex processing, backtracking and score revisions that require separation of the acts of composition and performance.

Figure 1-6 illustrates the close resemblance of the composer's traditional working method to the process of computer-assisted composition.

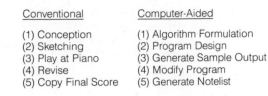

| Conventional | Computer-Aided |
|---|---|
| (1) Conception | (1) Algorithm Formulation |
| (2) Sketching | (2) Program Design |
| (3) Play at Piano | (3) Generate Sample Output |
| (4) Revise | (4) Modify Program |
| (5) Copy Final Score | (5) Generate Notelist |

**1-6** Parallel processes in conventional and computer-aided composition.

In the past, composers have conceived, worked on, tested, revised, and finely polished a composition before giving the final score to a soloist or ensemble for performance. In fact, composers have always used algorithms to aid in composition, but until recently they relied solely on the computation power of the human brain. Therefore, it is no surprise that the steps in algorithmic composition often parallel each step in the traditional process.

Figure 1-7 provides a picture of the relationship between algorithmic composer, software, and performance equipment. Notice that the keyboard synthesizer has been replaced by keyless tone generators to suggest the shift of emphasis from realtime data generation to the production of algorithmically composed music.

**Communications hardware** The key piece of hardware for MIDI communications between personal computers and synthesizers is the Computer-to-MIDI Interface Unit. This can take one of two forms. Either the interface hardware is contained within a "black box" external to the computer or synthesizer, or it takes the form of a computer card that fits into one of the personal computer's internal slots. In either case, the computer, interface, and synthesizer are interconnected by means of a serial transmission cable, running from the computer's communications port to the interface and the synthesizer.

MIDI units are provided with varying degrees of intelligence. That is, the simpler ones are only a kind of conduit that channels the flow of information back and forth. Other MIDI-interface units contain additional circuitry and logic to provide more sophisticated functions for the handling and timing of the musical data flow. In any event, the MIDI hardware alone is not very useful. What is required for powerful handling of musical data is a software package that provides automated means for the organization, manipulation, and transmission of information.

# INFORMATION TRANSMISSION

**Software** The communications interface proper is the traffic controller and data interpreter module that connects the computer's serial communications port to the MIDI port(s) of digital synthesizers. There are basically two categories of Computer-to-MIDI interfaces: smart and dumb. The terms are only a reference to the degree of processing accomplished by each type, not necessarily an indication of relative usefulness.

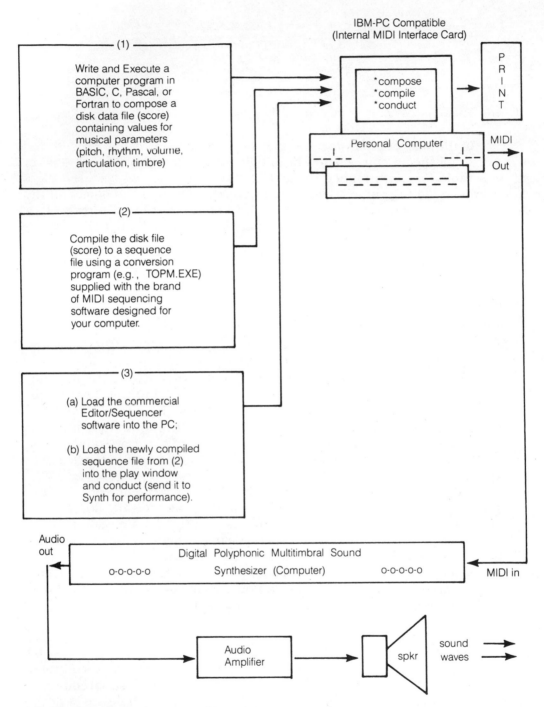

IBM-PC Compatible
(Internal MIDI Interface Card)

**(1)**

Write and Execute a
computer program in
BASIC, C, Pascal, or
Fortran to compose a
disk data file (score)
containing values for
musical parameters
(pitch, rhythm, volume,
articulation, timbre)

*compose
*compile
*conduct

P
R
I
N
T

Personal Computer

MIDI

Out

**(2)**

Compile the disk file
(score) to a sequence
file using a conversion
program (e.g., TOPM.EXE)
supplied with the brand
of MIDI sequencing
software designed for
your computer.

**(3)**

(a) Load the commercial
    Editor/Sequencer
    software into the PC;

(b) Load the newly compiled
    sequence file from (2)
    into the play window
    and conduct (send it to
    Synth for performance).

Audio
out

Digital Polyphonic Multitimbral Sound

o-o-o-o-o     Synthesizer (Computer)     o-o-o-o-o

MIDI in

Audio
Amplifier

spkr

sound
waves

**1-7** The process of using compositional algorithms to generate a music score for performance by
a digital synthesizer.

One important consideration is whether the interface/software combination uses the personal computer's Random Access Memory to an appreciable degree in recording notelist sequences (a notelist is simply a stream of note/event data containing several attributes: pitch, rhythm, articulation, volume, timbre, etc.). The reason for concern is that many sequencer/editor programs that reside in computer memory during recording use a good deal of the computer's limited RAM. If these programs also deal with recorded MIDI data by storing recorded data in RAM, then there is usually a serious constraint on the length of sequence that can be recorded without chaining (splicing) notelists together later in the editing software.

I therefore recommend the Promidi Studio System, which is supplied complete with interface and software for editing, archiving, and sequencing of data. The method used by this system of direct-to-disk sequence filing so that, in conjunction with the computer's internal hard disk drive, the notelist length is virtually unlimited. Moreover, the Promidi Studio System features extremely fine rhythmic resolution, and a superior editing method.

**The MIDI "language"**  If the protocol MIDI uses to transmit data can be termed a language, then it is the same, low-level language shared by all computers: machine language. Nothing other than bit patterns, called *bytes*, travel through the MIDI cables from computer to synthesizer. Although it is true that the bit patterns comprising the bytes must be sent in the proper order to represent the various musical data, there is a very simple reference code that uses a "status" or initial byte with a special flag at the front to tell the synthesizer exactly to what the following stream of bytes will refer. Unless you intend to experiment with the above-mentioned realtime applications, these low-level codes will be of little concern to you; all you need to learn is a few "templates" in decimal form that handle the various kinds of MIDI note and non-note messages for proper formatting of the ASCII disk file. The conversion program that translates, or compiles, the notelist data file handles the minor details.

As mentioned, the MIDI codes are all expressed in binary form, as sequences of Os and 1s. The method of transmission is *serial*—that is, bytes (themselves a stream of eight digits) are sent one at a time down the transmission cable to the synthesizer. The only reason this works reasonably well is that transmission is quite fast; the number of bytes that can be sent each second, represented by the *baud rate*, is 31,250.

There are only two major types and (several subtypes) of MIDI data: status bytes and data bytes. *Status* bytes tell the computer or synthesizer what kind of data is being sent; they indicate whether the information is to be applied to a key press, or modulation wheel, or pitch bend, etc. *Data* bytes follow on the heels of status bytes, and they give actual values to be applied within the general action indicated by the status byte (FIG. 1-8).

1  0 1 1 0 1 1 0

|<— indicates status byte

**1-8**  Status bytes and data bytes.

0 1 1 0 0 0 1 1

|<— indicates data byte

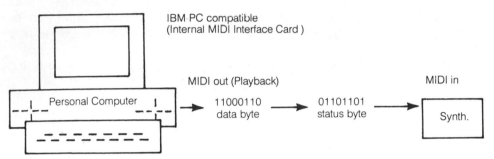

IBM-PC compatible
(Internal MIDI Interface Card )

MIDI out (Playback)        MIDI in

11000110 → 01101101 →
data byte    status byte

**1-9**  A simplified diagram of MIDI transmission.

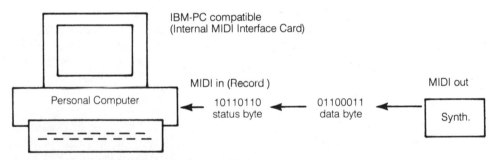

IBM-PC compatible
(Internal MIDI Interface Card)

MIDI in (Record )        MIDI out

← 10110110 ← 01100011 ←
status byte    data byte

**1-10**  Recording MIDI data from the synthesizer to the computer.

Status bytes carry a first (top) bit of value 1; data bytes carry a top bit of value 0.

Figure 1-9, a simplified diagram of MIDI transmission, will help you to understand the process.

The reverse process occurs when recording MIDI data from the synthesizer keyboard to the computer (FIG. 1-10).

**MIDI channels**  MIDI channels can be visualized as similar to the concept of a multitrack tape recorder. Current MIDI implementations provide for a maximum of 16 concurrent music channels, each capable of carrying an independent melodic line. How is this possible when a single, serial transmission cable is carrying the message to and from the computer?

Each status byte carries with it information about the specific channel to which the following data message(s) apply. In this way, many different messages for any of the 16 MIDI channels can be mixed and sent along a single transmission wire. The catch is that the software sending the messages must send each datum in the proper order and time. We will deal with this problem in relation to algorithmic composition in Chapter 7 when the Midifile( ) function is discussed. For now, just accept the statement that one MIDI-equipped personal computer plus two daisy-chained 8-voice polyphonic synthesizers equals a 16-piece orchestra capable of performing a fully contrapuntal composition. (See FIG. 1-11.)

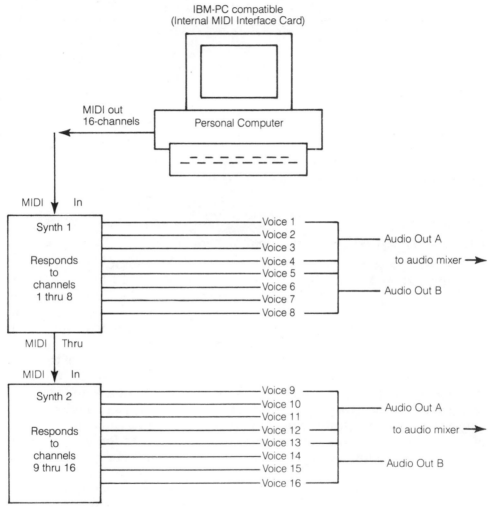

**1-11**  The equivalent of a 16-piece orchestra.

## TIME DURATION MEASUREMENT IN *MIDI*

Commercial sequencer software packages deal with time measurement in relation to a defined clock based on the computer's internal operating speed. While the exact method varies from one software package to the next, the same principle is shared by all: a reference value, called one *tick*, is accumulated in multiples to represent time durations of various lengths. The number of ticks per reference duration, for example the quarter-note, determines the rhythmic complexity that can be expressed by the system. Sequencing software that divides the quarter-note into 192 ticks (slices) by definition has a lower rhythmic resolution than software which divides the quarter-note into 96 ticks. See FIG. 1-12.

Quarter-note = 100 mm. (default tempo)

Whole-note = 768 clock ticks

Half-note = 384 clock ticks

Quarter-note = 192 clock ticks

|–| = 24 clock ticks

**1-12**  Time duration measurement in example MIDI sequencer.

Because it is convenient to use integers to represent rhythm values (note durations), I arbitrarily choose a reference value of 1 for the musical whole-note. This allows you to regard each of the other integers as the denominator of a fraction (of a whole-note). For example: $1/1$ = whole note, $1/2$ = half-note, $1/4$ = quarter-note, etcetera. In a monophonic melody, consider each note's rhythm value to be the amount of time, measured in clock ticks, from the attack point of one note to the attack point of the next note. (Rest notes can be viewed as notes having no amplitude; however, they still occupy note-space.) The number of ticks comprising the reference value can be called the "rhythmic resolution." If you could slice the whole-note into an infinite number of parts (ticks), you could achieve infinitely complex rhythmic patterns. However, our perception of time durations is limited. This fact accounts for the limited range of rhythmic values present in traditional music. For this reason, infinite resolution is not a desirable goal. Figure 1-13 is a map of the correspondence between the scalar ranges of MIDI parameters and those of musical elements.

## *ASCII* FILE FORMAT

Figure 1-14 is a list of variables required by the computer to define a musical event and direct it to the proper instrument.

The shell structure (ASCII file record) for each note-event is represented by FIG. 1-15.

| PITCH | | | RHYTHM | | VELOCITY | | TIMBRE | |
|---|---|---|---|---|---|---|---|---|
| G | 10 | 127 | 1 = Whole | 768 | fff | 127 | gong | 127 |
| F# | 10 | 126 | 2 = Half | 384 | | | bells | 126 |
| F | 10 | 125 | 4 = Quarter | 192 | | | sitar | 125 |
| E | 10 | 124 | 8 = Eighth | 96 | | | harpsi | 124 |
| D# | 10 | 123 | 16 = Sixteenth | 48 | | | harmon | 123 |
| D | 10 | 122 | 32 = 32nd | 24 | | | string | 122 |
| C# | 10 | 121 | 64 = 64th | 12 | | | picc | 121 |
| C | 10 | 120 | | | | | sax4 | 120 |
| | | | | | | | sax3 | 119 |
| | | | | | | | sax2 | 118 |
| C | 9 | 108 | | | | | sax1 | 108 |
| | | | | | ff | 100 | | |
| C | 8 | 96 | | | | | tymp | 96 |
| C | 7 | 84 | | | | | cymbal | 84 |
| | | | | | f | 80 | | |
| C | 6 | 72 | | | | | drum2 | 72 |
| | | | | | mf | | | |
| C | 5 | 60 | | | | 60 | drum1 | 60 |
| | | | | | mp | | | |
| C | 4 | 48 | | | | | organ | 48 |
| | | | | | p | 40 | | |
| C | 3 | 36 | | | | | glock | 36 |
| | | | | | pp | | | |
| C | 2 | 24 | | | | | snare | 24 |
| | | | | | | 20 | | |
| C | 1 | 12 | | | ppp | | piano | 12 |
| B | 0 | 11 | | | | | tuba | 11 |
| A# | 0 | 10 | | | | | fr.hn | 10 |
| A | 0 | 9 | | | | | tromb | 9 |
| G# | 0 | 8 | | | | | trump | 8 |
| F# | 0 | 6 | | | | | clar | 6 |
| G | 0 | 7 | | | | | bassn | 7 |
| F | 0 | 5 | | | | | oboe | 5 |
| E | 0 | 4 | | | | | flute | 4 |
| D# | 0 | 3 | | | | | bass | 3 |
| D | 0 | 2 | | | | | cello | 2 |
| C# | 0 | 1 | | | | | vla | 1 |
| C | 0 | 0 | | | | 0 | vln | 0 |

NOTE: The Timbre Table (Program Change) is arbitrarily assigned.

**1-13** Correspondence between integer ranges and MIDI note parameter scales.

The variable DURATION (number of clock ticks) is added to the variable NOTEON (note start time) to compute the time for the next note-event. For instance, to represent a sequence of 4 quarter-notes the variable, NOTEON, must be advanced by increments of 192 for each successive note-event, as in:

event #1    NOTEON = 0
event #2    NOTEON = 192
event #3    NOTEON = 384
event #4    NOTEON = 576

The value contained in the variable ARTDUR is normally the value of the variable DURATION (total space reserved for the note-event) shortened by an articulation factor.

(For use with Systems Design Associates TOPM.EXE File Conversion Software)

Protocol: TOPM     infile.dat outfile.v01

<u>NOTE MESSAGES</u>:

Variables:  (expressed in decimal form)
        NOTEON;      MIDI note event start time, measured in ticks
        PITCH;        MIDI note numbers, 0 – 127
        VELOCITY;    speed of key depression, 0 – 127
        DURATION;   time-space (in ticks) allotted for a note
        ARTDUR;     articulated duration (regulates the ratio of sound/silence for a given note time-space)
        CHANNEL;   MIDI channel number, 0 – 15
        PORT;       communication port number (remains constant; Promidi uses port 0)

**1-14**  A list of variables required by the computer to define a musical event and direct it to the instrument.

Note Message Format:

| Fields: | 1 | 2 | 3 | 4 | 5 | 6 |
|---|---|---|---|---|---|---|
| | NOTEON | PITCH | VELOCITY | ARTDUR | CHANNEL | PORT |
| | integer (ticks) | integer (0 – 127) | integer (0 – 127) | integer (time on) | integer (0 – 15) | integer (0) |

**1-15**  The ASCII file record for each note.

(When a synthesizer is set in monophonic mode to play only a single note at a time, each note is usually shortened to at least 85 percent of DURATION to allow for synthesizer gating; that is, the first note is allowed some decay time before the next note is attacked to prevent foreshortening of the envelope and guarantee clarity.)

This illustrates the required TOPM.EXE ASCII format:

```
100 60 127 163 0 0 gated  1/4 note, max  velocity,  ch 1,  middle C
192 61  90 163 0 0 gated  1/4 note, med  velocity,  ch 1,  middle C#
384 62  50 163 1 0 gated  1/4 note, low   velocity,  ch 2,  middle D
```

**Non-note messages**  Various synthesizer controller and program change messages can be included in the ASCII file. The same 6-field shell is used, but with fewer pieces of information.

Figure 1-16 is a list of non-note message types. Controller changes are accomplished by sending a message either before or after a note begins. The MIDI controllers in FIG. 1-17 are supported by many synthesizer makers.

Figure 1-18 is an example of a controller change message for the MIDI main volume controller.

Use the original format shell, but fill it as in FIG. 1-19.

Figure 1-20 is an output file using the main volume controller.

| Message | No. of Bytes | Code Number (in decimal) |
|---|---|---|
| Polyphonic Aftertouch | 3 | 160 – 175 (channels 0 – 15) |
| Controller Change | 3 | 176 – 191 (channels 0 – 15) |
| Program Change | 2 | 192 – 207 (channels 0 – 15) |
| Channel Aftertouch | 2 | 208 – 223 (channels 0 – 15) |
| Pitch Bender | 3 | 224 – 239 (channels 0 – 15) |

**1-16** A list of non-note message types.

| Controller | Number (decimal) | Value range (decimal) |
|---|---|---|
| Modulation Wheel | 1 | 0 – 127 |
| Breath Controller | 2 | 0 – 127 |
| Foot Controller | 4 | 0 – 127 |
| Portamento Time | 5 | 0 – 127 |
| Data Entry Slider | 6 | 0 – 127 |
| Main Volume | 7 | 0 – 127 |
| Sustain | 64 | OFF – 0; ON – 127 |
| Portamento | 65 | OFF – 0; ON – 127 |
| Sostenuto | 66 | OFF – 0; ON – 127 |
| Soft | 67 | OFF – 0; ON – 127 |
| Data Increment | 96 | 127 |
| Data Decrement | 97 | 127 |
| Local | 122 | OFF – 0; ON – 127 |
| All Note Off | 123 | OFF – 0 |
| Omni Off | 124 | OFF – 0 |
| Omni On | 125 | OFF – 0 |
| Mono On | 126 | 0 – 15 (# channels) |
| Poly On | 127 | 0 |

**1-17** These controllers are supported by many synthesizer makers.

Variables: (decimal form)

| | |
|---|---|
| STARTIME | start time (in ticks) |
| CONTROLLER; | refer. number of controller (Main Vol = 7) |
| CSTATCHANNEL; | status byte; type of message (176 + ch. no.) |
| VALUE; | data value, range 0 – 127 |
| PORT; | communication port number (remains constant; Promidi uses port 0) |

**1-18** An example of a controller change message for the MIDI main volume controller.

| Field | 1 | 2 | 3 | 4 | 5 | 6 |
|---|---|---|---|---|---|---|
| | STARTIME | CONTROLLER | VALUE | 0 | CSTATCHANNEL | PORT |
| | integer | integer | integer | | integer | integer |
| | (ticks) | | | | 176 + ch | |

**1-19** The Promidi Studio System format.

ASCII File Example:

| | | | | | | |
|---|---|---|---|---|---|---|
| 090 | 7 | 0 | 0 | 179 | 0 | set main volume on channel 4 to 0 |
| 100 | 60 | 127 | 163 | 3 | 0 | gated $1/4$ note, max velocity, ch 4, middle C |
| 104 | 7 | 10 | 0 | 179 | 0 | increment main volume for crescendo |
| 106 | 7 | 40 | 0 | 179 | 0 | increment main volume for crescendo |
| 108 | 7 | 60 | 0 | 179 | 0 | increment main volume for crescendo |
| 110 | 7 | 80 | 0 | 179 | 0 | increment main volume for crescendo |
| 175 | 7 | 127 | 0 | 179 | 0 | return main vol to max for next note |
| 192 | 61 | 90 | 163 | 3 | 0 | gated $1/4$ note, med velocity, ch 4, middle C# |
| 384 | 62 | 20 | 163 | 3 | 0 | gated $1/4$ note, low velocity, ch 4, middle D |

**1-20**  An output file using the main volume controller.

Program (timbre) change can be accomplished by sending a message between the end of one note and the beginning of another, as in FIG. 1-21.

Figure 1-22 is an output file using the program change when changing a controller or program change parameter setting from one note to the next, you can avoid "glitches" in the sound output of the synthesizer by allowing at least 10 clock ticks between the issuance of a non-note message and a note-on message.

Variables:   STARTIME        start time (in ticks)
             VOICENUM        Timbre (patch) number, 0 – n
             PSTATCHANNEL    status byte (192 + channel)

Program Change Message Format:

| Field | 1 | 2 | 3 | 4 | 5 | 6 |
|---|---|---|---|---|---|---|
| | STARTIME | VOICENUM | 0 | 0 | PSTATCHANNEL | PORT |
| | integer (ticks) | integer | | integer | (192 + ch) | integer |

**1-21**  Changing timbre.

ASCII File Example:

| | | | | | | |
|---|---|---|---|---|---|---|
| 090 | 12 | 0 | 0 | 192 | 0 | select Program (timbre) 12 for channel 1 |
| 100 | 60 | 127 | 163 | 0 | 0 | gated $1/4$ note, max velocity, ch 1, middle C |
| 180 | 12 | 0 | 0 | 192 | 0 | select Program (timbre) 12 for channel 1 |
| 192 | 61 | 90 | 163 | 0 | 0 | gated $1/4$ note, med velocity, ch 1, middle C# |
| 372 | 26 | 0 | 0 | 192 | 0 | select Program (timbre) 26 for channel 1 |
| 384 | 62 | 50 | 163 | 1 | 0 | gated $1/4$ note, low velocity, ch 2, middle D |

**1-22**  An output file using the program change message.

## FROM *MIDI* DATA TO STANDARD MUSIC NOTATION

**Conversion programs**  Transformation of MIDI (sequence) data to a form accepted by commercial music printing software is the final link in the chain which connects algorithmically composed data with the printed music score. Several software packages are currently available, but they vary widely in power and scope. It is advisable to test each package thoroughly before deciding which best meets your needs.

We used the IBM PC compatible Promidi Studio System to perform notelist data converted to sequencer format. This system provides conversion programs for use with two different music printing products: Personal Composer, and The Copyist.

For readers who own Macintosh as well as IBM PCs, a broad range of music printing software is accessible by means of interconnecting the MIDI OUT of the IBM to the MIDI IN of the Macintosh computer. The music can be transferred by playing it on the IBM source sequencer while recording it on the Macintosh host sequencer, such as The Performer. The recorded sequence can then be loaded into Finale or Professional Composer (or other) music printing software, edited, and printed.

Figure 1-23 illustrates the conversion process.

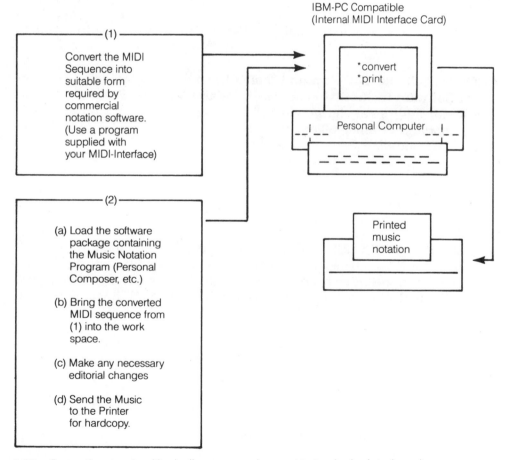

**1-23** Converting an algorithmically composed score to standard printed music.

## MUSIC-PRINTING SOFTWARE

There are several music notation software packages commercially available, but to date the most powerful and easy to use (for IBM PCs) is called Personal Composer/System 2. It can be obtained from music dealers around the world. In order to convert algorithmically generated music to notation, you must obtain a file conversion program to interface with the MIDI sequencer playback files with the music printing software. The Pro-midi Studio System, by Systems Design Associates, provides conversion programs for the Personal Composer/System 2 and for The Copyist Music Notation software.

## NAMES AND ADDRESSES OF RECOMMENDED COMPUTER-TO-*MIDI* INTERFACE MANUFACTURERS

At the time of this writing, only two manufacturers provided software that allows the algorithmic composer to directly convert and play back data files generated as score-file output of a user-written music composition computer program—undoubtedly the list will grow as interest in this field increases.

PROMIDI STUDIO SYSTEM (internal MIDI Interface, complete Sequencing Software included; expander for Roland MPU401 Emulation available for additional charge; conversion programs for ASCII-to-Promidi transfer and Promidi to Personal Composer Notation and Copyist Music Printing Software.

Order from: Systems Design Associates, Inc.
            5068 Plano Parkway
            Suite 121
            Plano, Texas 75075

PERSONAL COMPOSER Software, by Jim Miller, Honolulu, Hawaii, U.S.A., can be ordered through most synthesizer dealers who stock IBM-PC compatible computers. This music notation software package is recommended for use with the PROMIDI STUDIO SYSTEM and its notation conversion program: PCV.EXE

CAKEWALK Recorder/Editor (Software only, runs on IBM-compatibles interfaced with MIDI synthesizers by the Roland MPU401 MIDI interface). Provides ASCII-to-CAKEWALK and CAKEWALK-to-ASCII file conversion utilities. Software for Conversion of CAKEWALK sequences to standard notation is not available at present.

Order from: CMS Computer Music Supply
            382 N. Lemon Ave.
            Walnut, California 91789
            U.S.A.

# 2
# *Utilities*

## FUNCTION GROUP: Tunings.c

1. Tunings( )   MIC 2.1
2. Fpower( )   MIC 2.2

## Purpose

Compile a table of equal-tempered, octave-repeating, microtonal scale frequencies measured in cycles per second (Hertz).

One direct application of the scale compiler is to generate microtonal scales for the pitch output of a sound synthesizer. You will discover other interesting uses for this subroutine by mapping variously tuned scales to volume, rhythm, timbre, and articulation parameters.

To map one set of values onto another parameter, interpret the first data table (array) as a set of pointers to the addresses of values stored in the second data table.

## Notes

Variable "octdiv" controls the number of equal-size intervals contained within one octave, variable "freq1" sets the initial (tonic) scale pitch, and variable "numtones" builds the scale upward over the required number of tones. To illustrate, if numtones = 60 and octdiv = 12, then a five-octave scale will be compiled.

## Programming ideas

1. Experiment with several different tunings of your microcomputer sound synthesizer chip using output of the scale compiler.
2. Read the frequency data table into a program that converts the values via the modulus operator (%) to a small set of rhythmic durations.

# Program source code

```
/* TUNINGS.C (equal-tempered,octave-repeating,microtonal
                scale compiler) */
#include <stdio.h>
#include <math.h>
main()
{
 int tone[84],numtones,octdiv,j;
 double freq1;
 void Tunings();

 numtones = 84;
 octdiv = 19;
 freq1 = 61.735;   /*beginning frequency for scale computation*/
 Tunings(tone,freq1,octdiv,numtones);
 for (j = 0;j < numtones;j++)
     {
      if(j % 10 == 0)
        printf("\n");
      printf("%d ",tone[j]);
     }
} /* end of main */
/*=============== MIC 2.1 ===============*/
/* Tunings() function */
void Tunings(tone,freq1,octdiv,numtones)
int tone[],octdiv,numtones;
double freq1;
{
 double Fpower();
 double coeff,t9;
 double base=2.0;
 int j;

 t9 = 1.0/octdiv;
 coeff = Fpower(base,t9);
 tone[0]=freq1+.5;
 for (j = 1;j < numtones;j++)
    tone[j] = tone[j-1] * coeff + .5;
} /* end Tunings() function */
/*=============== MIC 2.2 ===============*/
/* Fpower() function */
double Fpower(value, tothe)
double value, tothe;
 {
  int sign;
  double result;

  sign = (tothe < 0.0) ? -1 : 1;
  tothe = fabs(tothe);
  result = exp( log(value) * tothe);
  if(sign < 0)
     result = 1.0 / result;
  return(result);
 } /* end of Fpower() function */
/*=====================================*/
/* END OF TUNINGS.C */
```

# Program Execution

```
TUNINGS.EXE

62  64  66  68  71  74  77  80  83  86
89  92  95  99  103  107  111  115  119  123
128  133  138  143  148  153  159  165  171  177
184  191  198  205  213  221  229  238  247  256
266  276  286  297  308  319  331  343  356  369
383  397  412  427  443  459  476  494  512  531
551  571  592  614  637  661  686  711  737  764
792  821  852  884  917  951  986  1023  1061  1100
1141  1183  1227  1273
```

# FUNCTION: Pitchtab( )   MIC 2.3

## Purpose

Provide a registrated pitch element table for conversion of integers to chromatic scale pitches from low-octave to high-octave.

## Notes

This function resembles the READ . . . . DATA method used in BASIC language to initialize a musical element table. (Itemize all pitches and octave registers in DATA statements—C1, C#1, D1, D#1, etc.—then READ them into an element table array during program execution. The difference is that table values are assigned to a static array in a single statement, eliminating the need for an iteration loop to sequentially read the data into the element array.

Although coded here as a function( ), the module can simply be included at the top of a main( ) routine as "in-line" code.

## Programming ideas

In interactive programs, a pitch table helps the user by converting the data to familiar terms.

1. Write a program that generates random integers and offers a user-option to view them either as pitches or numbers.
2. Modify the function to initialize element tables for other parameters such as rhythm or volume.

## Program source code

```
/* PITCHTAB.C   (initializes a pitch data table
                  corresponding to integer values 1-n) */
#include <stdio.h>
main()
{
 void Pitchtab();

 Pitchtab();

} /* end of main */
/*=============== MIC 2.3 ===============*/
/* Pitchtab() function */
void Pitchtab()
{
int j,total = 85;
static char *pitch[] = {
    "C0 ","C#0","D0 ","D#0","E0 ","F0 ","F#0","G0 ","G#0",
    "A0 ","A#0","B0 ","C1 ","C#1","D1 ","D#1","E1 ","F1 ",
    "F#1","G1 ","G#1","A1 ","A#1","B1 ","C2 ","C#2","D2 ",
```

```
        "G#2","E2 ","F2 ","F#2","G2 ","G#2","A2 ","A#2","B2 ",
        "C3 ","C#3","D3 ","D#3","E3 ","F3 ","F#3","G3 ","G#3",
        "A3 ","A#3","B3 ","C4 ","C#4","D4 ","D#4","E4 ","F4 ",
        "F#4","G4 ","G#4","A4 ","A#4","B4 ","C5 ","C#5","D5 ",
        "D#5","E5 ","F5 ","F#5","G5 ","G#5","A5 ","A#5","B5 ",
        "C6 ","C#6","D6 ","D#6","E6 ","F6 ","F#6","G6 ","G#6",
        "A6 ","A#6","B6 ","C7 "  };

    for (j = 0; j < total; j++)
        if (j % 15 == 0)
            printf("\n%s ",pitch[j]);
        else
            printf("%s ",pitch[j]);

} /* end of Pitchtab() function */
/*======================================*/
/* END OF PITCHTAB.C */
```

## Program execution

```
PITCHTAB.EXE

C0   C#0  D0   D#0  E0   F0   F#0  G0   G#0  A0   A#0  B0   C1   C#1  D1
D#1  E1   F1   F#1  G1   G#1  A1   A#1  B1   C2   C#2  D2   G#2  E2   F2
F#2  G2   G#2  A2   A#2  B2   C3   C#3  D3   D#3  E3   F3   F#3  G3   G#3
A3   A#3  B3   C4   C#4  D4   D#4  E4   F4   F#4  G4   G#4  A4   A#4  B4
C5   C#5  D5   D#5  E5   F5   F#5  G5   G#5  A5   A#5  B5   C6   C#6  D6
D#6  E6   F6   F#6  G6   G#6  A6   A#6  B6   C7
```

# FUNCTION GROUP: Vectors.c

1. Parstore( )   MIC 2.4
2. Parxtrct( )   MIC 2.5

## Purpose

To configure an event vector array by calling composite number storage [Parstore( )] and extraction [Parxtrct( )] functions. Each address in the array must hold pitch, rhythm, and volume parameter data for a single musical tone.

Although this program deals specifically with musical elements, there are other circumstances in which the need arises for compression of numeric data due to system memory limitations. These functions will come to the rescue.

## Notes

Composite number storage and extraction works by assigning each musical parameter value to a separate segment of the number:

| 000 | 000 | 000 |
|-----|-----|-----|
| v   | r   | p   |

For this reason, a double-precision variable is required. The only restriction is that the parameter value range must be $<= 999$. Any musical dimension that you wish to control may be substituted for program variables "p," "r," and "v."

## Programming ideas

1. Modify the program to store information about other compositional dimensions such as texture density, timbre, and articulation.
2. Shift program focus from the single sonic event level to the macroformal level by storing information to determine the number of melodic notes in a phrase, number of phrases in a phrase-group, and number of phrase-groups in a formal section.

## Program source code

```
/* VECTORS.C (creates event vectors by storing pitch, rhythm
                and volume data for a single musical event in
                one double precision number.)*/
#include <stdio.h>
main()
{
  int total = 10;
```

```
    void Parstore(),Parxtrct();
    double c[10];

    printf("%s %d %s","attributes being stored for",
           total,"notes are:\n");
    Parstore(c,total);
    printf("\nextracted note attributes are\n");
    Parxtrct(c,total);

} /* end of main */
/*=============== MIC 2.4 ===============*/
/* Parstore() function */
void Parstore(array,total)
double array[];
int total;
{
 int j;
 int v;          /* note volume parameter */
 double p;       /* note pitch parameter */
 double r;       /* note rhythm paramter */

 for (j = 0;j <total;j++)
    {
     p = rand() % 88 + 1;  /* load a random pitch number */
     r = rand() % 16 + 16; /* load a random rhythm value*/
     v = rand() % 100 + 1; /*load a random volume value*/
     printf("pitch = %.0f\t",p);
     printf("rhythm = %.0f\t",r);
     printf("volume = %d\n",v);
     p = p * 1000000.;
     r = r * 1000.;
     array[j] = p + r + v;
     printf("composite number = %.0f\n",array[j]);
    }

 } /* end of Parstore() function */
/*=============== MIC 2.5 ===============*/
/* Parxtrct() function */
void Parxtrct(c,total)
double c[];
int total;
{
 double d;
 int p,r,v,j;
 for (j = 0;j < total;j++)
    {
     d = c[j];
     d = d / 1000000.;
     p = d;
     r = (d - p) * 1000;
     d = d * 1000.;
     v = (d - (int)d) * 1000.+.5;
     printf("p = %d\tr = %d\tv = %d\n",p,r,v);
    }
} /* end of Parxtrct() function */
/*===================================*/
/* END OF VECTORS.C */
```

# Program execution

`VECTORS.EXE`

```
attributes being stored for 10 notes are:
pitch = 83        rhythm = 18      volume = 83
composite number = 83018083
pitch = 35        rhythm = 24      volume = 18
composite number = 35024018
pitch = 84        rhythm = 31      volume = 49
composite number = 84031049
pitch = 63        rhythm = 28      volume = 59
composite number = 63028059
pitch = 52        rhythm = 31      volume = 93
composite number = 52031093
pitch = 41        rhythm = 20      volume = 22
composite number = 41020022
pitch = 24        rhythm = 23      volume = 20
composite number = 24023020
pitch = 26        rhythm = 22      volume = 86
composite number = 26022086
pitch = 63        rhythm = 21      volume = 53
composite number = 63021053
pitch = 84        rhythm = 27      volume = 17
composite number = 84027017

extracted note attributes are
p = 83   r = 18   v = 83
p = 35   r = 24   v = 18
p = 84   r = 31   v = 49
p = 63   r = 28   v = 59
p = 52   r = 31   v = 93
p = 41   r = 20   v = 22
p = 24   r = 23   v = 20
p = 26   r = 22   v = 86
p = 63   r = 21   v = 53
p = 84   r = 27   v = 17
```

## FUNCTION GROUP: Curves.c

1. Lincurve( )    MIC 2.6
2. Expcurve( )    MIC 2.7
3. Logcurve( )    MIC 2.8

## Purpose

Generate ascending integer data sequences which conform to one of three available curves: linear, exponential, or logarithmic.

Although this group is especially appropriate for creating smooth accelerando of tempo, gradual increase of volume level, or incremental timbre shift, you can apply the curves to any compositional problem which requires discrete, continuously scaled integers for direct use, or for indirect use as pointers to other sets of data.

## Notes

Control parameters are "start," "end," and "num," all of which must be positive integers.

## Programming ideas

1. Write a program that directly applies the curves to pitch, rhythm, and volume parameters.
2. Generate curves in various ranges to serve as pointers to other musical parameter arrays which contain unsorted, random-order values.
3. Modify the curve algorithms to return negative as well as positive values.

## Program source code

```
/* CURVES.C (returns positive integers along three
            discrete curves:linear,exponential,logarithmic)*/
#include <stdio.h>
#include <math.h>
main()
{
 int x[300],start = 1,end = 200,num = 100,j1,j2;
 void Lincurve(),Expcurve(),Logcurve();

 printf("curve start will be %d,end will be %d ",start,end);
 printf("\nand number of elements will be %d.\n",num);
 for (j1 = 1; j1 <= 3;j1++)
    {
      if (j1 == 1)
         Lincurve(x,start,end,num);
      else
        if (j1 == 2)
            Expcurve(x,start,end,num);
```

```
          else Logcurve(x,start,end,num);
          for (j2 = 1;j2 <= num;j2++)
              if (j2 % 15 == 0)
                  printf("\n%d ",x[j2]);
              else
                  printf("%d ",x[j2]);
          printf("\n");
      }
} /* end of main */
/*=============== MIC 2.6 ===============*/
/* Lincurve() function */
void Lincurve(x,start,end,num)
int x[],start,end,num;
{
  int j,l;
  float a;

  printf("\nlinear curve:\n");
  for (j = 1;j <= num;j+=10)
      {
        for (l = j;l <= j + 9;l++)
            {
              a = (float) (l-1) / (num-1);
              x[l] = start + a * (end-start) +.5;
              if (l == num)
                 break;
            }
      }

} /* end of Lincurve() function */
/*=============== MIC 2.7 ===============*/
/* Expcurve() function */
void Expcurve(x,start,end,num)
int x[],start,end,num;
{
  int j,l;
  float a;

  printf("\nexponential curve:\n");
  for (j = 1;j <= num;j+=10)
      {
        for (l = j;l <= j + 9;l++)
            {
              a = (float)(l-1) * (l-1) / ((num-1) * (num-1));
              x[l] = start + a * (end-start)+.5;
              if (l == num)
                 break;
            }
      }

} /* end of Expcurve() function */
/*=============== MIC 2.8 ===============*/
/* Logcurve() function */
void Logcurve(x,start,end,num)
int x[],start,end,num;
{
  int j,l;
  float a,b,log();

  printf("\nlogarithmic curve:\n");
  for (j = 1;j <= num;j += 10)
```

```
    {
    for (l = j;l <= j + 9;l++)
        {
        a = l;
        b = num;
        x[l] = start + log(a)/log(b) * (end-start)+.5;
        if (l == num)
            break;
        }
    }

} /* end of Logcurve() function */
/*=======================================*/
/* END OF CURVES.C */
```

## Program execution

CURVES.EXE

curve start will be 1,end will be 200
and number of elements will be 100.

linear curve:
```
1 3 5 7 9 11 13 15 17 19 21 23 25 27
29 31 33 35 37 39 41 43 45 47 49 51 53 55 57
59 61 63 65 67 69 71 73 75 77 79 81 83 85 87
89 91 93 95 97 99 102 104 106 108 110 112 114 116 118
120 122 124 126 128 130 132 134 136 138 140 142 144 146 148
150 152 154 156 158 160 162 164 166 168 170 172 174 176 178
180 182 184 186 188 190 192 194 196 198 200
```

exponential curve:
```
1 1 1 1 1 2 2 2 2 3 3 3 4 4
5 6 6 7 8 8 9 10 11 12 13 14 15 16 17
18 19 21 22 23 24 26 27 29 30 32 33 35 37 39
40 42 44 46 48 50 52 54 56 58 60 62 65 67 69
72 74 77 79 82 84 87 89 92 95 98 100 103 106 109
112 115 118 121 125 128 131 134 138 141 144 148 151 155 158
162 165 169 173 177 180 184 188 192 196 200
```

logarithmic curve:
```
1 31 48 61 71 78 85 91 96 101 105 108 112 115
118 121 123 126 128 130 133 135 136 138 140 142 143 145 147
148 149 151 152 153 155 156 157 158 159 160 161 163 164 165
165 166 167 168 169 170 171 172 173 173 174 175 176 176 177
178 179 179 180 181 181 182 183 183 184 185 185 186 186 187
188 188 189 189 190 190 191 191 192 192 193 193 194 194 195
195 196 196 197 197 198 198 199 199 200 200
```

# FUNCTION: Fractab( )    MIC 2.9

## Purpose

Sum a sequence of rhythm durations that are expressed as fraction denominators ($1/2$, $1/4$, $1/8$, $1/16$, $1/32$, $1/64$, etc.).

It sometimes happens that a sequence of randomly generated melodic rhythm values must be reconciled to a preestablished time frame. This subroutine provides a tally of generated values that can be fed back to the program for adjustment of individual durations.

For example, if the situation requires that:

a. the melody must contain eight notes,
b. the note duration values must exactly equal two whole notes (thirty-two 16th-notes in total), and . . .
c. the subroutine returns the duration sequence $1/16$, $1/2$, $1/16$, $1/4$, $1/16$, $1/8$, $1/4$, $1/2$ (twenty-nine 16th-notes in total),

then the discrepancy between the tally and output requirements dictates that the shorter values be augmented by the appropriate amount—in this case three 16th-notes spread across three randomly selected notes.

## Notes

If you wish to generate duration fractions that are multivariant—$3/16$, $2/5$, $7/8$, etc.—then substitute Function Group: FRACTSUM.C (MIC 2.12 & MIC 2.13) for Fractab( ).

## Programming ideas

1. Write a program that generates random-order pitches and rhythms for a melodic line. Include Fractab( ) and additional statements to reconcile the melodic rhythm duration sum to a user-input time frame.

## Program source code

```
/* FRACTAB.C (tabulates rhythmic duration values in cases where
              each value can be expressed as a fraction which
              has 1 as the numerator (e.g. 1/8). The sum of all
              durations is returned in decimal.)*/
#include <stdio.h>
main()
{
  int x[50], j;
  int total = 50;
  float sum = 0.0;
  float Fractab();
```

```
    for (j = 0; j < total; j++)
        {
            x[j] = j + 1; /* load fraction denominators */
            if(j % 5 == 0)
                printf("\n1/%d\t",x[j]);
            else
                printf("1/%d\t", x[j]);
        }
    sum = Fractab(x, total); /* call tabulation */
    printf("\nThe sum of durations is %f whole notes", sum);
} /* end of main */
/*=============== MIC 2.9 ===============*/
/* Fractab() function */
float Fractab(x, total)
int x[], total;
{
    int j;
    float sum = 0.0;

    for (j = 0; j < total; j++)
        sum += 1.0 / x[j];
    return(sum);
} /* end of Fractab() function */
/*====================================*/
/* END OF FRACTAB.C */
```

## Program execution

```
FRACTAB.EXE

1/1     1/2     1/3     1/4     1/5
1/6     1/7     1/8     1/9     1/10
1/11    1/12    1/13    1/14    1/15
1/16    1/17    1/18    1/19    1/20
1/21    1/22    1/23    1/24    1/25
1/26    1/27    1/28    1/29    1/30
1/31    1/32    1/33    1/34    1/35
1/36    1/37    1/38    1/39    1/40
1/41    1/42    1/43    1/44    1/45
1/46    1/47    1/48    1/49    1/50
The sum of durations is 4.499206 whole notes
```

# FUNCTION: Durred( )   MIC 2.10

## Purpose

Reduce an array of rhythm duration fractions to lowest terms (consistent with rhythm pulse subdivision); return the reduced fractions to the program as a character string array.

## Notes

Circumstances arise in which computer-generated rhythms must be transcribed to conventional music notation. The process is simplified by reducing duration fractions ONLY to the level of the underlying metrical pulse (or subdivision thereof). For example, assuming a background meter of 6/8 time, it is more meaningful to a musician to see the fraction 12/16 expressed as 6/8, as opposed to 1/2, because 6/8 more adequately expresses the relationship between the background meter and the individual note durations.

If there is no need for a human being to interpret rhythmic fractions, e.g., when the values are for transmission to a digital synthesizer, then use Function Eucreduc( )—MIC 2.11; it will execute more efficiently.

## Programming ideas

1. Alter the main routine to generate random-order fraction denominators as well as numerators. Observe the effect that this method of reduction has on the intelligibility of returned duration fractions.
2. Write an interactive program that allows the user to request any (reasonable) length random-order melody, generates the appropriate number of rhythm durations, then adjusts the durations to conform to an input time reference.

## Program source code

```
/* DURRED.C   (Reduces an array of rhythm duration
                fractions to lowest terms [consistent with
                rhythm pulse subdivision and places them
                in a string array */
#include <stdio.h>
main()
{
  int j,x[20],y[20],total=20;
  void Durred();
  int seed = 2221;

  srand(seed);
  printf("random fraction numerators & denominators:\n");
  for (j = 0;j < total;j++)
```

```
      {
       if (j % 10 == 0)
           printf("\n");
       x[j] = rand() % 50 + 1;
       y[j] = 32;
       printf("%d/%d ",x[j],y[j]);
      }
 Durred(x,y,total);
 printf("\nthe reduced sequence:\n");
 for (j = 0;j < total;j++)
     {
      if (j % 10 == 0)
          printf("\n");
      printf("%d/%d ",x[j],y[j]);
     }
 } /* end of main */
 /*=============== MIC 2.10 =============*/
 /* Durred() function */
 void Durred(x,y,total)
 int x[],y[],total;
 {
  int j;
  for (j = 0;j < total;j++)
     {
      if (x[j] / 2.0 != x[j] / 2 || y[j] / 2.0 != y[j] / 2)
          continue;
      else
          {
           x[j]=x[j] / 2;
           y[j]=y[j] / 2;
          }
     }
 } /* end of Durred() function */
 /*=====================================*/
 /* END OF DURRED.C */
```

## Program execution

DURRED.EXE

random fraction numerators & denominators:

```
41/32 40/32 28/32 9/32 29/32 15/32 16/32 18/32 20/32 10/32
32/32 5/32 25/32 21/32 34/32 21/32 50/32 40/32 36/32 31/32
the reduced sequence:

41/32 20/16 14/16 9/32 29/32 15/32 8/16 9/16 10/16 5/16
16/16 5/32 25/32 21/32 17/16 21/32 25/16 20/16 18/16 31/32
```

# FUNCTION: Eucreduc( )  MIC 2.11

## Purpose

Reduce rhythm duration fractions to absolute lowest terms. (For use when consistency of pulse subdivision is not a concern.) Return the fractions to the program as a character string array.

## Notes

Durred, MIC 2.10 reduces fractions while limiting reduction to whole integer pulse subdivision. (For instance, $9/12$ would be reduced no further.) Eucreduc( ), however, relies on Euclid's Greatest Common Divisor algorithm to convert a fraction such as $9/12$ to even lower terms—$3/4$. When durations are being directed to a synthesizer, it is preferable to use this subroutine.

## Programming ideas

See MIC 2.10 Durred( ) applications.

## Program source code

```
/* EUCREDUC.C (reduces rhythm durations to absolute
              lowest terms using GCD - Euclid's algorithm;
              i.e. it doesn't preserve metrical
              pulse consistency. For example the fraction 9/12
              reduces to 3/4 )*/
#include <stdio.h>
main()
{
  int x[50],y[50],total = 50,seed = 17114,j;
  void Eucreduc();

  srand(seed);
  printf("%s%s","Loading random fraction",
         " numerator and denominator arrays---\n");
  for (j = 0;j < total;j++)
      {
      if (j % 10 == 0)
          printf("\n");
      x[j] = rand() % total + 1;
      y[j] = rand() % 16 + 1;
      printf("%d/%d ",x[j],y[j]);
      }
  printf("\nthe reduced fraction sequence ---\n");
  Eucreduc(x,y,total);
} /* end of main */
/*============== MIC 2.11 ============*/
/* Eucreduc() function */
void Eucreduc(x,y,total)
int x[],y[],total;
{
```

```
int a,b,c,d,j,temp,count=0;

for (j = 0;j < total;j++)
   {
    if (y[j] == 1)
       {
        printf("%d/%d ",x[j],y[j]);
        continue;
       }
    a = x[j];
    b = y[j];
    if (a > b)
      {
       temp = a;
       a = b;
       b = temp;
      }
    while(a > 0)
      {
       c = b / a;
       d = b - a * c;
       b = a;
       a = d;
      }
    printf("%d/%d ",x[j]/b,y[j]/b);
    count++;
    if (count % 10 == 0)
       printf("\n");
   }
}  /* end of Eucreduc() function */
/*=====================================*/
/* END OF EUCREDUC.C */
```

## Program execution

EUCREDUC.EXE

Loading random fraction numerator and denominator arrays---

```
13/12 27/16 44/15 23/7 3/1 48/4 28/9 7/5 2/8 14/12
22/5 34/3 22/5 6/12 19/14 46/13 46/13 19/10 44/5 28/4
26/9 2/2 45/12 46/14 25/8 15/2 4/13 19/3 12/12 41/14
36/3 12/1 23/10 8/11 28/14 25/7 14/13 2/5 49/1 17/11
29/1 20/11 7/6 46/5 22/10 41/16 35/6 30/4 22/12 13/10
the reduced fraction sequence ---
13/12 27/16 44/15 23/7 3/1 12/1 28/9 7/5 1/4 7/6 22/5
34/3 22/5 1/2 19/14 46/13 46/13 19/10 44/5 7/1 26/9
1/1 15/4 23/7 25/8 15/2 4/13 19/3 1/1 41/14 12/1
12/1 23/10 8/11 2/1 25/7 14/13 2/5 49/1 17/11 29/1 20/11 7/6 46/5
11/5 41/16 35/6 15/2 11/6 13/10
```

# FUNCTION GROUP: Fractsum.c

1. LeastCommonMultiple( )     MIC 2.12
2. GreatestCommonDivisor( )   MIC 2.13

## Purpose

Although the functions in this group have a number of individual applications, they are together here to sum an array of multivariant rhythm duration fractions.

## Notes

An alternative function, Fractab( ) MIC 2.9, sums fractions and expresses the result in decimal whole note values; however, the fractions must each have the numerator 1.

In contrast, FRACTSUM.C places no restriction on fraction type, and returns a fractional, not decimal, sum (e.g., $2/_1 + {}^{11}/_{16} = 2^{11}/_{16}$). Function LeastCommonMultiple( ) calls Function Greatest Common Divisor to total the sequence fractions.

There is one serious drawback to this particular fraction-summing method: When implemented for a computer with a small word-size, numeric overflow is quickly reached. (Add code to deal with this error condition.)

## Programming ideas

Write a program that generates random-order pitches and rhythms for a melodic line. Include Fractab( ) MIC 2.9 and additional code to reconcile the melodic rhythm duration sum to a user-input time frame.

## Program source code

```
/* FRACTSUM.C (sums a sequence of rhythm duration fractions;
              beware of potential overflow caused by overly
              complex fractions. */
#include <stdio.h>
main()
{
 unsigned long int x[50],y[50];
 int total = 50,seed = -231,j;
 unsigned long int GreatestCommonDivisor();
 void LeastCommonMultiple();

 srand(seed);
 printf("a sequence of fractions to be summed ----\n");
 for (j = 0;j < total;j++)
    {
      if (j % 10 == 0)
        printf("\n");
      x[j] = rand() % 10 + 1;
```

```c
      do
        y[j] = rand() % 8 + 1;
        /* accept only simple denominators */
        while(y[j] % 3 != 0  && y[j] % 4 != 0);
          printf("%d/",x[j]);
        printf("%d ",y[j]);
      }
  LeastCommonMultiple(x,y,total);
} /* end of main */
/*=============== MIC 2.12 ==============*/
/* LeastCommonMultiple() function
     (determines the least common multiple of two integers
      by calling the greatest common divisor function to supply
      that value, then divides the product of the two integers
      by the greatest common divisor.) */

void LeastCommonMultiple(x,y,total)
unsigned long int x[],y[];
int total;
{
 unsigned long int whole = 0,num=0,den=0,LCM,GCD,j,m,n;
 unsigned long int GreatestCommonDivisor();

 for (j= 1;j < total;j++)
    {
      m = y[0];  /* y[0] stores current denominator sum */
      n = y[j];/* next fraction denominator */
      GCD = GreatestCommonDivisor(m,n);
      LCM = m * n / GCD;
      m = LCM / y[0];
      n = LCM / y[j];
      /* x[0] stores current fraction denominator sum; x[j]
      holds next fraction denominator */
      num = (x[0] * m) + (x[j] * n);
      den = LCM;
      m = num;
      n = den;
      GCD = GreatestCommonDivisor(m,n);
      num = m / GCD;   /*num stores reduced numerator total */
      den = n / GCD;   /*den store reduced denominator total*/
      whole += num / den;
      x[0] = num % den;
      y[0] = den;
    }
 printf("\nsum of fractions = ");
 printf("%d + ",whole);
 printf("%d/",num % den);
 printf("%d",den);

} /* end of LeastCommonMultiple() function */
/*=============== MIC 2.13 ==============*/
/* GreatestCommonDivisor() function */
unsigned long int GreatestCommonDivisor(m,n)
unsigned long int m,n;
{
 unsigned long int a,b,c,d,temp;

 a = m;
 b = n;
 if (a > b)          /* swap */
    {
      temp = a;
```

```
      a = b;
      b = temp;
      }
  while(a > 0)
        {
        c = b / a;
        d = b - a * c;
        b = a;
        a = d;
        }
  return(b);
} /* end of GreatesCommonDivisor() function */
/*======================================*/
/* END OF FRACTSUM.C */
```

## Program execution

FRACTSUM.EXE

a sequence of fractions to be summed ----

```
1/4 7/6 7/4 2/6 2/8 6/6 8/3 9/8 2/6 10/3
1/6 7/6 2/3 6/4 1/6 7/8 4/8 1/6 8/4 5/3
3/8 3/4 4/6 8/3 5/8 4/8 8/3 2/8 9/3 9/4
3/6 9/8 4/8 8/3 7/3 7/4 1/3 1/6 7/3 1/6
4/3 1/6 7/6 4/6 10/6 6/4 1/3 5/8 8/8 3/6
sum of fractions = 55 + 2/3
```

## FUNCTION: Decfrac( )   MIC 2.14

## Purpose

Converts an array of decimal values (%) to fractions for use as rhythm durations.

## Notes

The main routine fills floating point array X[ ] with decimal values that convert to relatively simple fractions. The reason for controlling decimal complexity is that some synthesizers reject fractional input smaller than $1/128$ of a whole note; moreover, human perceptual limitations render extremely complex fractions useless—e.g., $121347/291385$. I set the practical minimum duration for rhythm applications at $1/100$ of a whole note, because few people are able to discriminate rhythmic nuance finer than this.

## Programming ideas

Generate decimal attack point rhythm durations for a sequence of pitches; use computer music format (each decimal duration is printed, followed by the current total of durations in decimal to be interpreted as elapsed time). Plot the rhythm attack points and durations on graph paper, then transcribe the output to proportional graphic notation for performance by an acoustic musical instrument such as the flute.

Apply the numerators of the converted set of duration fractions as scalar values (measured in %) for the articulation or volume parameter of the piece; either map them directly, or in random order.

Download the final data to a synthesizer, assign a flute timbre to the notelist, and play the electronic version.

## Program source code

```
/* DECFRAC.C   (converts decimals and decimal fractions
                 to rationals) */
#include <stdio.h>
main()
(
  float x[50];
  int total = 50,prec,base,seed = 3243,j;
  void Decfrac();

  srand(seed);
  printf("%s%s","Enter 1,2,or 3 for precision degree",
         " (1/10,1/100,or1/1000)\n");
  scanf("%d",&prec);
  printf("%s%s","Loading random decimals containing integer",
         " and fractional\nparts:\n");
```

```
    switch(prec)
        {
        case 1   : base = 10;
                   break;
        case 2   : base = 100;
                   break;
        case 3   : base = 1000;
                   break;
        default : base = 1000;
        }
    for (j = 0; j < total;j++)
        {
        x[j] = (rand() % 4) + (rand() % base) / (float)base;
        if (j % 6 == 0)
            printf("\n");
        printf("%g    ",x[j]);
        }
    printf("\n\nHere are the equivalent rational fractions:\n\n");
    Decfrac(x,total,base);
} /* end of main */
/*=============== MIC 2.14 ===============*/
/* Decfrac() function :NOTE for a higher degree of accuracy
                        when converting small decimal values,
                        raise base value exponentially,
                        ie. 1000,10000,etc. */
void Decfrac(x,total,base)
float x[];
int total,base;
{
int orig,num,denom,a,b,c,d,temp,j;

for (j = 0;j < total;j++)
    {
    orig = a = (x[j] * base) + .5;
    b = base;
    if (a > b)
        {
        temp = a;
        a = b;
        b = temp;
        }
    while(a > 0)
        {
        c = (b / a);
        d = b - a * c;
        b = a;
        a = d;
        }
    num = orig / b;
    denom = base / b;
    if (j % 6 == 0)
        printf("\n");
    printf("%d/%d    ",num,denom);
    }
} /* end of Decfrac() function */
/*=======================================*/
/* END OF DECFRAC.C */
```

# Program execution

DECFRAC.EXE

Enter 1,2,or 3 for precision degree (1/10,1/100,or1/1000)
Loading random decimals containing integer and fractional
parts:

```
0.6   2.1   3.7   0.2   0.2   3.9
3.8   3.2   1.6   0.1   0.5   3.9
2.2   2.1   3.7   2.6   1.6   1.1
0.4   0     3.5   2.8   3.4   1.4
3.4   0.1   3.1   1.6   0.6   1.6
0.7   1.9   2.3   3.6   0.6   2.9
0.1   2     0.1   3.9   1.5   3.7
2.5   1.4   1.1   0.9   2.1   1.6
3.4   1
```

Here are the equivalent rational fractions:

```
3/5    21/10   37/10   1/5    1/5    39/10
19/5   16/5    8/5     1/10   1/2    39/10
11/5   21/10   37/10   13/5   8/5    11/10
2/5    0/1     7/2     14/5   17/5   7/5
17/5   1/10    31/10   8/5    3/5    8/5
7/10   19/10   23/10   18/5   3/5    29/10
1/10   2/1     1/10    39/10  3/2    37/10
5/2    7/5     11/10   9/10   21/10  8/5
17/5   1/1
```

# FUNCTION: Fracdec( )   MIC 2.15

## Purpose

Convert an array of fractional rhythm values to an array of decimal values for transference to other musical parameters.

## Notes

You can translate a sequence of duration fractions—$1/2$, $3/7$, $5/9$, etc.—to decimal for mapping of the rhythm parameter to another parameter. In mapping, one set of value relationships is applied at some transpositional level to another dimension of the musical texture. For instance, to map rhythm onto volume, convert the durations to decimal, then scale the decimal values to fall within the volume parameter limits. (To do this, multiply each decimal number by the correct scaling factor, then truncate the result to integer.)

## Programming ideas

Generate an array of random-order, multivariant, rhythm duration fractions. Convert the fractions to decimal form, then scale and truncate the values for application to the articulation parameter of a piece for synthesizer or solo acoustic instrument.

Use the array contents, now converted and scaled, as pointers to the contents of other musical element arrays; e.g., generate the pitch, volume, and timbre parameters by applying the pointers in original or reverse order.

## Program source code

```
/* FRACDEC.C (converts fractional value to decimal
                for use as rhythm values;it also computes
                the sum of durations in whole notes )*/
#include <stdio.h>
main()
{
  int j,total = 20,seed = 323;
  double x[20],y[20],z[20],sum,Fracdec();

  srand(seed);
  printf("loading random fractions:\n");
  for (j = 0; j < total;j++)
      {
        x[j] = rand() % total + 1; /*load numerators*/
        y[j] = rand() % total + 1; /*lod denominators*/
      }
  sum = Fracdec(x,y,z,total);
  for (j = 0; j < total;j++)
      printf("%.0f/%.0f =%g\n",x[j],y[j],z[j]);
```

```
   printf("sum = %f whole notes.",sum);
} /* end of main */
/*=============== MIC 2.15 ==============*/
/* Fracdec() function */
double Fracdec(x,y,z,total)
int total;
double x[],y[],z[];
{
 double sum = 0.0;
 int j;

 for (j = 0;j < total;j++)
    {
     z[j] = x[j] / y[j];
     sum += z[j];
    }
 return(sum);
} /* end of Fracdec() function */
/*=====================================*/
/* END OF FRACDEC.C */
```

## Program execution

**FRACDEC.EXE**

```
loading random fractions:
13/13 =1
18/9 =2
14/4 =3.5
8/2 =4
6/16 =0.375
12/15 =0.8
7/17 =0.4117647
2/9 =0.2222222
19/18 =1.055556
3/9 =0.3333333
16/3 =5.333333
5/16 =0.3125
14/10 =1.4
20/18 =1.111111
4/15 =0.2666667
3/10 =0.3
4/1 =4
3/16 =0.1875
15/7 =2.142857
9/18 =0.5
sum = 29.251844 whole notes.
```

## FUNCTION GROUP: Decbidec.c

1. DecToBin( )    MIC 2.16
2. BinToDec( )    MIC 2.17
3. StringRev( )   MIC 2.18
4. StringLength( )  MIC 2.19

## Purpose

Convert an array of positive decimal integers to a character array of binary equivalents, and vice versa.

## Notes

There are a number of significant compositional applications for binary numbers. A particularly accessible one is as note attack-point determinants within a subdivided metrical continuum. Bit patterns that represent numbers are interpreted as "on-off" signals for musical tones, normally in one of two modes—open or closed. In open mode, a binary number is scanned from left to right. When a 1 is encountered a tone is sounded, which may continue (if the user so chooses) until the next 1 is reached, at which point another note is attacked. In closed mode, the instruction of each bit is literally adhered to: when a 1 is encountered, a note begins; it ends at the next bit, which will be either a new tone (1) or silence (0). Each bit of the number corresponds to a pulse unit predetermined by the composer, or to some other consistently assigned pattern.

For example, given the bit pattern 11001010, the pitches C#, G Ab C, and a quarter-note pulse unit, the following relationship would be produced in closed mode:

| (R = Rest) | | | | | | | | |
|---|---|---|---|---|---|---|---|---|
| P(itch) | C# | G | R | R | Ab | R | C | R |
| R(hythm) | 1/4 | 1/4 | 1/4 | 1/4 | 1/4 | 1/4 | 1/4 | 1/4 |

In open mode, the same set of givens will produce:

| P(itch) | C# | G | Ab | C |
|---|---|---|---|---|
| R(hythm) | 1/4 | 3/4 | 1/2 | 1/2 |

## Programming ideas

Write a program to apply binary numbers to rhythm using open and closed modes. Experiment with rules of your own for their application.

## Program source code

```c
/* DECBIDEC.C (converts a decimal integer value
                to a binary string, then back to decimal)*/
#include <stdio.h>
#define ToAscii(x) ((x >= 0 && x <=9) ? x + '0' : -1)
#define IsBinary(x) ((x == '0' || x == '1') ? 1 : 0)
#define ToDecimal(x) (x - '0')
#define TOTAL 20
main()
{
 char binary[12];
 unsigned int decnum;
 int DecToBin();
 int j;
 printf("%s%s","A sequence of decimal to binary",
       " to decimal conversions:\n");
 for (j = 0;j < TOTAL;j++)
     {
     decnum = (j+1) * 100;       /*compute a decimal value*/
     DecToBin(decnum,binary);
     printf("\ndecimal integer %d ",decnum);
     printf(" in binary = %s\n",binary);
     BinToDec(binary,decnum);
     printf("converted back to decimal = %d",decnum);
     }
} /* end of main */
/*=============== MIC 2.16 ===============*/
/* DecToBin() function (This function converts an array
                         of positive decimal integers to
                         an array of binary equivalents.) */

int DecToBin(decnum,binary)
unsigned int decnum;
char binary[12];
{
 int remainder,index = 0,count = 0;
 void StringRev();
 while (decnum / 2.0 != 0)
     {
     remainder = decnum % 2;
     binary[index++] = ToAscii(remainder);
     decnum = decnum / 2;
     count ++;
     }
 while (count++ <= 15)
     binary[index++] = '0';
 binary[index] = NULL;
 StringRev(binary,0,index);
 } /* end of DecToBin() function */
/*=============== MIC 2.18 ===============*/
 /* StringRev() function */
 void StringRev(string,start,end)
 char string[];
 int start,end;
 {
  int length;
  char temp;
  int StringLength();
  length = StringLength(string);
     if (end >= length)
```

```
                  end = length - 1;
     if (start >= end)
        return;
       else
          {
            temp = string[start];
            string[start] = string[end];
            string[end] = temp;
            StringRev(string,++start,--end);
          }
} /* end of StringRev() function */
/*=============== MIC 2.19 ===============*/
/* StringLength() function */
int StringLength(string)
char *string;
{
 if (*string == NULL)
     return(0);
  else
     return(1 + StringLength(++string));
} /* end of StringLength() function */
/*=============== MIC 2.17 ===============*/
/*BinToDec() function   (converts binary numbers to
                         their decimal equivalents.)*/
int BinToDec(binary,decnum)
char *binary;
unsigned int *decnum;
{
 *decnum = 0;

 while (*binary)
     if (IsBinary(*binary))
       *decnum = *decnum * 2 + ToDecimal(*binary++);
     else
        return(-1);
 return(0);
  ;
 }
 /* end of BinToDec */
/*=====================================*/
/* END OF DECBIDEC.C */
```

# Program execution

DECBIDEC.EXE

A sequence of decimal to binary to decimal conversions:

```
decimal integer 100   in binary = 0000000001100100
converted back to decimal = 100
decimal integer 200   in binary = 0000000011001000
converted back to decimal = 200
decimal integer 300   in binary = 0000000100101100
converted back to decimal = 300
decimal integer 400   in binary = 0000000110010000
converted back to decimal = 400
decimal integer 500   in binary = 0000000111110100
converted back to decimal = 500
decimal integer 600   in binary = 0000001001011000
converted back to decimal = 600
```

```
decimal integer 700  in binary = 0000001010111100
converted back to decimal = 700
decimal integer 800  in binary = 0000001100100000
converted back to decimal = 800
decimal integer 900  in binary = 0000001110000100
converted back to decimal = 900
decimal integer 1000  in binary = 0000001111101000
converted back to decimal = 1000
decimal integer 1100  in binary = 0000010001001100
converted back to decimal = 1100
decimal integer 1200  in binary = 0000010010110000
converted back to decimal = 1200
decimal integer 1300  in§nary = 0000010100010100
converted back to decimal = 1300
decimal integer 1400  in binary = 0000010101111000
converted back to decimal = 1400
decimal integer 1500  in binary = 0000010111011100
converted back to decimal = 1500
decimal integer 1600  in binary = 0000011001000000
converted back to decimal = 1600
decimal integer 1700  in binary = 0000011010100100
converted back to decimal = 1700
decimal integer 1800  in binary = 0000011100001000
converted back to decimal = 1800
decimal integer 1900  in binary = 0000011101101100
converted back to decimal = 1900
decimal integer 2000  in binary = 0000011111010000
converted back to decimal = 2000
```

# FUNCTION: Stirling( ) MIC 2.20

## Purpose

To provide a "shortcut" method of calculating the factorial of an integer. Called *Stirling's approximation*, the function is used in statistical applications to compute probabilities, permutations, and combinations.

## Notes

The algorithm computes factorials by approximating the natural logarithm for factorials greater than 10; for factorials smaller than eleven, the exact log of n! is returned. It works quickly, and the degree of accuracy is sufficient for most situations.

## Programming ideas

See MIC 2.21 Permutot( ) and MIC 2.22 Combntot( ).

## Program source code

```
/* STIRLING.C  (computes factorial approximations) */
#include <stdio.h>
#include <math.h>
main()
{
 int j;
 double num;/*number for which factorial is to be computed*/
 double Stirling(),exp();
 double appr;/*Stirling's approximation of log of number*/

 for (j = 9; j <= 12;j++)
     {
      num = j;
      printf("%s%s%.0f","Integer for which factorial",
             " will be computed is:",num);
      appr = Stirling(num);
      printf("\nlog of factorial is appr. %f\n",appr);
      if (num < 34.)
          printf("factorial is appr.%.0f\n",(exp(appr)+.5));
     }
} /* end of main */
/*=============== MIC 2.20 ===============*/
/* Stirling() function */
double Stirling(num)
double num;
{
 double appr = 1.0;
 double log();
 int j;
 if (num <=0.0)
     {
      appr = 0.0;
```

```
        return(appr);
    }
  for (j = 1;j <= 10;j++)
      {
       appr = appr * j;
       if (num == j)
           {
            appr = log(appr);
            return(appr);
           }
      }
  appr = log(6.283186L) / 2.0 + log(num) *
         (num + .5) - num + 1 / (12 * num);
  return(appr);
} /* end of Stirling() function */
/*====================================*/
/* END OF STIRLING.C */
```

## Program execution

STIRLING.EXE

```
Integer for which factorial will be computed is:9
log of factorial is appr. 12.801827
factorial is appr.362880
Integer for which factorial will be computed is:10
log of factorial is appr. 15.104413
factorial is appr.3628801
Integer for which factorial will be computed is:11
log of factorial is appr. 17.502310
factorial is appr.39916886
Integer for which factorial will be computed is:12
log of factorial is appr. 19.987216
factorial is appr.479002395
```

# FUNCTION GROUP: Permutot.c

1. Permutot( )   MIC 2.21
2. Stirling( )    MIC 2.20

## Purpose

Compute the number of permutations (potential reorderings) of n elements taken m at a time.

## Notes

Composers often wish to know the number of potential arrangements of a finite set of elements. This does not mean that all possibilities will be used within a particular composition. It is simply a point of departure for the decision-making process. In fact, a composition that used all permutations of the one-octave chromatic pitch series—only 12 notes—would take one lifetime to compose and a second lifetime to perform. There are 12! factorial—479,001,600 permutations.

The number of permutations of a given element set can be kept within human perceptual limits by taking fewer than the total number of elements at a time. For example, if one exploits all permutations of the 12-tone chromatic, taken 2 at a time, the possibilities are reduced to 132.

Why do you need a function to do this computation, when a hand calculator will do the job? The answer is to provide information for programmed structuring of data on higher organizational levels.

## Programming ideas

1. Write a program to feed-back permutational information to an algorithm that employs it to provide systematically permuted melodic pitch sets.
2. Write a program that "observes" various permutational possibilities of one randomly generated parameter (e.g., pitch), then returns that data to the program to control a second parameter.

## Program source code

```
/* PERMUTOT.C   (computes the number of permutations
                 of n elements taken m at a time.) */
#include <stdio.h>
#include <math.h>
main()
{
  int elements = 1; /*number of items to permute*/
  int many = 1; /*items to be taken at a time*/
  int j;
  double permutations,Permutot();
  for (j = 0;j < 10; j++)
```

```
    {
     permutations = Permutot(elements,many);
     printf("permutations of %d elements", elements);
     printf(" taken %d at a time",many);
     printf("\nare %.0f\n",permutations);
     elements += 3;
     many += 2;
    }
} /* end of main */
/*=============== MIC 2.21 ===============*/
double Permutot(elements,many)
int elements,many;
{
 double num;
 double elemfact = 0.0; /*log of 'elements' factorial*/
 double manyfact = 0.0; /*log of 'many' factorial*/
 double permutations = 0.0;
 double Stirling(),exp();
 double appr;

 num = elements;
 elemfact = Stirling(num);
 num = elements-many;
 manyfact = Stirling(num);
 permutations = exp(elemfact-manyfact);
 return(permutations);
} /* end of Permutot() function */
/*=============== MIC 2.20 ===============*/
/* Stirling() function */
double Stirling(num)
double num;
{
 double appr = 1.0;
 double log();
 int j;
 if (num <= 0.0)
   {
    appr = 0.0;
    return(appr);
   }
 for (j = 1;j <= 10;j++)
   {
    appr = appr * j;
    if (num == j)
       {
        appr = log(appr);
        return(appr);
       }
   }
 appr = log(6.283186L) / 2.0 + log(num) *
        (num + .5) - num + 1 / (12 * num);
 return(appr);
} /* end of Stirling() function */
/*====================================*/
/* END OF PERMUTOT.C */
```

# Program execution

```
permutations of 1 elements taken 1 at a time
are 1
permutations of 4 elements taken 3 at a time
are 24
permutations of 7 elements taken 5 at a time
are 2520
permutations of 10 elements taken 7 at a time
are 604800
permutations of 13 elements taken 9 at a time
are 259459542
permutations of 16 elements taken 11 at a time
are 174356710124
permutations of 19 elements taken 13 at a time
are 168951606028845
permutations of 22 elements taken 15 at a time
are 223016087856331552
permutations of 25 elements taken 17 at a time
are 3.84702719613062152e+020
permutations of 28 elements taken 19 at a time
are 8.40190696613826175e+023
```

## FUNCTION GROUP: Combntot.C

1. Combntot( )   MIC 2.22
2. Stirling( )    MIC 2.20

## Purpose

Compute the number of combinations of n elements taken m at a time. (The order of elements has no significance in combinations.)

## Notes

While permutations are arrangements of objects, combinations are simply selections. To illustrate: It is like asking "How many different ways can a set of twelve pitches appear with a set of three rhythm durations." (The answer is 220.) When you are interested only in the number of unique combinations of n elements taken m at a time, a vastly reduced set of possibilities is at hand, one which can be exploited within the boundaries of a single composition.

Suppose you wish to compose the pitch dimension of a process-oriented piece by generating random-order sets of six notes from the 1-octave chromatic. Not considering permutations, there are only 924 different sets to be generated, each consisting of six notes, for a total of 5,544 pitches in the piece. (The maximum number of combinations for a given set of n elements occurs around the "taken m" midpoint, after which the number of combinations recedes as its complement modulo n; e.g., 12 elements taken 7 at a time equals 792 unique combinations, as does 12 elements taken 5 at a time.)

## Programming ideas

Develop a program that will compute and file all the possible combinations of 12 elements after the user has selected the number to be taken at a time.

## Program source code

```
/* COMBNTOT.C  (computes the number of combinations
                of n elements taken m at a time.) */
#include <stdio.h>
#include <math.h>
main()
{
  int elements = 10;/* number of items */
  int many = 2;  /* number of items taken at a time */
  int j;
  double combinations,Combntot();
  for(j = 0;j < 10; j++)
    {
```

```
        combinations = Combntot(elements,many);
        printf("combinations of %d elements",elements);
        printf (" taken %d at a time",many);
        printf("\nare %.0f\n",combinations);
        elements += 3;
        many += 3;
        }
} /* end of main */
/*=============== MIC 2.22 ===============*/
/* Combntot() function */
double Combntot(elements,many)
int elements,many;
{
 double num;
 double elemfact; /*log of 'elements' factorial*/
 double manyfact; /*log of 'many' factorial*/
 double diffact;  /*log of (elemfact-manyfact) factorial*/
 double combinations;
 double Stirling(),exp();
 double appr;

 num = elements;
 elemfact = Stirling(num);
 num = many;
 manyfact = Stirling(num);
 num = elements - many;
 diffact = Stirling(num);
 combinations = exp(elemfact - (manyfact + diffact));
 return(combinations);
} /* end of Combntot() function */
/*=============== MIC 2.20 ===============*/
/* Stirling() function */
double Stirling(num)
double num;
{
 double appr = 1.0;
 double log();
 int j;
 if(num <= 0.0)
    {
     appr = 0.0;
     return(appr);
    }
 for(j = 1;j <= 10;j++)
     {
       appr = appr * j;
       if(num == j)
          {
           appr = log(appr);
           return(appr);
          }
     }
 appr = log(6.283186L) / 2.0 + log(num) *
        (num + .5) - num + 1 / (12 * num);
 return(appr);
} /* end of Stirling() function */
/*===================================*/
/* END OF COMBNTOT.C */
```

# Program execution

COMBNTOT.EXE

```
combinations of 10 elements taken 2 at a time
are 45
combinations of 13 elements taken 5 at a time
are 1287
combinations of 16 elements taken 8 at a time
are 12870
combinations of 19 elements taken 11 at a time
are 75582
combinations of 22 elements taken 14 at a time
are 319770
combinations of 25 elements taken 17 at a time
are 1081575
combinations of 28 elements taken 20 at a time
are 3108104
combinations of 31 elements taken 23 at a time
are 7888724
combinations of 34 elements taken 26 at a time
are 18156202
combinations of 37 elements taken 29 at a time
are 38608018
```

## FUNCTION GROUP: Normtabl.c

1. Freqtabl( )    MIC 2.23
2. Datanorm( )   MIC 2.24
3. Zeromat( )    MIC 2.25

## Purpose

Test probability distribution functions for applicability to specific musical parameters.

## Notes

To adequately test probability distribution functions, a characteristic curve must be produced by using many samples. Although you might not wish to view a detailed graph of the distribution, you do need to observe the curve's shape for comparison to the idealized function. Therefore, you must normalize data—Datanorm( )—to fit within a viewable CRT range. Most importantly, a table of occurrence frequency must be generated—Freqtabl( )—to provide the data for generating a bargraph or similar video display.

## Programming ideas

1. Modify the main routine to generate data by the use of functions found in Chapter 4 "Probability distribution functions."
2. Adapt NORMTABL.C to allow CRT viewing of a Histogram of the distribution.

## Program source code

```
/* NORMTABL.C   (create a data frequency
                  table and normalize values for the table)*/
#include <stdio.h>
main()
{
  int x[20],range = 20,total = 1000,seed = -1011,j;
  float y[20];
  int srand();
  void Freqtabl(),Datanorm(),Zeromat();

  srand(seed);
  printf("integer value\tnormalized value\tfrequency\n");
  Zeromat(x,y,range);
  Freqtabl(x,range,total);
  Datanorm(x,y,range);
  for (j = 0;j < range;j++)
      printf("\t%d\t\t %.3f\t\t\t%d\n",j,y[j],x[j]);
} /* end of main */
/*============== MIC 2.23 ==============*/
/* Freqtabl() function */
```

```
void Freqtabl(x,range,total)
int x[],range,total;
{
 int num,j,rand();

 for (j = 0; j < total;j++)
     {
      num = rand() % range;
      x[num] = x[num] + 1;
     }
} /* end of Freqtabl() function */
/*=============== MIC 2.24 ===============*/
/* Datanorm() function */
void Datanorm(x,y,range)
int x[],range;
float y[];
{
 int j;
 float sum = 0.0;

 for (j = 0;j < range;j++)
     sum += x[j];
 for (j = 0;j < range;j++)
     y[j] = x[j] / sum;
} /* end of Datanorm() function */
/*=============== MIC 2.25 ===============*/
/* Zeromat() function */
void Zeromat(x,y,range)
int x[],range;
float y[];

{
 int j;
 for (j = 0;j < range;j++)
     {
      x[j] = 0;
      y[j] = 0.0;
     }
} /* end of Zeromat() function */
/*=====================================*/
/* END OF NORMTABL.C */
```

## Program execution

NORMTABL.EXE

| integer value | normalized value | frequency |
|---|---|---|
| 0 | 0.059 | 59 |
| 1 | 0.044 | 44 |
| 2 | 0.043 | 43 |
| 3 | 0.052 | 52 |
| 4 | 0.053 | 53 |
| 5 | 0.056 | 56 |
| 6 | 0.048 | 48 |
| 7 | 0.049 | 49 |
| 8 | 0.041 | 41 |
| 9 | 0.036 | 36 |
| 10 | 0.051 | 51 |
| 11 | 0.042 | 42 |

| | | |
|---|---|---|
| 12 | 0.047 | 47 |
| 13 | 0.045 | 45 |
| 14 | 0.052 | 52 |
| 15 | 0.063 | 63 |
| 16 | 0.067 | 67 |
| 17 | 0.060 | 60 |
| 18 | 0.043 | 43 |
| 19 | 0.049 | 49 |

## FUNCTION GROUP: Scaler.c

1. AllScaler( )   MIC 2.35
2. scaler( )      MIC 2.36
3. Inverse( )     MIC 2.37

## Purpose

Normalize an input array of integers to any (or all) of 84 distinct ranges; conversion of data for one parameter to the ranges of other parameters.

## Notes

Allscaler( ) gives all gamuts from 1 to 84, each normalized to 0; scaler( ) gives the specified gamut.

## Attention

Notice that three additional subprogram files must be available to the compiler (from Appendix B):

    array.c        MIC_SP1.0
    synclavi.c     MIC_SP7.0
    randmain.c     MIC_SP19.0

These files, in turn, may call other subprograms so list them first to determine dependencies.

To adequately test data generated in the pitch parameter, for example, the composer might wish to map the normalized sequence to the rhythm or timbre parameters to test the applicability of the data. Therefore, the data must be scaled to fit within the range limits of the target parameter.

## Programming ideas

1. Modify the main routine to generate data by the use of functions found in Chapter 4, "Probability distribution functions."
2. Adapt SCALER.C to allow CRT viewing of a histogram of the distribution.
3. Modify the main routine to allow the user to specify the specific output conversion(s).

## Program source code

SCALER.C

```
#include <stdio.h>
#define MAXDATA 100
```

```c
#include "randmain.c"
#include "synclavi.c"
#include "array.c"
main()
{
    int datarray[MAXDATA], inverse[MAXDATA], j, size;

    size = RandMain(datarray);
    printf("\n\n\nInverse\n");
    Inverse(datarray, inverse, size);
    for(j = 0; j < size; j++)
        printf("%d ", inverse[j]);
    printf("\n\noriginal scaled to gamut of 20");
    scaler(datarray, size, 20);
    printf("\n\ninverse scaled to gamut of 20");
    scaler(inverse, size, 20);
    printf("\n\nall gamuts");
    AllScaler(datarray, size);
} /* end of main() */
/*=============== MIC 2.35 ============*/
AllScaler(datarray, size)
    int datarray[], size;

{
int j,  max, min, pc[MAXDATA];
float factor, pc_float, min1 = 214000.0;
float  k,range;

 max = getmax(datarray, size);
 min = getmin(datarray, size);
 range = max - min;
 for(k = 1; k <= 84; k++)
    {
    factor =  k / (range + (range / k));
    printf("\n\ngamut = %f scaling factor = %f\n", k, factor);
    min1 =210000.0;

        for(j = 0; j < size; j++)
            {
            pc_float = datarray[j] * factor;
            if (pc_float < min1)
                min1 = pc_float;
            }
        for(j = 0; j < size; j++)
            {
            pc_float = datarray[j] * factor - min1;
            pc[j] = (int)(pc_float  + 0.5);
            }
            PutArray(pc, size);
            ScriptArray(pc,' ', size);

    }
}
/*=============== MIC 2.36 ============*/
scaler(int datarray[], int size, float gamut)
{
    int disarray[MAXDATA], j, min, max;
    float range, factor;

    max = getmax(datarray, size);
    min = getmin(datarray, size);
    range = max - min;
    factor =  gamut / (range + (range / gamut));
```

```
        printf("\n\ngamut = %f scaling factor = %f\n", gamut, factor);
        for(j = 0; j < size; j++)
            printf("%d ",  (int)(datarray[j] * factor - min  + 0.5));
}
/*=============== MIC 2.37 ============*/
Inverse(int datarray[], int inv[], int size)
{
    int j, min, max, range;

    max = getmax(datarray, size);
    min = getmin(datarray, size);
    range = max - min;
      for(j = 0; j < size; j++)
            inv[j] = abs(datarray[j] - (range + 1));  /* invert */
} /* end of scaler() function */
/*====================================*/
```

## Example program run

```
How many random numbers do you want?      10
Enter lowest number in gamut     0
Enter highest number in gamut    10
4 10 0 0 7 3 5 9 6 5

Inverse
7 1 11 11 4 8 6 2 5 6

original scaled to gamut of 20

gamut = 20.000000 scaling factor = 1.904762
8 19 0 0 13 6 10 17 11 10

inverse scaled to gamut of 20

gamut = 20.000000 scaling factor = 1.904762
12 1 20 20 7 14 10 3 9 10

all gamuts

gamut = 1.000000 scaling factor = 0.050000
   0   1   0   0   0   0   0   0   0   0

   C0  C#0 C0  C0  C0  C0  C0  C0  C0  C0

gamut = 2.000000 scaling factor = 0.133333
   1   1   0   0   1   0   1   1   1   1

   C#0 C#0 C0  C0  C#0 C0  C#0 C#0 C#0 C#0

gamut = 3.000000 scaling factor = 0.225000
   1   2   0   0   2   1   1   2   1   1

   C#0 D0  C0  C0  D0  C#0 C#0 D0  C#0 C#0

gamut = 4.000000 scaling factor = 0.320000
   1   3   0   0   2   1   2   3   2   2

   C#0 D#0 C0  C0  D0  C#0 D0  D#0 D0  D0
```

Function group: Scaler.c   75

```
gamut = 5.000000 scaling factor = 0.416667
  2    4    0    0    3    1    2    4    3    2

   D0  E0  C0  C0  D#0 C#0 D0   E0   D#0 D0

gamut = 6.000000 scaling factor = 0.514286
  2    5    0    0    4    2    3    5    3    3

   D0  F0  C0  C0  E0  D0  D#0  F0   D#0 D#0

gamut = 7.000000 scaling factor = 0.612500
  2    6    0    0    4    2    3    6    4    3

   D0  F#0 C0  C0  E0  D0  D#0  F#0  E0  D#0

gamut = 8.000000 scaling factor = 0.711111
  3    7    0    0    5    2    4    6    4    4

   D#0 G0  C0  C0  F0  D0  E0   F#0  E0  E0

gamut = 9.000000 scaling factor = 0.810000
  3    8    0    0    6    2    4    7    5    4

   D#0 G#0 C0  C0  F#0 D0  E0   G0   F0  E0

gamut = 10.000000 scaling factor = 0.909091
  4    9    0    0    6    3    5    8    5    5

   E0  A0  C0  C0  F#0 D#0 F0   G#0  F0  F0

gamut = 11.000000 scaling factor = 1.008333
  4   10    0    0    7    3    5    9    6    5

   E0  A#0 C0  C0  G0  D#0 F0   A0   F#0 F0

gamut = 12.000000 scaling factor = 1.107692
  4   11    0    0    8    3    6   10    7    6

   E0  B0  C0  C0  G#0 D#0 F#0  A#0  G0  F#0
                         .
                         .
                         .
                         .
                         .
                         .
gamut = 48.000000 scaling factor = 4.702041
 19   47    0    0   33   14   24   42   28   24

   G1  B3  C0  C0  A2  D1  C2   F#3  E2  C2

gamut = 49.000000 scaling factor = 4.802000
 19   48    0    0   34   14   24   43   29   24

   G1  C4  C0  C0  A#2 D1  C2   G3   F2  C2

gamut = 50.000000 scaling factor = 4.901961
 20   49    0    0   34   15   25   44   29   25

   G#1 C#4 C0  C0  A#2 D#1 C#2  G#3  F2  C#2
```

```
gamut = 51.000000 scaling factor = 5.001923
  20  50   0   0  35  15  25  45  30  25

   G#1 D4  C0  C0  B2  D#1 C#2 A3  F#2 C#2

gamut = 52.000000 scaling factor = 5.101887
  20  51   0   0  36  15  26  46  31  26

   G#1 D#4 C0  C0  C3  D#1 D2  A#3 G2  D2

gamut = 53.000000 scaling factor = 5.201852
  21  52   0   0  36  16  26  47  31  26

   A1  E4  C0  C0  C3  E1  D2  B3  G2  D2

gamut = 54.000000 scaling factor = 5.301818
  21  53   0   0  37  16  27  48  32  27

   A1  F4  C0  C0  C#3 E1  D#2 C4  G#2 D#2

gamut = 55.000000 scaling factor = 5.401786
  22  54   0   0  38  16  27  49  32  27

   A#1 F#4 C0  C0  D3  E1  D#2 C#4 G#2 D#2

gamut = 56.000000 scaling factor = 5.501754
  22  55   0   0  39  17  28  50  33  28

   A#1 G4  C0  C0  D#3 F1  E2  D4  A2  E2

gamut = 57.000000 scaling factor = 5.601724
  22  56   0   0  39  17  28  50  34  28

   A#1 G#4 C0  C0  D#3 F1  E2  D4  A#2 E2

gamut = 58.000000 scaling factor = 5.701695
  23  57   0   0  40  17  29  51  34  29

   B1  A4  C0  C0  E3  F1  F2  D#4 A#2 F2

gamut = 59.000000 scaling factor = 5.801667
  23  58   0   0  41  17  29  52  35  29

   B1  A#4 C0  C0  F3  F1  F2  E4  B2  F2

gamut = 60.000000 scaling factor = 5.901639
  24  59   0   0  41  18  30  53  35  30

   C2  B4  C0  C0  F3  F#1 F#2 F4  B2  F#2
                       .
                       .
                       .
                       .
                       .
                       .

gamut = 76.000000 scaling factor = 7.501299
  30  75   0   0  53  23  38  68  45  38

   F#2 D#6 C0  C0  F4  B1  D3  G#5 A3  D3
```

```
gamut = 77.000000 scaling factor = 7.601282
 30  76   0   0  53  23  38  68  46  38

   F#2 E6  C0  C0  F4  B1  D3  G#5 A#3 D3

gamut = 78.000000 scaling factor = 7.701266
 31  77   0   0  54  23  39  69  46  39

   G2  F6  C0  C0  F#4 B1  D#3 A5  A#3 D#3

gamut = 79.000000 scaling factor = 7.801250
 31  78   0   0  55  23  39  70  47  39

   G2  F#6 C0  C0  G4  B1  D#3 A#5 B3  D#3

gamut = 80.000000 scaling factor = 7.901235
 32  79   0   0  55  24  40  71  47  40

   G#2 G6  C0  C0  G4  C2  E3  B5  B3  E3

gamut = 81.000000 scaling factor = 8.001220
 32  80   0   0  56  24  40  72  48  40

   G#2 G#6 C0  C0  G#4 C2  E3  C6  C4  E3

gamut = 82.000000 scaling factor = 8.101205
 32  81   0   0  57  24  41  73  49  41

   G#2 A6  C0  C0  A4  C2  F3  C#6 C#4 F3

gamut = 83.000000 scaling factor = 8.201191
 33  82   0   0  57  25  41  74  49  41

   A2  A#6 C0  C0  A4  C#2 F3  D6  C#4 F3

gamut = 84.000000 scaling factor = 8.301176
 33  83   0   0  58  25  42  75  50  42

   A2  B6  C0  C0  A#4 C#2 F#3 D#6 D4  F#3
```

# 3
# *Series and motive operations*

## FUNCTION GROUP: Motforms.c

1. Printpitch( )  MIC 3.1
2. Motretro( )  MIC 3.2
3. Motinvrt( )  MIC 3.3
4. Motrnpz( )  MIC 3.4

## Purpose

Process pitch sequences (motifs) of varying length by any of three standard methods:

a. retrograde order
b. intervallic inversion
c. intervallic transposition

## Notes

Main routine variable, "total," can be changed to accommodate any length sequence, but the array dimension statements must also be altered accordingly.

Care should be taken to prevent overrun of the pitch element table range limits when modifying the driver program to allow user input of melodic sequences. Program failure can be prevented by the insertion of additional code to reset output data within pitch limits if overrun occurs.

# Programming ideas

1. Change the main routine to interactive. Allow the user to input pitch sequences and select program options.
2. Alter the program to read pitch data from a source file, process the data in various ways, then send the output to a destination file.

# Program source code

```
/* MOTFORMS.C (processes pitch sequences - motifs - by any of
                 3 methods:retrograde,inversion,transposition) */
#include <stdio.h>
main()
{
  int orig[12];        /*stores original pitch motif*/
  int retro[12];       /*stores retrograde motif*/
  int invert[12];      /*stores inverted motif*/
  int motrans[12];     /*stores motif transposition*/
  int transint = -3;   /*transposition interval*/
  int total = 12,j,seed = -22215;
  void Printpitch(),Motretro(),
       Motinvrt(),Motrnpz();

  srand(seed);
  printf("\noriginal pitch motif --\n");
    for (j = 0;j < total;j++)
         /*generate a midrange random-order pitch motif*/
         orig[j] = rand() % 12 + 30;
  Printpitch(orig,total);
  Motretro(orig,retro,total);
  printf("\nretrograde motif --\n");
  Printpitch(retro,total);
  Motinvrt(orig,invert,total);
  printf("\ninverted motif --\n");
  Printpitch(invert,total);
  Motrnpz(orig,motrans,transint,total);
  printf("\nmotif transposed by %d interval--\n",transint);
  Printpitch(motrans,total);
}/* end of main */
/*================= MIC 3.1 ==============*/
/* Printpitch() function  - an adaptation of MIC 2.3,
                                Pitchtab() function */
  void Printpitch(array,total)
  int array[],total;
  {
    static char *pitch[] = {
    "C0 ","C#0","D0 ","D#0","E0 ","F0 ","F#0","G0 ","G#0",
    "A0 ","A#0","B0 ","C1 ","C#1","D1 ","D#1","E1 ","F1 ",
    "F#1","G1 ","G#1","A1 ","A#1","B1 ","C2 ","C#2","D2 ",
    "G#2","E2 ","F2 ","F#2","G2 ","G#2","A2 ","A#2","B2 ",
    "C3 ","C#3","D3 ","D#3","E3 ","F3 ","F#3","G3 ","G#3",
    "A3 ","A#3","B3 ","C4 ","C#4","D4 ","D#4","E4 ","F4 ",
    "F#4","G4 ","G#4","A4 ","A#4","B4 ","C5 ","C#5","D5 ",
    "D#5","E5 ","F5 ","F#5","G5 ","G#5","A5 ","A#5","B5 ",
    "C6 ","C#6","D6 ","D#6","E6 ","F6 ","F#6","G6 ","G#6",
    "A6 ","A#6","B6 ","C7 "   };
    int j;

    for (j = 0;j < total;j++)
```

```
        printf("%s " ,pitch[array[j]]);
printf("\n");
  } /* end Printpitch() function */
/*=============== MIC 3.2 ===============*/
/* Motretro() function - accepts an input pitch
                         sequence and outputs its
                         retrograde form.*/
  void Motretro(array1,array2,total)
  int array1[],array2[],total;
  {
   int j,l;

      for (j = 0;j < total;j++)
        {
         l = total - j - 1;
         array2[l] = array1[j];
        }

  } /* end Motretro() function */
/*=============== MIC 3.3 ===============*/
/* Motinvrt() function  - accepts an input pitch sequence
                          and outputs its mirror image
                          form */
  void Motinvrt(array1,array2,total)
  int array1[],array2[],total;
  {
   int j;

   array2[0] = array1[0];
      for (j = 1;j < total;j++)
         array2[j] = array2[j-1] -
         (array1[j] - array1[j-1]);

  } /* end Motinvrt() function */
/*=============== MIC 3.4 ===============*/
/* Motrnpz() function  -  transposes an input motif by
             a specified number of 1/2 steps. Transposition
             direction is determined by the sign of the
             transposition interval.*/
void Motrnpz(array1,array2,tintval,total)
int array1[],array2[],tintval,total;
{
 int j;

   for (j = 0;j < total;j++)
      array2[j] = array1[j] + tintval;

} /* end Motrnpz() function */
/*====================================*/
/* END OF MOTFORMS.C */
```

## Program execution

MOTFORMS.EXE

original pitch motif --
A#2  B2   G#2 A#2 D3   G2   A2   C3   F3   A#2 G2   G2

retrograde motif --
G2   G2   A#2 F3   C3   A2   G2   D3   A#2 G#2 B2   A#2

```
inverted motif --
A#2 A2   C3   A#2 F#2 C#3 B2   G#2 G#2 A#2 C#3 C#3

motif transposed by -3 interval--
G2   G#2 F2   G2   B2   E2   F#2 A2   D3   G2   E2   E2
```

# FUNCTION GROUP: Displace.c

1. Displace( )     MIC 3.5
2. Printpitch( )   MIC 2.3

## Purpose

Vary registrated pitch sequences by individually displacing notes a specific number of octaves.

## Notes

The main routine can be converted to an interactive main routine by dimensioning arrays orig[ ], final[ ], and disp[ ] to accommodate longer pitch sequences. Add appropriate input loop statements which prompt the user to enter the pitch sequence and corresponding octave displacements.

## Programming ideas

1. Convert the main routine to an interactive routine that will accept any length pitch sequence (up to 100 notes).
2. Write a program that uses an array of random order rhythm values (range 1–6) to displace a pitch sequence. Avoid parametric unity, i.e., duration 1 (a whole note) should not result in displacement by 1 octave.

   *Hint*: use the durations as pointers to the addresses of an array which contains random-order octave displacements.

3. Write an interactive program that offers the user options to invert, retrograde, transpose, and displace an input melodic sequence.
4. Convert the integers of the octave-displaced sequence to binary form; map the binary numbers to the rhythm parameter in an interesting way.

## Program source code

```
/* DISPLACE.C  (individually displaces the pitches of an input
               pitch sequence by a specific number of octaves) */
#include <stdio.h>
main()
{
   int orig[20];            /*prime sequence*/
   int final[20];           /*sequence after displacement*/
   int displint[20];        /*displacement interval array*/
   int total,j,seed = 554;
   void Printpitch(),Displace();
   total = 10;
```

```c
      srand(seed);
      printf("\na random-order pitch sequence --\n");
        for (j = 0;j < total;j++)
          {
             orig[j] = rand() % 12+24;      /*gen. a r-o sequence*/
             displint[j] = rand() % 5 - 2; /*gen. displacements*/
          }
        Printpitch(orig,total);
        printf("\nrespective octave displacements:\n");
        for (j = 0;j < total;j++)
           printf("%d    ",displint[j]);
        Displace(orig,final,displint,total);
        printf("\nthe registrated pitch sequence:\n");
        Printpitch(final,total);
} /* end of main */
/*=============== MIC 3.1 ===============*/
/* Printpitch function */
  void Printpitch(array,total)
  int array[],total;
  {
   static char *pitch[] = {
    "C0 ","C#0","D0 ","D#0","E0 ","F0 ","F#0","G0 ","G#0",
    "A0 ","A#0","B0 ","C1 ","C#1","D1 ","D#1","E1 ","F1 ",
    "F#1","G1 ","G#1","A1 ","A#1","B1 ","C2 ","C#2","D2 ",
    "D#2","E2 ","F2 ","F#2","G2 ","G#2","A2 ","A#2","B2 ",
    "C3 ","C#3","D3 ","D#3","E3 ","F3 ","F#3","G3 ","G#3",
    "A3 ","A#3","B3 ","C4 ","C#4","D4 ","D#4","E4 ","F4 ",
    "F#4","G4 ","G#4","A4 ","A#4","B4 ","C5 ","C#5","D5 ",
    "D#5","E5 ","F5 ","F#5","G5 ","G#5","A5 ","A#5","B5 ",
    "C6 ","C#6","D6 ","D#6","E6 ","F6 ","F#6","G6 ","G#6",
    "A6 ","A#6","B6 ","C7 "   };

    int j;

      for (j = 0;j < total;j++)
           printf("%s " ,pitch[array[j]]);
     printf("\n");

   } /* end Printpitch() function */
/*=============== MIC 3.5 ===============*/
/* Displace() function (individually displaces the pitches
                        of an input pitch sequence by a
                        specific number of octaves.) */
void Displace(array1,array2,array3,total)
int array1[],array2[],array3[],total;
{
 int j;

    for (j = 0;j < total;j++)
       array2[j] = array1[j] + 12 * array3[j];

} /* end Displace() function */
/*===================================*/
/* END OF DISPLACE.C */
```

## Program execution

`DISPLACE.EXE`

```
a random-order pitch sequence --
F#2 C#2 C#2 C2  G2  G2  D2  C2  A2  A2

respective octave displacements:
0    -2   -1   1   0   -2   0   -2   -2   -1
the registrated pitch sequence:
F#2 C#0 C#1 C3  G2  G0  D2  C0  A0  A1
```

# FUNCTION GROUP: Alterseq.c

1. Alterseq( )     MIC 3.6
2. Printpitch( )   MIC 3.1

## Purpose

Modify a pitch sequence via interval expansion or contraction by a constant factor.

## Notes

Variable "intsize," if negative, contracts the melodic interval (measured in 1/2-steps) between adjacent notes of the pitch sequence. If "intsize" is positive, the interval is expanded.

There is built-in protection against repeated tones resulting from compression; The algorithm prevents the generation of intervals smaller than a minor second. However, repeated tones contained in the original sequence are allowed to remain.

## Programming ideas

1. Convert the main routine to an interactive routine that allows the user to input a sequence of integers representing registered pitches. Run the program several times using the same pitch sequence, but expand or contract the intervals by a markedly different factor during each run. Map the prime order output data to the pitch parameter, then map the same data in retrograde form to the rhythm parameter.
2. Run the interactive program version three times using the same input integer sequence, but alter the interval of expansion/contraction with each run. Apply the original integer sequence to the pitch parameter; map the three altered output integer sequences to the rhythm, volume, and articulation parameters.

## Program source code

```
/* ALTERSEQ.C  (alters a value sequence by interval expansion
                or contraction. Positive integers expand the
                sequence,negative integers contract it.) */
#include <stdio.h>
#define abs_val(x) ((x >= 0) ? x : 0 - x)
main()
{
  int orig[10];        /* prime pitch sequence */
  int final[10];       /* expanded/contracted sequence */
  int intsize = 2;     /* interval-size for exp/contr */
  int total = 10,j,seed = 9164;
  void Printpitch(),Alterseq();
```

```
        srand(seed);
        printf("\na random-order pitch sequence --\n");
           for (j = 0;j <= total-1;j++)
               orig[j] = rand() % 22 + 22; /*gen. a r-o sequence*/
        Printpitch(orig,total);
        printf("\nthe sequence expanded by");
        printf(" %d semitones:\n",intsize);
        Alterseq(orig,final,intsize,total);
        Printpitch(final,total);
        printf("\nthe sequence contracted by");
        printf(" %d semitones:\n",intsize);
        intsize = -2;
        Alterseq(orig,final,intsize,total);
        Printpitch(final,total);
} /* end of main */
/*=============== MIC 3.1 ===============*/
/* Printpitch() function */
        void Printpitch(array,total)
        int array[],total;
        {
        static char *pitch[] = {
           "C0 ","C#0","D0 ","D#0","E0 ","F0 ","F#0","G0 ","G#0",
           "A0 ","A#0","B0 ","C1 ","C#1","D1 ","D#1","E1 ","F1 ",
           "F#1","G1 ","G#1","A1 ","A#1","B1 ","C2 ","C#2","D2 ",
           "D#2","E2 ","F2 ","F#2","G2 ","G#2","A2 ","A#2","B2 ",
           "C3 ","C#3","D3 ","D#3","E3 ","F3 ","F#3","G3 ","G#3",
           "A3 ","A#3","B3 ","C4 ","C#4","D4 ","D#4","E4 ","F4 ",
           "F#4","G4 ","G#4","A4 ","A#4","B4 ","C5 ","C#5","D5 ",
           "D#5","E5 ","F5 ","F#5","G5 ","G#5","A5 ","A#5","B5 ",
           "C6 ","C#6","D6 ","D#6","E6 ","F6 ","F#6","G6 ","G#6",
           "A6 ","A#6","B6 ","C7 "   };

           int j;

              for (j = 0;j <= total-1;j++)
                  printf("%s " ,pitch[array[j]]);
           printf("\n");

        } /* end Printpitch() function */
/*=============== MIC 3.6 ===============*/
/* Alterseq() function */
void Alterseq(array1,array2,expcont,total)
int array1[],array2[],expcont,total;
{
int j,oldintvl,intdir,newintvl;

        array2[0] = array1[0];
        for (j = 1;j <= total-1;j++)
           {
             if (array1[j] == array1[j-1])
                 { array2[j] = array2[j-1];
                   continue;
                 }
             oldintvl = array1[j] - array1[j-1];
             if (oldintvl > 0)
                 intdir = 1;
             else if (oldintvl < 0)
                      intdir = -1;
             else intdir = 0;
             newintvl = abs_val(oldintvl) + expcont;
```

```
        if (newintvl < 1)
            newintvl = 1;
        array2[j] = array2[j-1] + intdir * newintvl;
    }
}/* end Alterseq() function */
/*=======================================*/
/* END OF ALTERSEQ.C */
```

# Program execution

`ALTERSEQ.EXE`

```
a random-order pitch sequence --
C2   A#2 F3   C#2 E3   C2   E2   D#2 F#3 A#1

the sequence expanded by 2 semitones:
C2   C3   A3   D#2 G#3 D2   G#2 F2   A#3 C2

the sequence contracted by 2 semitones:
C2   G#2 C#3 B1   C3   A#1 C2   B1   C3   F#1
```

# FUNCTION GROUP: Setflag.c   MIC 3.7

1. Setflag( )      MIC 3.7
2. Zeromat( )    MIC 2.27

## Purpose

Generate random-order integer series by the array flag method; repeated invocation returns random-order permutations.

## Notes

This sampling-without-replacement subroutine is inefficient, but works well when the number of elements to be serialized is relatively small. It generates a random number within range limits, then checks the content of the array cum[ ] address pointed to by the random number to determine whether a flag (1) is present. If the address is empty, it receives the flag, and the random integer is placed in array set[ ] as a series member. If the address already has the flag, the number is discarded and another generated.

Repeated invocation of this subroutine for the purpose of generating series permutations requires the invocation of Function MIC 2.25 Zeromat( ) to reset to 0 the flags in array cum[ ] prior to each call.

Depending upon programming circumstances, it may be more appropriate to invoke either of the two shuffling subroutines (MIC 3.8 or MIC 3.9) to generate random-order permutations of an element set.

## Programming ideas

1. Write an interactive main routine that allows the user to input "low" and "high" element values. Run the program several times setting "low" to 1 and "high" to various values (try 500) to get a feeling for the limited usefulness of the algorithm.
2. Generate series containing non-continuous scalar components (12,14,23,45,47,61,etc.) by treating the function output as a set of pointers to an element table.

## Program source code

```
/* SETFLAG.C (array-flag method random-order series generator) */
#include <stdio.h>
main()
{
 int set[12];
 int low = 0; /* first series element */
 int high = 11; /* last series element */
 int range = high - low + 1; /* series span */
 int total = 12; /*number of series elements */
 int j,seed = 21118;
```

```
  void Setflag();

  srand(seed);
  Setflag(set,low,range,total);
  printf("\na random-order 12-value series:\n");
    for (j = 0;j < total;j++)
       printf("%d ",set[j]);
} /* end of main */
/*================ MIC 3.7 ==============*/
/* Setflag() function */
void Setflag(array,bottom,span,total)
int array[],bottom,span,total;
{
 int j,u,cum[12];
 void Zeromat();

 Zeromat(cum,total);
 for (j = 0;j < total;j++)
     {
      do
         u = rand() % span + bottom;
      while (cum[u] == 1);
      cum[u] = 1;
      array[j] = u;
     }
} /* end of Setflag() function */
/*============== MIC 2.25 ==============*/
/* Zeromat() function */
void Zeromat(x,range)
int x[],range;

{
 int j;
 for (j = 0;j < range;j++)
    {
     x[j] = 0;
    }
} /* end of Zeromat() function */
/*==================================*/
/* END OF SETFLAG.C */
```

## Program execution

SETFLAG.EXE

enter a random number generator seed: 9122
a random-order 12-value series:
3 5 10 11 7 1 8 9 6 4 0 2

# FUNCTION: Conshufl( )   MIC 3.8

## Purpose

Randomly reorder (shuffle) the contents of an element table array.

## Notes

This algorithm shuffles an element table by first generating a random sequence of pointers, then swapping corresponding array address contents. However, after shuffling, the prime order element table is no longer available to the program. (See function MIC 3.9 Addshufl( ) for a non-disruptive randomization of array addresses.)

## Programming ideas

1. Write a program that will randomize (shuffle) any reasonable-length list of parameter values. Provide options for accessing any of four element tables: Pitch, rhythm, and volume.
2. Add Function Group: VECTORS.C to the above program to organize the output data into event vectors.
3. Write a program to randomize a data table containing numbers corresponding to a six-octave microtonal scale (MIC 2.1). Use the output of 4 runs to generate a four-voice texture whose rhythms are also derived from a shuffled duration element table.

## Program source code

```
/* CONSHUFL.C  (disruptive shuffle program - array contents
                    reordered) */
#include <stdio.h>
main()
 {
 int x[20]; /* stores the integer sequence to be shuffled */
 int total,j,seed = 441;
 void Conshufl();

 srand(seed);
 total = 20;

 printf("\noriginal integer sequence:\n");
 for (j = 0;j < total;j++)
    {
    x[j] = j + 1;
    printf("%d ",x[j]);
    }
 printf("\nshuffled integer sequence:\n");
 Conshufl(x,total);
 for (j = 0;j < total;j++)
    printf("%d ",x[j]);
 } /* end of main */
```

```
/*=============== MIC 3.8 ===============*/
/* Conshufl() function */
void Conshufl(array,total)
int array[],total;
{
 int j,u,s;
 for (j = 0;j < total;j++)
     {
      /* swap address contents */
      u = rand() % total;
      s = array[j];
      array[j] = array[u];
      array[u] = s;
     }
} /* end of Conshufl() function */
/*======================================*/
/* END OF CONSHUFL.C */
```

## Program execution

CONSHUFL.EXE

```
original integer sequence:
1 2 3 4 5 6 7 8 9 10 11 12 13 14 15 16 17 18 19 20
shuffled integer sequence:
13 6 14 9 7 2 3 11 12 8 5 1 15 17 20 10 18 19 16 4
```

# FUNCTION: Addshufl( )   MIC 3.9

## Purpose

Randomly reorder (shuffle) a list of pointers to an element table.

## Notes

This function differs form MIC 3.8: Conshufl( ), in that it is non-disruptive; that is, pointers to an array are shuffled instead of array contents, thereby leaving the original list intact for future access by the program main routine.

## Programming ideas

1. Write a program that intersperses the four standard pitch modification operations (retrograde, inversion, retrograde-inversion, and transpositions) with random-order permutations of a prime order pitch sequence.
2. Write a program based upon Function Group: CURVES.C (MIC 2.6, MIC 2.7, MIC 2.8) to generate random-order permutations of parameter data tables consisting of linearly, exponentially, and logarithmically scaled value sequences.

## Program source code

```
/* ADDSHUFL.C (nondisruptive shuffle program: list of array
                address pointers reordered instead of array
                contents) */
#include <stdio.h>
main()
  {
  int table[20],pointers[20],total,j,seed = -4491;
  void Addshufl();

  srand(seed);
  total = 20;

  printf("\noriginal array holding integer sequence:\n");
  for (j = 0;j < total;j++)
      {
      table[j] = j + 1;
      printf("%d ",table[j]);
      pointers[j] = j;
      }
  printf("%s%s","\noriginal array accessed ",
          "by shuffled address pointers:\n");
  Addshufl(pointers,total);
  for (j = 0;j < total;j++)
      printf("%d ",table[pointers[j]]);
  } /* end of main */
/*=============== MIC 3.9 ===============*/
```

```
/* Addshufl() function */
void Addshufl(ptrlist,total)
int ptrlist[],total;
{
 int j,u,s,rand();
 for (j = 0;j <= total-1;j++)
     {
      u = rand() % total;
      s = ptrlist[j];
      ptrlist[j] = ptrlist[u];
      ptrlist[u] = s;
     }
} /* end Addshufl() function */
/*===================================*/
/* END OF ADDSHUFL.C */
```

## Program execution

ADDSHUFL.EXE

```
original array holding integer sequence:
1 2 3 4 5 6 7 8 9 10 11 12 13 14 15 16 17 18 19 20
original array accessed by shuffled address pointers:
15 1 13 7 18 5 4 19 12 20 11 10 6 16 14 17 9 3 8 2
```

## FUNCTION GROUP: Rowforms.c

1. Printpitch   MIC 3.1
2. Conshufl    MIC 3.8
3. Rowretro    MIC 3.10
4. Rowinvrt    MIC 3.11
5. Rowtrnpz    MIC 3.12

## Purpose

Generate commonly found 12-tone row forms: original, retrograde, inversion, and transpositions.

## Notes

The 12-tone row forms produced by this set of subroutines are not register-specific. However, octave assignments may be derived from the row in a number of ways, or they may be randomly generated as the result of a separate, unrelated process.

## Programming ideas

1. Write a program that generates random-order 12-tone rows, then maps pitch octave assignments from a compressed scale representing the interval sizes between the row pitches.

   Hint: Because the largest possible interval in $1/2$-steps is 11 and the normal pitch range is 1 to 6 octaves, one obvious method is to "wrap-around" the interval scale on the octave range scale.
2. Expand the above program to generate rhythm durations derived from the random-order 12-tone rows. [Add Function MIC 3.21: Timpoint( )]
3. Use Function MIC 3.5: Displace( ) to generate pitch octave assignments.

## Program source code

```
/* ROWFORMS.C   (produces commonly used 12-tone rowforms) */
#include <stdio.h>
main()
{
 int orig[12];        /* stores prime-order 12-tone series */
 int nextform[12];    /* stores related series forms */
 int transint;        /* interval of series transposition */
 int total=12;
 int j,seed = 5131;
 void Printpitch(),Conshufl(),Rowretro(),
      Rowinvrt(),Rowtrnpz();

 srand(seed);
```

```c
    printf("\n(--loading integer array to be shuffled--)\n");
    for (j = 0;j < total;j++)
        orig[j] = j;
    printf("\na random-order 12-tone series:\n");
    Conshufl(orig,total);
    Printpitch(orig,total);
    printf("\nretrograde order:\n");
    Rowretro(orig,nextform,total);
    Printpitch(nextform,total);
    printf("\ninverted form:\n");
    Rowinvrt(orig,nextform,total);
    Printpitch(nextform,total);
    transint = 4;
    printf("\noriginal form transposed");
    printf(" by %d semitones:\n",transint);
    Rowtrnpz(orig,nextform,transint,total);
    Printpitch(nextform,total);
} /* end of main */
/*================ MIC 3.8 ==============*/
/* Conshufl() function */
void Conshufl(array,total)
int array[],total;
{
 int j,u,s,rand();

 for (j = 0;j < total;j++)
     {
      u = rand() % total;
      s = array[j];
      array[j] = array[u];
      array[u] = s;
     }
} /* end Conshufl() function */
/*================ MIC 3.10 ==============*/
/* Rowretro() function */
void Rowretro(array1,array2,total)
int array1[],array2[],total;
{
 int j,l;

 for (j = 0;j < total;j++)
     {
      l = (total - 1 - j) % total;
      array2[l] = array1[j];
     }
} /* end Rowretro() function */
/*================ MIC 3.11 ==============*/
/* Rowinvrt() function */
void Rowinvrt(array1,array2,total)
int array1[],array2[],total;
{
 int j;

 for (j = 0;j < total;j++)
     array2[j] = (total-array1[j]) % total;
} /* end Rowinvrt() function */
/*================ MIC 3.1 ==============*/
/* Rowtrnpz() function */
void Rowtrnpz(array1,array2,intval,total)
int array1[],array2[],intval,total;
{
```

```
  int j;

  for (j = 0;j < total;j++)
      array2[j] = (array1[j] + intval) % total;
} /* end Rowtrnpz() function */
/*================ MIC 3.12 =============*/
/* Printpitch() function */
void Printpitch(array,total)
int array[],total;
{
  int j;
  static char *pitch[] =
              {"C ","C# ","D ","D# ","E ","F ","F# ",
               "G ","G# ","A ","A# ","B " };
  printf("\n");
  for (j = 0;j < total;j++)
      printf("%s",pitch[array[j]]);
} /* end of Printpitch() function */
/*======================================*/
/* END OF ROWFORMS.C */
```

## Program execution

ROWFORMS.EXE

--loading integer array to be shuffled--

a random-order 12-tone series:

C A B D D# C# E G A# F F# G#
retrograde order:

G# F# F A# G E C# D# D B A C
inverted form:

C D# C# A# A B G# F D G F# E
original form transposed by 4 semitones:

E C# D# F# G F G# B D A A# C

# FUNCTION GROUP: Rowsquar.c

1. Setflag     MIC 3.7
2. Rowmat     MIC 3.13

## Purpose

Generate and display a square matrix containing all forms and transpositions of a random-order 12-tone row.

## Notes

Composers who use serial techniques sometimes like to visualize combinatorial pitch row possibilities by printing a compressed version of the 48 transpositions of a particular set. It may seem awkward to shift one's reading style from unidirectional to multidirectional mode, but the serial matrix affords one an uncluttered view of compositional potential.

The row expressed as a matrix has also been adapted to non-serial applications by composers. Although traditional 12-tone technique interprets the matrix in a rigid, literal fashion, one might imagine many conceptual extensions that simply use the square as pretext for a musical event. For example, each of the 12 chromatic pitches could represent a complex of sounds rather than a single note; or, indeterminacy might be introduced into performance by giving individual players different serial matrices to read in a prescribed manner.

## Programming ideas

1. Convert the DRIVER PROGRAM to an interactive main routine that allows the user to input pitch rows.
2. Modify the above program to store the matrix in a 2-dimension array, then add code to generate a random four-directional walk through the matrix. [See Function MIC 6.9: Matwalk( )]
3. Devise other strategies for traversing the matrix.

## Program source code

```
/* ROWSQUAR.C  (produces square rowforms matrix) */
#include <stdio.h>
main()
 {
 int orig[12];   /* stores original 12-tone series */
 int invers[12]; /* stores inverted 12-tone series */
 int seed = 665;
 void Rowmat();    /* configures and prints the matrix */
 void Setflag();

 srand(seed);
 printf("\nhere is a random-order, 12-tone series matrix:\n");
```

```
    printf("(of all available O,RO,I, and RI forms)\n");
    Setflag(orig,invers);          /* call series generator */
    Rowmat(orig,invers);           /* print the matrix */
} /* end of main */
/*================ MIC 3.7 ==============*/
/* Setflag() function  -- modified to program specs */
void Setflag(array1,array2)
int array1[12],array2[12];
{
 int cum[12],u,j,trans;
 for (j = 0;j <= 11;j++)
    {
        do    u = rand() % 12;
        while (cum[u] == 1);
        cum[u]=1;
          if (j == 0)
            trans = u;
          if (u - trans <0)
        array1[j] = u - trans + 12;
        else array1[j] = u - trans;
        array2[j] = (12-array1[j]) % 12;
      }
 } /* end Setflag() function */
/*================ MIC 3.13 ==============*/
/* Rowmat function */
void Rowmat(array1,array2)
int array1[],array2[];
{
   int j,k,nextnote,intval;
   static char *pitch[] =
           {"C ","C# ","D ","D# ","E ","F ","F# ",
            "G ","G# ","A ","A# ","B "};

   printf("\n");
   for (j = 0;j <=11;j++)
      {
        intval = array2[j];
        for (k = 0;k <= 11;k++)
           {
            nextnote = (array1[k] + intval) % 12;
            printf("%s",pitch[nextnote]);
           }
        printf("\n");
        }
} /* end Rowmat() function */
/*===================================*/
/* END OF ROWSQUAR.C */
```

# Program execution

ROWSQUAR.EXE

```
here is a random-order, 12-tone series matrix:
(of all available O,RO,I, and RI forms)

C B G C# A# F D# E A D F# G#
C# C G# D B F# E F A# D# G A
F E C F# D# A# G# A D G B C#
B A# F# C A E D D# G# C# F G
D C# A D# C G F F# B E G# A#
```

```
G  F#  D  G#  F  C  A#  B  E  A  C#  D#
A  G#  E  A#  G  D  C  C#  F#  B  D#  F
G#  G  D#  A  F#  C#  B  C  F  A#  D  E
D#  D  A#  E  C#  G#  F#  G  C  F  A  B
A#  A  F  B  G#  D#  C#  D  G  C  E  F#
F#  F  C#  G  E  B  A  A#  D#  G#  C  D
E  D#  B  F  D  A  G  G#  C#  F#  A#  C
```

# FUNCTION GROUP: Modops.c

1. PrintPitch( )    MIC 3.1
2. Conshufl         MIC 3.8
3. M5setM7          MIC 3.14

## Purpose

Generate related transformations of a 12-tone series via multiplicative operations.

## Notes

Although the M5 and M7 operations are said to produce transformations of a tone row, in a broader sense they generate nonrandom-order permutations of the 12 notes of the chromatic scale (just as intervallic transposition produces series-related nonrandom permutations of the chromatic set).

The distinction between a simple permutation and a transformation lies in the orderly propagation of new sets from a reference set in a manner that preserves some of the characteristics of the original (or model) set. The "relatedness" in multiplicative operations is manifest by virtue of the fact that ordered pairs of notes within the series exchange their positions. Moreover, the M5 operation represents a mapping of a chromatic scale ordering onto the cycle of fourths, while the M7 operation is a mapping onto the cycle of fifths.

## Programming ideas

1. Explore other multiplication factors modulo 12. What happens to series integrity?
2. Experiment with various length series using a number of different multiplication factors.

## Program source code

```
/* MODOPS.C (produces related transformations of a 12-tone row)*/
#include <stdio.h>
main()
  {
  int orig[12];        /* stores original series */
  int perm[12];        /* stores series permutation */
  int op;              /* toggles m5 or m7 operation */
  int total,j,seed = -9112;
  void Conshufl(),M5setM7(),Printpitch();

  srand(seed);
  total = 12;
  printf("\na random-order 12-tone series:\n");
  for (j = 0;j < total;j++)
```

```c
      orig[j] = j;
 Conshufl(orig,total);
 Printpitch(orig,total);
 printf("\nthe permutation resulting from M5 operation:\n");
 op = 5;
 M5setM7(orig,perm,op,total);
 Printpitch(perm,total);
 printf("\nthe permutation resulting from M7 operation:\n");
 op = 7;
 M5setM7(orig,perm,op,total);
 Printpitch(perm,total);
} /* end of main */
/*=============== MIC 3.8 ==============*/
/* Conshufl() function */
void Conshufl(array,total)
int array[],total;
{
 int j,u,s;

 for (j = 0;j < total;j++)
     {
      u = rand() % total;
      s = array[j];
      array[j] = array[u];
      array[u] = s;
     }
}/* end Conshufl() function */
/*=============== MIC 3.14 ==============*/
/* M5setM7() function   (outputs a permutation of an input
                series by the "M5" or "M7" operation.) */
void M5setM7(array1,array2,op,total)
int array1[],array2[],op,total;
{
 int j;

 for (j = 0;j < total;j++)
     array2[j] = (array1[j] * op) % 12;
}/* end M5setM7() function */
/*=============== MIC 3.1 ==============*/
/* Printpitch() function */
void Printpitch(array,total)
int array[],total;
{
 int j;
 static char *pitch[] =
            {"C ","C# ","D ","D# ","E ","F ","F# ",
             "G ","G# ","A ","A# ","B " };
 printf("\n");
 for (j = 0;j < total;j++)
     printf("%s",pitch[array[j]]);
} /* end of Printpitch() function  */
/*=====================================*/
/* END OF MODOPS.C */
```

## Program execution

`MODOPS.EXE`

a random-order 12-tone series:

E G# A D# A# B F# C D F C# G
the permutation resulting from M5 operation:

G# E A D# D G F# C A# C# F B
the permutation resulting from M7 operation:

E G# D# A A# F F# C D B G C#

# FUNCTION GROUP: Pstnperm.c

1. Setflag( )     MIC 3.7
2. Pstnperm( )    MIC 3.15

## Purpose

Permute a prime order 12-tone series by swapping pitch class numbers with position-in-set numbers.

## Notes

A member of the class of permutations consisting of derived series transformations, this algorithm has an interesting special case: when the ascending or descending chromatic scale is the prime order series, its retrograde is returned.

This method of systematic set permutation may be applied to value series of any reasonable length. Moreover, derived set propagation is nearly endless if one submits every transportation of all four forms of each permuted set to the swapping process.

## Programming ideas

1. Modify the DRIVER PROGRAM to allow the user to input a numeric series of variable length; add necessary code to generate the retrograde, inversion, and retrograde-inversion forms, as well as all chromatic transpositions. Include a user option to submit any or all forms and transpositions to the Pstnperm( ) function.
2. Write an interactive program using MIC 3.15 which interprets the permuted output series as pointers to values contained in the data tables of other musical parameters.

## Program source code

```
/* PSTNPERM.C (generates a series permutation by swapping
               series position and pitch class number) */
#include <stdio.h>
main()
{
 int set[12];     /*stores original series */
 int posit[12];   /*stores permutation */
 int low = 0;
 int high = 11;
 int range = high - low + 1;
 int total = 12,seed = 9182;
 void Setflag(),Pstnperm(),Printpitch();

 srand(seed);
 Setflag(set,low,range,total);
 printf("\na random-order 12-value series:\n");
```

```
     Printpitch(set,total);
     printf("\npermutation resulting from ");
     printf("swap of PC number and position\n");
     Pstnperm(set,posit,total);
     Printpitch(posit,total);
} /* end of main */
/*=============== MIC 3.7 ===============*/
/* Setflag() function */
void Setflag(array,bottom,span,total)
int array[],bottom,span,total;
{
 int j,u,cum[12],rand();

 for (j = 0;j < total;j++)
     {
       do    u = rand() % span + bottom;
       while (cum[u] == 1);
       cum[u] = 1;
       array[j] = u;
     }
} /* end Setflag() function */
/*=============== MIC 3.15 ==============*/
/* Pstnperm() function  (generates a permutation of a
             prime order series by swapping pitch class numbers
             with position-in-set numbers. If the series is
             the chromatic scale, then, of course, no alteration
             of the set will take place - the retrograde will
             be generated.)    */
void Pstnperm(array1,array2,total)
int array1[],array2[],total;
{
 int j;

 for (j = 0;j < total;j++)
     array2[array1[j]] = j;

} /* end Pstnperm() function */
/*=============== MIC 3.1 ===============*/
/* Printpitch() function  (adapted to print pitches
                           as integers) */
void Printpitch (array,total)
int array[],total;
{
 int j;

 printf("\n");
 for (j = 0;j < total;j++)
     printf("%d ",array[j]);

} /* end Printpitch() function  */
/*===================================*/
/* END OF PSTNPERM.C */
```

# Program execution

**PSTNPERM.EXE**

a random-order 12-value series:

7 2 4 8 9 10 1 0 6 5 11 3
permutation resulting from swap of PC number and position

7 6 1 11 2 9 8 0 3 4 5 10

# FUNCTION: Samplset( )   MIC 3.16

## Purpose

Generate permutations of a number series via cyclical, exhaustive sampling of the source set at a selected interval (start at set member n and place $n^{th}$ set member in a destination set, looping back through the series until all values have been transferred).

## Notes

This algorithm is derived from the classic Josephus' Problem, which is:

1. Arrange a group of men in a circle;
2. Move around the circle;
3. Remove every $n^{th}$ man;
4. Repeat 2 and 3 until all men are gone.

Although there are other methods of accomplishing exhaustive sampling, this function works by using two "bounce" arrays to hold transient versions of the set which is being sampled. During the sampling process each member of the destination series is sent to the screen as it is removed from a copy of the source set. The source set is not disrupted.

If this function is called by a program which requires run-time storage of the set permutations, then another array must be included to receive the destination series as they are printed to the screen.

## Programming ideas

1. Write a program using MIC 3.16 which generates and files permutations of a user-input value series. (Treat the destination series as a set of pointers to element tables holding pitch, rhythm, articulation, or volume data.)
2. Write a program that derives sampling factors for a group of set permutations from the input series, thereby systematizing the generation of new series from a source set.

## Program source code

```
/* SAMPLSET.C   (generates and prints numeric series
                 permutations by set-sampling at a selected
                 series-position interval) */
#include <stdio.h>
main()
{
int orig[100];
```

```
int currsetl = 12;   /*current set length */
int cycle;           /* permutation loop index */
int target;          /* current targeted set sample */
int factor = 2;      /* set sampling interval */
int permut = 5;      /* total number of permutations */
int j;               /* loop index,pointer to original set */
void Samplset();

printf("a sequential set:\n");
for (j = 1;j <= currsetl;j++)
    {
     orig[j] = j;
     printf("%d ",orig[j]);
    }
for (cycle = 1;cycle <= permut;cycle++)
    {
     printf("\npermutation %d\n",cycle);
     target = 1;
     printf("start position = %d\n",target);
     printf("target factor = %d\n",factor);
     Samplset(orig,target,factor,currsetl);
     factor = factor + 2;
    }
} /* end of main */
/*=============== MIC 3.16 =============*/
/* Samplset() function  */
void Samplset(array1,target,factor,currsetl)
int array1[],target,factor,currsetl;
{
 int a[100],b[100],acnt,bcnt,j;

 for (j = 1;j <= currsetl;j++)
     a[j] = array1[j];
 loop: bcnt = 0;
 for (j = 1;j <= currsetl;j++)
     {
      if (j == target)
          {
           printf("%d ",a[j]);
           target = target + factor;
          }
        else
          {
           bcnt = bcnt +1;
           b[bcnt] = a[j];
          }
     }
     if (bcnt < 1)
         {
          printf("\n");
          return;
         }
     target = target - currsetl;
     acnt = 0;
     if (target % bcnt != 0)
         target = target % bcnt;
     else target = bcnt;
     for (j = 1;j <=bcnt;j++)
         if (j == target)
             {
              printf("%d ",b[j]);
```

```
            target = target + factor;
            }
        else
            {
            acnt = acnt + 1;
            a[acnt] = b[j];
            }
    if (acnt < 1)
        {
        printf("\n");
        return;
        }
    currsetl = acnt;
    target = target - bcnt;
    if (target % currsetl != 0)
        target = target % currsetl;
    else target = currsetl;
    goto loop;
} /* end of Samplset() function */
/*=======================================*/
/* END OF SAMPLSET.C */
```

# Program execution

SAMPLSET.EXE

```
a sequential set:
1 2 3 4 5 6 7 8 9 10 11 12
permutation 1
start position = 1
target factor = 2
1 3 5 7 9 11 2 6 10 4 12 8

permutation 2
start position = 1
target factor = 4
1 5 9 2 7 12 8 4 3 6 11 10

permutation 3
start position = 1
target factor = 6
1 7 2 9 5 3 12 4 8 6 11 10

permutation 4
start position = 1
target factor = 8
1 9 6 4 3 5 8 12 11 7 2 10

permutation 5
start position = 1
target factor = 10
1 11 10 12 3 6 2 9 5 7 4 8
```

## FUNCTION GROUP: Rotate.c

1. Conshufl( )             MIC 3.8
2. Setrotat( )             MIC 3.17
3. Zerotrnp( )             MIC 3.18
4. Segrotat( )             MIC 3.19
5. GreatestCommonDivisor( )  MIC 2.13
6. Matprint( )             MIC 3.20

## Purpose

Perform rotation and transposition operations on a 12-element set of values.

## Notes

Set member rotation is one of the common 12-tone row transformation operations. In this group of functions, integers are output instead of pitch classes to underscore applications to other musical parameters. (The set members can also serve as array pointers.) The numbers 0 to 11 symbolize the 12 pitch classes of the chromatic scale in a form suitable for further modulo operations as in MIC 3.14, but the function can be easily rewritten using the numbers 1 – 12 if the composer/programmer wishes.

Function Setrotat( ) works by moving a given number of consecutive set members from the front to the end of the series. It also calculates the number of unique transformations of the row before repetition occurs and prevents the program from continuing beyond that point. The rotations are placed in array "mat1[ ]" for printout and later use by Function Zerotrnpz( ).

Function Segrotat( ) rotates partitioned-set segment members. Segments must equally subdivide the row (2 groups of 6 notes, 3 groups of 4 notes, etc.). After the number of unique transformations is calculated, the rotations are placed in array "mat3[ ]" for printout.

## Programming ideas

Write an interactive program based on ROTATE.C which prompts the user to input source series, performs set rotations, then call MIC 3.15: Pstnperm( ) to derive the next set to be subjected to rotations.

## Program source code

```
/* ROTATE.C (set of functions to perform serial rotation
            and transposition operations)*/
#include <stdio.h>
main()
{
 int orig[12];       /* stores original series */
```

```
        int mat1[12][12];   /* stores unpartitioned set rotation */
        int mat2[12][12];   /* stores '0' start-point transposition */
        int mat3[12][12];   /* stores partitioned set rotation */
        int setotal = 12;   /* number of series elements */
        int rotegroup; /* number of contiguous elements to rotate */
        int numsegs;          /* symmetrical set partitions */
        int segmems;    /* number of elements within each partition */
        int cycles,j,k;    /* loop indices */

        int seed = 11;
        int GreatestCommonDivisor(),Segrotat();
        void Matprint(),Conshufl(),Setrotat(),Zerotrnp();

        srand(seed);
        printf("a random-order 12-value series:\n");
        for (j = 0;j <= setotal-1;j++)   /*load set elements*/
            orig[j] = j;
        Conshufl(orig,setotal);          /*call shuffle function*/
        for (j = 0;j <= setotal-1;j++)
            printf("%d ",orig[j]);
        rotegroup = 4;
        cycles = GreatestCommonDivisor(setotal,rotegroup);
        printf("\ntotal number of unique cycles = %d\n",cycles);
        printf("here is the rotation matrix:\n");
        Setrotat(orig,mat1,rotegroup,setotal,cycles);
        Matprint(mat1,cycles,setotal);
        printf("\n'0' start point transposition:\n");
        Zerotrnp(mat1,mat2,cycles,setotal);
        Matprint(mat2,cycles,setotal);
        numsegs = 4;
        printf("\npartitioned series,rotation within segment --\n");
        printf("--  divided into %d equal segments.\n",numsegs);
        cycles = Segrotat(orig,mat3,numsegs,setotal);
        Matprint(mat3,cycles,setotal);
} /* end of main */
/*=============== MIC 3.20 =============*/
/* Matprint() function*/
void Matprint(matrix,cycles,setotal)
int matrix[][12],cycles,setotal;
{

  int l,k;
  for (l = 0;l <= cycles-1;l++)
      {
        for (k = 0;k <= setotal-1;k++)
            printf("%d ",matrix[l][k]);
        printf("\n");
      }
  } /* end Matprint() function */
/*=============== MIC 3.8 =============*/
/* Conshufl() function */
void Conshufl(array1,total)
int array1[],total;
{
  int m,u,s,rand();

  for (m = 0;m <= total-1;m++)
      {
        u = rand() % total;
        s = array1[m];
        array1[m] = array1[u];
```

```
                array1[u] = s;
            }
} /* end Conshuf1() function */
/*================ MIC 2.13 =============*/
/* GreatestCommonDivisor() function */
int GreatestCommonDivisor(a,b)
int a,b;
{
 int temp,c,d,series,cycles;

 series = a;
 if (a > b)     /*<<< swap function*/
   {
    temp = a;
    a = b;
    b = temp;
   }
 while(a > 0)
   {
    c = b/a;
    d = b - a * c;
    b = a;
    a = d;
   }
 cycles = series/b;
 return(cycles);
} /* end GreatestCommonDivisor() function */
/*================ MIC 3.17 =============*/
/* Setrotat() function */
void Setrotat(array1,array2,rotegroup,setotal,cycles)
int array1[],array2[][12],rotegroup,setotal;
{
 int l,k,u,s,t;

 rotegroup = rotegroup -1;
 u = 0;
 s = 0;
 for (k = rotegroup;k <= setotal-1+rotegroup;k++)
     {
      for (l = 1;l <= setotal;l++)
         {
          t = (k + l + u) % setotal;
          array2[s][l-1] = array1[t];
         }
      u = u + rotegroup;
      s = s + 1;
      if (s >= cycles)
         break;
     }
} /* end Setrotat() function */
/*================ MIC 3.18 =============*/
/* Zerotrnp() function */
void Zerotrnp(matrix1,matrix2,cycles,setotal)
int matrix1[][12],matrix2[][12],cycles,setotal;
{
 int intval,l,k,s;

 for (k = 0;k <= cycles-1;k++)
     {
      intval = matrix1[k][0];
      for (l = 0;l <= setotal-1;l++)
```

```
                    {
                      s = matrix1[k][l] - intval;
                      if (s < 0)
                         s = s + 12;
                      matrix2[k][l] = s;
                    }
            }
} /* end Zerotrnp() function */
/*=============== MIC 3.19 =============*/
/* Segrotat() function */
int Segrotat(array1,matrix,numsegs,setotal)
int array1[],matrix[][12],numsegs,setotal;
{
  int k,l,m,s,t,segmems;
  s = 0;

  segmems = setotal / numsegs;
  for (k = 1;k <= segmems;k++)
      {
        t = 0;
        for (l = 0;l <= setotal-1;l+=segmems)
            {
              for (m = s + 1;m <= segmems + s;m++)
                  {
                    matrix[s][t] = array1[m % segmems + l];
                    t += 1;
                  }
            }
        s += 1;
      }
  return(segmems);
} /* end Segrotat() function */
/*===================================*/
/* END OF ROTATE.C */
```

# Program execution

```
ROTATE.EXE

a random-order 12-value series:
11 4 2 6 5 0 8 9 1 7 3 10
total number of unique cycles = 3
here is the rotation matrix:
5 0 8 9 1 7 3 10 11 4 2 6
1 7 3 10 11 4 2 6 5 0 8 9
11 4 2 6 5 0 8 9 1 7 3 10

'0' start point transposition:
0 7 3 4 8 2 10 5 6 11 9 1
0 6 2 9 10 3 1 5 4 11 7 8
0 5 3 7 6 1 9 10 2 8 4 11

partitioned series,rotation within segment -
--  divided into 4 equal segments.
4 2 11 5 0 6 9 1 8 3 10 7
2 11 4 0 6 5 1 8 9 10 7 3
11 4 2 6 5 0 8 9 1 7 3 10
```

# FUNCTION GROUP: Timpoint.c

1. Printpitch( )   MIC 3.1
2. Setflag( )      MIC 3.7
3. Timpoint( )     MIC 3.21
4. Zeromat( )      MIC 2.25

## Purpose

Derive a rhythm duration series from a 12-tone pitch series using the timepoint system.

## Notes

Sometimes composers wish to map the internal interval relations of a 12-tone series onto the rhythm domain. The timepoint system is commonly used to produce a one-to-one correspondence between pitch interval-size and note attack-point. As it is the time intervals between pitch attacks that are of importance to this system, the sound-to-silence ratio between pitch onsets should be determined by an independent articulation parameter. A modulus is often used to keep numeric series computation within the one-octave pitch class boundaries (0 to 11, mod 12); similarly, a time modulus is employed to match the pitch modulus when correlation is desirable.

This function first computes the distance in $1/2$-steps between consecutive set members; it then returns a series of durations, articulated by a modulus which determines the number of metrical pulses allowed within each bar.

## Programming ideas

1. Write a program that allows the user to input a 12-tone series, then transforms the original row via cyclical sampling [MIC 3.16: Samplset( )]. Map the pitch series to attack timepoints.
2. Modify the above program to include the set rotation and transposition functions MIC 3.18, MIC 3.19, and MIC 3.20. Allow the user to derive articulation and volume parameters from the input series transformations as well as rhythm.
3. Write a program to automatically generate random-order 12-tone rows, produce transformations, then file data for four musical parameters.

## Program source code

```
/* TIMPOINT.C (produces note duration values using the
                serial timepoint system) */
#include <stdio.h>
main()
```

```c
{
int orig[12]; /* prime 12-element series */
int prpitch = 1; /* flag to print notenames or numbers */
int median;   /* basic metrical pulse unit */
int modulus;   /* transform modulus */
int seed = -9121;
int j;         /* loop index */
void Setflag(),Timpoint(),Printpitch(),Zeromat();

srand(seed);
printf("\nenter modulus (2,3,4,6, or 12):\n");
scanf("%d",&modulus);
printf("enter median (2,4,8, or 16:)\n");
scanf("%d",&median);
printf("\na random-order 12-tone pitch series,");
printf(" mod %d:\n",modulus);
Setflag(orig,modulus);
Printpitch(orig,prpitch);
printf("\nthe pitch series expressed as numbers,");
printf(" mod %d:\n",modulus);
prpitch = 0;
Printpitch(orig,prpitch);
printf("%s%s","\ndurations representing the ",
       "distance between time points,\n");
printf("%s%s","using a 1/%d note pulse base",
       " and a measure \n",median);
printf("of %d -1/%d notes.\n",modulus,median);
Timpoint(orig,modulus,median);
} /* end of main */
/*================ MIC 3.7 ==============*/
/* Setflag() function */
void Setflag(array,modulus)
int array[],modulus;
{
 int j,u,cum[12];
 void Zeromat();

Zeromat(cum);
for (j = 0;j < 12;j++)
    {
    do    u = rand() % 12;
    while (cum[u] == 1);
    cum[u] = 1;
    array[j] = u % modulus;
    }
} /* end of Setflag() function */
/*================ MIC 3.21 =============*/
/* Timpoint() function  (produces rhythm duration values
                using the serial 'timepoint system'.*/
void Timpoint(set,modulus,median)
int set[],modulus,median;
{
 int tally,dur,j;
 tally = 0;

 for (j = 0;j < 11;j++)
    {
     if (set[j+1] <= set[j])
        dur = modulus - set[j] + set[j+1];
     else dur = set[j+1] - set[j];
     tally = tally + dur;
```

```
            printf("%d/%d ",dur,median);
        }
dur = modulus - set[j];
printf("%d/%d ",dur,median);
} /* end of Timpoint() function */
/*=============== MIC 3.1 ===============*/
/* Printpitch() function    (modified to program specs) */
void Printpitch(array,p)
int array[],p;
{
   int j;
   static char *pitch[] =
                {"C ","C# ","D ","D# ","E ","F ","F# ",
                 "G ","G# ","A ","A# ","B " };

   printf("\n");
   for (j = 0;j < 12;j++)
        if (p)
            printf("%s",pitch[array[j]]);
        else printf("%d ",array[j]);
} /* end of Printpitch() function */
/*=============== MIC 2.25 =============*/
/* Zeromat function*/
void Zeromat(array)
int array[];
{
  int j;

  for (j = 0;j < 12;j++)
       array[j] = 0;
} /* end Zeromat function */
/*===================================*/
/* END OF TIMPOINT.C */
```

## Program execution

TIMPOINT.EXE

enter modulus (2,3,4,6, or 12): 4
enter median (2,4,8, or 16): 4

a random-order 12-tone pitch series, mod 4:

D# D# D D C# C C# C C# C D D#
the pitch series expressed as numbers, mod 4:

3 3 2 2 1 0 1 0 1 0 2 3
durations representing the distance between time points,
using a 1/%d note pulse base and a measure
of 4 -1/4 notes.
4/4 3/4 4/4 3/4 3/4 1/4 3/4 1/4 3/4 2/4 1/4 1/4

# FUNCTION GROUP: Alintseq.c

1. Alintseq( )    MIC 3.22
2. Conshufl( )    MIC 3.8

## Purpose

Map a set of 11 unique numeric intervals (sizes 1–11) to chromatic scale pitch classes.

## Notes

Although the random-order interval set generated by the program contains only one of each interval, it is quite likely that the mapping process will result in the repetition of one or more pitch classes. (The production of all-interval, pitch class series requires a more laborious algorithm.) Nevertheless, the repetition of tones in an all-interval sequence can be used intentionally to achieve tonal emphasis through pitch omission and redundancy.

The tones of numeric pitch class, interval-derived series and sequences can be octave-displaced without destroying the basic internal relationships; all that needs to be done is to convert an interval to its octave-contained complement when displacement causes a change of direction (e.g., minor 3rd up to Major 6th down).

## Programming ideas

1. Write a program to test randomly generated interval series for pitch class omissions and redundancy. Tabulate the total number of absent pitches, specific pitch omissions, total number of pitch redundancies, and specific pitch repetitions.
2. Augment the program in 1 to increase its intelligence; i.e., give it conditional guidelines for creating a continuity factor when testing and selecting rows for placement in a file of totally related series.
3. Use the file generated in 2 as a set of pointers for pitch, rhythm, articulation, and volume parameters.
4. Modify ALINTSEQ.C to include a function for pitch octave-displacement which uses interval complementation to deal with line direction change.

## Program source code

```
/* ALINTSEQ.C   (maps a set of 11 unique intervals [in
                 semitones, size 1-11] to the pitch class
                 numbers of the chromatic scale.) */
#include <stdio.h>
main()
{
```

```
int intset[12]; /* array of unique interval-sizes */
int pclass[12]; /* pitch class sequence array */
int total = 10; /* number of sequences to generate */
int intervals = 11; /* number of intervals between notes*/
int j,k;        /* loop indices */
int seed = 445;
void Alintseq(),Conshufl();

srand(seed);
for (j = 0;j < total;j++)
    {
     for (k = 0;k < intervals;k++)
         intset[k] = k + 1;
     Conshufl(intset,intervals);
     printf("\n\nrandom-order interval-class series #%d:\n",j);
     for (k = 0;k < 11;k++)
         printf("%d ",intset[k]);
     Alintseq(pclass,intset);
     printf("\n\n-- mapped to pitchclass numbers --\n");
     for (k = 0;k < 12;k++)
         printf("%d ",pclass[k]);
    }
} /* end of main */
/*================ MIC 3.22 =============*/
/* Alintseq() function (generates
                        all-interval pitch sequences) */
 void Alintseq(pclass,intset)
 int pclass[],intset[];
 {
  int j;

  pclass[0] = 0;
  for (j = 1;j < 12;j++)
      pclass[j] = (pclass[j-1] + intset[j-1]) % 12;
 } /* end of Alintseq() function */
/*================ MIC 3.8 ==============*/
/* Conshufl() function */
void Conshufl(intset,intervals)
int intset[],intervals;
{
 int j,u,s,rand();

 for (j = 0;j < intervals;j++)
     {
      u = rand() % 11;
      s = intset[j];
      intset[j] = intset[u];
      intset[u] = s;
     }
} /* end of Conshufl() function */
/*===================================*/
/* END OF ALINTSEQ.C */
```

## Program execution

```
ALINTSEQ.EXE

random-order interval-class series #1:
1 11 6 5 10 4 7 2 8 9 3
-- mapped to pitchclass numbers --
```

```
0 1 0 6 11 9 1 8 10 6 3 6
random-order interval-class series #2:
5 6 10 1 3 11 8 9 2 4 7
-- mapped to pitchclass numbers --
0 5 11 9 10 1 0 8 5 7 11 6
random-order interval-class series #3:
8 4 6 1 10 5 3 7 2 9 11
-- mapped to pitchclass numbers --
0 8 0 6 7 5 10 1 8 10 7 6
random-order interval-class series #4:
5 8 6 3 9 7 10 11 4 1 2
-- mapped to pitchclass numbers --
0 5 1 7 10 7 2 0 11 3 4 6
random-order interval-class series #5:
2 1 11 5 8 6 3 9 10 4 7
-- mapped to pitchclass numbers --
0 2 3 2 7 3 9 0 9 7 11 6
random-order interval-class series #6:
6 4 11 2 10 3 7 9 8 1 5
-- mapped to pitchclass numbers --
0 6 10 9 11 9 0 7 4 0 1 6
random-order interval-class series #7:
11 7 2 4 8 3 9 5 10 1 6
-- mapped to pitchclass numbers --
0 11 6 8 0 8 11 8 1 11 0 6
random-order interval-class series #8:
1 6 4 10 9 11 8 2 3 7 5
-- mapped to pitchclass numbers --
0 1 7 11 9 6 5 1 3 6 1 6
random-order interval-class series #9:
2 4 9 6 3 10 8 5 11 7 1
-- mapped to pitchclass numbers --
0 2 6 3 9 0 10 6 11 10 5 6
random-order interval-class series #10:
2 8 5 3 11 9 7 1 6 10 4
-- mapped to pitchclass numbers --
0 2 10 3 6 5 2 9 10 4 2 6
```

# FUNCTION GROUP: Alintset.c

1. Alintset( )   MIC 3.23
2. Zeromat( )   MIC 2.25

## Purpose

Generate all-interval 12-tone series. (Pitch class repetition is disallowed.)

## Notes

The algorithm in Function Alintset( ) relies on the computer's ability to sample/test, then discard/keep huge amounts of data in a short period of time. Although the method employed is one of "brute force," it is similar to the way composers go about discovering all-interval pitch series. As the computer randomly generates the tones of the series, it tests the pitch classes and melodic intervals for uniqueness. If redundancy is encountered, the offending pitch is discarded and progress resumes. The catch is that, as more and more pitches are added to the series, it becomes increasingly difficult to find tones that pass the redundancy tests. In fact, many trial sets have to be abandoned near the end because no solution can be found (given the previous choices). Nevertheless, execution of the algorithm on a 16-bit micro is quite fast.

## Programming ideas

1. Alter the program to include MIC 3.1: Printpitch( ).
2. Write a program to rotate the intervals of the all-interval series returned by the program; note the effects of interval rotation on pitch redundancy, then find ways to exploit row characteristics.
3. Modify Function Group: ALINTSET.C to include a function for pitch octave-displacement which uses interval complementation to deal with line direction change.

## Program source code

```
/* ALINTSET.C (all-interval 12-tone series generator) */
#include <stdio.h>
main()
{
  int pclass[12]; /* pitch class array */
  int j,k;        /* loop indices */
  int seed = -11519;
  void Alintset();

  srand(seed);
  for (j = 0;j < 20;j++)
      {
      Alintset(pclass);
      printf("\n");
```

```
            for (k = 0;k < 12;k++)
                printf("%d ",pclass[k]);
        }
 printf("\n");
} /* end of main */
/*=============== MIC 3.23 =============*/
/* Alintset() function ( generates all-interval 12-note
        series by the sample-test-discard/keep method. */
void Alintset(pclass)
int pclass[];
{
 int pcum[12],icum[12],temp[12];
 int j,l,m,u,intsize;
 void Zeromat();

 loop: Zeromat(pclass);
        Zeromat(icum);
        Zeromat(pcum);
        pclass[0] = 0;
        pclass[11] = 6;
        for (j = 1;j < 11;j++)
            {
             do
                u = (rand() % 11)+1;
             while (u == 6 || pcum[u] == 1);
             temp[j] = u;
             pcum[u] = 1;
            }
        for (l = 1;l < 12;l++)
            {
             for (m = 1;m < 11;m++)
                {
                 if (temp[m] > 0)
                    intsize = temp[m] - pclass[l-1];
                 else continue;
                 if (intsize < 0)
                    intsize = 12 + intsize;
                 if (icum[intsize] < 1)
                    {
                     pclass[l] = temp[m];
                     temp[m] = 0;
                     icum[intsize] = 1;
                     break;
                    }
                } /* end inner loop */
             if (m > 10 && pclass[l] == 0)
                goto loop;
            } /* end outer loop */
} /* end of Alintset() function */
/*=============== MIC 2.25 =============*/
/* Zeromat function */
void Zeromat(array)
int array[];
{
 int j;

 for (j = 0;j < 12;j++)
     array[j] = 0;
} /* end of Zeromat function*/
/*====================================*/
/* END OF ALINTSET.C */
```

# Program execution

`ALINTSET.EXE`

```
0  1  5  2  8 10  3 11  9  4  7  6
0 11  9 10  3  5  8  4  1  7  2  6
0 10  5  4  7  3  9 11  8  1  2  6
0 10  7  8  4  3  5 11  2  9  1  6
0  1  8  7  9  5 10  4  2 11  3  6
0  8  1 11  3  9 10  7  2  5  4  6
0  9 11  4  7  3 10  8  2  1  5  6
0  3  7  2 10  8  9 11  5  4  1  6
0  3  4 10  8  5  9 11  7  2  1  6
0 11  7  5  2  9 10  4  8  1  3  6
0 10 11  7  1  8  5  9  2  4  3  6
0  9  7  3  8 10  4 11  2  1  5  6
0  7 11  1  4  5  2 10  3  9  8  6
0  8  2  3  5  9  7  4 11 10  1  6
0  8  3  4 10  7  5  9 11  2  1  6
0  2  1  7  3 10  8 11  4  5  9  6
0  5  9  7  8  4 10  1  3  2 11  6
0  9  3  4  8  1 11  2 10  5  7  6
0  8  2  5  3  4 11 10  7  9  1  6
0  9  2  4  5  8  3  1  7 11 10  6
```

# FUNCTION GROUP: Intlink.c

1. Intlink( )    MIC 3.24
2. Matprint( )   MIC 3.20
3. Zeromat( )    MIC 2.25

## Purposes

Generate a stream of 12-tone series linked at the point of interval redundancy.

## Notes

This group of functions represents one of the most unrigorous serial functions imaginable. First, Intlink( ) builds a random order number series (1 – 12). It then locates the set position at which interval redundancy occurs and uses the remaining tones in the row (in order) as the nucleus of the next series to be generated; the values needed to complete the new row are then randomly generated. Thus, pitch-group repetitions of various lengths are produced—within an overall serial context—as a method of generating new, obliquely related series for use as pointers to any or all musical element tables.

Although it is theoretically possible that an order correspondence of from two to twelve pitches will be maintained between consecutively generated series, probabilities are skewed toward the carry-over of smaller groups of tones.

## Programming ideas

Write a program which:

1. derives rhythm parameter timepoints from each series returned
2. randomly assigns octave-displacements to the series tones,
3. invokes MIC 3.6: Alterseq( ), to expand contract the lines resulting from 2).
4. files the pitch and rhythm data.

## Program source code

```c
/* INTLINK.C (Generates a stream of redundant-interval-linked
               12-tone series) */
#include <stdio.h>
main()
 {
  int total = 10,seed = -2929;
  void Intlink();

  srand(seed);
  Intlink(total);
```

```
} /* end of main */
/*================ MIC 3.24 =============*/
/* Intlink function()
 -- generates a random-order series,locates the
    series position at which interval-size
    redundancy occurs, then links subsequent set
    permutations by moving remaining values from flag-
    point in the current series to the beginning of the
    next series to form its nucleus. Appropriate values
    are then permuted to complete the (now) current
    series. Thus, value-group repetitions of various
    lengths are produced - within an overall serial
    context - as a method of generating new related
    sequences for use as pointers to pitch, rhythm,
    volume, articulation, or other parameter elements. */

void Intlink(total)
int total;
{
 int pclass[12];/* array holding current series */
 int pcum[12];  /* array of pitch class repetition flags */
 int icum[12];/* array of interval class repetition flags */
 int j,k;      /* loop indices */
 int u;         /* random integer */
 int intsize;   /* interval between pitch classes */
 int redpt;     /* interval redundancy point marker */
 int shift;     /* shiftpoint for remaining set members */
 void Zeromat(),Matprint();

 Zeromat(pclass);
 Zeromat(icum);
 Zeromat(pcum);
 for (j = 0;j < total;j++)
     {
     for (k = 0;k < 12;k++)
         if (pclass[k] > 0)
             pcum[pclass[k]] = 1;
     for (k = 0;k < 12;k++)
         {
          if (pclass[k] > 0)
             continue;
          do
             u = (rand() % 12);
          while (pcum[u] == 1);
          pcum[u] = 1;
          pclass[k] = u;
         }
     for (k = 0;k < 11;k++)
         {
          intsize = pclass[k+1] - pclass[k];
          if (intsize < 0)
          intsize = 12 + intsize;
          if (icum[intsize] == 1)
             break;
          icum[intsize] = 1;
         }
     redpt = k+1;
     printf("\ninterval redundancy occurs");
     printf(" at position %d\n",redpt+1);
     Matprint(pclass,redpt);
     Zeromat(icum);
```

```
        Zeromat(pcum);
        shift = 0;
        for (k = redpt;k <=12;k++)
            {
            pclass[shift] = pclass[k];
            shift = shift + 1;
            }
        for (k = shift;k < 12;k++)
            pclass[k] = 0;
        }
} /* end of Intlink() function */
/*=============== MIC 3.20 =============*/
/* Matprint function */
void Matprint(pclass,redpt)
int pclass[],redpt;
{
 int j;
 printf("pc set: ");
 for (j = 0;j < 12;j++)
     {
     printf("%d ",pclass[j]);
     if (j == redpt-1)
         printf("||");
     }
} /* end of Matprint() function */
/*=============== MIC 2.25 =============*/
/* Zeromat() function */
void Zeromat(array)
int array[];
{
 int j;

 for (j = 0;j < 12;j++)
     array[j] = 0;
} /* end of Zeromat() function */
/*======================================*/
/* END OF INTLINK.C */
```

# Program execution

`INTLINK.EXE`

`enter a random number generator seed: 4912`

```
interval redundancy occurs at position 6
pc set: 10 6 0 7 11 ||3 2 8 1 4 5 9
interval redundancy occurs at position 8
pc set: 3 2 8 1 4 5 9 ||0 11 7 6 10
interval redundancy occurs at position 4
pc set: 0 11 7 ||6 10 5 9 8 1 4 2 3
interval redundancy occurs at position 4
pc set: 6 10 5 ||9 8 1 4 2 3 7 0 11
interval redundancy occurs at position 8
pc set: 9 8 1 4 2 3 7 ||6 11 10 0 5
interval redundancy occurs at position 7
pc set: 6 11 10 2 5 0 ||3 4 7 8 9 1
interval redundancy occurs at position 4
pc set: 3 4 7 ||8 9 1 0 5 2 6 11 10
interval redundancy occurs at position 7
```

```
pc set: 8 9 1 0 5 2 ||6 11 10 4 3 7
interval redundancy occurs at position 5
pc set: 6 11 10 4 ||3 7 9 0 5 8 1 2
interval redundancy occurs at position 8
pc set: 3 7 9 4 5 8 1 ||2 11 6 10 0
```

# FUNCTION: Valratio( )   MIC 3.25

## Purpose

Control the ratio of repeated integers to unique integers in a random-order stream of values.

## Notes

The algorithm imposes a kind of "sliding series" on a continuously generated sequence of bounded values. It works by preventing repetition of any number falling within an arbitrary window of predetermined size. For instance, if 100 random numbers within the range 1 – 10 are to be returned, and a window of 9 is specified, then the output sequence will be a non-repeating set. However, if a smaller window is entered, say 4, then redundancy will only be disallowed within any group of four adjacent numbers.

## Programming ideas

1. Modify the main routine to allow user input of values for "total," "range," and "window" variables.
2. Write a program based on Valratio( ) that returns (over separate runs) pointers to pitch, octave-displacement, rhythm duration, volume, and articulation element tables.
3. Expand program 2) to include MIC 3.6: Alterseq( ); add file-writing code to send the output of multiple program executions to four separate files, each of which should contain Pitch, Rhythm, Articulation, and Volume data for a single musical line. Perform the four files concurrently on a digital synthesizer.

## Program source code

```
/* VALRATIO.C  (Controls the ratio of repeated integers to
                unique integers in a random-order stream
                of values. */
#include <stdio.h>
#include <math.h>
int finalseq[100];
main()
{
 extern finalseq[]; /* array holding filtered values */
 int j;  /* loop index */
 int total = 100;
 int seed = -1922;
 int range = 12; /* range of integers, start - 0 */
 int window = 4; /* size of repetition-prevent window */
 void Valratio();

 srand(seed);
 Valratio(range,window,total);
```

```
    printf("\napplied to random-order pitches (0-11)\n");
    printf("\nrepetition-prevent window is %d ;",window);
    for(j = 0;j < total;j++)
        if(j % 20 == 0)
            printf("\n");
        else
            printf("%d ",finalseq[j]);
}
/* end of main */
/*=============== MIC 3.25 =============*/
/* Valratio() function */
void Valratio(span,gap,total)
int span,gap;
{
  extern finalseq[];
  int pcum[12]; /* array of integer occurrence flags */
  int j;         /* loop index */
  int u;         /* random integer */

  for(j = 0;j < total;j++)
      {
       do
          u = rand() % span;
       while (pcum[u] == 1);
       pcum[u] = 1;
       finalseq[j] = u;
       if(j <= gap)
          continue;
       pcum[finalseq[j-gap]] = 0;
      }
} /* end of Valratio() function */
/*====================================*/
/* END OF VALRATIO.C */
```

## Program execution

VALRATIO.EXE

applied to random-order pitches (0-11)

repetition-prevent window is 4 ;
11 4 6 0 10 11 8 1 4 6 11 0 5 1 9 8 4 5 3
10 11 7 5 9 3 10 7 1 6 8 0 4 7 11 9 10 4 1 0 8
3 6 11 1 10 8 9 7 3 0 10 4 7 11 9 10 4 1 0
6 3 10 7 0 9 11 3 10 0 7 11 5 3 6 0 8 9 1
6 3 9 8 5 6 0 10 4 5 3 1 0 9 7 3 5 4 9

## FUNCTION GROUP: Markov.c

1. Markov( )    MIC 3.26
2. Zeromat( )    MIC 2.25
3. Freqtab2( )    MIC 3.27
4. Seedtest( )    MIC 3.28

## Purpose

Generate a Markovian integer summation residue cycle conforming to parameters passed from main; provide a table of integer occurrence frequencies.

## Notes

This subroutine was adapted from an algorithm devised by composer Peter Armstrong. Peter's goal was to harness various kinds of numeric series (other than 12-tone) for application to musical elements such as microtonal pitch scales, rhythm tables, etc.

Control parameters "order" and "apply" provide the beautiful flexibility of this algorithm. You can generate many types of ascending integer series, depending upon the number and value of seeds input and the summation application mode. (If "apply" is set to EXCLUSIVE then only the outer pair of seed terms is added to generate the next; if "apply" is set to INCLUSIVE then all seeds are summed to produce the next term.) Simplest cases of this Markovian concept are the Fibonacci and Lucas series.

Control variable "modulus" converts the ascending number series to a manageable form (series generated in this manner quickly transcend musical element table bounds). It has been set to 12 for the runs produced by the main routine; output falls within range 0 – 11 to accommodate the numbering system used in several Chapter 2 programs that deal with the 12 pitch classes of the chromatic scale. Other "modulus" values may be substituted to "wrap-around" the integer output on any desirable range.

## Programming ideas

Write an interactive program that includes MIC 3.26: Markov and MIC 2.1: Tunings( ) to generate a number of different octave-repeating microtonal series on a digital synthesizer. (The variable "modulus" sets the number of pitches per octave.)

## Program source code

```
/* MARKOV.C  (Markovian integer Summation Residual Cycle
             Generator) */
#include <stdio.h>
main()
{
  int cycle[5001]; /* stores generated integer cycle */
```

```
int seed[10];    /* array of seeds (initial terms to sum)*/
int freq[88]; /* array of integer occurrence frequencies */
int order; /*num. of preceding terms to sum for next term*/
int modulus; /*integer-range modulus imposed on each sum */
int total;    /* total terms generated */
int apply; /*signal: inclusive or exclusive seed addition*/
int j;        /* loop index */
int Markov();
void Zeromat(),Freqtab2();

printf("enter modulus:\n");
scanf("%d",&modulus);
printf("%s%s","enter 0 for inclusive or",
       " 1 for exclusive seed addition:\n");
scanf("%d",&apply);
printf("\nhow many seeds will you enter (min=2)?\n");
scanf("%d",&order);
while (order < 2)
       {
       printf("\nyou must enter at least TWO seeds:\n");
       printf("how many seeds?");
       scanf("%d",&order);
       }
for (j = 1;j <= order;j++)
   {
     printf("enter seed %d\n",j);
     scanf("%d",&seed[j]);
   }
printf("\n");
for (j = 1;j <= order;j++)
     printf("seeds=%d ",seed[j]);
total = Markov(cycle,seed,order,apply,modulus);
Zeromat(freq,modulus,total);
Freqtab2(cycle,freq,modulus,total);
printf("\ntotal =%d\n",total);
for (j = 1;j <=total;j++)
     {
       printf("%d ",cycle[j]);
       if (j % 15  == 0)
          printf("\n");
     }
printf("\n\noccurrence frequency table\n");
for (j = 1;j <= modulus;j++)
     {
      printf("%d : %d   ",j-1,freq[j]);
       if (j % 5 == 0)
          printf("\n");
     }
 printf("\n\n");
}/* end of main */
/*================ MIC 3.26 =============*/
/* Markov() function */
int Markov(cycle,seed,order,apply,mod)
int cycle[],seed[],order,apply,mod;
{
  int nxterm,total,done,j,l,Seedtest();
    for (j = 1;j <= order;j++)
       cycle[j] = seed[j];
    total = order;
    for (j = 1;j <= 5000;j++)
       {
```

```
            nxterm = seed[order];
            for (l = 1;l <= order-1;l++)
               nxterm += seed[l];
            if (apply == 1)
               nxterm = seed[order] + seed[1];
            nxterm = nxterm % mod;
            cycle[j+order] = nxterm;
            for (l=1;l <= order-1;l++)
               seed[l] = seed[l+1];
            seed[order] = nxterm;
            total += 1;
            done =Seedtest(order,seed,cycle);
            if (done == 1)
               {
                total -= order;
                break;
               }
        }
 return(total);
 } /* end of Markov() function */
/*=============== MIC 2.25 =============*/
/* Zeromat() function */
void Zeromat(array,mod)
int array[],mod;
{
 int j;

 for (j = 0;j <= mod;j++)
     array[j] = 0;
} /* end of Zeromat() function */
/*=============== MIC 3.27 =============*/
/* Freqtab2() function */
void Freqtab2(array1,array2,mod,total)
int array1[],array2[],mod,total;
{
 int j,k;

 for (j = 1;j <= mod;j++)
     {
      for (k = 1;k <= total;k++)
          if (array1[k] + 1 == j)
              array2[j] = array2[j] + 1;
     }
} /* end of Freqtab2() function */
/*=============== MIC 3.28 =============*/
/* Seedtest() function */
int Seedtest(order,seed,cycle)
int order,seed[],cycle[];
{
 int k,done=1;

 for (k = 1;k <= order;k++)
     if (seed[k] != cycle[k])
         {
          done = 0;
          break;
         }
 return(done);
} /* end of Seedtest() function */
/*=====================================*/
/* END OF MARKOV.C */
```

# Program execution

`MARKOV.EXE`

```
enter modulus: 12
enter 0 for inclusive or 1 for exclusive seed addition: 1

how many seeds will you enter (min=2)? 5
enter seed 1
enter seed 2
enter seed 3
enter seed 4
enter seed 5

seeds=1 seeds=2 seeds=3 seeds=4 seeds=5
total =312
1  2  3  4  5  3  5  8  1  10  3  3  1  6  11
0  9  3  5  4  9  6  3  3  1  10  11  4  5  7
1  4  9  2  11  3  5  6  3  4  9  3  1  8  1
10  11  7  1  6  11  0  1  7  1  8  5  10  7  7
1  6  7  4  1  7  1  8  9  2  3  11  9  10  11
8  1  3  9  8  5  2  3  3  9  10  3  4  5  7
5  0  9  2  11  3  1  2  7  0  1  11  9  4  1
2  3  7  5  6  11  8  1  7  9  0  1  6  11  3
9  6  11  4  9  3  9  0  1  10  11  7  5  10  7
4  9  11  5  0  5  6  3  7  9  6  7  8  1  7
5  4  1  6  11  3  1  10  7  8  5  7  1  4  1
6  7  7  1  10  7  8  9  11  9  8  9  10  11  11
1  6  3  8  5  11  9  0  9  10  3  7  5  10  11
0  9  11  5  0  1  2  7  3  1  2  3  4  1  11
9  4  5  6  11  11  1  10  3  0  1  3  5  0  9
6  11  7  9  6  3  0  1  7  5  4  5  10  7  7
9  2  11  0  5  3  9  4  9  6  7  11  1  10  11
4  1  3  5  0  1  10  7  11  5  10  7  4  1  3
1  4  1  10  7  11  9  2  3  8  9  7  5  8  1
6  3  11  5  2  3  0  9  7  9  4  5  10  11  3
9  2  11  0  1  11  1  0  1  2  3  7

occurrence frequency table
0 : 18    1 : 43    2 : 14    3 : 36    4 : 20
5 : 28    6 : 18    7 : 34    8 : 14    9 : 33
10 : 20   11 : 34
```

# FUNCTION GROUP: Tropes.c

1. Tropes( )       MIC 3.27
2. Zeromat( )      MIC 2.25
3. Setflag( )      MIC 3.7
4. Matprint( )     MIC 3.20

## Purpose

Systematically generate permutations of an original integer series array by cyclical selection of series elements at uniform position-in-series intervals.

## Notes

The routine Tropes( ) outputs 11 permutations of the prime series by increasing the magnitude of the selection-step (order) with each iteration of the loop in function main( ). In practical terms, this simply means that every other set member is selected sequentially during the second loop cycle, every third element is selected during the third iteration, and so on. The array holding the prime array is left intact for further use, and the permutations are stored in a temporary array for printout by Matprint( ).

## Programming ideas

1. Alter the Function Group to allow storage of all permutations in a 2-dimensional matrix.
2. Convert the main routine to interactive form, with user-options to select permutation orders (set-element selection step-size) and enter their own series from the keyboard.
3. Write a program based upon Function Group: CURVES.C (MIC 2.6, MIC 2.7, & MIC 2.8) to generate systematic permutations of parameter data tables consisting of linearly, exponentially, and logarithmically scaled value sequences.
4. Add a function to the above program to allow further "troping" of the newly generated tropes.

## Program source code

```
/* TROPES.C (returns systematic permutations of a numeric
            series array */
#define MAXDATA 12
main()
{
 int x[MAXDATA], y[MAXDATA];
 int j,k;         /* loop indices */
 int bottom = 0; /* lowest integer value to generate */
 int range = 12; /* value range of integers to generate */
 int total = 12; /* number of integers in series */
```

```
int seed = -9033;
void Setflag();
void Matprint();

srand(seed);
printf("generating a random-order number series:\n");
Setflag(x,bottom,range,total);
Matprint(x,total);
printf("\nnow tropes (permutations) will be output:");
for (j = 1; j < total; j++)
    {
     printf("\n order %d\n", j);
     Tropes(x, total, j);
    }
} /* end of main() */
/*=============== MIC 3.27 ===============*/
Tropes(array1, size, order)
int array1[], size, order;
{
 int j, k, offset, array2[MAXDATA];
 void Matprint();
 for (offset = 0, k = 0; offset < order; offset++)
    for (j = offset; j < size; j += order)
        array2[k++] = array1[j];
 Matprint(array2,size);

} /* end of Tropes() function */
/*=============== MIC 2.25 ===============*/
/* Zeromat() function ( adapted to program specs) */
void Zeromat(array,range)
int array[],range;
{
 int j;

 for (j = 0;j < range;j++)
    array[j] = 0;
} /* end of Zeromat() function */
/*=============== MIC 3.7 ===============*/
/* Setflag() function */
void Setflag(array,bottom,span,total)
int array[],bottom,span,total;
{
 int j,u,cum[12];
 void Zeromat();

 Zeromat(cum,total);
 for (j = 0;j < total;j++)
    {
     do
       u = rand() % span + bottom;
     while (cum[u] == 1);
     cum[u] = 1;
     array[j] = u;
    }
} /* end of Setflag() function */
/*=============== MIC 3.20 ===============*/
/* Matprint() function  (adapted to program specs) */
void Matprint(array,total)
int array[],total;
{
  int k;
```

```
  for (k = 0;k < total;k++)
     printf("%d ",array[k]);
  printf("\n");
} /* end of Matprint() function */
/*====================================*/
/* END OF TROPES.C */
```

## Program execution

TROPES.EXE

generating a random-order number series:
3  6  8  1  4  7  0  11  9  2  10  5

now tropes (permutations) will be output:
 order 1
3  6  8  1  4  7  0  11  9  2  10  5

 order 2
3  8  4  0  9  10  6  1  7  11  2  5

 order 3
3  1  0  2  6  4  11  10  8  7  9  5

 order 4
3  4  9  6  7  2  8  0  10  1  11  5

 order 5
3  7  10  6  0  5  8  11  1  9  4  2

 order 6
3  0  6  11  8  9  1  2  4  10  7  5

 order 7
3  11  6  9  8  2  1  10  4  5  7  0

 order 8
3  9  6  2  8  10  1  5  4  7  0  11

 order 9
3  2  6  10  8  5  1  4  7  0  11  9

 order 10
3  10  6  5  8  1  4  7  0  11  9  2

 order 11
3  5  6  8  1  4  7  0  11  9  2  10

# FUNCTION GROUP: Mirror.c

## Purpose

Build chords around a central pitch as a mirror according to the interval sequence of the input pitches.

## Notes

The central pitch can be based on the input, thereby causing a change with each chord, or a stationary F#3 (middle of synthesizer keyboard controllers) may be chosen. Each interval sequence is rotated, and the resulting mirror chord is defined as a motif. (The user is asked if all or part of the input pattern is to be used.) Often the best-sounding sequences are obtained by using a short interval pattern. The rhythm is output either as uniform note durations, or as a stream of values representing the mirror pattern.

## Attention

We have departed from our normal method of presentation in this Function Group. Instead of providing source code that demonstrates the algorithms noninteractively, we have chosen to introduce an organizational method widely used by C programmers to reduce code redundancy and provide enhanced data type-checking in lengthy routines. To successfully execute this program, you should fully understand the computer's expectations in terms of input data; furthermore, the concept of note-list score format should be grasped (see Chapter 7 Function Group Scorform.c) before attempting to use the program in a meaningful way.

Notice that the C Preprocessor instruction #include "filename" has been invoked several times to reduce the amount of text space required to contain program source code. Because many of the constituent functions have been listed elsewhere in this book, it is more efficient to ask the Preprocessor to include them at compilation time rather than type them in again. You will find this technique invaluable as programming skills and algorithmic needs develop.

Notice also that prototyping has been introduced with this program. Function prototypes are stored in files having the name of the master source code file, but ending in the filename extension ".PRO" instead of ".C." A recent addition to C language, prototyping may not be available on your compiler; in this case, simply omit the #include "filename" directive to the Preprocessor. If you are running TurboC, however, try to make use of the enhanced error-proofing provided by the use of prototype files.

One further programming refinement is present in Function Group: MIRROR.C. The fact that multiple #include "filename" directives are present means that these files in their own right may require a number of specific header (.H) files. All nonstandard header files used herein are listed in Appendix A and must be available in your .H subdirectory or resident in the top-level compiler directory during compilation, or else the compiler will search unsuccessfully and deliver an error message to that effect.

All "include" subprograms with the .C extension are listed in Appendix B and must be available to the calling program at compilation time. They are:

1. array.c      MIC_SP1.0
2. scorform.c   MIC_SP6.0
3. getpart.c    MIC_SP3.0
4. getfnam.c    MIC_SP4.0
5. inputyou.c   MIC_SP2.0

All "include" prototype files (.PRO) can be found in Appendix C.

## Program source code

```
/* MIRROR.C   (Builds chords around a central pitch as a mirror
                according to the interval sequence of a stream
                of input pitches) */
#include <stdio.h>
#define MAXDATA 200
#include "array.c"
#include "inputyou.c"
#include "getpart.c"
#include "scorform.c"
#include "getfnam.c"
#include "mirror.pro"

main()
{
    int shape[MAXDATA], datarray[MAXDATA];
    int inv[MAXDATA], disarray[MAXDATA];
    int size, ShapeSize, usescore, j, which;
```

```
        char motname[8];
        FILE *outputfile;

        outputfile = getfnam("Output","w");
        size = InputYourOwn(disarray);
        size = getpart(disarray, datarray, size, 1);
        ShapeSize = size - 1;
        getshape(datarray, shape, size);
        printf("\nWhat do you want to call the motifs?\n");
        scanf("%s", &motname);
        printf("(1) Default center is F#3 (2) moving center\n");
        scanf("%d", &which);
        WriteComment(outputfile, datarray, size,"Pitches");
        for(j = 0; j < ShapeSize; j++)
            {
            RotateArray(shape, shape, ShapeSize, j);
            WriteComment(outputfile, shape, ShapeSize,"Intervals");
            printf("\nRotation no %d\n", j);
            if(which == 1)
              loop(outputfile, shape, ShapeSize, j, 42, motname);
            else
              loop(outputfile, shape, ShapeSize, j, datarray[j], motname);
            PutLn();
            FputLn(outputfile);
            }
        PutPeform(outputfile, ShapeSize, motname);
}
/*=============== MIC 3.28 ==============*/
PutPeform(fp, ShapeSize, motname)
    FILE *fp;
    int ShapeSize;
    char motname[];
{
    int j;
    fprintf(fp, "\nNotelist using R 1-1\n");
    for(j = 0; j < ShapeSize; j++)
        fprintf(fp, "Perform %s%d\nP  R\nR  4\n", motname, j);
}
/*=============== MIC 3.29 ==============*/
WriteComment(fp, data, size, comment)
    FILE *fp;
    int data[], size;
    char comment[];
{
        printf("\n/*\n");
        printf("%s\n", comment);
        PutArray(data, size);
        printf("*/\n");

        fprintf(fp, "\n/*\n");
        fprintf(fp, "%s\n", comment);
        FputArray(fp, data, size);
        fprintf(fp, "*/\n");
}
/*=============== MIC 3.30 ==============*/
loop(fp, shape, ShapeSize, num, center, motname)
    FILE *fp;
    int shape[], ShapeSize, num, center;
    char motname[];
{
    int up[MAXDATA], down[MAXDATA], chord[MAXDATA], ChordSize;
```

```
            fprintf(fp, "\n/* center = %d ", center);
            printf("\n/* center = %d ", center);
            PutPitch(center);
            FputPitch(fp, center);
            printf(" */\n");
            fprintf(fp, " */\n");
            GetCenter(up, down, center);
            GetPatterns(shape, up, down, ShapeSize);
            ChordSize = GetChord(up, down, chord, ShapeSize);
            OpenMot(fp, motname);
            printf("%d", num);
            fprintf(fp, "%d", num);
            OpenChord(fp);
            PutChord(fp, chord, ChordSize);
            EndChord(fp);
            PutRhythm(fp, chord, ChordSize);
            EndMot(fp, motname);
            printf("%d\n", num);
            fprintf(fp, "%d\n", num);
        }




/*=============== MIC 3.31 ===============*/
PutChord(fp, chord, ChordSize)
    FILE *fp;
    int chord[], ChordSize;
{
    int j;

    for(j = 0; j < ChordSize; j++)
        {
        if(chord[j] != chord[j + 1])    /* no repeated pitches */
            {
            PutPitch(chord[j]);
            FputPitch(fp, chord[j]);
            }
        }
}
/*=============== MIC 3.32 ===============*/
GetChord(up, down, chord, size)
    int up[], down[], chord[], size;
{
    int j, ChordSize;

    ChordSize = 0;
    for(j = size; j > 0; j--)
        if(down[j] >= 0 && down[j] <= 85)
            chord[ChordSize++] = down[j];
    for(j = 0; j <= size; j++)
        if(up[j] >= 0 && up[j] <= 85)
            chord[ChordSize++] = up[j];
    return(ChordSize);
}
/*=============== MIC 3.33 ===============*/
GetPatterns(disarray, up, down, size)
    int disarray[], up[], down[], size;
{
```

```
    int j;

    for(j = 0; j < size; j++)
        {
        up[j + 1] = up[j] + abs(disarray[j]);
        down[j + 1] = down[j] - abs(disarray[j]);
        }
}
/*=============== MIC 3.34 ==============*/
OpenChord(fp)
    FILE *fp;
{
    printf("\n P  [ ");
    fprintf(fp, "\n P   [ ");
}




/*=============== MIC 3.35 ==============*/
EndChord(fp)
    FILE *fp;
{
    printf("]\n");
    fprintf(fp, "]\n");
}
/*=============== MIC 3.36 ==============*/
GetCenter(up, down, center)
    int up[], down[], center;
{
    up[0] = center;
    down[0] = center;
}
/*=============== MIC 3.37 ==============*/
PutRhythm(fp, chord, ChordSize)
    FILE *fp;
    int chord[], ChordSize;
{
    int j, count;

    count = 0;
    printf(" R    ");
    fprintf(fp, "/*R   ");
    for( j = 0; j < ChordSize; j++)
        {
        if(chord[j] != chord[j + 1])   /* no repeated pitches */
            {
            printf("%3d ", chord[j] + 1); /* no 0 on rhythm lines */
            fprintf(fp, "%3d ", chord[j] + 1);
            count++;
            }
        }
    fprintf(fp, " */");
    fprintf(fp, "\n R   (1)%d ", count);
}
/*=============== MIC 3.38 ==============*/
OpenMot(fp, motname)
    FILE *fp;
    char motname[];
```

```
{
    printf("\n Def Mot %s", motname);
    fprintf(fp, "\n Def Mot %s", motname);
}
/*=============== MIC 3.39 ===============*/
EndMot(fp, motname)
    FILE *fp;
    char motname[];
{
    printf("\n End %s", motname);
    fprintf(fp, "\n End %s", motname);
}



/*=============== MIC 3.40 ===============*/
InvertShape(shape, inv, size)
    int shape[], inv[], size;
{
    int j;

    for(j = 0; j < size; j++)
        {
        if(shape[j] > 0)
            inv[j] = shape[j] - abs(shape[j] * 2);
        else
            inv[j] = shape[j] + abs(shape[j] * 2);
        }
}
/*======================================*/
```

## Sample output of Mirror.c

(output file takes this form)

```
/*
Pitches
  5    6    7    8    9   10
*/

/*
Intervals
  1    1    1    1    1
*/

/* center = 42 F#3  */

 Def Mot tune0
 P  [ C#3 D3   D#3 E3   F3   F#3 G3   G#3 A3   A#3 B3   ]
/*R    38  39   40  41   42   43  44   45  46   47  48  */
 R  (1)11
 End tune0

/*-----------------------------------------------------------*/

/*
Intervals
  1    1    1    1    1
*/
```

```
/* center = 42 F#3  */

 Def Mot tune1
 P  [ C#3  D3   D#3  E3   F3   F#3  G3   G#3  A3   A#3  B3   ]
/*R    38   39   40   41   42   43   44   45   46   47   48   */
 R   (1)11
 End tune1

/*------------------------------------------------------------*/

/*
Intervals
  1    1    1    1    1
*/

/* center = 42 F#3  */

 Def Mot tune2
 P  [ C#3  D3   D#3  E3   F3   F#3  G3   G#3  A3   A#3  B3   ]
/*R    38   39   40   41   42   43   44   45   46   47   48   */
 R   (1)11
 End tune2

/*------------------------------------------------------------*/

/*
Intervals
  1    1    1    1    1
*/

/* center = 42 F#3  */

 Def Mot tune3
 P  [ C#3  D3   D#3  E3   F3   F#3  G3   G#3  A3   A#3  B3   ]
/*R    38   39   40   41   42   43   44   45   46   47   48   */
 R   (1)11
 End tune3

/*------------------------------------------------------------*/

/*
Intervals
  1    1    1    1    1
*/

/* center = 42 F#3  */

 Def Mot tune4
 P  [ C#3  D3   D#3  E3   F3   F#3  G3   G#3  A3   A#3  B3   ]
/*R    38   39   40   41   42   43   44   45   46   47   48   */
 R   (1)11
 End tune4

/*------------------------------------------------------------*/

Notelist using R 1-1
Perform tune0
P  R
R  4
Perform tune1
P  R
```

```
R  4
Perform tune2
P  R
R  4
Perform tune3
P  R
R  4
Perform tune4
P  R
R  4
```

# FUNCTION GROUP: Sets.c

(Includes FUNCTIONS MIC 3.40 – MIC 3.81

## Purpose

Perform analytic operations on pitch class series.

## Notes

SETS.C is a collection of pitch class set analysis functions. The user inputs pitch data via keyboard or by reading a script file. The options are for imbrication and set size. By imbricating the input, sometimes hidden sets can be found. The input pitches are put into normal order, and the set identified by its standard set number. Information is given about the identified set, and some set complex information is also provided. Finally there is a summary of which sets have occurred. The user may also print a set table.

## Attention

In order for this FUNCTION GROUP to execute properly, you must place all "include" files referenced by the main program and header file "sets.h" in the compiler directory. So, if you look at a listing of the main routine "include" files, you will notice that they, in turn, need access to the following subprograms (.c extension):

1. array.c        MIC_SP1.0
2. inputyou.c     MIC_SP2.0
3. scrptprs.c     MIC_SP13.0
4. quicksort.c    MIC_SP12.0
5. ansi.c         MIC_SP5.0

## Programming ideas

Only 3,4,5, and 6 note sets are given here, but sets of a higher cardinal number may be also used. Also the set complexes are for sets of adjacent cardinality. The user may wish to have a complete list of set complexes. The method of initializing arrays is clear but might require too much memory. In that case, the information should be stored as bit fields.

# Program source code

```
/* SETS.C  (Series Analysis Routines) */

#include <stdlib.h>
#include "sets.h"
#include "sets.pro"

main()
{
  register int k;
  int index, imsize, imbeg, totsize, setnumber[MAXDATA], ask;
  int pcarray[MAXDATA],size;
  int setfq[50], setsize, original[12], vector[6];
  int imarray[MAXDATA], test[12], testshape[12], ordered[12];
  FILE *fopen();

  outputfile = fopen("set.dat","w");
  Cls();
  centerf("Set Analysis\n");
  size = GetData(datarray, setfq, pcarray);
  showdata(outputfile, datarray, pcarray, size);
  imsize = GetImsize();
  ShowImbricated(outputfile, pcarray, imarray, imsize, size);
  setsize = GetSetSize();
  index = GetIndex(imsize, size, setsize);

 for(k = 0; k < index; k++)
   {
   GetTestSets(test, pcarray, datarray, original, imarray,
             setsize, imsize,k);
   ShowOriginal(outputfile, original, test, setsize);
   Order(test, ordered, vector, setnumber, setsize, k);
   if(setnumber[k] == 0)
     NotSetError(outputfile, setsize);
   else if(setnumber[k] != 0)
     PutSetData(outputfile, test, setsize, vector,
             setnumber[k], setfq);
   }
  PutSetSummary(outputfile, setfq, setsize);
  PutTable(outputfile);
  printf("\n\nAnalysis is in file: set.dat\n\n");
  fclose(outputfile);
}
/*=============== MIC 3.40 ==============*/
GetIndex(imsize, size, setsize)
   int imsize, size, setsize;
{
  if(imsize == 0)
    return(size / setsize);
  else
    return(size - (imsize-1) );
}
/*=============== MIC 3.41 ==============*/
GetSetSize()
{
  int setsize;
  printf("\nEnter set size 3, 4, 5 or 6 ");
  scanf("%d", &setsize);
  return(setsize);
```

```
}
/*=============== MIC 3.42 ===============*/
GetImsize()
{
  int imsize;
  printf("\nEnter size of imbrication (0 for no imbrication) ");
  scanf("%d", &imsize);
  return(imsize);
}
/*=============== MIC 3.43 ===============*/
Order(test, ordered, vector, setnumber, setsize, k)
    int test[], ordered[], vector[], setnumber[], setsize, k;
{
    QuickSort(test, 0, setsize-1);
    NormalOrder(test, ordered, setsize);
    getshape(ordered, vector, setsize);
    endvector(vector, setsize);
    setnumber[k] = GetSetnumber(vector, setsize);
}
/*=============== MIC 3.44 ===============*/
ShowOriginal(fp, original, test, setsize)
    FILE *fp;
    int original[], test[], setsize;
{
    PutLn();
    FputLn(fp);
    printf("\nOriginal pitches:");
    fprintf(fp, "\nOriginal pitches:");
    ScriptArray(original, ' ', setsize);
    FscriptArray(fp, original, ' ', setsize);
    printf("Pc array:           ");
    PutArray(test, setsize);
    fprintf(fp, "Pc array:              ");
    FputArray(fp, test, setsize);
}
/*=============== MIC 3.45 ===============*/
GetTestSets(test, pcarray, datarray, original, imarray,
            setsize, imsize, k)
   int test[], pcarray[], datarray[], original[], imarray[],
            setsize, imsize, k;
{
    int j;

    if (imsize == 0)
       for(j = 0; j < setsize; j++)
           {
           test[j] = pcarray[j + k * setsize];
           original[j] = datarray[j + k * setsize];
           }
      else
         for(j = 0; j < imsize; j++)
             {
             test[j] = imarray[j + k * imsize];
             original[j] = datarray[j + k];
             }
}
/*=============== MIC 3.46 ===============*/
GetSetnumber(ordered, setsize)
    int ordered[], setsize;
{
    int setnumber;
```

```
      switch(setsize)
      {
      case 3 : setnumber = set3cmp(ordered);
                break;
      case 4 : setnumber = set4cmp(ordered);
                break;
      case 5 : setnumber = set5cmp(ordered);
                break;
      case 6 : setnumber = set6cmp(ordered);
                break;
      }
      return(setnumber);
}
/*=============== MIC 3.47 ===============*/
NotSetError(fp, setsize)
    FILE *fp;
    int setsize;
{
    PutLn();
    FputLn(fp);
    printf("\n\t\t\t**** NOT A %d NOTE SET ***\n",setsize);
    fprintf(fp, "\n\t\t\t**** NOT A %d NOTE SET ***\n",setsize);
    putchar(7);
    notset++;

}
/*=============== MIC 3.48 ===============*/
PutSetData(fp, test, setsize, ordered, setnumber, setfq)
    FILE *fp;
    int test[], setsize, ordered[], setnumber, setfq[];
{
    printf("Ordered pc array:       ");
    PutArray(test, setsize);
    fprintf(fp, "Ordered pc array:       ");
    FputArray(fp, test, setsize);
    printf("As pitches:");
    fprintf(fp, "As pitches:");
    ScriptArray(test, ' ', setsize);
    FscriptArray(fp, test, ' ', setsize);
    printf("Ordered interval array:");
    PutArray(ordered, setsize);
    fprintf(fp, "Ordered interval array:");
    FputArray(fp, ordered, setsize);
    printf("Set = %d-%d\n", setsize, setnumber);
    fprintf(fp, "Set = %d-%d\n", setsize, setnumber);
    setfq[setnumber - 1]++;
    switch(setsize)
      {
      case 3: PrintSetInfo(set3, setnumber, setsize);
                FprintSetInfo(fp, set3, setnumber, setsize);
                break;
      case 4: PrintSetInfo(set4, setnumber, setsize);
                FprintSetInfo(fp, set4, setnumber, setsize);
                break;
      case 5: PrintSetInfo(set5, setnumber, setsize);
                FprintSetInfo(fp, set5, setnumber, setsize);
                break;
      case 6: PrintSetInfo(set6, setnumber, setsize);
                FprintSetInfo(fp, set6, setnumber, setsize);
                break;
      }

}
```

```
/*=============== MIC 3.49 ==============*/
PutSetSummary(fp, setfq, setsize)
    FILE *fp;
    int setfq[], setsize;
{
 int j;
  PutLn();
  FputLn(fp);
  printf( "\n\nSet summary: \n");
  fprintf(fp, "\n\nSet summary: \n");
  for(j = 0; j < amt[setsize - 3]; j++)
        {
        if(setfq[j] != 0)
           {
        printf("\nSet %d-%d occurs %d ", setsize, j+1 ,
                setfq[j]);
        fprintf(fp, "\nSet %d-%d occurs %d ", setsize, j+1,
                setfq[j]);
          if(setfq[j] == 1)
             {
             printf("time");
             fprintf(fp, "time");
             }
          else
             {
              printf("times");
              fprintf(fp, "times");
             }
           }
        }
    printf("\nThere were %d non-sets", notset);
    fprintf(fp, "\nThere were %d non-sets", notset);
   PutLn();
   FputLn(fp);
}
/*=============== MIC 3.50 ==============*/
PutTable(fp)
    FILE *fp;
{
    int ask, j;
   do
     {
      printf("Do you want a set table? yes = 1, no = 2\n");
      scanf("%d",&ask);
      } while(ask < 1 || ask > 2);

  if(ask == 1)
    {
    printf( "\n\nHere is the 3 note set table\n");
    fprintf(fp, "\n\nHere is the 3 note set table\n");
    PrintSetTable(set3,3);
    FprintSetTable(fp, set3,3);
    printf( "\n\nHere is the 4 note set table\n");
    fprintf(fp, "\n\nHere is the 4 note set table\n");
    PrintSetTable(set4,4);
    FprintSetTable(fp, set4,4);
    printf( "\n\nHere is the 5 note set table\n");
    fprintf(fp, "\n\nHere is the 5 note set table\n");
    PrintSetTable(set5, 5);
    FprintSetTable(fp, set5, 5);
    printf( "\n\nHere is the 6 note set table\n");
```

```
      fprintf(fp, "\n\nHere is the 6 note set table\n");
      PrintSetTable(set6, 6);
      FprintSetTable(fp, set6, 6);
      }
}
/*=============== MIC 3.51 ===============*/
GetData(datarray, setfq, pcarray)
   int datarray[], setfq[], pcarray[];
{
   int ask, j, size;
   psize = rsize = asize = vsize = tsize = 0;

   do {
   printf("\nDo you wish to type in integers (1) or ");
   printf("Read in a Script score (2) ");
   printf("\nType a 1 or 2\t?\b");
   scanf("%d",&ask);
   } while (ask < 1 || ask > 2);
   if(ask == 1)
     size = InputYourOwn(datarray);
   else
       {
       inputfile = getfnam("input","r");
       GetLines(inputfile);
       fclose(inputfile);
       switch(WhichArray())
          {
          case 1 : size = psize;
                   printf("\nUsing Pitch Array \n\n");
                   for(j = 0; j < psize; j++)
                        datarray[j] = parray[j];
                   break;
          case 2 : size = rsize;
                   printf("\nUsing Rhythm Array \n\n");
                   for(j = 0; j < rsize; j++)
                        datarray[j] = rarray[j];
                   break;
          case 3 : size = asize;
                   printf("\nUsing Articulation Array \n\n");
                   for(j = 0; j < asize; j++)
                        datarray[j] = aarray[j];
                   break;
          case 4 : size = vsize;
                   printf("\nUsing Volume Array \n\n");
                   for(j = 0; j < vsize; j++)
                        datarray[j] = varray[j];
                   break;
          case 5 : size = tsize;
                   printf("\nUsing Rte Array \n\n");
                   for(j = 0; j < tsize; j++)
                        datarray[j] = tarray[j];
                   break;
          }
       }
   for(j = 0; j < 50; j++)
      setfq[j] = 0;
   for(j = 0; j < size; j++)
      pcarray[j] = datarray[j] % 12;
   printf("\nUsing %d pitches\n", size);
   return(size);
}
```

```
/*=============== MIC 3.52 ==============*/
WhichArray()
{
    char string[80];
    int j = 0;

    printf("\nWhich data set do you wish to analyze\n");
    if(psize != 0)
       printf("(1) Pitch data   ");
    if(rsize != 0)
       printf("(2) Rhythm data   ");
    if(asize != 0)
      printf("(3) Articulation data   ");
    if(vsize != 0)
       printf("(4) Volume data   ");
    if(tsize != 0)
       printf("(5) Rte data ");
   do {
      gets(string);
      j = atoi(string);
      } while(j < 1 || j > 5);
    return(j);
}
/*=============== MIC 3.53 ==============*/
showdata(fp, datarray,pcarray,size)
    FILE *fp;
    int datarray[], pcarray[], size;
    {
  printf("\nInput pitches\n");
  fprintf(fp, "\nInput pitches\n");
  ScriptArray(datarray, ' ', size);
  FscriptArray(fp, datarray, ' ', size);
  PutLn();
  FputLn(fp);
  printf("\nPitch classes of input data:\n");
  PutArray(pcarray, size);
  fprintf(fp, "\nPitch classes of input data:\n");
  FputArray(fp, pcarray, size);
  PutLn();
  FputLn(fp);
}
/*=============== MIC 3.54 ==============*/
ShowImbricated(fp, pcarray, imarray, imsize, size)
    FILE *fp;
    int pcarray[],imarray[], imsize, size;
    {
    int j, totsize, imbeg;

   if(imsize == 0)
      return;
    for(j = 0,imbeg = 0; j < size - (imsize-1); j++, imbeg+=imsize)
       imbricate(pcarray, imarray, j, imsize, imbeg);

    totsize = imsize * (size - (imsize - 1));
    printf("\nImbricated array (in blocks of %d)\n", imsize);
    PutArray(imarray, totsize);
     printf("\n");
   fprintf(fp, "\nImbricated array (in blocks of %d)\n", imsize);
   FputArray(fp, imarray, totsize);
   fprintf(fp, "\n");
    PutLn();
```

```
  FputLn(fp);
fprintf(fp, "\nImbricated array as pitches\n");
printf("\nImbricated array as pitches\n");
 ScriptArray(imarray, ' ', totsize);
 FscriptArray(fp, imarray, ' ', totsize);
 PutLn();
 FputLn(fp);
}
/*=============== MIC 3.55 ===============*/
NormalOrder(pcarray, ordered, setsize)
   int pcarray[], ordered[], setsize;
{
    int j, min, temp, test, t1,k, norm;
    int temparray[6], ordered2[6];

    t1 = 0;
    test = 0;           /* to see if requirement 2 is needed */
    for(j = 0; j < setsize; j++)
        {
        ordered[j] = pcarray[j];
        temparray[j] = pcarray[j];
        }
        j = 0;
        min = abs(ordered[0] - ordered[setsize-1]);
    do {
        rotate(ordered, ordered, setsize);
        temp = abs(ordered[0] - ordered[setsize-1]);
        if(temp < min)
            {
            min = temp;
            for(k = 0; k < setsize; k++)
                temparray[k] = ordered[k];
            }
        else if (temp == min)
            {
            test = 1;
            for(k = 0; k < setsize; k++)
                ordered2[k] = ordered[k];
            break;
            }
        j++;
    } while ( j < setsize-1 && test == 0);
    if(min < temp)
        {
        rotate(ordered, ordered, setsize);
        rotate(temparray, temparray, setsize);
        }
    if(test == 1)  /* compare temparray with ordered */
        {
        for(j = 0; j < setsize-1; j++)
            {
        if(abs(ordered2[j+1] - ordered2[j]) >
            abs(temparray[j+1] - temparray[j]))
                {
                t1 = 1;
                break;  /* use ordered */
                }
            }
        if(t1 == 0 )
            {
            norm = ordered2[0];
```

```
       for(j = 0; j < setsize; j++)
          ordered[j] = ordered2[j] - norm;
          return;
          }
       else
          {
          norm = temparray[0];
           for(j = 0; j < setsize; j++)
              ordered[j] = abs(temparray[j] - norm);
          return;
          }
       }
}
/*=============== MIC 3.56 ===============*/
endvector(vector, size)
   int vector[], size;
{
   int j, temp=0;
   for(j = 0; j < size-1; j++)
      temp += vector[j];
   vector[size-1] = 12 - temp;
}
/*=============== MIC 3.57 ===============*/
rotate(datarray, disarray, size)
    int datarray[];
    int disarray[];
    int size;
{
   int  j;

   disarray[size] = datarray[0] + 12;
   for(j = 0; j < size; j++)
      disarray[j] = datarray[j+1];
}
/*=============== MIC 3.58 ===============*/
set3cmp(test)
   int test[];
{
   int j = 0;
   int k = 0;
   int setname = 0;

   for(j = 0; j < 12; j++)
      {
         if(
            (test[k] == set3[j].set_array[k]) &&
            (test[k+1] == set3[j].set_array[k+1])
           )
           {
           setname = j + 1;
           return(setname);
           }
      }
   return(0);    /* not found */
}
/*=============== MIC 3.59 ===============*/
set4cmp(test)
   int test[];
{
   int j = 0;
   int k = 0;
```

```
    int setname = 0;

    for(j = 0; j < 29; j++)
        {
        if(
            (test[k] == set4[j].set_array[k]) &&
            (test[k+1] == set4[j].set_array[k+1]) &&
            (test[k+2] == set4[j].set_array[k+2])
            )
            {
            setname = j + 1;
            return(setname);
            }
        }
    return(0);    /* not found */
}
/*=============== MIC 3.60 ===============*/
set5cmp(test)
    int test[];
{
    int j = 0;
    int k = 0;
    int setname = 0;

    for(j = 0; j < 38; j++)
        {
        if(
            (test[k] == set5[j].set_array[k]) &&
            (test[k+1] == set5[j].set_array[k+1]) &&
            (test[k+2] == set5[j].set_array[k+2]) &&
            (test[k+3] == set5[j].set_array[k+3])
            )
            {
            setname = j + 1;
            return(setname);
            }
        }
    return(0);    /* not found */
}
/*=============== MIC 3.61 ===============*/
set6cmp(test)
    int test[];
{
    int j = 0;
    int k = 0;
    int setname = 0;

    for(j = 0; j < 50; j++)
        {
        if(
            (test[k] == set6[j].set_array[k]) &&
            (test[k+1] == set6[j].set_array[k+1]) &&
            (test[k+2] == set6[j].set_array[k+2]) &&
            (test[k+3] == set6[j].set_array[k+3]) &&
            (test[k+4] == set6[j].set_array[k+4])
            )
            {
            setname = j + 1;
            return(setname);
            }
        }
```

```c
    return(0);    /* not found */
}
/*=============== MIC 3.62 ===============*/
PrintSetTable(set, setsize)
    struct sets set[];
    int setsize;
    {
    register int j = 0;
    int k;

    for(j = 0; j < amt[setsize - 3]; j++)
        {
        k = 0;
        printf("\nSet %d-%d", setsize, j+1);

        printf("\nSet array:\t ");
        for(k = 0; k < setsize; k++)
            printf("%d ", set[j].set_array[k]);

        printf("\nInversion:\t ");
        if(set[j].array_inversion[0] != 0)
            for(k = 0; k < setsize; k++)
                printf("%d ", set[j].array_inversion[k]);

        printf("\nVector:  \t ");
        for(k = 0; k < 6; k++)
            printf("%d ", set[j].icvector[k]);

        PutSubset(j, setsize);
        PutSimilar(j, setsize);
        PutContains(j, setsize);
        }
}
/*=============== MIC 3.63 ===============*/
FprintSetTable(fp, set, setsize)
    FILE *fp;
    struct sets set[];
    int setsize;
    {
    register int j = 0;
    int k;

    for(j = 0; j < amt[setsize - 3]; j++)
        {
        k = 0;
        fprintf(fp, "\nSet %d-%d", setsize, j+1);

        fprintf(fp, "\nSet array:\t ");
        for(k = 0; k < setsize; k++)
            fprintf(fp, "%d ", set[j].set_array[k]);

        fprintf(fp, "\nInversion:\t ");
        if(set[j].array_inversion[0] != 0)
            for(k = 0; k < setsize; k++)
                fprintf(fp, "%d ", set[j].array_inversion[k]);

        fprintf(fp, "\nVector:  \t ");
        for(k = 0; k < 6; k++)
            fprintf(fp, "%d ", set[j].icvector[k]);

        FputSubset(fp, j, setsize);
```

```
      }
}
/*================ MIC 3.64 ==============*/
PutSubset(setnumber, setsize)
    int setnumber, setsize;
{
    int k = 0;
    int subset;

    if(setsize == 6)
      return;
    setsize += 1;
    printf("\nIs a subset of: ");
    switch(setsize - 1)
        {
        case 3 : while(subset3of[setnumber][k] != 0 &&
                      k <= 9)        /* 0 = flag */
          {
            subset = subset3of[setnumber][k++];
            printf("\n\t %d-%d\t",  setsize , subset);
            PutSetArray(set4[subset-1].set_array, setsize );
            printf("\t");
            PutSetArrayPitches(set4[subset-1].set_array,
                            setsize );
            printf("\n\t\t");
            PutSetInversion(set4[subset-1].array_inversion,
                        setsize );
            printf("\t");
            PutSetInversionPitches(set4[subset-1].array_inversion,
                              setsize);
          };
              printf("\n");
              break;
        case 4 : while(subset4of[setnumber][k] != 0 && k <= 9)
          {
            subset = subset4of[setnumber][k++];
            printf("\n\t %d-%d\t",  setsize , subset);
            PutSetArray(set5[subset-1].set_array, setsize );
            printf("\t");
            PutSetArrayPitches(set5[subset-1].set_array,
                            setsize);
            printf("\n\t\t");
            PutSetInversion(set5[subset-1].array_inversion,
                        setsize);
            printf("\t");
            PutSetInversionPitches(set5[subset-1].array_inversion,
                              setsize);
          }
              printf("\n");
              break;
        case 5 : while(subset5of[setnumber][k] != 0 && k <= 9)
          {
            subset = subset5of[setnumber][k++];
            printf("\n\t %d-%d\t",  setsize , subset);
            PutSetArray(set6[subset-1].set_array, setsize);
            printf("\t");
            PutSetArrayPitches(set6[subset-1].set_array, setsize);
            printf("\n\t\t");
            PutSetInversion(set6[subset-1].array_inversion,
                        setsize);
            printf("\t");
```

```
                  PutSetInversionPitches(set6[subset-1].array_inversion,
                                      setsize);
          };
                  printf("\n");
                  break;
      }
}
/*=============== MIC 3.65 ==============*/
FputSubset(fp, setnumber, setsize)
    FILE *fp;
    int setnumber, setsize;
{
    int k = 0;
    int subset;

    if(setsize == 6)
      return;
    setsize += 1;
    fprintf(fp, "\nIs a subset of: ");
    switch(setsize-1)
        {
    case 3 : while(subset3of[setnumber][k] != 0 && k <= 9)
            {
            subset = subset3of[setnumber][k++];
            fprintf(fp, "\n\t %d-%d\t",  setsize , subset);
            FputSetArray(fp, set4[subset-1].set_array, setsize);
            fprintf(fp, "\t");
            FputSetArrayPitches(fp, set4[subset-1].set_array,
                              setsize);
            fprintf(fp, "\n\t\t");
            FputSetInversion(fp, set4[subset-1].array_inversion,
                              setsize);
            fprintf(fp, "\t");
        FputSetInversionPitches(fp,set4[subset-1].array_inversion,
                              setsize);
            };
            fprintf(fp, "\n");
            break;
    case 4 : while(subset4of[setnumber][k] != 0 && k <= 9)
            {
            subset = subset4of[setnumber][k++];
            fprintf(fp, "\n\t %d-%d\t",  setsize , subset);
            fprintf(fp, "\t");
            FputSetArray(fp, set5[subset-1].set_array, setsize);
            fprintf(fp, "\t");
            FputSetArrayPitches(fp, set5[subset-1].set_array,
                              setsize);
            fprintf(fp, "\n\t\t");
            FputSetInversion(fp, set5[subset-1].array_inversion,
                              setsize);
            fprintf(fp, "\t");
            FputSetInversionPitches(fp,
                    set5[subset-1].array_inversion, setsize);
            }
            fprintf(fp, "\n");
            break;
    case 5 : while(subset5of[setnumber][k] != 0 && k <= 9)
            {
            subset = subset5of[setnumber][k++];
            fprintf(fp, "\n\t %d-%d\t",  setsize , subset);
            FputSetArray(fp, set6[subset-1].set_array, setsize);
```

```
                    fprintf(fp, "\t");
                    FputSetArrayPitches(fp, set6[subset-1].set_array,
                                    setsize);
                    fprintf(fp, "\n\t\t");
                    FputSetInversion(fp, set6[subset-1].array_inversion,
                                    setsize);
                    fprintf(fp, "\t");
                FputSetInversionPitches(fp,set6[subset-1].array_inversion,
                                    setsize);
                    };
                    fprintf(fp, "\n");
                    break;
                    }
}
/*=============== MIC 3.66 ==============*/
PutSetArray(SetArray, setsize)
    int SetArray[], setsize;
{
    int k;
        for(k = 0; k < setsize; k++)
            printf("%d ",SetArray[k]);
}

/*=============== MIC 3.67 ==============*/
PutSetInversion(SetInversion, setsize)
    int SetInversion[], setsize;
{
    int k;
        if(SetInversion[0] == 0)
            {
            printf("No inversion");
            return;
            }
        else
            for(k = 0; k < setsize; k++)
                printf("%d ", SetInversion[k]);
}
/*=============== MIC 3.68 ==============*/
PutSetArrayPitches(SetArray, setsize)
    int SetArray[], setsize;
{
    int k, pitch = 0;
        PutPitch(pitch);
        for(k = 0; k < setsize; k++)
            {
            pitch += SetArray[k];
            PutPitch(pitch);
            }
}
/*=============== MIC 3.69 ==============*/
PutSetInversionPitches(SetInversion, setsize)
    int SetInversion[], setsize;
{
    int k, pitch = 0;
        if(SetInversion[0] == 0)
            return;
        else
            {
            PutPitch(pitch);
            for(k = 0; k < setsize; k++)
                {
```

```
                pitch += SetInversion[k];
                PutPitch(pitch);
                }
            }
    }
/*=============== MIC 3.70 ===============*/
FputSetArrayPitches(fp, SetArray, setsize)
    FILE *fp;
    int SetArray[], setsize;
{
    int k, pitch = 0;
        FputPitch(fp, pitch);
        for(k = 0; k < setsize; k++)
            {
            pitch += SetArray[k];
            FputPitch(fp, pitch);
            }
    }
/*=============== MIC 3.71 ===============*/
FputSetInversionPitches(fp, SetInversion, setsize)
    FILE *fp;
    int SetInversion[], setsize;
{
    int k, pitch = 0;
        if(SetInversion[0] == 0)
          return;
        else
            {
            FputPitch(fp, pitch);
            for(k = 0; k < setsize; k++)
                {
                pitch += SetInversion[k];
                FputPitch(fp, pitch);
                }
            }
    }
/*=============== MIC 3.72 ===============*/
PutSetVector(SetVector)
    int SetVector[];
{
    int k;
        for(k = 0; k < 6; k++)
            printf("%d ", SetVector[k]);
    }
/*=============== MIC 3.73 ===============*/
FputSetArray(fp, SetArray, setsize)
    FILE *fp;
    int SetArray[], setsize;
{
    int k;
        for(k = 0; k < setsize; k++)
            fprintf(fp, "%d ",SetArray[k]);
    }
/*=============== MIC 3.74 ===============*/
FputSetInversion(fp, SetInversion, setsize)
    FILE *fp;
    int SetInversion[], setsize;
{
    int k;
        if(SetInversion[0] == 0)
    {
```

```
                    fprintf(fp, "No inversion");
                    return;
                    }
                else
                  for(k = 0; k < setsize; k++)
                     fprintf(fp, "%d ", SetInversion[k]);
}
/*=============== MIC 3.75 ===============*/
FputSetVector(fp, SetVector)
     FILE *fp;
    int SetVector[];
{
    int k;
       for(k = 0; k < 6; k++)
          fprintf(fp, "%d ", SetVector[k]);
}
/*=============== MIC 3.76 ===============*/
PrintSetInfo(set, setnumber, setsize)
     struct sets set[];
     int setnumber, setsize;
     {
    int j;

       j = setnumber - 1;
       setnumber -= 1;
       printf("\nSet info:");
       printf("\nSet array:\t ");
       PutSetArray(set[j].set_array, setsize);
       printf("\nInversion:\t ");
       PutSetInversion(set[j].array_inversion, setsize);
       printf("\nVector:  \t ");
       PutSetVector(set[j].icvector);
       PutSubset(j, setsize);
       PutSimilar(j, setsize);
       PutContains(j, setsize);
}
/*=============== MIC 3.77 ===============*/
FprintSetInfo(fp, set, setnumber, setsize)
     FILE *fp;
     struct sets set[];
     int setnumber, setsize;
     {
    int j;
    j = setnumber - 1;

       fprintf(fp, "\nSet info:");
       fprintf(fp, "\nSet array:\t ");
       FputSetArray(fp, set[j].set_array, setsize);
       fprintf(fp, "\nInversion:\t ");
       FputSetInversion(fp, set[j].array_inversion, setsize);
       fprintf(fp, "\nVector:  \t ");
       FputSetVector(fp, set[j].icvector);
       FputSubset(fp, j, setsize);
       FputSimilar(fp, j, setsize);
       FputContains(fp, j, setsize);
}
/*=============== MIC 3.78 ===============*/
PutContains(setnumber, setsize)
     int setnumber, setsize;
{
       int k = 0;
```

```
      int contained;

      if (setsize == 3)
         return;
       printf("Contains: ");
       switch(setsize)
          {
          case 4 : while(contains3[setnumber][k] != 0 && k <= 11)
             {
              contained = contains3[setnumber][k++];

              printf("\n\t %d-%d\t", setsize - 1, contained);
              PutSetArray(set3[contained-1].set_array, 3);
              printf("\t   ");
              PutSetArrayPitches(set3[contained-1].set_array, 3);
              printf("\n\t\t");
     PutSetInversion(set3[contained-1].array_inversion, 3);
      printf("\t   ");
 PutSetInversionPitches(set3[contained-1].array_inversion, 3);
 };
      printf("\n")
      break;
          case 5 : while(contains4[setnumber][k] != 0 && k <= 11)
             {
              contained = contains4[setnumber][k++];
              printf("\n\t %d-%d\t", setsize - 1, contained);
              PutSetArray(set4[contained-1].set_array, 4);
              printf("\t");
              PutSetArrayPitches(set4[contained-1].set_array, 4);
              printf("\n\t\t");
            PutSetInversion(set4[contained-1].array_inversion, 4);
              printf("\t");
 PutSetInversionPitches(set4[contained-1].array_inversion, 4);
             };
              printf("\n")
              break;
          case 6 : while(contains5[setnumber][k] != 0 && k <= 11)
              {
               contained = contains5[setnumber][k++];
               printf("\n\t %d-%d\t", setsize - 1, contained);
               PutSetArray(set5[contained-1].set_array, 5);
               printf("\t");
               PutSetArrayPitches(set5[contained-1].set_array, 5);
               printf("\n\t\t");
            PutSetInversion(set5[contained-1].array_inversion, 5);
               printf("\t");
 PutSetInversionPitches(set5[contained-1].array_inversion, 5);
          };
                 printf("\n")
                 break;
          }
}
/*=============== MIC 3.79 ==============*/
PutSimilar(setnumber, setsize)
     int setnumber, setsize;
{
      int k = 0;
      int similar;
      if (setsize == 3)
         return;
```

```
        printf("\nIs similar to: ");
        switch(setsize)
          {
            case 4 : while(SimilarTo4[setnumber][k] != 0 &&
                           k <= 12)
                    {
                    similar = SimilarTo4[setnumber][k++];
                    printf("\n\t %d-%d\t", setsize , similar);
                    PutSetArray(set4[similar-1].set_array, setsize);
                    printf("\t");
                PutSetArrayPitches(set4[similar-1].set_array, setsize);
                    printf("\n\t\t");
             PutSetInversion(set4[similar-1].array_inversion, setsize);
                    printf("\t");
                  PutSetInversionPitches(set4[similar-1].array_inversion,
                            setsize);
                    };
                    printf("\n");
                    break;
            case 5 : while(SimilarTo5[setnumber][k] != 0 && k <= 12)
                    {
                    similar = SimilarTo5[setnumber][k++];
                    printf("\n\t %d-%d\t", setsize , similar);
                    PutSetArray(set5[similar-1].set_array, setsize);
                    printf("\t");
                    PutSetArrayPitches(set5[similar-1].set_array,
                                setsize);
                    printf("\n\t\t");
                    PutSetInversion(set5[similar-1].array_inversion,
                                setsize);
                    printf("\t");
                  PutSetInversionPitches(set5[similar-1].array_inversion,
                                setsize);
                    };
                    printf("\n");
                    break;
            case 6 : while(SimilarTo6[setnumber][k] != 0 && k <= 15)
                    {
                    similar = SimilarTo6[setnumber][k++];
                    printf("\n\t %d-%d\t", setsize , similar);
                    PutSetArray(set6[similar-1].set_array, setsize);
                    printf("\t");
                    PutSetArrayPitches(set6[similar-1].set array,
                                setsize);
                    printf("\n\t\t");
                    PutSetInversion(set6[similar-1].array_inversion,
                                setsize);
                    printf("\t");
                  PutSetInversionPitches(set6[similar-1].array_inversion,
                                setsize);
                    };
                    printf("\n");
                    break;
          }
}
/*=============== MIC 3.80 ==============*/
FputContains(fp, setnumber, setsize)
    FILE *fp;
    int setnumber, setsize;
{
    int k = 0;
```

```
      int contained;

      if (setsize == 3)
        return;
      fprintf(fp, "Contains: ");
      switch(setsize)
        {
        case 4 : while(contains3[setnumber][k] != 0 && k <= 11)
            {
            contained = contains3[setnumber][k++];
            fprintf(fp,"\n\t %d-%d\t", setsize - 1, contained);
            FputSetArray(fp,set3[contained-1].set_array, 3);
            fprintf(fp,"\t   ");
            FputSetArrayPitches(fp,set3[contained-1].set_array, 3);
            fprintf(fp,"\n\t\t");
            FputSetInversion(fp,
                set3[contained-1].array_inversion, 3);
            fprintf(fp,"\t\t ");
            FputSetInversionPitches(fp,
                    set3[contained-1].array_inversion, 3);
            };
          fprintf(fp,"\n");
          break;
        case 5 : while(contains4[setnumber][k] != 0 && k <= 11)
              {
              contained = contains4[setnumber][k++];
              fprintf(fp,"\n\t %d-%d\t", setsize - 1, contained);
              FputSetArray(fp,set4[contained-1].set_array, 4);
              fprintf(fp,"\t");
          FputSetArrayPitches(fp,set4[contained-1].set_array, 4);
            fprintf(fp,"\n\t\t");
            FputSetInversion(fp,
                    set4[contained-1].array_inversion, 4);
            fprintf(fp,"\t");
            FputSetInversionPitches(fp,
                    set4[contained-1].array_inversion, 4);
                };
              fprintf(fp,"\n");
              break;
        case 6 : while(contains5[setnumber][k] != 0 && k <= 11)
                {
                contained = contains5[setnumber][k++];
                fprintf(fp,
                    "\n\t %d-%d\t", setsize - 1, contained);
                FputSetArray(fp,set5[contained-1].set_array, 5);
                fprintf(fp,"\t");
                FputSetArrayPitches(fp,
                    set5[contained-1].set_array, 5);
                fprintf(fp,"\n\t\t");
                FputSetInversion(fp,
                    set5[contained-1].array_inversion, 5);
                fprintf(fp,"\t");
            FputSetInversionPitches(fp,
                    set5[contained-1].array_inversion, 5);
                };
                fprintf(fp,"\n");
                break;
        }
}
/*=============== MIC 3.81 ===============*/
FputSimilar(fp, setnumber, setsize)
```

```
        FILE *fp;
        int setnumber, setsize;
{
    int k = 0;
    int similar;
    if (setsize == 3)
        return;
    fprintf(fp, "\nIs similar to: ");
    switch(setsize)
      {
        case 4 : while(SimilarTo4[setnumber][k] != 0 &&
                        k <= 12)
                {
                similar = SimilarTo4[setnumber][k++];
                fprintf(fp, "\n\t %d-%d\t", setsize , similar);
                FputSetArray(fp,set4[similar-1].set_array,
                            setsize);
                fprintf(fp,"\t");
                FputSetArrayPitches(fp,set4[similar-1].set_array,
                                setsize);
                fprintf(fp,"\n\t\t");
                FputSetInversion(fp,
                        set4[similar-1].array_inversion, setsize);
                fprintf(fp,"\t");
        FputSetInversionPitches(fp,
                        set4[similar-1].array_inversion, setsize);
                };
                fprintf(fp,"\n");
                break;
        case 5 : while(SimilarTo5[setnumber][k] != 0 && k <= 12)
                {
                similar = SimilarTo5[setnumber][k++];
                fprintf(fp,"\n\t %d-%d\t", setsize , similar);
                FputSetArray(fp,set5[similar-1].set_array,
                            setsize);
                fprintf(fp,"\t");
                FputSetArrayPitches(fp,set5[similar-1].set_array,
                                setsize);
                fprintf(fp,"\n\t\t");
                FputSetInversion(fp,
                        set5[similar-1].array_inversion, setsize);
                fprintf(fp,"\t");
        FputSetInversionPitches(fp,
                        set5[similar-1].array_inversion, setsize);
                };
                fprintf(fp, "\n");
                break;
        case 6 : while(SimilarTo6[setnumber][k] != 0 && k <= 15)
                {
                similar = SimilarTo6[setnumber][k++];
                fprintf(fp,"\n\t %d-%d\t", setsize , similar);
                FputSetArray(fp,set6[similar-1].set_array,
                            setsize);
                fprintf(fp,"\t");
                FputSetArrayPitches(fp,set6[similar-1].set_array,
                                setsize);
                fprintf(fp,"\n\t\t");
                FputSetInversion(fp,
                        set6[similar-1].array_inversion, setsize);
                fprintf(fp,"\t");
                FputSetInversionPitches(fp,
```

```
                        set6[similar-1].array_inversion, setsize);
              };
              fprintf(fp,"\n");
              break;
          }
} /* END OF MAIN */
/*=======================================*/
```

## Sample program output (sets.exe)

```
    no imbrication, 5 note sets

Input pitches

    D#0 E0  C0  C#0 D0  C#0 D0  D#0 F0  C0  D0  E0  F0  C0  C#0

/*-----------------------------------------------------------*/

Pitch classes of input data:
    3   4   0   1   2   1   2   3   5   0   2   4   5   0   1

/*-----------------------------------------------------------*/

/*-----------------------------------------------------------*/

Original pitches:
    D#0 E0  C0  C#0 D0
Pc array:                 3   4   0   1   2
Ordered pc array:         0   1   2   3   4
As pitches:
    C0  C#0 D0  D#0 E0
Ordered interval array:   1   1   1   1   8
Set = 5-1

Set info:
Set array:        1 1 1 1 8
Inversion:        No inversion
Vector:           4 3 2 1 0 0
Is a subset of:
        6-1       1 1 1 1 1 7      C0  C#0 D0  D#0 E0  F0  C1
                  No inversion
        6-2       1 1 1 1 2 6      C0  C#0 D0  D#0 E0  F#0 C1
                  2 1 1 1 1 6      C0  D0  D#0 E0  F0  F#0 C1

Is similar to:
        5-2       1 1 1 2 7        C0  C#0 D0  D#0 F0  C1
                  2 1 1 1 7        C0  D0  D#0 E0  F0  C1
Contains:
        4-1       1 1 1 9          C0  C#0 D0  D#0 C1
                  No inversion
        4-2       1 1 2 8          C0  C#0 D0  E0  C1
                  2 1 1 8          C0  D0  D#0 E0  C1
        4-3       1 2 1 8          C0  C#0 D#0 E0  C1
                  No inversion

/*-----------------------------------------------------------*/

Original pitches:
    C#0 D0  D#0 F0  C0
```

```
Pc array:                    1   2   3   5   0
Ordered pc array:            0   1   2   3   5
As pitches:
   C0  C#0  D0   D#0  F0

Ordered interval array:  1   1   1   2   7
Set = 5-2

Set info:
Set array:         1 1 1 2 7
Inversion:         2 1 1 1 7
Vector:            3 3 2 1 1 0
Is a subset of:
        6-1    1 1 1 1 1 7    C0  C#0 D0  D#0 E0  F0  C1
               No inversion
        6-2    1 1 1 1 2 6    C0  C#0 D0  D#0 E0  F#0 C1
               2 1 1 1 1 6    C0  D0  D#0 E0  F0  F#0 C1
        6-8    2 1 1 1 2 5    C0  D0  D#0 E0  F0  G0  C1
               No inversion
        6-9    1 1 1 2 2 5    C0  C#0 D0  D#0 F0  G0  C1
               2 2 1 1 1 5    C0  D0  E0  F0  F#0 G0  C1

Is similar to:
        5-1    1 1 1 1 8      C0  C#0 D0  D#0 E0  C1
               No inversion
        5-3    1 1 2 1 7      C0  C#0 D0  E0  F0  C1
               1 2 1 1 7      C0  C#0 D#0 E0  F0  C1
        5-4    1 1 1 3 6      C0  C#0 D0  D#0 F#0 C1
               3 1 1 1 6      C0  D#0 E0  F0  F#0 C1
        5-23   2 1 2 2 5      C0  D0  D#0 F0  G0  C1
               2 2 1 2 5      C0  D0  E0  F0  G0  C1
Contains:
        4-1    1 1 1 9        C0  C#0 D0  D#0 C1
               No inversion
        4-2    1 1 2 8        C0  C#0 D0  E0  C1
               2 1 1 8        C0  D0  D#0 E0  C1
        4-4    1 1 3 7        C0  C#0 D0  F0  C1
               3 1 1 7        C0  D#0 E0  F0  C1
        4-10   2 1 2 7        C0  D0  D#0 F0  C1
               No inversion
        4-11   1 2 2 7        C0  C#0 D#0 F0  C1
               2 2 1 7        C0  D0  E0  F0  C1


/*------------------------------------------------------------*/

Original pitches:
   D0  E0  F0  C0  C#0
Pc array:                    2   4   5   0   1
Ordered pc array:            0   1   2   4   5
As pitches:
   C0  C#0  D0   E0  F0
Ordered interval array:  1   1   2   1   7
Set = 5-3

Set info:
Set array:         1 1 2 1 7
Inversion:         1 2 1 1 7
Vector:            3 2 2 2 1 0
Is a subset of:
        6-1    1 1 1 1 1 7    C0  C#0 D0  D#0 E0  F0  C1
               No inversion
        6-14   1 2 1 1 3 4    C0  C#0 D#0 E0  F0  G#0 C1
```

```
              3 1 1 2 1 4      C0  D#0 E0   F0   G0   G#0 C1
     6-15     1 1 2 1 3 4      C0  C#0 D0   E0   F0   G#0 C1
              3 1 2 1 1 4      C0  D#0 E0   F#0  G0   G#0 C1

Is similar to:
     5-2      1 1 1 2 7        C0  C#0 D0   D#0  F0   C1
              2 1 1 1 7        C0  D0  D#0  E0   F0   C1
     5-4      1 1 1 3 6        C0  C#0 D0   D#0  F#0  C1
              3 1 1 1 6        C0  D#0 E0   F0   F#0  C1
     5-11     2 1 1 3 5        C0  D0  D#0  E0   G0   C1
              3 1 1 2 5        C0  D#0 E0   F0   G0   C1
     5-27     1 2 2 3 4        C0  C#0 D#0  F0   G#0  C1
              2 2 1 4 3        C0  D0  E0   F0   A0   C1
Contains:
     4-2      1 1 2 8          C0  C#0 D0   E0   C1
              2 1 1 8          C0  D0  D#0  E0   C1
     4-3      1 2 1 8          C0  C#0 D#0  E0   C1
              No inversion
     4-4      1 1 3 7          C0  C#0 D0   F0   C1
              3 1 1 7          C0  D#0 E0   F0   C1
     4-7      1 3 1 7          C0  C#0 E0   F0   C1
              No inversion
     4-11     1 2 2 7          C0  C#0 D#0  F0   C1
              2 2 1 7          C0  D0  E0   F0   C1


/*--------------------------------------------------------------*/


Set summary:

Set 5-1 occurs 1 time
Set 5-2 occurs 1 time
Set 5-3 occurs 1 time
There were 0 non-sets
/*--------------------------------------------------------------*/
```

## FUNCTION GROUP: Constel.c

1. con( )                 MIC3.82
2. FindFreq( )            MIC3.83
3. GetPitchStats( )       MIC3.84
4. FusionMain( )          MIC3.85
5. PutFusPitch( )         MIC3.86

## Purpose

Intervallic analysis.

## Notes

This group of functions performs elementary statistical analysis on the pitches in a given sequence. The linear interval sequence is extracted and frequency tables of register and interval occurrence are compiled. The last part of the program fuses adjacent intervals to reveal the outline of parts of the sequence or framing intervals. There are several levels of fusions, from simple interval pairs to triple fusions (if the sequence is long enough).

## Attention

Don't forget to list the "include" files to learn which addition (.c,.h,.pro) files they must have access to.

## Programming ideas

1. Add program code to graphically plot the statistical data.
2. Use the fusion functions in a generative rather than analytical fashion.

## Program source code

```
/* CONSTELL.C   (Intervallic Analysis Program) */

#include <stdio.h>
#include <ctype.h>
#define MAXDATA 500
#include "array.c"
#include "synclavie.c"
#include "statfunc.c"
#include "inputyou.c"
#include "matrix.c"
#include "screen.c"
#include "getnum.c"
#include "fusarray.c"

struct pitchrec
```

```
        {
        int pc;
        int freq;
        } pit[MAXDATA], regist[MAXDATA], odat[MAXDATA];

#include "constel.pro"
/* ARRAYS */
int datarray[MAXDATA];
int statarray[MAXDATA];
int constellation[MAXDATA];
int fusarray[MAXDATA][2];
int fusfreq[MAXDATA];
int pcarray[MAXDATA];
int imarray[MAXDATA];
int sorted[MAXDATA];
int pcsort[MAXDATA];
int shapearray[MAXDATA];

int size, i, consize, fusize, j, s;

FILE *inputfile;
FILE *outputfile;
main()
{
   outputfile = fopen("const.dat", "w");
   size = InputYourOwn(datarray);
   con();
   FusionMain();
   fclose(outputfile);
   printf("\nAnalysis is in file: const.dat\n");
}
/*=============== MIC 3.82 ==============*/
/******************************************************************/
con()
{
  register int j = 0;
  register int k = 0;
  int form, start, last, incr, nt, trans;

   Cls();
   PutLn();
    fprintf(outputfile, "\n\tConstellation Analysis \n\n");
    FputLn(outputfile);
    fprintf(outputfile, "\n\nInput data :\n");
    FscriptArray(outputfile, datarray, ' ', size);
    FputLn(outputfile);
    fprintf(outputfile, "\nInput data as integers :\n");
    FputArray(outputfile, datarray, size);
    FputLn(outputfile);
    fprintf(outputfile, "\nLinear interval sequence:\n");
    getshape(datarray, shapearray, size);
    FputArray(outputfile, shapearray, size-1);
printf("\nHow many transpositions do you want (0-12)\n");
scanf("%d", &nt);
for(trans = 0; trans <= nt; trans++)
{
if(trans != 0)
   {
   PutLn();
    FputLn(outputfile);
   printf("\n\n\nTransposition no. %d \n", trans);
```

```
    fprintf(outputfile, "\n\n\nTransposition no. %d \n",trans);
}
  for(j = 0; j < size; j++)
      {
        pit[j].freq = 0;
        pit[j].pc = 0;
        regist[j].pc = 0;
        regist[j].freq = 0;
        odat[j].pc = 0;
        odat[j].freq = 0;
        pcsort[j] = (datarray[j] + trans) % 12;
        sorted[j] = datarray[j] + trans;
      }


  QuickSort(sorted, 0, size -1);
  QuickSort(pcsort, 0, size -1);
  k = 0;
  for(j=0; j < size; j++)
      {
        if(sorted[j] != sorted[j + 1])
          constellation[k++] = sorted[j];
      }

      consize = k;
if(trans == 0)
{
fprintf(outputfile,"\n\nThere are %d pitches in the constellation\n", co
printf("\n\nThere are %d pitches in the constellation\n", consize);
}

      fprintf(outputfile, "Constellation:\n");
      printf("Constellation:\n");
       ScriptArray(constellation, ' ', consize);
       FscriptArray(outputfile, constellation, ' ', consize);

       getshape(constellation, shapearray, consize);

      for(j = 0; j < size; j++)
          {
            pit[j].pc = pcsort[j];
            regist[j].pc = sorted[j] / 12;
            odat[j].pc = sorted[j];
            statarray[j] = datarray[j] + trans;
          }

  GetPitchStats(outputfile, statarray, size);
  getshape(constellation, shapearray, consize);
  FindFreq(pit, size);
  FindFreq(regist, size);
  FindFreq(odat, size);
   PutLn();
    FputLn(outputfile);

  printf("\n\npitch class\t\tfrequency\n");
      printf("-----------\t\t---------\n");
    fprintf(outputfile,"\n\npitch class\t\tfrequency\n");
      fprintf(outputfile,"-----------\t\t---------\n");
    for(j=0; j < size; j++)
      {
        if(pit[j].pc != pit[j+1].pc)
```

```
            {
            printf("      %d", pit[j].pc);
            printf("\t\t\t   %d\n", pit[j].freq);
            fprintf(outputfile, "     %d", pit[j].pc);
            fprintf(outputfile, "\t\t\t   %d\n", pit[j].freq);
            }
        }

   PutLn();
    FputLn(outputfile);
 k = consize - 2;
    printf("\n\npitch\t\tfrequency\t\tinterval\n");
        printf("-----\t\t---------\t\t--------\n");
     fprintf(outputfile,"\n\npitch\t\tfrequency\t\tinterval\n");
        fprintf(outputfile,"-----\t\t---------\t\t--------\n");
   for(j =  size; j >= 0; j--)
        {
        if(odat[j].pc != odat[j + 1].pc)
            {
            PutPitch(odat[j].pc);
            FputPitch(outputfile, odat[j].pc);
            printf("\t\t   %d\n", odat[j].freq);
            fprintf(outputfile, "\t\t   %d\n", odat[j].freq);
            if(j > 0)
                {
                printf("\t\t\t\t          %d\n", shapearray[k]);
                fprintf(outputfile, "\t\t\t\t %d\n", shapearray[k--]);
                }
            }
        }
   PutLn();
    FputLn(outputfile);
    printf("\n\nregister\t\tfrequency\n");
        printf("--------\t\t---------\n");
   fprintf(outputfile, "\n\nregister\t\tfrequency\n");
        fprintf(outputfile, "--------\t\t---------\n");
   for(j=0; j < size; j++)
        {
        if(regist[j].pc != regist[j + 1].pc)
            {
            printf("     %d", regist[j].pc);
            printf("\t\t\t   %d\n", regist[j].freq);
            fprintf(outputfile, "     %d", regist[j].pc);
            fprintf(outputfile, "\t\t\t   %d\n", regist[j].freq);
            }
        }
}
}
/*=============== MIC 3.83 ===============*/
FindFreq(pit, size)
    struct pitchrec pit[];
    int size;

{
    int j, k, key;

for(j = 0; j< size; j++)
    {
    key = pit[j].pc;
    for(k = 0; k< size; k++)
        {
```

```
            if(key == pit[k].pc)
                pit[k].freq += 1;
            }
        }
    }
/*=============== MIC 3.84 ===============*/
GetPitchStats(outputfile,statarray, size)
    FILE *outputfile;
    int statarray[];
    int size;
    {
    float mea, sdev;
    int mod, med, min, max, dev;

        med = median(statarray, size);
        printf("\nmedian = ");
            PutPitch(med);
        fprintf(outputfile,"\nmedian = ");
            FputPitch(outputfile, med);

        mea = mean(statarray, size);
        printf("\nmean = ");
        i = mea;    /* cast */
        PutPitch(i);
        fprintf(outputfile,"\nmean = ");
        FputPitch(outputfile,i);
        sdev = StdDev(statarray, size);
        printf("\nstandard deviation from the mean = %3.2f", sdev);
        fprintf(outputfile,"\nstandard deviation from the mean = %3.2f", sd
        dev = sdev; /* cast */
        printf("\nThat means that the tessitura is from ");
        PutPitch(i - dev / 2);
        printf("to ");
        PutPitch(i + dev / 2);
        printf("\n");
        fprintf(outputfile, "\nThat means that the tessitura is from ");
        FputPitch(outputfile, i - dev / 2);
        fprintf(outputfile, "to ");
        FputPitch(outputfile, i + dev / 2);
        fprintf(outputfile, "\n");

        mod = FindMode(statarray, size);
        printf("\nstatistical mode = ");
         PutPitch(mod);
        fprintf(outputfile, "\nstatistical mode = ");
         FputPitch(outputfile, mod);

        max = getmax(statarray, size);
        printf("\nhighest pitch = ");
         PutPitch(max);
        fprintf(outputfile, "\nhighest pitch = ");
         FputPitch(outputfile, max);

        min = getmin(statarray, size);
        printf("\nlowest pitch = ");
         PutPitch(min);
        fprintf(outputfile, "\nlowest pitch = ");
         FputPitch(outputfile, min);

        regress(statarray, size);
```

```
     }
/*=============== MIC 3.85 ==============*/
FusionMain()
{

     int last, incr;

     fprintf(outputfile, "\n\tFusions\n");
     FputLn(outputfile);
     fprintf(outputfile, "\n\nInput data :\n");
     FscriptArray(outputfile, datarray, ' ', size);
     FputLn(outputfile);
     fprintf(outputfile, "\nInput data as integers :\n");
     FputArray(outputfile, datarray, size);
     FputLn(outputfile);

     PutLn();
     FputLn(outputfile);
     ZeroMatrix(fusarray, size, 2);
     getshape(datarray, shapearray, size-1);
     fusize = 0;
          {
       fusize = FusePair(outputfile, shapearray, fusarray, size - 1);
       printf("\nInterval pairs\n");
       fprintf(outputfile, "\nInterval pairs\n");
       PutMatrix(fusarray, fusize, 2);
       MatrixSort(fusarray, fusize, 2);
       FindMatrixFreq(fusarray, fusfreq, fusize);
       PutMatrixFq(fusarray, fusfreq, fusize, 2);
       FputMatrixFq(outputfile, fusarray, fusfreq, fusize, 2);
       PutFusPitch(outputfile, fusarray, fusize);
       ZeroMatrix(fusarray, fusize, 2);

     PutLn();
     FputLn(outputfile);

       fusize = fusion(datarray, fusarray, size - 1, 24);
       printf("\nSingle datum with multiple fusions\n");
       printf("upper limit = 24\n");
       fprintf(outputfile, "\nSingle datum with multiple fusions");
       fprintf(outputfile, "\nupperlimit = 24\n");
       PutMatrix(fusarray, fusize, 2);
       MatrixSort(fusarray, fusize, 2);
       FindMatrixFreq(fusarray, fusfreq, fusize);
       PutMatrixFq(fusarray, fusfreq, fusize, 2);
       FputMatrixFq(outputfile, fusarray, fusfreq, fusize, 2);
       PutFusPitch(outputfile, fusarray, fusize);
       ZeroMatrix(fusarray, fusize, 2);

     PutLn();
     FputLn(outputfile);

       fusize = fusion2(datarray, fusarray, size - 1);
       printf("\nDouble fusions\n");
       fprintf(outputfile, "\nDouble fusions\n");
       PutMatrix(fusize, fusize, 2);
       MatrixSort(fusarray, fusize, 2);
       FindMatrixFreq(fusarray, fusfreq, fusize);
       PutMatrixFq(fusarray, fusfreq, fusize, 2);
       FputMatrixFq(outputfile, fusarray, fusfreq, fusize, 2);
```

```
            PutFusPitch(outputfile, fusarray, fusize);
            ZeroMatrix(fusarray, fusize, 2);

        PutLn();
        FputLn(outputfile);

            fusize = fusion3(datarray, fusarray, size - 1);
                if(fusize > 0)
                {
            printf("\nTriple fusions\n");
            fprintf(outputfile, "\nTriple fusions\n");
            PutMatrix(fusarray, fusize, 2);
            MatrixSort(fusarray, fusize, 2);
            FindMatrixFreq(fusarray, fusfreq, fusize);
            PutMatrixFq(fusarray, fusfreq, fusize, 2);
            FputMatrixFq(outputfile, fusarray, fusfreq, fusize, 2);
            PutFusPitch(outputfile, fusarray, fusize);
            ZeroMatrix(fusarray, fusize, 2);
                }

        PutLn();
        FputLn(outputfile);
            }
        }
/*=============== MIC 3.86 ==============*/
PutFusPitch(fp, fusarray, size)
    FILE *fp;
    int fusarray[][2], size;
{
    int pc, j;

    printf("\nAs pitches from C1\n\n");
    fprintf(fp, "\nAs pitches from C1\n\n");
    for(j = 0; j < size; j++)
        {
            pc = 12;
            PutPitch(pc);
            PutPitch(pc += fusarray[j][0]);
            PutPitch(pc += fusarray[j][1]);
            printf("\n");
            pc = 12;
            FputPitch(fp, pc);
            FputPitch(fp, pc += fusarray[j][0]);
            FputPitch(fp, pc += fusarray[j][1]);
            fprintf(fp, "\n");
            }
} /* end of function */
```

## Sample output: constel.c

```
            Constellation Analysis
/*------------------------------------------------------------*/

Input data :

    C0  D#0  E0   C#1 C3   D4   G3
```

```
/*------------------------------------------------------------*/

Input data as integers :
   0    3    4   13   36   50   43

/*------------------------------------------------------------*/

Linear interval sequence:
   3    1    9   23   14   -7


There are 7 pitches in the constellation
Constellation:

   C0   D#0  E0   C#1  C3   G3   D4

median = C#1
mean = A1
standard deviation from the mean = 19.52
That means that the tessitura is from C1  to F#2

statistical mode = C0
highest pitch = D4
lowest pitch = C0
/*------------------------------------------------------------*/

pitch class              frequency
-----------              ---------
      0                       2
      1                       1
      2                       1
      3                       1
      4                       1
      7                       1


/*------------------------------------------------------------*/

pitch         frequency              interval
-----         ---------              --------
D4                1
                                        7
G3                1
                                        7
C3                1
                                       23
C#1               1
                                        9
E0                1
                                        1
D#0               1
                                        3
C0                1

/*------------------------------------------------------------*/

register                 frequency
--------                 ---------
      0                       3
      1                       1
```

```
           3                        2
           4                        1

        Fusions

/*------------------------------------------------------------*/

Input data :

    C0  D#0  E0   C#1 C3  D4  G3

/*------------------------------------------------------------*/

Input data as integers :
    0    3    4   13   36   50   43

/*------------------------------------------------------------*/

/*------------------------------------------------------------*/

        FUSIONS

        Intervals to be fused :
            3    1    9   23   14    7

Interval pairs

   fusion                    frequency
   ------                    ---------
1        9                       1
3        1                       1
9        23                      1
14       7                       1
23       14                      1

As pitches from C1

C1   C#1 A#1
C1   D#1 E1
C1   A1  G#3
C1   D2  A2
C1   B2  C#4
/*------------------------------------------------------------*/

Single datum with multiple fusions
upperlimit = 24

   fusion                    frequency
   ------                    ---------
0        7                       1
0        20                      1
3        17                      1
4        3                       1
13       7                       2
36       17                      1
36       20                      2

As pitches from C1

C1   C1  G1
C1   C1  G#2
```

```
C1   D#1  G#2
C1   E1   G1
C1   C#2  G#2
C1   C#2  G#2
C1   C4   F5
C1   C4   G#5
C1   C4   G#5
```

/*----------------------------------------------------------------*/

Double fusions

| fusion | | frequency |
|--------|----|-----------|
| 3      | 17 | 1 |
| 7      | 49 | 1 |
| 17     | 86 | 1 |

As pitches from C1

```
C1   D#1  G#2
C1   G1   G#5
C1   F2   R
```

/*----------------------------------------------------------------*/

Triple fusions

| fusion | | frequency |
|--------|----|-----------|
| 0      | 20 | 1 |
| 3      | 53 | 1 |
| 7      | 13 | 1 |
| 20     | 36 | 1 |

As pitches from C1

```
C1   C1   G#2
C1   D#1  G#5
C1   G1   G#2
C1   G#2  G#5
```

/*----------------------------------------------------------------*/

# 4
# *Probability distribution functions*

Many compositional algorithms entail the testing of large amounts of data derived from the uniform random number generator found on mainframes and micros. Music based on sets of syntactical rules and constraints often requires many calls to integerized RND function by way of the sample-test/keep-discard method, which can be viewed as a process of "filtering" nonconforming values from a stream of data destined for a given musical parameter. Normally, textures composed in this manner are arrived at most efficiently via the computer's intrinsic uniform random distribution algorithm.

Nonuniform probability distributions, on the other hand, are fundamental to an important method of composition in which the details of selected musical parameters are directly calculated without reference to table-based syntactical rules. Often the goal of this approach is to map the characteristic curve exhibited by the function onto one or more musical parameters. There is no further contextual or historical contingency other than the appropriate scaling of data to meet parameter range requirements. The collection of algorithms presented in this chapter is by no means exhaustive; it is, however, broad enough to cover most compositional situations.

Each function deals with either a continuous or discrete random variable. Random variables normally assume their values as the result of a random process based on probabilities of occurrence. A continuous random variable can take on an infinite number of states, subject to the precision of the computer word, and is normally expressed as a real number falling between zero and one. A discrete random variable can only take on a limited number of (normally integer) states.

The sum of all the probabilities of all possible outcomes of a random process is always equal to one, and is customarily expressed as a line or bar graph. The continuous random variable graph is typified by a solid line curve. The discrete random variable graph resembles a histogram, but differs in that a histogram records actual frequencies of occurrence of specific values during a program run. The probability distribution graph represents the likelihood of occurrence of points along an infinite or discrete scale of values during a hypothetical program run. Comparison of an occurrence frequency histogram with a probability distribution graph for a particular algorithm provides a method of verifying correct subroutine operation. It also clarifies the correlation between number of samples generated and fidelity to the ideal probability distribution. (Usually, a lot of data must be generated before the characteristic curve develops.)

Real number values of continuous variables may be converted to integer and mapped to any numerical range by taking the integer portion after multiplication by the appropriate scaling factor.

# FUNCTION GROUP: Beta.c

1. Beta( )      MIC 4.1
2. Fpower( )    MIC 2.2

## Purpose

Generate a random number data set exhibiting Beta Probability Distribution characteristics.

## Notes

The algorithm returns continuous, random-order real numbers greater than zero and less than or equal to one. The shape of its curve changes with the values of its controlling parameters: "prob0" and "prob1." The parameter "prob0" determines the probability of values nearest zero; "prob1" determines probabilities nearest one. Smaller parameter values produce higher probabilities at the respective boundary; if "prob0" and "prob1" are equal, the curve is a symmetric around .5, otherwise the curve tilts in favor of the boundary controlled by the smaller parameter. The mean is:

prob0 / (prob 0 + prob 1)

The curve produced by this function can be made to resemble the bell-shaped (so-called normal) GAUSSIAN curve by setting both "prob0" and "prob1" greater than one. It can be toggled to output uniform distribution by setting "prob0" and "prob1" equal to one.

Example curve:                    prob0 = prob1 = 0.5

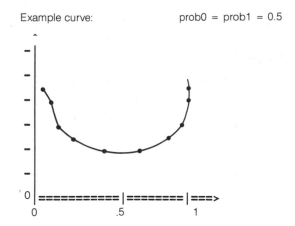

## Program source code

```
/* BETA.C (Eulerian Beta Probability Distribution Function */
#include <stdio.h>
#include <math.h>
main()
{
 int seed = -43;
 int j;              /* loop index */
 float parm0 = .4; /* controls values nearer to 0 */
 float parm1 = .2; /* controls values nearer to 1 */
 double x[100];       /* array storing Beta distribution */
 double Beta();

 srand(seed);
 for (j = 0;j < 100;j++)
     {
      if (j % 5 == 0)
         printf("\n");
      x[j] = Beta(parm0,parm1);
      printf("%f ",x[j]);
      }
} /* End of main */
/*============== MIC 4.1 ==============*/
/* Beta() Function */
double Beta(prob0,prob1)
double prob0,prob1;
{
 double u1;       /* random real number 1 ( > 0 < 1.) */
 double u2;       /* random real number 2 ( > 0 < 1.) */
 double t1;       /* computed probability 1 */
 double t2;       /* computed probability 2 */
 double sum;      /* total of probabilities 1 and 2 */
 double result; /* final Beta value */
 double Fpower();

 prob0 = 1. / prob0;
 prob1 = 1. / prob1;
 do
   {
     u1 = rand() / 32767.;
     u2 = rand() / 32767.;
     t1 = Fpower(u1,prob0);
     t2 = Fpower(u2,prob1);
     sum = t1 + t2;
   }
 while (sum > 1.0);
 result = t1 / sum;
 return result;
} /* end of Beta() function */
/*============== MIC 2.2 ==============*/
/* Fpower() function */
double Fpower(value, tothe)
double value, tothe;
{
 int sign;
 double result;

 sign = (tothe < 0.0) ? -1 : 1;
 tothe = fabs(tothe);
 result = exp( log(value) * tothe);
```

```
  if (sign < 0)
     result = 1.0 / result;
  return(result);
} /* end of Fpower() function */
/*========================================*/
/* END OF BETA.C */
```

## Program execution

BETA.EXE

```
0.010990 0.359585 0.999128 0.223860 0.999807
0.704022 0.003031 0.817014 0.999484 0.553148
0.399195 0.752755 0.992644 0.833937 0.964797
0.010715 0.979119 0.813143 0.898935 0.997926
0.014646 0.589775 0.988215 0.936789 0.685888
0.957545 0.961579 0.000084 0.177708 0.880190
0.131819 0.974886 0.063196 0.645864 0.007146
0.982604 0.104106 0.799257 0.057739 0.009879
0.909136 0.183087 0.999559 0.057684 0.950676
0.940050 0.916770 1.000000 0.989211 0.893537
0.107457 0.960971 0.469452 0.553147 0.992217
0.998132 0.993824 0.778849 0.214022 0.999997
0.328246 0.999494 0.159273 0.826219 0.894953
0.021496 0.164498 0.954909 0.020334 0.489878
0.999218 0.970606 0.841927 0.926379 0.951947
0.289238 0.316517 0.019442 0.467412 0.723952
0.875365 0.432815 0.016803 0.997326 0.963250
0.023208 0.000203 0.999992 0.080765 0.117176
0.999984 0.882339 0.634970 0.045995 0.000184
0.995582 0.000001 0.990730 0.565506 0.065421
```

# FUNCTION: Bilexp( )   MIC 4.2

## Purpose

Generate a random number data set exhibiting Bilateral Exponential Probability Distribution characteristics.

## Notes

This function returns continuous, random-order numbers centered about zero. The negative to positive values are distributed exponentially on either side of the mean (0) and its range is unbounded both above and below the mean. Sometimes referred to as the first law of LaPlace, the distribution is controlled by the parameter "spread" which increases the range of generated values in inverse proportion to its magnitude (must be > 0).

Example curve:                                    spread = 1.5

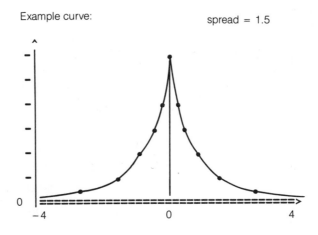

## Program source code

```
/*  BILEXP.C  (Bilexp Probability Distribution Function) */
#include <stdio.h>
#include <math.h>
main()
{
 int total;
 int j;
 int seed = 1231;
 double x[100];
 double parm = .43;
 double Bilexp();

 srand(seed);
 for (j = 0;j < 100;j++)
     {
      if (j % 5 == 0)
```

```
            printf("\n");
            x[j] = Bilexp(parm);
            printf("%f ",x[j]);
        }
} /* end of main*/
/*=============== MIC 4.2 ===============*/
/* Bilexp function */
double Bilexp(spread)
double spread;   /* horizontal scaling parameter */
{
 double u;        /* stores random number > 0 & < 1.0 */

 u = (rand() / 32767.) * 2.;
 if (u > 1)
    {
    u = 2. - u;
    u = -log(u);
    u = u / spread;
    return u;
    }
 else
    {
    u = log(u);
    u = u / spread;
    return(u);
    }
} /* end of Bilexp() function */
/*=======================================*/
/* END OF BILEXP.C */
```

## Program execution

```
BILEXP.EXE

-9.167392 3.958152 1.022059 1.434329 5.896396
2.602305 2.699034 0.132822 -1.119226 3.941086
3.685882 4.670400 1.026690 -0.146841 3.263379
7.529966 -1.578920 0.944291 2.946929 1.676083
0.609170 -2.078071 3.870297 0.029786 0.909192
1.703087 3.531165 0.695605 2.618004 0.824504
1.078923 -0.425182 -0.592079 2.712210 0.912972
3.035803 2.853083 4.297001 8.846820 -0.438513
0.172841 -5.431838 1.076441 5.679309 -3.017546
0.509518 3.933370 5.396888 -1.176897 -0.088462
-0.349235 12.001710 -1.333447 2.050826 2.027968
1.243777 -0.324134 3.142967 -4.409566 -1.921140
1.913694 -0.824301 2.136380 -2.165372 -0.952828
-1.011729 3.226710 0.918233 -0.386982 -2.437891
-3.826480 -0.001207 1.592393 -1.965663 -2.653718
6.766148 -0.978414 1.015241 0.798746 -3.436567
-2.990685 -2.170781 5.507898 -1.109370 0.472875
-0.848095 0.851163 4.914367 0.656311 -0.916970
-1.901765 -0.512170 0.338702 -0.202539 0.668011
-0.628061 0.387317 -0.632715 1.519237 1.196048
```

# FUNCTION: Cauchy( )  MIC 4.3

## Purpose

Generate a random number data set exhibiting Cauchy Probability Distribution characteristics.

## Notes

This function returns continuous real numbers in a symmetrical, positive-to-negative distribution centered around the mean. It is similar to the Gaussian distribution in that it is unbounded above and below the mean (0), but it approaches zero probabilities more slowly at the extremes. In practical terms, this causes values quite remote from the mean to have a higher probability of occurrence than in a Gaussian distribution. The control parameter "spread" determines the horizontal dispersion of values along the curve.

Example curve:  spread = .5

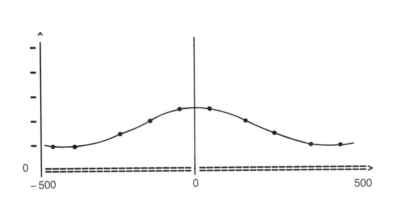

## Program source code

```
/* CAUCHY.C (Cauchy Probability Distribution Function */
#include <stdio.h>
#include <math.h>
main()
{
 int j,total = 100,seed = -7743;
 float parm1 = 2.0;    /* horizontal scaling factor */
 double x[100],Cauchy();

 srand(seed);
 for (j = 0;j < total;j++)
    {
     if (j % 5 == 0)
        printf("\n");
     x[j] = Cauchy(parm1);
```

```
        printf("%f ",x[j]);
        }
}/* end of main */
/*=============== MIC 4.3 ===============*/
/* Cauchy() function */
double Cauchy(spread)
double spread;              /* horizontal scaling factor */
{
 double PI= 3.1415927;
 double u;       /* random number > 0 & < 1.0 */
 double result; /* final Cauchy value */

 do {
     u = rand() / 32767.;
     u = u * PI;
     result = spread * tan(u);
     }
 while (u == .5);
 return result;
} /* end of Cauchy() function */
/*====================================*/
/* END OF CAUCHY.C */
```

## Program execution

CAUCHY.EXE

```
-1.656243 -3.923872 29.991776 1.649789 -0.193504
-1.220800 1.274069 -0.379132 1.709961 166.208393
-2.871423 4.153552 -0.587291 3.542630 -3.298190
-7.998833 0.614049 0.835203 1.325619 -0.070594
-2.643495 0.673091 -1.684563 9.269187 -1.267878
0.784315 -0.819707 2.680699 0.689140 -0.445706
-1.862281 0.651387 -0.901293 37.114822 -1.486634
-3.061565 -3.951926 -27.344761 1.132015 -7.810809
-0.576683 5.213639 -1.365731 -3.399563 -3.362575
2.484867 -1.282442 -2.418642 -3.585061 0.001342
-0.348426 -0.725384 -0.523466 1.745793 -99.557471
-1.506074 2.471255 -87.448481 4.539351 1.890403
-1.453261 0.171462 1.810333 1.468552 14.542320
1.252875 -0.220444 0.958665 2.047835 1.238769
0.910769 2.536231 0.403222 -5.209158 -10.168957
-0.527566 1.943379 2.570015 0.006136 2.681771
144.351696 0.736905 -1.859777 2.979780 -0.730378
-43.655568 8.373116 11.068622 -7.056781 0.798287
6.920014 0.820603 1.367419 0.503232 -6.877964
0.758542 1.238238 -0.869416 -2.999004 -0.179385
```

# FUNCTION: Expon( )   MIC 4.4

## Purpose

Generate a random number data set exhibiting Exponential Probability Distribution characteristics.

## Notes

This algorithm returns continuous, random-order real numbers greater than zero. Samples closer to zero are most likely to occur, with the probabilities of higher numbers falling off exponentially.

The control parameter "spread" determines the dispersion of values along the curve; larger values for "spread" increase the probability of returning a small number result. Although there is no upper limit to the size of an individual sample, it is very unlikely that a large number will be generated. The distribution mean is .69315 / spread.

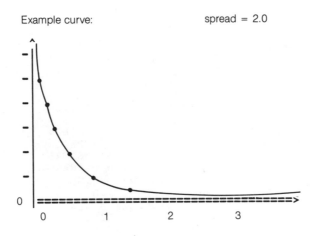

Example curve:                    spread = 2.0

## Program source code

```
/* EXPON.C (Exponential Probability Distribution Function */
#include <stdio.h>
#include <math.h>
main()
{
    int j, total = 100, seed = 1296;
    double x[100];
    double parm = 2.0; /* horizontal scaling factor */
    double Expon();

    srand(seed);
    for (j = 0;j < total;j++)
        {
        if (j % 5 == 0)
```

```
            printf("\n");
          x[j] = Expon(parm);
          printf("%f ",x[j]);
        }
} /* end of main */
/*============== MIC 4.4 ===============*/
/* Expon() function */
double Expon(spread)
double spread;      /* horizontal scaling factor */
{
  double u; /* random number > 0 & < 1.0 */
  double result; /* final Expon value */

  u = rand() / 32767.;
  result = -log(u) / spread;
  return result;
} /* end of Expon() function */
/*=======================================*/
/* END OF EXPON.C */
```

## Program execution

EXPON.EXE

```
0.180739 0.365910 0.794703 1.110815 0.042149
0.091451 0.232745 0.524669 1.125089 1.021958
2.075535 0.025336 0.062012 0.130476 0.874127
0.001268 0.617594 0.033362 0.442071 0.062548
0.160141 0.125176 0.112022 0.006961 0.088674
0.445965 0.551570 0.558935 0.401843 0.223618
0.475922 0.470184 1.138146 0.026509 0.657392
0.075263 0.534616 0.209291 0.740604 0.380785
0.618276 0.134294 0.136595 0.195792 0.224406
0.447681 0.281466 0.420242 0.214841 0.401196
0.003384 0.196018 0.691122 1.125814 0.636633
0.074093 0.109148 0.948260 0.320428 0.848748
0.193922 0.256131 0.222998 0.159805 0.831309
0.472102 0.930189 0.628147 2.353409 0.000779
0.665758 1.706694 0.222021 0.360358 0.060253
0.115490 1.418809 0.044496 0.981031 1.105078
1.229544 0.235206 1.553101 0.086746 0.229161
0.547129 0.110573 0.340763 0.503426 0.316562
0.341669 1.216163 0.046183 1.079452 0.242886
0.327693 0.828420 0.120960 1.543648 0.281788
```

# FUNCTION: Gamma( )    MIC 4.5

## Purpose

Generate a random number data set exhibiting Gamma Probability Distribution characteristics.

## Notes

This algorithm returns continuous, random-order, real numbers over an asymmetrical curve. It is often used in rhythmic applications to provide a sense of "rubato." The shape of the curve is drastically altered by the value of control parameter "spread." Generally, "spread" values larger than 10 are not used because the algorithm tends toward a Gaussian distribution as the value rises.

Because there are several possible special cases (radically altered curve shapes), it will pay to experiment with a diversity of "spread" values, and tally actual occurrence frequencies on a bargraph.

Example curve:                              spread = 2.0

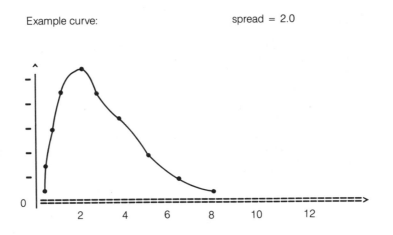

## Program source code

```
/* GAMMA.C (Gamma Probability Distribution Function)*/
#include <stdio.h>
#include <math.h>
main()
{
  int j, total = 100, seed = -296;
  double x[100];
  double parm = 5.0;   /* governs shape of curve */
  double Gamma();

  srand(seed);
  for (j = 0;j < total;j++)
     {
      if (j % 5 == 0)
```

```
        printf("\n");
     x[j] = Gamma(parm);
     printf("%f ",x[j]);
     }
} /* end of main*/
/*=============== MIC 4.5 ================*/
/* Gamma function */
double Gamma(spread)
double spread;      /* governs shape of curve */
{
 int j;
 double result;
 double u;
 double sum = 1.0;

 for (j = 0;j < spread;j++)
     {
     u = rand() / 32767.;
     sum = sum * u;
     }
 result = -log(sum);
 return result;
} /* end of Gamma() function */
/*=======================================*/
/* END OF GAMMA.C */
```

## Program execution

**PROGRAM EXECUTION:**

```
4.848656 5.199660 3.569251 4.148325 3.887295
6.240203 2.291942 8.424481 2.148828 4.512343
4.736967 2.425011 10.381698 5.558272 5.695244
4.181691 10.828009 2.878646 3.905727 6.334919
5.569885 5.586389 5.296786 6.745270 3.607900
6.461507 3.272248 5.986170 5.965548 4.750306
8.802918 4.376763 5.606261 5.760528 5.642366
3.233463 3.460231 3.356096 13.866656 11.360364
5.034211 4.132257 7.248348 3.646231 5.223305
3.665702 2.708764 5.592431 6.282181 4.858055
6.351133 7.570575 4.328890 3.382579 4.026595
4.739250 8.057736 5.242775 5.275028 4.829192
5.234377 5.567001 13.246912 4.799805 9.367443
1.652347 3.675683 7.101449 8.029843 3.478084
1.757624 3.910659 6.071557 6.232306 5.305021
4.664670 6.978143 1.963472 4.177363 1.742774
2.888380 8.907016 4.846449 3.649949 5.951984
4.907827 6.991382 3.371839 5.651329 5.365534
8.148632 4.952009 4.453359 10.597573 2.977761
1.790738 3.856396 4.101259 5.823742 1.009400
```

# FUNCTION: Gauss( )  MIC 4.6

## Purpose

Generate a random number data set exhibiting Gaussian Probability Distribution characteristics.

## Notes

Also referred to as the "normal distribution" and the Gauss-Laplace Distribution, this algorithm generates a bell-shaped curve comprised of random-order real numbers larger than zero and centered about the mean. The distribution is arrived at via the summation of uniform random numbers. The standard deviation "dev" and the mean "mean" are the control parameters.

Example curve:

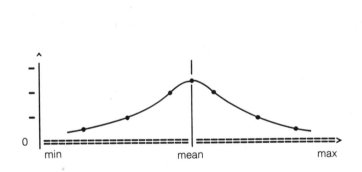

## Program source code

```
/* GAUSS.C  (Gaussian Probability Distribution Function)*/
#include <stdio.H>
main()
{
  int j, total = 100, seed = -30261;
  double x[100];
  double parm1 = 2.0; /* controls standard deviation */
  double parm2 = 10.0;/* controls statistical mean */
  double Gauss();

  srand(seed);
  for (j = 0;j < total;j++)
    {
      if (j % 5 == 0)
         printf("\n");
      x[j] = Gauss(parm1,parm2);
      printf("%f ",x[j]);
```

```
        }
} /* end of main*/
/*=============== MIC 4.6 ==============*/
/* Gauss() function */
double Gauss(dev,mean)
double dev,mean; /* control std. deviation and stat. mean */
{
 int j;
 int num = 12;/* number of random values used to compute */
 double result; /* final gaussian value */
 double u;        /* random number > 0 & < 1.0 */
 double sum = 0.0; /* sum of random numbers */
 double scale = 1.0; /* internal scaling factor */
 double halfnum = num / 2.0;

 for (j = 0; j < num;j++)
     {
      u = rand() / 32767.;
      sum = sum + u;
     }
 result = dev * scale * (sum - halfnum) + mean;
 return result;
} /* end of Gauss() function */
/*====================================*/
/* END OF GAUSS.C */
```

## Program execution

GAUSS.EXE

```
12.314890 11.178503 9.634877 9.220191 11.122166
8.813440 11.201880 10.544145 7.378399 10.718406
9.766533 9.392193 11.623035 7.404767 12.876492
10.408704 12.660665 11.900815 10.844020 9.254128
10.561968 8.749046 11.747734 9.604541 7.663137
11.009064 10.431471 12.151799 7.566149 9.254494
9.504807 5.602710 10.138371 10.576189 12.343272
9.680593 12.512589 7.579394 10.087466 12.124088
12.087832 9.385601 8.644002 11.686636 9.528184
10.631855 7.684927 13.138890 7.763482 8.470412
9.648122 12.265572 12.989715 9.569933 8.736778
8.868007 11.667776 11.113926 9.920225 11.762871
7.524155 7.801813 11.932737 11.782220 10.551958
10.849147 10.274422 10.774316 8.008606 8.986236
10.211615 10.602374 11.418500 9.459456 7.775445
8.145451 11.570360 13.030915 12.763390 12.298898
11.519150 8.978057 7.737785 8.972320 9.585559
10.093875 9.027192 14.092532 8.355785 9.687735
7.725517 8.600543 11.681753 8.583819 12.692770
11.454146 11.680715 10.122257 9.553697 6.625690
```

# FUNCTION: Hypcos( )   MIC 4.7

## Purpose

Generate a random number data set exhibiting Hyperbolic Cosine Probability Distribution characteristics.

## Notes

This algorithm produces a symmetrical curve comprised of random-order, continuous, positive-to-negative real numbers. Although it is centered on zero, the mean is missing.

Example curve:

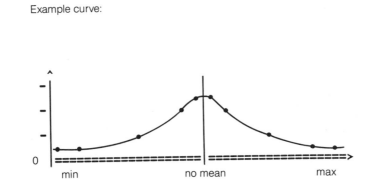

## Program source code

```c
/* Hypcos.c (Hyperbolic Cosine Prob. Distr. Function) */
#include <stdio.h>
#include <math.h>
main()
{
 int j, total = 100, seed = 602;
 double x[100], Hypcos();

 srand(seed);
 for (j = 0;j < total;j++)
     {
     if (j % 5 == 0)
        printf("\n");
     x[j] = Hypcos();
     printf("%f ",x[j]);
     }
} /* end of main*/
/*=============== MIC 4.7 ===============*/
/* Hypcos() function */
double Hypcos()
{
 double PI = 3.1415927;
 double result;
 double u;
```

```
u = rand() / 32767.;
result = log(tan(PI * u /2.0));
return result;
} /* end of Hypcos() function */
/*======================================*/
/* END OF HYPCOS.C */
```

## Program execution

HYPCOS.EXE

```
-0.447231 -2.572166 -0.420027 0.345758 -1.470294
2.936152 0.727509 -1.509629 2.373300 2.281548
0.118348 -0.614872 0.280250 1.323721 -1.892836
1.298349 -0.068269 0.444909 0.291530 -1.382082
1.333989 -0.947991 -0.242169 -2.306029 2.470149
1.679118 -0.950269 -0.702250 -1.222725 3.248058
1.628220 -0.402434 -1.260111 -0.351151 1.598450
-2.672303 3.205711 -1.852299 -0.061352 -0.993282
0.081634 -0.782678 2.320216 -2.191268 -0.516507
0.337636 5.456957 4.408213 0.581376 -2.312364
-0.538412 -1.208829 -2.419484 1.055535 2.295396
0.287633 0.131779 -0.435220 -3.175371 1.022303
0.016156 -1.158313 0.635731 0.756782 -0.583516
-1.519456 0.733271 1.784108 1.133905 -0.995934
1.111261 0.837414 0.562116 0.272882 0.603109
1.737879 -3.736815 -0.512806 -0.561559 -1.382488
3.085284 0.673695 0.787758 0.938209 0.077402
1.989971 -0.312087 0.890590 1.006447 -0.320245
-0.859009 -2.078297 0.001870 0.554442 1.180315
-0.571498 -0.517161 -0.614185 -0.134874 0.097806
```

# FUNCTION: Linear( )   MIC 4.7

## Purpose

Generate a random number data set exhibiting Linear Probability Distribution characteristics.

## Notes

This function returns continuous, random-order, real numbers larger than zero and less than one. Results closer to zero are most likely to occur.

A reverse linear distribution can be achieved by altering the algorithm to select the larger rather than the smaller random value ("u1" or "u2"). In this case, results farther removed from 0 will be more likely to occur.

Example distribution:

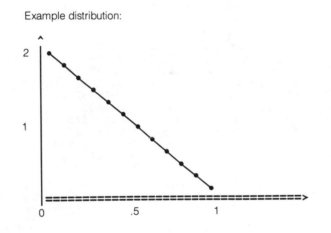

## Program source code

```
/* LINEAR.C (Linear Probability Distribution Function) */
#include <stdio.h>
main()
{
  int j, total = 100, seed = -29454;
  float x[100],Linear();

  srand(seed);
  for (j = 0;j < total;j++)
      {
       if (j % 5 == 0)
          printf("\n");
       x[j] = Linear();
       printf("%f ",x[j]);
       }
} /* end of main*/
/*=============== MIC 4.8 ===============*/
/* Linear() function */
```

```
float Linear()
{
 float result; /* final Linear value */
 float u1;     /* random number > 0 & < 1.0 */
 float u2;     /* random number > 0 & < 1.0 */

 u1 = rand() / 32767.;
 u2 = rand() / 32767.;
 if (u2 < u1)
    u1 = u2;
 result = u1;
 return result;
} /* end of Linear() function */
/*====================================*/
/* END OF LINEAR.C */
```

## Program execution

LINEAR.EXE

```
0.329173 0.172735 0.249733 0.592700 0.308481
0.279214 0.241523 0.391552 0.548906 0.316172
0.280038 0.931639 0.049013 0.370434 0.064028
0.753685 0.092654 0.807520 0.307291 0.687429
0.439161 0.011170 0.160588 0.550127 0.631031
0.874813 0.412732 0.048433 0.072085 0.460189
0.444960 0.278146 0.512284 0.115085 0.192480
0.135044 0.875149 0.660482 0.765038 0.761589
0.070711 0.035188 0.395642 0.149815 0.110202
0.157750 0.186773 0.577593 0.135319 0.549364
0.679556 0.051119 0.700674 0.481307 0.292367
0.848354 0.195502 0.081668 0.940184 0.075472
0.599048 0.533006 0.456160 0.374554 0.220649
0.554918 0.216803 0.289743 0.115116 0.065889
0.167730 0.456160 0.666372 0.066744 0.087008
0.002960 0.073061 0.428480 0.148473 0.483139
0.225043 0.249672 0.189795 0.625721 0.213416
0.243507 0.498978 0.043641 0.563585 0.216010
0.140690 0.377972 0.222083 0.467910 0.267037
0.458419 0.296976 0.050081 0.179754 0.016602
```

# FUNCTION: Logistic( )   MIC 4.9

## Purpose

Generate a random number data set exhibiting Logistic Probability Distribution characteristics.

## Notes

This function returns continuous, random-order, negative-to-positive, real numbers. The control parameters "par1" and "par2" determine the mean and dispersion of values along the curve.

Example curve:

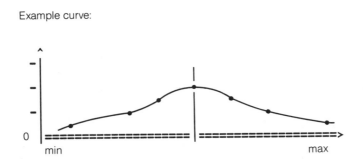

## Program source code

```
/* LOGISTIC.C (Logistic Probability Distribution Function) */
#include <stdio.h>
#include <math.h>
main()
{
 int j, total = 100, seed = 742;
 double x[100],val1,val2,Logist();
 val1 = 1.0; /* controls mean of distribution */
 val2 = 5.0; /* controls dispersion of curve values */

 srand(seed);
 for (j = 0;j < total;j++)
     {
      if (j % 5 == 0)
         printf("\n");
      x[j] = Logist(val1,val2);
      printf("%f ",x[j]);
      }
} /* end of main*/
/*=============== MIC 4.9 ===============*/
/* Logistic() function */
double Logist(mean,dispersion)
double mean,dispersion;
{
 double result;         /* final Logistic value */
 double u;              /* random number > 0 & < 1.0 */
```

```
 u = rand() / 32767.;
 result = (-mean * -log(1.0 / u - 1.0)) / dispersion;
 return result;
} /* end of Logistic() function */
/*=====================================*/
/* END OF LOGISTIC.C */
```

## Program execution

LOGISTIC.EXE

```
-0.334279 0.385297 -0.203285 0.127533 0.183139
-0.059083 0.015939 0.105260 -0.063907 -0.386510
0.748888 0.606583 -0.119194 0.142856 0.123525
-0.111957 -0.263996 -0.148164 0.081190 0.281807
-0.159932 -0.171647 -0.290905 0.446928 -0.044533
0.579250 -0.609667 -0.052188 -0.281729 0.005970
-0.341987 -0.173226 0.438072 0.162793 0.734264
-0.625013 0.425829 0.515534 -1.032069 0.005213
-0.237870 -0.006068 0.140399 0.026664 -0.000110
-0.130833 0.647482 -0.117517 0.398488 0.521853
0.229236 0.133987 -0.326322 0.243300 -0.324898
0.338804 0.299817 -0.680044 0.341563 0.022106
0.266573 0.655870 0.201163 0.319182 -0.261182
-0.069228 0.894464 -0.032556 0.105600 -0.238758
0.157768 -0.414888 0.563798 0.315804 -0.546233
-0.203472 0.188492 0.153015 0.227505 0.351556
0.894464 -0.516280 1.202541 0.370372 -0.236474
0.284291 -0.600000 -0.070410 0.170335 -0.209556
0.443941 -0.181169 0.152227 -0.036147 0.077002
0.024237 0.591258 0.004798 -0.646812 -0.548048
```

# FUNCTION: Poisson( )   MIC 4.10

## Purpose

Generate a random number data set exhibiting Poisson Probability Distribution characteristics.

## Notes

This algorithm generates random-order, non-negative integers. The control parameter "spread" determines the distribution of values, which are unbounded at the upper end.

The mean of the distribution is the value of control parameter "spread" (must be > 0).

Discrete variable
Example distribution of probabilities

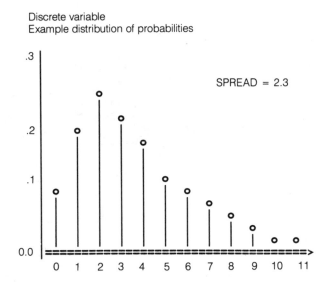

## Program source code

```
/* POISSON.C (Poisson Probability Distribution Function */
#include <stdio.h>
#include <math.h>
main()
{
  int x[100],j,total = 100,seed = 9213;
  int Poisson();
  double parm1 = 4.5; /* controls distribution of values */

  srand(seed);
  for (j = 0;j < total;j++)
      {
       if (j % 10 == 0)
           printf("\n");
```

```
        x[j] = Poisson(parm1);
        printf("%d ",x[j]);
        }
}
/* end of main */
/*=============== MIC 4.10 ===============*/
/* Poisson() function */
int Poisson(spread)
double spread; /* controls distribution of values */
{
 int num = 0;
 double u,t;

 u = rand() / 32767.;
 t = exp(-spread);
 while (u > t)
      {
       num = num + 1;
       u = u * (rand() / 32767.);
      }
 return num;
} /* end of Poisson() function */
/*====================================*/
/* END OF POISSON.C */
```

## Program execution

POISSON.EXE

```
5 6 2 4 2 6 8 4 3 2
3 7 0 5 2 1 7 1 1 4
5 6 6 3 6 5 6 5 5 0
4 2 5 7 4 3 6 1 3 8
1 2 3 8 0 6 6 9 1 1
7 4 4 6 4 9 5 3 1 7
2 7 5 1 6 4 4 4 6 2
1 4 6 1 4 3 6 5 1 4
4 5 1 5 5 8 2 4 2 6
4 3 3 2 6 6 4 4 6 2
```

# FUNCTION: Rnd-rnd( )   MIC 4.11

## Purpose

Generate a random number data set exhibiting Rnd-rnd Probability Distribution characteristics.

## Notes

This function uses a random decaying function to determine distribution of discrete values. Occurrence frequency falls off with magnitude, similar to the Exponential Probability distribution, but with more variability. To obtain the random-order integers, the random number generator is made to call itself recursively.

Discrete variable
Example distribution of probabilities:

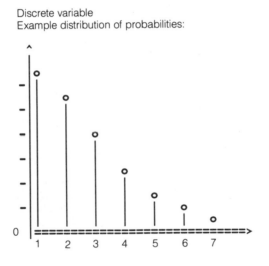

## Program source code

```
/* RND_RND.C   (Recursive Random Distribution Function */
#include <stdio.h>
main()
{
    int x[300],j,total = 300,srand(),Rnd_rnd(),seed = -8112;
    int bottom = 1;      /* lowest possible random integer */
    int top = 5;         /* highest possible random integer */
    int span;                    /* range of random integers */
    span = top - bottom + 1;
    srand(seed);
    for (j = 0;j < total;j++)
      {
      if (j % 15 == 0)
        printf("\n");
      x[j] = Rnd_rnd(bottom,span);
```

```
        printf("%d ",x[j]);
    }
} /* end of main */
/*=============== MIC 4.11 ===============*/
/* Rnd_rnd() function */
int Rnd_rnd(low,range)
int low,range;
{
 long int u;

 u = ((rand(rand()) / 32767.) *
     (rand(rand()) / 32767.)) * range + low;
 return u;
} /* end of Rnd_rnd() function */
/*======================================*/
/* END OF RND_RND.C */
```

## Program execution

```
1 4 2 3 1 2 4 2 2 2 2 2 2 1 1
4 2 2 1 2 2 1 3 3 1 3 2 2 2 1
2 4 2 1 1 4 3 1 1 1 2 1 1 3 1
1 3 3 1 1 1 2 2 5 1 2 2 1 1 4
2 4 2 2 1 1 3 1 3 4 4 3 3 1 1
1 3 2 1 1 1 1 1 1 4 1 1 3 1 4
1 1 1 3 2 1 3 2 5 1 1 1 1 1 3
1 1 1 1 1 1 2 2 4 1 4 1 1 3 1
2 4 4 1 2 3 1 2 1 1 1 1 3 1 3
1 3 3 1 1 3 1 2 1 3 1 2 2 1 2
4 1 1 1 1 1 1 5 1 1 1 1 1 1 1
4 2 1 4 1 1 1 3 2 1 2 2 3 1 3
1 1 1 1 1 1 1 2 1 2 4 1 2 2 1
1 1 1 1 2 1 2 1 2 3 1 1 1 1 2
3 2 1 2 1 4 1 1 2 1 2 1 1 3 3
1 5 1 3 2 1 1 4 1 3 3 1 2 1 1
1 1 2 1 1 4 2 2 4 2 2 4 1 2 1
2 4 1 3 3 1 1 1 1 2 1 1 3 4 1
1 2 1 1 1 3 1 2 4 1 1 1 3 2 1
3 1 3 1 1 1 2 2 1 1 4 2 2 1 1
```

# FUNCTION GROUP: Weibull.c

    1.  Weibull( )   MIC 4.12
    2.  Fpower( )   MIC 2.2

## Purpose

Generate a random number data set exhibiting Weibull Probability Distribution characteristics.

## Notes

This function returns random-order, continuous, real numbers larger than 0. Its curve can assume a variety of shapes in accordance with the value of its input parameter "denshape." The "spread" parameter controls only the horizontal scale. There is no upper limit to values generated.

Example curve:                    denshape = 3

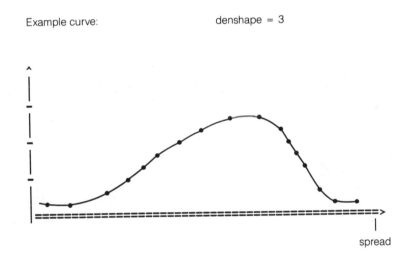

spread

## Program source code

```
/* WEIBULL.C (Weibull Probability Distribution Function) */
#include <stdio.h>
#include <math.h>
main()
{
  int j, total = 100, seed = -212;
  double x[100], Weibull();
  double parm1 = 20.0;    /* controls horizontal scale */
  double parm2 = 1.0;     /* controls curve shape */

  srand(seed);
  for (j = 0;j < total;j++)
      {
      if (j % 5 == 0)
          printf("\n");
```

```
        x[j] = Weibull(parm1,parm2);
        printf("%f ",x[j]);
        }
} /* end of main*/
/*=============== MIC 4.12 ==============*/
/* Weibull() function */
double Weibull(spread,denshape)
double spread,denshape;
{
 double result,u,s,t,Fpower();

 u = rand() / 32767.;
 u = 1. / (1. - u);
 s = log(u);
 t = 1. / denshape;
 result = spread * Fpower(s,t);
 return result;
} /* end of Weibull() function */
/*=============== MIC 2.2 ===============*/
/* Fpower() function */
 double Fpower(value,tothe)
 double value, tothe;
 {
  int sign;
  double result;

  sign = (tothe < 0.0) ? -1 : 1;
  tothe = fabs(tothe);
  result = exp( log(value) * tothe);
  if (sign < 0)
     result = 1.0 / result;
  return(result);
 } /* end of Fpower() function */
/*===================================*/
/* END OF WEIBULL.C */
```

## Program execution

WEIBULL.EXE

```
9.256420 1.783166 15.610108 34.076964 6.735427
19.655075 7.211167 10.621601 1.357983 52.974343
13.436001 43.025359 23.690789 56.055919 8.077893
6.189065 7.029050 11.152833 18.695120 38.007816
79.543645 13.530627 2.979317 5.078500 12.622286
16.670149 7.720935 5.551414 1.866082 10.388356
13.914892 20.878987 6.146691 0.482472 16.970183
16.528776 0.825547 0.865023 18.412676 16.580450
30.764799 11.036971 40.634751 16.881971 20.357077
1.325999 2.702130 5.801103 32.787871 4.461040
11.886781 4.059244 6.891604 2.410134 13.801391
12.433870 3.633861 1.957418 16.889070 0.155638
64.757706 2.649799 5.305600 5.924664 6.595733
6.439314 55.431642 13.284815 5.387735 5.853380
10.810385 12.529569 30.022734 1.943960 5.393329
22.488511 15.304719 11.708425 7.636705 30.993471
5.898415 11.543599 32.819342 21.242887 11.070916
18.298062 2.244881 13.819654 3.896902 27.620571
11.292975 15.761214 1.588600 10.376047 25.559315
31.585740 41.637108 19.486188 6.024230 3.691772
```

# FUNCTION: Triangle( )    MIC 4.13

## Purpose

Generate a random number data set exhibiting Triangular Probability Distribution characteristics.

## Notes

Triangle( ) function returns continuous, random-order; real numbers larger than zero and less than one. Middle-valued results are most likely to occur. The algorithm works by taking the average of two uniformly distributed random numbers.

Example distribution:

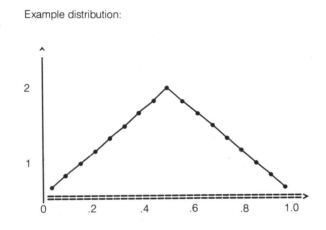

## Program source code

```
/* TRIANGLE.C (Triangular Prob. Distr. Function */
#include <stdio.h>
main()
{
  int j, total = 100, seed = 62;
  double x[100];
  double Triangle();

  srand(seed);
  for (j = 0;j < total;j++)
      {
       if (j % 5 == 0)
          printf("\n");
       x[j] = Triangle();
       printf("%f ",x[j]);
      }
} /* end of main */
/*=============== MIC 4.13 ===============*/
/* Triangle() function */
```

```
double Triangle()
{
 double result;
 double u1;
 double u2;

 u1 = rand() / 32767.;
 u2 = rand() / 32767.;
 result = .5 * (u1 + u2);
 return result;
} /* end of Triangle() function */
/*=====================================*/
/* END OF TRIANGLE.C */
```

## Program execution

TRIANGLE.EXE

```
0.628880 0.577883 0.396084 0.212683 0.325755
0.438734 0.648640 0.273400 0.595340 0.666875
0.345592 0.075426 0.483612 0.493866 0.740211
0.477966 0.303598 0.188696 0.479629 0.488952
0.482910 0.624317 0.140080 0.519089 0.286431
0.218863 0.637074 0.510666 0.414014 0.752235
0.510422 0.441496 0.973098 0.057405 0.584567
0.203803 0.326273 0.586886 0.503586 0.358211
0.314219 0.854076 0.641469 0.762551 0.853038
0.249657 0.387188 0.575732 0.407086 0.233100
0.804895 0.636799 0.836619 0.398984 0.669057
0.718787 0.620334 0.418439 0.874676 0.657476
0.453246 0.355480 0.722297 0.355495 0.719169
0.358562 0.578356 0.661214 0.838313 0.726859
0.410199 0.122440 0.490173 0.351650 0.196265
0.615619 0.211005 0.032868 0.711310 0.349467
0.366543 0.670415 0.686453 0.744087 0.499634
0.330485 0.844417 0.684759 0.552904 0.687185
0.809671 0.650899 0.466399 0.338710 0.393536
0.719932 0.150304 0.498917 0.754418 0.446211
```

# 5
# *Sorting and searching*

## FUNCTION: Shellsrt( )   MIC 5.1

### Purpose

Arrange a table of integers in ascending order.

### Notes

The Shell sort algorithm is fast, compact, and easy to decipher. Although under certain conditions the common bubble sorting algorithm (a variation is given in this book) might be faster, musical sequences consisting of randomly-generated data normally are so long and disjunct that bubble sort is useless. However, when the list to be processed is ten items or less and is "almost sorted," bubble sort is quicker.

An in-place binary sort, Shellsrt works by successively splitting the unordered list into smaller halves, rearranging contents along the way via a switching algorithm. If the original unsorted list must be preserved for future use by the calling program, it can be copied to array X[ ] before entering the Shellsrt( ) function.

Shellsrt( ) (and the other sorting functions in Chapter 5) have interesting secondary applications. For example, if the internal "footsteps" of the sorting process are mapped to the pitch element table, patterns of the algorithm-in-motion will be engraved in sound. To observe the subroutine's internal function, modify the source code to print out the values in array x[ ] as the sorting is in process.

### Programming ideas

1. Modify the main routine and sort function to generate real numbers instead of integers.
2. Map the sorting process (not final sorted list) to the pitch parameter.

# Program source code

```c
/* SHELLSRT.C (Shell Sort routine, quite fast for long
                lists)*/
#include <stdio.h>
main()
{
 int x[200];      /* stores list to be sorted */
 int total = 200,seed = 16213,j;
 void ShellSrt();

 srand(seed);
 printf("an array of random-order integers to be sorted:\n");
 for (j = 0;j < total;j++)
    {
     if (j % 10 == 0)
        printf("\n");
     x[j] = rand() % 1000 + 1;
     printf("%d ",x[j]);
    }
 printf("\n\nthe array sorted in ascending order:\n");
 ShellSrt(x,total);
 for (j = 0;j < total;j++)
    {
     if (j % 10 == 0)
        printf("\n");
     printf("%d ",x[j]);
    }
} /* end of main */
/*=============== MIC 5.1 =============*/
/* ShellSrt() function */
void ShellSrt(x,total)
int x[];
int total;
{
 register int j,k,l,s,w,y;
 int sortinc[5];

 sortinc[0] = 9;sortinc[1] = 5;sortinc[2] = 3;
 sortinc[3] = 2;sortinc[4] = 1;

 for (w = 0;w < 5;w++)
    {
     l = sortinc[w]; s = -1;
     for (j = 1;j < total;++j)
        {
         y = x[j];
         k = j - 1;
         if (s == 0)
           {
            s = -1;
            s++;
            x[s] = y;
           }
         while (y < x[k] && k >= 0 && k <= total)
           {
            x[k+1] = x[k];
            k = k - 1;
           }
        x[k+1] = y;
```

```
            }
        }
    } /* end of ShellSrt() function */
/*========================================*/
/* END OF SHELLSRT.C */
```

## Program execution

`SHELLSRT.EXE`

`an array of random-order integers to be sorted:`

```
324 23 160 518 156 997 606 119 486 527
284 949 401 554 689 959 56 95 158 630
475 46 368 371 331 887 673 695 416 949
26 299 518 507 869 913 688 971 705 810
196 268 349 385 505 923 762 384 348 30
715 961 714 820 239 224 18 889 706 54
617 473 15 345 67 978 681 18 742 334
291 542 562 273 493 225 392 736 472 368
119 195 300 262 605 316 314 129 477 767
189 501 828 980 989 217 642 411 245 561
678 528 731 67 816 62 369 621 422 424
27 215 504 462 314 525 782 373 214 680
556 554 145 677 67 759 331 141 75 343
713 566 630 790 211 585 655 485 836 166
731 900 523 909 800 496 890 342 420 703
222 451 264 609 800 516 590 506 82 627
663 333 973 425 48 843 105 48 630 107
716 442 1000 108 176 650 230 753 671 905
8 963 505 4 768 245 880 324 267 788
634 333 556 198 416 594 227 741 70 89
```

`the array sorted in ascending order:`

```
4 8 15 18 18 23 26 27 30 46
48 48 54 56 62 67 67 67 70 75
82 89 95 105 107 108 119 119 129 141
145 156 158 160 166 176 189 195 196 198
211 214 215 217 222 224 225 227 230 239
245 245 262 264 267 268 273 284 291 299
300 314 314 316 324 324 331 331 333 333
334 342 343 345 348 349 368 368 369 371
373 384 385 392 401 411 416 416 420 422
424 425 442 451 462 472 473 475 477 485
486 493 496 501 504 505 505 506 507 516
518 518 523 525 527 528 542 554 554 556
556 561 562 566 585 590 594 605 606 609
617 621 627 630 630 630 634 642 650 655
663 671 673 677 678 680 681 688 689 695
703 705 706 713 714 715 716 731 731 736
741 742 753 759 762 767 768 782 788 790
800 800 810 816 820 828 836 843 869 880
887 889 890 900 905 909 913 923 949 949
959 961 963 971 973 978 980 989 997 1000
```

# FUNCTION: Shaksort( )   MIC 5.2

## Purpose

Arrange a table of values in ascending order.

## Notes

The Shaker sorting algorithm is a variation on the classic bubble sort. It is an improved, in-place sort; therefore if the calling program must preserve the unsorted table for future reference, a copy can be placed in a separate array prior to entering the subroutine. Use this function for short lists.

To observe the internal workings of Shaksort( ), modify the source code to print out array contents as they are being sorted.

## Programming ideas

1. Alter—as explained in comments for MIC5.1—the main routine and function Shaksort( ) to place the internal steps of the sorting process in a new array of data pointers. Use the collection of pointers to sequence the elements of a volume parameter table.
2. Write a program that invokes a probability distribution function from Chapter 4 to generate an array of 100 random-order integers, range 1–100. First, use the list items as pointers to the pitch parameter; then, sort the list and use the items as pointers to a table of volume or articulation data. (The effect of the sorted list will be a variation on one of the curve-types introduced in Function Group: Curves.C, in Chapter 2.)

## Program source code

```
/* SHAKSORT.C (Improved version of Bubble sort, but sill
                good only for short lists)*/
#include <stdio.h>
main()
{
  int x[200];      /* stores list to be sorted */
  int total = 200,seed = -11933,j;
  void ShakSort();

  srand(seed);
  printf("an array of random-order integers to be sorted:\n");
  for (j = 0;j < total;j++)
    {
     if (j % 10 == 0)
        printf("\n");
     x[j] = rand() % 1000 + 1;
     printf("%d ",x[j]);
    }
```

```
   printf("\n\nthe array sorted in ascending order:\n");
   ShakSort(x,total);
   for (j = 0;j < total;j++)
      {
       if (j % 10 == 0)
          printf("\n");
       printf("%d ",x[j]);
      }
   printf("\n");
} /* end of main */
/*==============================*/
/* ShakSort() function */
void ShakSort(x,total)
int x[];
int total;
{
 register int j,k,l,m,temp;
 l = 1;
 k = total - 1;
 m = total - 1;

 do
    {
     for (j = m;j >= l;--j)
        {
          if (x[j-1] > x[j])
             {   /* swap */
               temp = x[j-1];
               x[j-1] = x[j];
               x[j] = temp;
               k = j;
             }
        }
     l = k + 1;
     for (j = l;j < m + 1;++j)
        {
          if (x[j-1] > x[j])
             {   /* swap */
               temp = x[j-1];
               x[j-1] = x[j];
               x[j] = temp;
               k = j;
             }
        }
     m = k - 1;
    }
 while (l <= m);
 } /* end of ShakSort() function */
/*====================================*/
/* END OF SHAKSORT.C */
```

## Program execution

SHAKSRT.EXE

an array of random-order integers to be sorted:

326 414 325 137 606 456 479 733 908 578
363 585 30 124 325 519 166 55 821 127

```
672 595  99 479 303 337 864 404 492 107
358 281 279 738 916 166 481 672 795 333
834 855 837 602  96 666 496 233 312 523
958 364 920 980 672 308 572  17 746 775
681 126 113  99 471 348 500 905 875 490
504  22 573 425 975 966  46 560 673 969
 53 393 500 114  66 835 569  77 459  66
 32  42 766 851 935 215 416 220 229 970
484 140 932 798 110 455 927 357 185 284
321 616 118 905 407 163 832 767 967  68
548 298 834 204 229 988 286 342 592 323
872 616 124 839 873 456 397 176 695 865
937 303 830 781 507 364 487 468 360  64
969 278 927 131 502 670 205 992  24 520
984 527 740 971 194 716 742 810 122 190
822 215 614 298 290 401 188 904  21 400
610 462 607 574 652 116   6 720 413 999
700  44 312 770 922 877 519 881 420 164
```

the array sorted in ascending order:

```
  6  17  21  22  24  30  32  42  44  46
 53  55  64  66  66  68  77  96  99  99
107 110 113 114 116 118 122 124 124 126
127 131 137 140 163 164 166 166 176 185
188 190 194 204 205 215 215 220 229 229
233 278 279 281 284 286 290 298 298 303
303 308 312 312 321 323 325 325 326 333
337 342 348 357 358 360 363 364 364 393
397 400 401 404 407 413 414 416 420 425
455 456 456 459 462 468 471 479 479 481
484 487 490 492 496 500 500 502 504 507
519 519 520 523 527 548 560 569 572 573
574 578 585 592 595 602 606 607 610 614
616 616 652 666 670 672 672 672 673 681
695 700 716 720 733 738 740 742 746 766
767 770 775 781 795 798 810 821 822 830
832 834 834 835 837 839 851 855 864 865
872 873 875 877 881 904 905 905 908 916
920 922 927 927 932 935 937 958 966 967
969 969 970 971 975 980 984 988 992 999
```

## FUNCTION: Quiksort( )    MIC 5.3

## Purpose

Arrange a table of values in ascending order.

## Notes

While the Quicksort function is one of the fastest sorting algorithms, its drawbacks are that it is long, complex, and difficult to decipher.

To observe the internal workings of Quiksort( ), make the following code changes, and print out the values as they are being internally manipulated by the algorithm.

## Programming ideas

1. Alter—as explained in comments for CTB5.1—the main routine and function Quiksort( ) to map the internal sorting process to an array of data table pointers. Use the pointer list to sequence the pitches of a melodic line.
2. Write a program that invokes MIC4.11: Rnd-rnd( ) Probability Distribution Function to fill an array with unsorted integers, range 1–64; sort the array using Quiksrt, then assign the table of pointers to the rhythm parameter. Build a file of durations using Function Group: MOTFORMS.C (Chapter 3) to generate retrograde, inversion, retrograde-inversion and transposed forms of the duration values.

## Program listing

```
/* QUIKSORT.C (one of the fastest sorts for long lists )*/
#include <stdio.h>
main()
{
 int x[800];     /* stores list to be sorted */
 int total = 800,seed = 1993,j;
 void QuikSort();

 srand(seed);
 printf("an array of random-order integers to be sorted:\n");
 for (j = 0;j < total;j++)
    {
     if (j % 10 == 0)
        printf("\n");
     x[j] = rand() % 1000 + 1;
     printf("%d ",x[j]);
    }
 printf("\n\nthe array sorted in ascending order:\n");

 QuikSort(x,0,total-1);
 for (j = 0;j < total;j++)
```

```
     {
     if (j % 10 == 0)
         printf("\n");
     printf("%d ",x[j]);
     }
} /* end of main */
/*================================*/
/* QuikSort() function */
void QuikSort(x,left,right)
int x[];
int left,right;
{
 register int j,k,y,z;
 j = left;
 k = right;
 y = x[(left + right)/2];
 do
    {
     while (x[j] < y && j < right) j++;
     while (y < x[k] && k > left) k--;
     if (j <= k)
       {
        z = x[j];
        x[j] = x[k];
        x[k] = z;
        j++;
        k--;
       }
    }
     while (j <= k);
         if (left <= k)
           QuikSort(x,left,k);
         if (j < right)
           QuikSort(x,j,right);

 } /* end of QuikSort() function */
/*================================*/
/* END OF QUIKSORT.C */
```

## Program execution

QUIKSORT.C

an array of random-order integers to be sorted:

```
59 288 35 47 685 302 431 640 678 378
357 85 659 531 897 535 539 48 683 682
398 508 281 408 28 593 280 788 759 56
172 209 763 615 721 129 118 387 625 793
988 552 144 341 301 839 357 96 570 87
131 15 148 472 560 838 207 939 84 162
174 765 965 817 159 461 832 543 552 875
707 41 411 92 738 159 975 828 744 53
992 683 120 243 825 122 355 414 239 63
155 710 689 422 143 449 934 635 729 567
261 358 965 463 987 830 228 26 282 865
352 982 382 193 113 638 396 179 937 784
437 964 140 62 216 909 603 865 248 816
50 234 141 915 191 739 837 237 891 182
```

```
980 806 679 523 554 691 768 920 990 850
620 124 729 819 344 299 596 823 977 889
109 629 859 721 86 115 680 613 392 425
290 779 223 300 723 917 174 585 19 25
198 136 914 514 513 443 424 414 596 95
865 409 838 106 574 490 618 389 697 893
92 916 176 953 163 251 221 234 218 459
995 641 772 524 604 794 575 61 690 917
449 907 907 682 298 614 961 151 953 354
778 291 762 99 884 824 806 122 948 147
668 304 872 368 392 832 442 708 474 1
502 2 10 931 711 26 129 234 677 62
233 185 195 279 464 313 871 424 162 98
578 393 590 984 17 790 899 361 451 296
315 70 646 612 367 400 620 363 51 917
963 801 300 851 419 466 345 996 945 769
862 690 893 74 895 308 616 171 132 441
393 430 513 645 256 66 232 338 715 211
865 24 480 87 154 807 732 522 322 764
570 859 3 131 806 824 968 420 971 295
20 192 226 351 28 277 589 510 318 488
348 620 378 786 711 696 721 302 844 488
933 874 794 375 840 980 37 178 808 407
507 859 489 989 719 593 900 463 485 927
192 155 607 308 479 844 22 315 395 608
740 933 953 990 552 211 325 518 42 735
191 998 304 541 861 1 840 830 946 498
440 125 654 898 780 989 599 782 135 82
959 20 676 791 6 647 365 480 803 353
12 625 973 792 258 470 384 884 293 260
829 695 70 288 665 70 194 278 482 519
656 348 126 859 571 368 493 558 409 743
616 812 876 415 787 102 152 223 768 853
821 989 221 398 342 352 112 278 914 623
184 152 314 217 302 932 923 494 125 74
212 310 967 784 67 665 576 807 891 127
887 380 834 879 107 198 578 701 579 155
972 768 306 184 188 473 594 144 658 139
694 188 654 407 517 412 983 71 365 732
500 189 541 730 314 932 782 791 216 703
811 125 904 57 759 992 480 581 263 118
977 798 769 67 270 9 628 633 296 929
185 109 585 403 688 655 446 979 390 747
121 406 479 635 750 202 232 127 740 523
735 503 48 871 461 216 414 3 51 638
416 295 684 273 178 672 754 466 382 916
548 575 436 843 183 853 517 979 259 14
409 964 897 739 79 285 498 619 92 31
2 644 949 665 750 273 129 419 322 732
81 239 487 662 499 724 756 45 487 228
154 252 815 785 797 289 477 338 81 595
433 180 90 890 80 527 120 492 940 750
905 45 937 44 215 566 460 746 884 960
906 157 309 82 102 312 180 874 387 925
25 641 148 986 154 641 657 505 73 259
700 984 478 252 612 491 821 719 128 590
722 377 759 38 122 384 302 858 181 237
458 470 922 892 839 737 658 953 800 56
433 5 385 889 641 529 507 572 400 962
127 847 115 94 69 744 611 909 102 184
936 683 375 533 677 661 456 633 531 137
```

```
133 466 337 107 323 985 458 5 758 879
432 7 505 92 305 935 62 745 32 122
239 265 438 235 493 507 505 595 608 858
628 530 247 856 232 813 498 705 922 136
5 604 869 277 662 887 227 749 696 579
```

the array sorted in ascending order:

```
1 1 2 2 3 3 5 5 5 6
7 9 10 12 14 15 17 19 20 20
22 24 25 25 26 26 28 28 31 32
35 37 38 41 42 44 45 45 47 48
48 50 51 51 53 56 56 57 59 61
62 62 62 63 66 67 67 69 70 70
70 71 73 74 74 79 80 81 81 82
82 84 85 86 87 87 90 92 92 92
92 94 95 96 98 99 102 102 102 106
107 107 109 109 112 113 115 115 118 118
120 120 121 122 122 122 122 124 125 125
125 126 127 127 127 128 129 129 129 131
131 132 133 135 136 136 137 139 140 141
143 144 144 147 148 148 151 152 152 154
154 154 155 155 155 157 159 159 162 162
163 171 172 174 174 176 178 178 179 180
180 181 182 183 184 184 184 185 185 188
188 189 191 191 192 192 193 194 195 198
198 202 207 209 211 211 212 215 216 216
216 217 218 221 221 223 223 226 227 228
228 232 232 232 233 234 234 234 235 237
237 239 239 239 243 247 248 251 252 252
256 258 259 259 260 261 263 265 270 273
273 277 277 278 278 279 280 281 282 285
288 288 289 290 291 293 295 295 296 296
298 299 300 300 301 302 302 302 302 304
304 305 306 308 308 309 310 312 313 314
314 315 315 318 322 322 323 325 337 338
338 341 342 344 345 348 348 351 352 352
353 354 355 357 357 358 361 363 365 365
367 368 368 375 375 377 378 378 380 382
382 384 384 385 387 387 389 390 392 392
393 393 395 396 398 398 400 400 403 406
407 407 408 409 409 409 411 412 414 414
414 415 416 419 419 420 422 424 424 425
430 431 432 433 433 436 437 438 440 441
442 443 446 449 449 451 456 458 458 459
460 461 461 463 463 464 466 466 466 470
470 472 473 474 477 478 479 479 480 480
480 482 485 487 487 488 488 489 490 491
492 493 493 494 498 498 498 499 500 502
503 505 505 505 507 507 507 508 510 513
513 514 517 517 518 519 522 523 523 524
527 529 530 531 531 533 535 539 541 541
543 548 552 552 552 554 558 560 566 567
570 570 571 572 574 575 575 576 578 578
579 579 581 585 585 589 590 590 593 593
594 595 595 596 596 599 603 604 604 607
608 608 611 612 612 613 614 615 616 616
618 619 620 620 620 623 625 625 628 628
629 633 633 635 635 638 638 640 641 641
641 641 644 645 646 647 654 654 655 656
657 658 658 659 661 662 662 665 665 665
```

```
668  672  676  677  677  678  679  680  682  682
683  683  683  684  685  688  689  690  690  691
694  695  696  696  697  700  701  703  705  707
708  710  711  711  715  719  719  721  721  721
722  723  724  729  729  730  732  732  732  735
735  737  738  739  739  740  740  743  744  744
745  746  747  749  750  750  750  754  756  758
759  759  759  762  763  764  765  768  768  768
769  769  772  778  779  780  782  782  784  784
785  786  787  788  790  791  791  792  793  794
794  797  798  800  801  803  806  806  806  807
807  808  811  812  813  815  816  817  819  821
821  823  824  824  825  828  829  830  830  832
832  834  837  838  838  839  839  840  840  843
844  844  847  850  851  853  853  856  858  858
859  859  859  859  861  862  865  865  865  865
869  871  871  872  874  874  875  876  879  879
884  884  884  887  887  889  889  890  891  891
892  893  893  895  897  897  898  899  900  904
905  906  907  907  909  909  914  914  915  916
916  917  917  917  920  922  922  923  925  927
929  931  932  932  933  933  934  935  936  937
937  939  940  945  946  948  949  953  953  953
953  959  960  961  962  963  964  964  965  965
967  968  971  972  973  975  977  977  979  979
980  980  982  983  984  984  985  986  987  988
989  989  989  990  990  992  992  995  996  998
```

# FUNCTION: Insertst( )  MIC 5.4

## Purpose

Arrange a table of values in ascending order using the insertion sort algorithm.

## Notes

This insertion sort algorithm is surprisingly fast, yet simple to code and understand. It is also called the card player's sort because during processing each unsorted item is inserted in its appropriate slot relative to already sorted values.

## Programming ideas

1. Write a program using CTB3.6: Alterseq( ) and Insertst( ) which:

   a. sorts an array of random-order integers,
   b. assigns the unsorted list to the pitch parameter,
   c. assigns the original and retrograde forms of the sorted list to the volume parameter, and,
   d. assigns the array created from mapping of the internal function steps to the rhythm parameter.

2. Write a program using MIC3.25: Valratio( ), MIC3.5 Displace( ), and Insertst( ) to:

   a. fill an array with a random-order integer sequence that is redundancy-rate controlled;
   b. sort the array, then process it through function Displace( );
   c. use the processed array as a list of pointers to a rhythm data table.

## Program source code

```
/* INSERTST.C (insertion sort,aka card player's sort)*/
#include <stdio.h>
main()
{
  int x[200];      /* stores list to be sorted */
  int total = 200,seed = 31213,j;
  void InsertSt();

  srand(seed);
  printf("an array of random-order integers to be sorted:\n");
  for (j = 0;j < total;j++)
    {
      if (j % 10 == 0)
        printf("\n");
      x[j] = rand() % 1000 + 1;
```

```
            printf("%d ",x[j]);
        }
    printf("\n\nthe array sorted in ascending order:\n");
    InsertSt(x,total);
    for (j = 0;j < total;j++)
        {
        if (j % 10 == 0)
            printf("\n");
        printf("%d ",x[j]);
        }
} /* end of main */
/*================================*/
/* InsertSt() function */
void InsertSt(x,total)
int x[];
int total;
{
 register int j,k,temp;
 for (j = 1;j < total;j++)
    {
    temp = x[j];
    k = j - 1;
    while (k >= 0 && temp < x[k])
        {
        x[k+1] = x[k];
        k--;
        }
    x[k+1] = temp;
    }

 } /* end of InsertSt() function */
/*===================================*/
/* END OF INSERTST.C */
```

## Program execution

`INSERTST.EXE`

an array of random-order integers to be sorted:

```
562 151 603 434 419 178 340 309 769 652
951 769 173 829 200 873 429 444 592 204
93 886 530 396 414 725 542 43 508 739
397 187 293 575 13 797 56 358 279 605
211 638 774 203 640 862 200 52 393 970
58 578 947 413 584 617 288 680 356 892
752 530 808 183 569 664 974 541 628 551
14 100 395 206 856 456 57 137 556 957
538 444 503 457 252 397 303 137 740 388
442 162 156 807 282 547 196 281 948 465
536 762 563 371 266 805 407 558 96 302
235 523 287 474 453 288 296 699 415 828
411 428 991 455 738 921 811 825 377 546
832 129 723 946 596 208 695 675 137 447
739 412 92 135 688 693 477 583 448 57
232 706 404 165 236 970 218 865 811 7
541 605 794 229 214 157 370 157 482 311
727 586 52 164 800 623 486 756 111 918
```

```
83 383 722 4 984 994 841 738 698 38
49 303 514 391 274 293 39 91 29 673
```

the array sorted in ascending order:

```
4 7 13 14 29 38 39 43 49 52
52 56 57 57 58 83 91 92 93 96
100 111 129 135 137 137 137 151 156 157
157 162 164 165 173 178 183 187 196 200
200 203 204 206 208 211 214 218 229 232
235 236 252 266 274 279 281 282 287 288
288 293 293 296 302 303 303 309 311 340
356 358 370 371 377 383 388 391 393 395
396 397 397 404 407 411 412 413 414 415
419 428 429 434 442 444 444 447 448 453
455 456 457 465 474 477 482 486 503 508
514 523 530 530 536 538 541 541 542 546
547 551 556 558 562 563 569 575 578 583
584 586 592 596 603 605 605 617 623 628
638 640 652 664 673 675 680 688 693 695
698 699 706 722 723 725 727 738 738 739
739 740 752 756 762 769 769 774 794 797
800 805 807 808 811 811 825 828 829 832
841 856 862 865 873 886 892 918 921 946
947 948 951 957 970 970 974 984 991 994
```

# FUNCTION: Selecsrt( )   MIC 5.5

## Purpose

Arrange an array of values in ascending order.

## Notes

The selection sort algorithm is faster than the bubble sort, but still slow for long lists. SelecSrt( ) function first finds the list item with the lowest value, then swaps it with the first list item; it then repeats the action with next lowest, second list item, and so on.

## Programming ideas

Write a program using MIC3.25: Valratio( ), MIC3.5 Displace( ), and Insertst( ) to:

1. fill an array with a random-order integer sequence that is redundancy-rate controlled;
2. sort the array, then process it through function Displace( );
3. use the processed array as a list of pointers to a rhythm data table.

## Program source code

```
/* SELECSRT.C (selection sort, faster than the bubble sort,
               but slow for long lists.)*/
#include <stdio.h>
main()
{
 int x[200];     /* stores list to be sorted */
 int total = 200,seed = 9226,j;
 void SelecSrt();

 srand(seed);
 printf("an array of random-order integers to be sorted:\n");
 for (j = 0;j < total;j++)
    {
     if (j % 10 == 0)
        printf("\n");
     x[j] = rand() % 1000 + 1;
     printf("%d ",x[j]);
    }
 printf("\n\nthe array sorted in ascending order:\n");
 SelecSrt(x,total);
 for (j = 0;j < total;j++)
    {
     if (j % 10 == 0)
        printf("\n");
     printf("%d ",x[j]);
    }
} /* end of main */
```

```
/*===================================*/
/* SelecSrt() function  (First finds the item with the
                lowest value, then swaps it with the first
                list item;repeats the action with next lowest,
                second list item, and so on.)   */
void SelecSrt(x,total)
int x[];
int total;
{
 register int j,k,l,temp;
 for (j = 0;j < total-1;++j)
    {
     l = j;

     temp = x[j];
     for (k = j+1;k < total;++k)
        {
          if (x[k] < temp)
            {
             l = k;
             temp = x[k];
            }
        }
        x[l] = x[j];
        x[j] = temp;
    }
 } /* end of SelecSrt() function */
/*===================================*/
/* END OF SELECSRT.C */
```

# Program execution

SELECSRT.EXE

an array of random-order integers to be sorted:

```
519 513 274 512 179 902 969 467 693 485
584 564 834 793 433 716 141 969 374 801
687 134 295 150 896 255 815 700 908 371
561 376 58 352 431 246 641 891 796 933
499 56 530 908 38 795 597 212 576 574
121 22 275 533 641 912 633 255 994 962
9 407 816 79 299 938 214 945 192 786
363 756 485 644 859 463 42 950 300 822
645 44 242 909 188 883 517 385 891 877
840 272 770 543 461 955 443 153 712 721
234 229 360 31 781 682 309 421 997 585
630 91 445 705 393 76 67 79 985 211
77 457 507 477 358 124 809 782 785 611
611 462 876 442 226 942 840 410 678 286
160 990 427 258 632 462 527 221 424 443
326 725 624 531 210 273 118 542 157 31
342 665 432 369 801 537 849 905 305 731
832 643 963 499 442 27 349 883 730 584
714 645 269 424 756 210 997 596 569 612
15 566 153 402 760 953 935 748 797 33
```

the array sorted in ascending order:

```
9 15 22 27 31 31 33 38 42 44
```

```
56 58 67 76  77 79 79 91 118 121
124 134 141 150 153 153 157 160 179 188
192 210 210 211 212 214 221 226 229 234
242 246 255 255 258 269 272 273 274 275
286 295 299 300 305 309 326 342 349 352
358 360 363 369 371 374 376 385 393 402
407 410 421 424 424 427 431 432 433 442
442 443 443 445 457 461 462 462 463 467
477 485 485 499 499 507 512 513 517 519
527 530 531 533 537 542 543 561 564 566
569 574 576 584 584 585 596 597 611 611
612 624 630 632 633 641 641 643 644 645
645 665 678 682 687 693 700 705 712 714
716 721 725 730 731 748 756 756 760 770
781 782 785 786 793 795 796 797 801 801
809 815 816 822 832 834 840 840 849 859
876 877 883 883 891 891 896 902 905 908
908 909 912 933 935 938 942 945 950 953
955 962 963 969 969 985 990 994 997 997
```

# FUNCTION: Tsearch1( )   MIC 5.6

## Purpose

Search an unsorted table for the locations of specific entries or keys (linear method).

## Notes

The linear unsorted table search is the simplest and slowest of the four search algorithms included in this chapter. It scans the input array from front to back looking for occurrences of target items. In this main routine, the search is for array positions that store the lowest and highest values of the random number generator range—information that might be required by other parts of a long program, or which will be displayed to provide a runtime view of linear excursion. The position(s) and occurrence frequency of each item is returned to the main routine; if the search is unsuccessful, a message to that effect is printed.

In this implementation, datum and key are treated interchangeably; however, some applications necessitate interpretation of the stored values as keys (pointers) to the addresses of a secondary array.

## Programming ideas

Write an interactive program that:

1. generates and displays an array of random-order integers (range 1–88) that will be converted to registrated pitches,
2. searches the array for the locations of a small group of pitch classes that, after viewing the sequence, the user designates to receive volume accents. (Use the modulus operator to convert the array integers to octave-contained pitch classes.)
3. assigns 100% levels to corresponding addresses in the volume parameter array, then
4. fills the remaining volume array addresses with low-level (20–60%) volume data.

## Program source code

```
/* TSEARCH1.C (sequential table searching routine )*/
              /*useful in situations where a scondary event
              or parameter change is tied to the occurrence
              of a specific value */


#include <stdio.h>
main()
{
```

```
        int x[200];      /* stores list to be sorted */
        int total = 200,tablekey,tally,seed = 1993,j;
        int Tsearch1();

        srand(seed);
        printf("an array of random-order integers to be searched:\n");
        for (j = 0;j < total;j++)
            {
            if (j % 10 == 0)
                printf("\n");
            x[j] = rand() % 12; /* pitch-classes of the scale */
            printf("%d ",x[j]);
            }

        tablekey =   9;
        printf("\nsearch item will be the integer %d\n",tablekey);
        tally = Tsearch1(x,total,tablekey);
        if (tally == 0)
            printf("\nnot found\n");
        else
            printf("\n%d appeared % d times",tablekey,tally);
        printf("\n");
} /* end of main */
/*================================*/
/* Tsearch1() function (sequential search returns frequency &
                  location(s) of keys */
int Tsearch1(x,total,key)
int x[],total,key;
{
    int j,sum = 0;
    for (j = 0;j < total;j++)
        if (x[j] == key)
            {
            sum ++;
            printf("\nitem found at location %d",j);
            }
    return (sum);
} /* end of Tsearch1() function */
/*=====================================*/
/* END OF TSEARCH1.C */
```

## Program execution

TSEARCH1.EXE

an array of random-order integers to be searched:

```
6 7 2 6 0 1 2 11 9 1
8 0 6 2 8 10 10 11 10 9
9 11 8 7 7 8 7 7 10 11
11 8 10 2 0 8 1 6 0 0
11 3 7 4 4 10 0 11 5 10
2 6 11 7 7 5 6 10 11 1
1 4 8 0 2 8 3 6 7 2
2 4 6 11 1 6 6 7 3 0
11 10 7 6 0 9 6 5 10 6
10 9 4 9 10 4 1 2 0 2
0 9 4 2 2 1 7 5 9 8
7 1 1 0 4 5 7 6 4 3
```

```
8 7 11 9 3 4 10 8 3 11
5 5 8 10 2 2 8 8 6 5
11 5 6 2 1 6 3 3 9 9
7 3 4 6 11 10 7 2 4 0
0 4 6 4 5 2 3 0 11 8
1 10 10 3 2 8 1 4 2 0
9 7 5 1 0 6 7 9 11 2
8 4 1 5 5 5 5 0 0 4
search item will be the integer 9

item found at location 8
item found at location 19
item found at location 20
item found at location 85
item found at location 91
item found at location 93
item found at location 101
item found at location 108
item found at location 123
item found at location 148
item found at location 149
item found at location 180
item found at location 187
9 appeared  13 times
```

## FUNCTION GROUP: Tsearch2.c

1. Quiksort( )    MIC 5.3
2. Tsearch2( )    MIC 5.7

## Purpose

Search a sorted table for the locations of specific entries or keys (binary method).

## Notes

This binary search subroutine requires a sorted table of unique entries (keys). It is the fastest algorithm in common use, but might not be as appropriate as MIC5.6: Tsearch1( ) in many musical situations, because the sorting process significantly increases execution time. Moreover, because the algorithm functions by successively cutting its search in half until it finds the key, repeated items must be culled from the list or the subroutine will simply report the first redundant item it locates and return to the main program.

This condition can be circumvented by treating the array entries as pointers to an array containing redundant items. For example, suppose you shuffle an array of unique (not necessarily consecutive) integers to serve as pointers—keys—to a second, character string array that stores several items of information in each address. The entries at a number of different array locations may be identical, but the keys to the addresses will be unique; furthermore, while the keys will be sorted in ascending order, they need not be continuous. In this manner, sorted data of one musical parameter can be searched for target items to be mapped onto another parameter having a completely different value range.

## Programming ideas

1. Write a program that sorts and searches the data of one musical parameter to obtain pointers to another parameter that is then altered in some manner.
2. Write a program that "filters" or zeros-out specific values at keyed locations in the volume parameter in accordance with a list provided by a sorted search of the pitch parameter for particular items.

## Program source code

```
/* TSEARCH2.C (binary SORTED table searching routine
                finds 1st occurrence of key in list )*/


#include <stdio.h>
main()
```

```
{
    int x[200];      /* stores list to be sorted */
    int total = 200,tablekey,position,seed = 4132,j;
    int Tsearch1();
    void QuikSort();

    srand(seed);
    printf("an array of random-order integers to be searched:\n");
    for (j = 0;j < total;j++)
        {
        if (j % 10 == 0)
            printf("\n");
        x[j] = rand() % 50; /* pitch-classes of the scale */
        printf("%d ",x[j]);
        }
    printf("\n---array now being sorted (ascending-order)---\n");
    QuikSort(x,0,total-1);
    tablekey =   21;
    printf("\nsearch item will be the integer %d\n",tablekey);

    position = Tsearch1(x,total,tablekey);
    if (position == -1)
        printf("\nnot found\n");
    else
        printf("\n%d found at location % d",tablekey,position);
    printf("\n");
} /* end of main */
/*=================MIC 5.3 ==============*/
/* QuikSort() function */
void QuikSort(x,left,right)
int x[];
int left,right;
{
    register int j,k,y,z;
    j = left;
    k = right;
    y = x[(left + right)/2];
    do
        {
        while (x[j] < y && j < right) j++;
        while (y < x[k] && k > left) k--;
        if (j <= k)
            {
            z = x[j];
            x[j] = x[k];
            x[k] = z;
            j++;
            k--;
            }
        }
        while (j <= k);
            if (left <= k)
                QuikSort(x,left,k);
            if (j < right)
                QuikSort(x,j,right);

    } /* end of QuikSort() function */
/*===================================*/
/* Tsearch2() function (binary SORTED table search returns
                        location of key */
int Tsearch1(x,total,key)
```

```
int x[],total,key;
{
  int bottom,mid,top;

  bottom = 0; top = total-1;
  while (bottom <= top)
    {
      mid = (bottom + top) / 2;
      if (key < x[mid])
         top = mid-1;
      else if (key > x[mid])
         bottom = mid+1;
      else
         return mid;
    }
  return -1;
} /* end of Tsearch2() function */
/*====================================*/
/* END OF TSEARCH2.C */
```

## Program execution

TSEARCH2.EXE

an array of random-order integers to be searched:

```
10 42 46 6 22 23 27 19 19 0
36 5 45 15 47 35 46 22 36 40
24 11 14 7 48 19 28 34 39 11
11 46 20 35 21 24 31 34 8 11
0 13 17 44 22 21 46 34 21 44
44 1 42 11 15 6 34 37 40 23
49 6 0 4 15 20 0 9 17 26
15 43 45 25 26 45 19 42 48 39
14 34 35 2 23 7 14 17 3 26
6 48 43 6 39 43 47 42 9 43
13 20 31 33 34 11 16 46 16 13
47 25 49 5 27 29 35 37 26 35
1 23 27 47 49 2 45 30 30 43
13 10 48 43 13 1 20 39 44 38
3 43 37 8 49 27 47 0 21 21
34 23 45 30 37 11 9 8 45 22
45 44 35 18 36 39 43 4 9 9
29 15 7 9 7 19 17 21 30 8
29 23 1 49 29 10 33 5 15 8
36 31 22 27 39 26 6 43 24 36
```

---array now being sorted (ascending-order)---

search item will be the integer 21

21 found at location  80

# FUNCTION GROUP: Tsearch3.c

1. Quiksort( )  MIC 5.3
2. Tsearch3( )  MIC 5.8

## Purpose

Search a sorted list for targeted values using the proximity search method.

## Notes

This algorithm requires a sorted list of unique items. More powerful than either the binary or the interpolation search, it returns a subset of the array on either side of the value under search (even if the target item is missing).

This approach is applicable to musical situations in which a prioritized range of solutions to contextual requirements must be retrieved from a table of rules governing linear or vertical aggregates. For instance, melodic sequences might be generated by causing an input melodic interval class to trigger subsequent interval choices based upon generation rules stored in proximity to a target value. Or, random integers might dictate locations for random walks across a cluster of values.

## Programming ideas

1. Write an interactive program which:

    a. fills a driver array with 20 random-order integers, range 1–76 (redundancy OK),
    b. fills a reference array with a 44-member, random-order series, range 1–88,
    c. invokes proximity search to locate values supplied by the driver array,
    d. takes a random walk around the integers returned by the proximity search, then
    e. prints the random walk as registrated pitches.

2. Write an interactive program in which melodic interval succession is governed by a set of production rules stored in a reference array; use values derived from a secondary parameter as search arguments for CTB5.8.

## Program source code

```
/* TSEARCH3.C (SORTED table proximity search routine
              returns subset around 1st occurrence of
              search key  )*/
```

```c
#include <stdio.h>
main()
{
 int x[100];      /* stores list to be sorted */
 int total = 100,tablekey,swidth,seed = 1993,j;
 void Tsearch3();
 void QuikSort();
 srand(seed);
 printf("an array of random-order integers to be searched:\n");
 for (j = 0;j < total;j++)
    {
    if (j % 10 == 0)
       printf("\n");
    x[j] = rand() % 200; /* pitch-classes of the scale */
    printf("%d ",x[j]);
    }
 printf("\narray now being sorted (ascending-order)\n");
 QuikSort(x,0,total-1);

 tablekey =  21;
 swidth = 5;
 printf("\nsearch item will be the integer %d\n",tablekey);

 Tsearch3(x,total,tablekey,swidth);
} /* end of main */
/*================MIC 5.3 ===============*/
/* QuikSort() function */
void QuikSort(x,left,right)
int x[];
int left,right;
{
 register int j,k,y,z;
 j = left;
 k = right;
 y = x[(left + right)/2];
 do
    {
    while (x[j] < y && j < right) j++;
    while (y < x[k] && k > left) k--;
    if (j <= k)
       {
        z = x[j];
       x[j] = x[k];
       x[k] = z;
       j++;
       k--;
       }
    }
      while (j <= k);
         if (left <= k)
           QuikSort(x,left,k);
         if (j < right)
           QuikSort(x,j,right);

 } /* end of QuikSort() function */
/*===================================*/
/* Tsearch3() function (proximity search returns
           a subset of the list on either side
           of the search key */
void Tsearch3(x,total,key,subset)
int x[],total,key,subset;
```

```
{
   int bottom,top,j,flag = 1;

   for (j = 0;j < total;++j)
      if (key <= x[j])
         {
            flag = 0;
            break;
         }
   if (flag )
      j = total + 1;
   if (x[j] == key)
      top = j + subset;
   else
      top = j + subset - 1;
   bottom = j - subset;
   if (top > total)
      top = total;
   if (bottom < 1)
      bottom = 1;
for (j = bottom;j <= top;j++)
   printf("%d ",x[j]);
} /* end of Tsearch3() function */
/*===================================*/
/* END OF TSEARCH3.C */
```

## Program execution

an array of random-order integers to be searched:

```
58 87 34 46 84 101 30 39 77 177
156 84 58 130 96 134 138 47 82 81
197 107 80 7 27 192 79 187 158 55
171 8 162 14 120 128 117 186 24 192
187 151 143 140 100 38 156 95 169 86
130 14 147 71 159 37 6 138 83 161
173 164 164 16 158 60 31 142 151 74
106 40 10 91 137 158 174 27 143 52
191 82 119 42 24 121 154 13 38 62
154 109 88 21 142 48 133 34 128 166
```
array now being sorted (ascending-order)

search item will be the integer 21
```
10 13 14 14 16 21 24 24 27 27 30
```

# 6
# *Sound/Text composition*

The use of and manipulation of text has been used by many composers in different contexts, from music for live performers based on parts of words to the processing of speech components in computer-based electroacoustic music. This chapter contains four complete programs that deal with text in one way or another:

1. Poem.c
2. Phone.c
3. Txtparse.c
4. Drivel.c

The component functions should be stored together in a file such as "textlib.c" and accessed for program development by including the Preprocessor directive—#include "textlib.c"—at the top of your program; or, alternatively, you can add the directive to the text processing header file listed below:

```
/* text.h  (definitions for text processing)
/* #include "textlib.c" (add this line for automatic inclusion */
                        /* of all text-processing functions) */
#include <stdio.h>
#include <ctype.h>
#include <alloc.h>
#include "randmain.c"
#define MAXDATA 100
#define MAXVOCAB 100
#define MAXWORDSIZE 80
#define TRUE 1
#define FALSE -1
static char vowels[6] = {"AEIOU"};
static char punctuation[10] = {".,;:'!-/?"};
char *phones[MAXVOCAB];
char *dipth[MAXVOCAB];
char *words[MAXVOCAB];
char *verbs[MAXVOCAB];
```

```c
char *adjectives[MAXVOCAB];
char *nouns[MAXVOCAB];
char *articles[3] = {"a", "the", "an"};
int wct = 0;
int dip = 0;
int ph = 0;                    /* size of arrays */
int vbct = 0;
int adct = 0;
int nct = 0;
int act = 3;
/*****************************************/
```

# FUNCTION GROUP: Poem.c

1. GetVocab( )        MIC. 6.1
2. assign( )          MIC. 6.2
3. MakePoem( )        MIC. 6.4
4. VocabSummary( )    MIC. 6.3
5. SelectWord( )      MIC. 6.5

## Purpose

Generate nonsense poems.

## Notes

This program reads parts of speech from data files. A summary of the vocabulary is given sorted by part of speech. A "poem" is then created by MakePoem( ). The pattern of parts of speech used in MakePoem( ) should be altered to make different word patterns.

The syntax and verse structure of POEM.C's output is quite stilted and might not be to everyone's taste. Frequently, juxtaposition of remote imagery and unusual linkage of parts of speech occurs. To control the "nonsense factor," reduce the number of words in the adjective, noun, verb, and preposition categories to include only those which produce minimal ambiguity in any possible combination. Conversely, increased ambiguity and metaphorical madness is achieved by imaginative augmentation of program vocabulary.

## Programming ideas

Write an interactive program which:

1. reads in vocabulary from a file,
2. allows the user to control poem ambiguity level via a variable which gradually increases or decreases vocabulary size,
3. converts the returned poems to data for the pitch, rhythm, and articulation parameters of a melodic line for soprano voice, then
4. outputs the completed notelist to a disk file

## Program source code

```
POEM.C
#include <stdio.h>
#include "fgetword.c"
#include "text.h"
int GetVocab(FILE *fp, char *part[]);
void MakePoem(FILE *fp);
void VocabSummary(void);
main()
```

```
{
    FILE *fp;
    extern char *adjectives[];

    fp = fopen("adj.dat", "r");
    adct = GetVocab(fp, adjectives);
    fclose(fp);
    fp = fopen("verbs.dat", "r");
    vbct = GetVocab(fp, verbs);
    fclose(fp);
    fp = fopen("nouns.dat", "r");
    nct = GetVocab(fp, nouns);
    fclose(fp);
    VocabSummary();
    fp = fopen("poem.dat", "w");
    MakePoem(fp);
    fclose(fp);
}
/**********************************************/
GetVocab(fp, part)
    FILE *fp;
    char *part[];
{
    int j = 0;

    while(!feof(fp))
            j = assign(fp, part, j);

        return(j);
}
/****************************************************************/
assign(fp, part, position)
    FILE *fp;
    char *part[];
    int position;
{
    char *string;

        string = (char *) malloc(MAXWORDSIZE);
        fgetword(string, MAXWORDSIZE, fp);
            if(!isspace(string[0]))
                    part[position++] = string;
            return(position);
}
/****************************************************************/
void VocabSummary()
{
    int j;

        printf("\nVocabulary:\n");
        for(j = 0; j < nct; j++)
                printf("nouns %d = %s\n", j, nouns[j]);
        for(j = 0; j < adct; j++)
                printf("adjectives %d = %s\n", j, adjectives[j]);
        for(j = 0; j < vbct; j++)
                printf("verbs %d = %s\n", j, verbs[j]);
        for(j = 0; j < 3; j++)
                printf("articles %d = %s\n", j, articles[j]);
}
/****************************************************************/
```

```
void MakePoem(fp)
    FILE *fp;
{
    int j, num, howmany, prt,seed;

    printf("\nHow many lines do you want?\t");
    howmany = getnum();
    printf("\nWrite to file? (1) = yes\t");
    prt = getnum();
    randomize();
        for(j = 0; j < howmany; j++)
            {
        SelectWord(fp, articles, 3, prt);
        SelectWord(fp, adjectives, adct, prt);
        SelectWord(fp, nouns, nct, prt);
        SelectWord(fp, verbs, vbct, prt);
        SelectWord(fp, articles, 3, prt);
        SelectWord(fp, adjectives, adct, prt);
        SelectWord(fp, nouns, nct, prt);

                printf("\n");
                if(prt == 1)
                    fprintf(fp, "\n");
                }
}
/*************************************************************/
SelectWord(fp, part, ct, flag)
    FILE *fp;
    char *part[];
    int ct, flag;
{
    int num;
    num = irand(0, ct - 1);
    printf("%s ", part[num]);
    if(flag == 1)
        fprintf(fp, "%s ", part[num]);
}
/*************************************************************/
```

## Program execution

```
POEM.EXE

Vocabulary:
nouns 0 = thing
nouns 1 = book
nouns 2 = computer
nouns 3 = desk
nouns 4 = sky
nouns 5 = ocean
nouns 6 = floor
nouns 7 = ceiling
nouns 8 = girl
nouns 9 = boy
nouns 10 = tree
nouns 11 = cat
nouns 12 = table
nouns 13 = car
nouns 14 = ball
adjectives 0 = blue
```

```
adjectives 1 = wind-swept
adjectives 2 = short
adjectives 3 = long
adjectives 4 = fat
adjectives 5 = skinny
adjectives 6 = azure
adjectives 7 = pretty
adjectives 8 = handsome
adjectives 9 = fast
verbs 0 = insert
verbs 1 = show
verbs 2 = licks
verbs 3 = flick
verbs 4 = walk
verbs 5 = talk
verbs 6 = run
verbs 7 = acts
verbs 8 = asked
verbs 9 = wrote
verbs 10 = executed
articles 0 = a
articles 1 = the
articles 2 = an

How many lines do you want?      5
Write to file? (1) = yes         2

the blue computer show the pretty thing
the handsome book run a wind-swept sky
a blue table licks a pretty ball
the blue ocean acts a short floor
the azure floor talk the long ball
```

# FUNCTION GROUP: Phone.c

1. chop( )              MIC 6.35
2. SoundSummary( )      MIC 6.29
3. MakeText( )          MIC 6.32
4. getphonews( )        MIC 6.38
5. isvowel( )           MIC 6.36
6. getdipthws           MIC 6.37
7. ExtractWord( )       MIC 6.39

## Purpose

Phone extraction.

## Notes

This program reads text a line at a time from "stdin." The line is sorted into phones and dipthongs (or simply consonants and vowels) and stored in the global arrays phones[ ] and dipth[ ]. A summary of the contents of these arrays is given. MakeText( ) creates new words by randomly selecting from these arrays in the pattern consonant-vowel. This pattern can be changed to make new word structures.

## Programming ideas

1. Modify the program to generate more complicated patterns by using user-prescribed sequences of consonants and vowels; e.g., v-c-c-c-v-v-c-v-c.
2. Use routines found in Function Group: TEXTPARSE.C to convert the phones and dipthongs to musical pitches and rhythms.

## Program source code

```
PHONE.C
#include "text.h"
#include "fgetline.c"  /* MICSP_15.0 */
main()
{
    int j, k, howmany;
    char string[80];
    FILE *fp;

    fp = fopen("junk.txt", "w");
    printf("\nInclude newline? (1) yes\t");
        j = getnum();
    printf("\nHow many lines?\t");
        howmany = getnum();
    for(k = 0; k < howmany; k++)
            {
        printf("Input string\t");
                if(j == 1)
```

```
                    fgetline(stdin, string, 80);
                else
                    gets(string);
                puts(string);
                chop(string);
                }
        SoundSummary();
            MakeText(fp);
            fclose(fp);
} /* end of main */
/*================= MIC 6.35 ===============*/
chop(string)
    char string[];
{
    int position = 0;

    while(position < strlen(string))
        {
            if(isvowel(string[position]) == FALSE)
                    position = getphonews(string, position);
            else if(isvowel(string[position])  == TRUE)
                    position = getdipthws(string, position);
            else
                position++;
        }
}
/*================= MIC 6.29 ==============*/
SoundSummary()
{
    int j;

        printf("\nSounds\n");
        for(j = 0; j < ph; j++)
                printf("phones %d = %s\n", j, phones[j]);
        printf("%d phones\n", ph);
        for(j = 0; j < dip; j++)
                printf("dipthongs %d = %s\n", j, dipth[j]);
        printf("%d dipthongs\n", dip);
}
/*================= MIC 6.32 ==============*/
MakeText(fp)
    FILE *fp;
{
    int j, num, howmany, prt;

    printf("\nHow many words do you want?\t");
    howmany = getnum();
    printf("\nWrite to file? (1) = yes\t");
    prt = getnum();

        for(j = 0; j < howmany; j++)
                {
                num = irand(0, ph - 1);
                printf("%s", phones[num]);
                if(prt == 1)
                    fprintf(fp, "%s", phones[num]);
                num = irand(0, dip - 1);
                printf("%s", dipth[num]);
                if(prt == 1)
                    fprintf(fp, "%s", dipth[num]);
                }
```

```
}
/*================= MIC 6.36 ==============*/

isvowel(ch)
   char ch;
{
   int j;

   for(j = 0; j < 5; j++)
       if(toupper(ch) == vowels[j])
            return(TRUE);
         return(FALSE);
}
/*================= MIC 6.37 ==============*/
getdipthws(string, position)    /* keep the spaces */
   char string[];
   int position;
{
   char *vstr;
   int j = 0;

   vstr = (char *) malloc(80);
            while(isvowel(string[position]) == TRUE)
             vstr[j++] = string[position++];
             vstr[j] = '\0';
               if(strlen(vstr) > 0)
             dipth[dip++] = vstr;       /* dip is global counter */
         return(position);
}
/*================= MIC 6.38 ==============*/
getphonews(string, position)
   char string[];
   int position;
{
   char *cstr;
   int j = 0;

      cstr = (char *) malloc(80);
      while(isvowel(string[position]) == FALSE)
             {
          cstr[j++] = string[position++];
                  if(ispunct(cstr[j - 1]))
                      cstr[j++] = ' ';
             }
          cstr[j] = '\0';
          if(strlen(cstr) > 0)
            phones[ph++] = cstr;         /* ph is global counter */
         return(position);
}
/*================= MIC 6.39 ==============*/
ExtractWord(string, position)
   char string[];
   int position;
{
   int j = 0;
   char *word;

   word = (char *) malloc(80);
   while(!isspace(string[position]))
       word[j++] = string[position++];
```

```
    word[j++] = '\0';
    words[wct++] = word;
    return(position);
}
/*========================================*/
```

## Program execution

PHONE.EXE

```
Include newline? (1) yes          1
How many lines? 1
Input string
four score and seven years ago


Sounds
phones 0 = f
phones 1 = r sc
phones 2 = r
phones 3 =
phones 4 = nd s
phones 5 = v
phones 6 = n y
phones 7 = rs
phones 8 = g
phones 9 =

10 phones
dipthongs 0 = ou
dipthongs 1 = o
dipthongs 2 = e
dipthongs 3 = a
dipthongs 4 = e
dipthongs 5 = e
dipthongs 6 = ea
dipthongs 7 = a
dipthongs 8 = o
9 dipthongs

How many words do you want?       100
Write to file? (1) = yes          2

n yeron yavagend ser scororou ou
efond sera
ar scevend so
or scou
en yearan you
ors ovogars and sa
en yeafaveafe ovo en yefen yearours en yan yegor scoveveafears
e ero end sean yon yend ser scen yond sorea and segou
eveva agors eage a
efouva
ond sefour scou ero arer scarearago
eareavou
ora
o
afa egou ouve
```

## FUNCTION GROUP: Txtparse.c

1. copytxt( )                    MIC 6.6
2. PutTotals( )                  MIC 6.7
3. Putrhythm( )                  MIC 6.8
4. PutConsonants( )              MIC 6.9
5. PutPunctuation( )             MIC 6.10
6. PutVowels( )                  MIC 6.11
7. transpose( )                  MIC 6.12
8. PutCharSummary( )             MIC 6.13
9. PutData( )                    MIC 6.14
10. gettrans( )                  MIC 6.15
11. getstring( )                 MIC 6.16
12. getarray( )                  MIC 6.17
13. showarray( )                 MIC 6.18
14. Zero( )                      MIC 6.19
15. PutScore( )                  MIC 6.20
16. numvowel( )                  MIC 6.21
17. numpunctuation( )            MIC 6.22
18. numconsonants( )             MIC 6.23
19. WhichVowels( )               MIC 6.25
20. WhichPunctuation( )          MIC 6.26
21. WhichConsonants( )           MIC 6.27
22. hasvowel( )                  MIC 6.28

## Notes

This program reads a text file for input. Two files are opened by the program; one for the analysis of the text, and another for a script score based on the analysis. The analysis is done a line at a time. The script score is a simple ASCII text file that lists all the significant parameter values for each note-event. The most common note attributes used are: P(itch), R(hythm), A(rticulation), V(olume), and T(imbre). So, complete information for a sequence of five tones in a melody might be:

| | | | | | | |
|---|---|---|---|---|---|---|
| P | C#4 | D4 | F4 | A4 | E4 | Letter = note-name, number = octave-placement) |
| R | 1 | 8 | 8 | 1 | 1 | (expressed as fractions of a whole-note) |
| A | 100 | 50 | 50 | 100 | 100 | (% of note-time-space the tone actually sounds) |
| V | 40 | 80 | 80 | 40 | 40 | (% of maximum possible tone loudness) |
| T | 12 | 43 | 2 | 55 | 73 | (instrument number or tone-color change index) |

# Programming ideas

Modify the program to generate rhythm values derived from the text. Assign the rhythms to the pitches of the output melody.

# Program source code

```
TXTPARSE.C
#include "textlib.c"
#include "getfnam.c"
#include "array.c"
#include "synclavi.c"
#include "fgetline.c"
int wordcnt, lnwordcnt, globaltrans;
FILE *input;
FILE *output;
FILE *score;
FILE *getfnam();
/*****************************************************************/
main()
{
    int j, k, size, numv, numc, nump, trans, ask, max, min,
        datarray[80];
    int punctarray[80], carray[80], varray[80], slen, usepunct;
    char string[80];

    input = getfnam("input text","r");
    output = getfnam("output data","w");
    score = getfnam("Script score","w");
    globaltrans = trans = wordcnt =  0;
    trans = gettrans();
        printf("\nTransposition factor = %d\n", trans);
    printf("\nKeep the punctuation? (1) = yes ");
    scanf("%d", &usepunct);
    if(usepunct != 1)
        usepunct = FALSE;
    copytxt(input, output, TRUE);   /* echo text */
    copytxt(input, score, FALSE);
    fprintf(score, "\nNotelist using R 1-1\n");
  do {
    lnwordcnt = 0;
    Zero(datarray);
    getstring(string);
    slen = strlen(string);
    size = getarray(string, slen, datarray, usepunct);
    if(size != 0)
      {
        showarray(datarray, size);
        max = getmax(datarray, size);
        min = getmin(datarray, size);
        printf("\nMax = %d Min = %d\n", max, min);
        fprintf(output, "\nMax = %d Min = %d\n", max, min);
        if(globaltrans == FALSE)
          {
            trans = 0 - min;
            transpose(datarray, size, trans);
    fprintf(output, "\nData normalized to 0, rhythm to 1\n");
   fprintf(score, "\n/* Data normalized to 0, rhythm to 1 */\n");
  fprintf(stdout, "\n/* Data normalized to 0, rhythm to 1 */\n");
```

```
                PutData(datarray, size, string);
            }
                else
                {
            transpose(datarray, size, trans);
            fprintf(stdout, "\nData transposed %d\n", trans);
            fprintf(output, "\nData transposed %d\n", trans);
            fprintf(score, "\nData transposed %d\n", trans);
            PutData(datarray, size, string);
                }
        numv = numvowel(string);
        numc = numconsonants(string);
        nump = numpunctuation(string);
        PutCharSummary(numv, numc, nump);
        PutVowels(varray, numv, trans, string);
        PutConsonants(carray, numc, trans, string);
      PutPunctuation(punctarray, nump, trans, usepunct, string);
        }
        PutTotals(wordcnt, lnwordcnt);
    } while (!feof(input));

  fclose(input);
  fclose(output);
  fclose(score);
}
/***************************************************************/
copytxt(fpi, fpo, echo)
    FILE *fpi, *fpo;
    int echo;
{
    char string[80];

    if(echo)
      printf("\nOriginal complete text:\n");
    fprintf(fpo, "\n/* Original complete text:\n");
    do {
        fgetline(fpi, string, 80);
        if(echo)
          puts(string);
        fputs(string, fpo);
        } while (!feof(fpi));
    fprintf(fpo, "\n*/\n");
    rewind(fpi);
}
/***************************************************************/
PutTotals(wordcnt, lnwordcnt)
    int wordcnt, lnwordcnt;
{
 printf("\nThere are %d words total\n", wordcnt);
 printf("There are %d words in this line\n\n", lnwordcnt);
 printf( "---------------------------------------\n");
 fprintf(output, "\nThere are %d words total\n", wordcnt);
 fprintf(output, "There are %d words in this line\n\n",
                  lnwordcnt);
 fprintf(output,"---------------------------------------\n");
}
/***************************************************************/
Putrhythm(fp, darray, size)
   FILE *fp;
   int darray[], size;
{
```

```
        int j;

    for(j = 0; j < size; j++)
        darray[j] += 1;
    FscriptArray(fp, darray, 'R', size);
}
/*****************************************************************/
PutConsonants(carray, numc, trans, string)
    int carray[], numc, trans;
    char string[];
{
    printf("\nThe consonants are:\n");
    fprintf(output, "\nThe consonants are:\n");
    fprintf(score, "\n/* The consonants are: */\n");
    WhichConsonants(output, string, carray, trans);
    ScriptArray(carray, 'P', numc);
    FscriptArray(score, carray, 'P', numc);
    Putrhythm(score, carray, numc);
}
/*****************************************************************/
PutPunctuation(punctarray, nump, trans, usepunct, string)
    int punctarray[], nump, trans, usepunct;
    char string[];
{
    if(usepunct)
        {
        printf("\nThe punctuations marks are:\n");
        fprintf(score, "\n/* The punctuation marks are: */\n");
        fprintf(output, "\nThe punctuation marks are: \n");
        WhichPunctuation(output, string, punctarray, trans);
        ScriptArray(punctarray, 'P', nump);
        FscriptArray(score, punctarray, 'P', nump);
        Putrhythm(score, punctarray, nump);
        }
    else
        {
        printf("\nThe punctuations marks are not used\n\n");
fprintf(score, "\n/* The punctuation marks are not used */\n\n");
fprintf(output, "\nThe punctuation marks are not used \n\n");
        }
}
/*****************************************************************/
PutVowels(varray, numv, trans, string)
    int varray[], numv, trans;
    char string[];
{
    printf("\nThe vowels are:\n");
    fprintf(output, "\nThe vowels are:\n");
    fprintf(score, "\n/* The vowels are: */\n");
    WhichVowels(output, string, varray, trans);
    ScriptArray(varray, 'P', numv);
    FscriptArray(score, varray, 'P', numv);
    Putrhythm(score, varray, numv);
}
/*****************************************************************/
transpose(datarray, size, trans)
    int datarray[], size, trans;
{
    int k;
```

```
        for(k = 0; k < size; k++)
            datarray[k] += trans;
}
/************************************************************/
PutCharSummary(numv, numc, nump)
    int numv, numc, nump;
{
    printf("\nit has %d vowels", numv);
    printf("\nit has %d consonants", numc);
    printf("\nit has %d punctuation", nump);
    fprintf(output, "\nit has %d vowels", numv);
    fprintf(output, "\nit has %d consonants", numc);
    fprintf(output, "\nit has %d punctuation", nump);
}
/************************************************************/
PutData(datarray, size, string)
    int datarray[], size;
    char string[];
{
    PutArray(datarray, size);
    FputArray(output, datarray, size);
    ScriptArray(datarray, 'P', size);
    PutScore(score, string, datarray, size);
}
/************************************************************/
gettrans()
{
  int trans;
  printf("\nDo you want a global transposition value? (1) yes ");
  scanf("%d", &globaltrans);
  if(globaltrans != 1)
      {
      globaltrans = FALSE;
          return(0);
          }

      if(globaltrans)
          {
          printf("\nEnter transposition value for the array ");
          scanf("%d", &trans);
          }

    return(trans);
}
/************************************************************/
getstring(string)
    char string[];
{
    printf("\nCurrent string:\n");
    fprintf(output, "\nCurrent string:\n");
    fgetline(input, string, 80);
    puts(string);
    fputs(string, output);
    printf("\nIt is %d characters long (including spaces)",
            strlen(string) );
    fprintf(output,
                "\nIt is %d characters long (including spaces)",
        strlen(string) );
}
/************************************************************/
getarray(string, slen, datarray, usepunct)
```

```
        char string[];
        int slen, datarray[], usepunct;
{

        int k, size;

        size = 0;
        for(k = 0; k < slen; k++)
            {
            if(string[k] == ' ' || string[k] == '\n')
                {
                lnwordcnt++;
                wordcnt++;
                }
            if(usepunct != FALSE)
                {
                if( isalpha(string[k]) || ispunct(string[k]) )
                    datarray[size++] = string[k];
                }
            else
                if( isalpha(string[k]) )
                    datarray[size++] = string[k];
            }
        return(size);
}
/****************************************************************/
showarray(datarray, size)
    int datarray[], size;
{
        printf("\nThe string as integers:\n");
        fprintf(output, "\nThe string as integers:\n");
        PutArray(datarray, size);
        FputArray(output, datarray, size);

}
/****************************************************************/
Zero(datarray)
    int datarray[];
{
    int j;
    for(j = 0; j < 80; j++)
        datarray[j] = 0;
}
/****************************************************************/
PutScore(fp, string, datarray, size)
    FILE *fp;
    char string[];
    int datarray[], size;
{

        fprintf(fp, "\n\n/* Text: \n");
        fprintf(fp, " \n%s\n", string);
        fprintf(fp, " As pitch and rhythm\n*/\n");
        FscriptArray(fp, datarray, 'P', size);
        Putrhythm(fp, datarray, size);
}
/****************************************************************/
numvowel(string)
    char string[];
{
    int j, k, numvowels;

    numvowels = 0;
```

```
        for(j = 0; j < strlen(string); j++)
          for(k = 0; k < 5; k++)
            if(toupper(string[j]) == vowels[k])
               numvowels++;
      return(numvowels);
}
/*************************************************************/
numpunctuation(string)
   char string[];
{
   int j, k, numpunct;

   numpunct = 0;
   for(j = 0; j < strlen(string); j++)
      for(k = 0; k < 10; k++)
         if(string[j] == punctuation[k])
            numpunct++;
   return(numpunct);
}
/*************************************************************/
numconsonants(string)
   char string[];
{
   int j, k, numconsonants, isvowel;

    numconsonants = 0;
   for(j = 0; j < strlen(string); j++)
      {
      isvowel = FALSE;
      for(k = 0; k < 5; k++)
         if(toupper(string[j]) == vowels[k] ||
              isalpha(string[j]) == 0)
            isvowel = TRUE;
      if(isvowel != TRUE)
        numconsonants++;
      }
   return(numconsonants);
}
/*************************************************************/
WhichVowels(fp, string, disarray, trans)
   FILE *fp;
   char string[];
   int disarray[], trans;
{
   int j, k, m;

   m = 0;
   for(j = 0; j < strlen(string); j++)
      for(k = 0; k < 5; k++)
         if(toupper(string[j]) == vowels[k])
            {
            printf("%c ",string[j]);
            fprintf(fp, "%c ",string[j]);
            disarray[m++] = string[j] + trans;
            }
}
/*************************************************************/
WhichPunctuation(fp, string, disarray, trans)
   FILE *fp;
   char string[];
   int disarray[], trans;
```

```
{
    int j, k, m;

    m = 0;
    for(j = 0; j < strlen(string); j++)
        for(k = 0; k < 10; k++)
            if(string[j] == punctuation[k])
                {
                printf("%c ",string[j]);
                fprintf(fp, "%c ",string[j]);
                disarray[m++] = string[j] + trans;
                }
}
/*********************************************************/
WhichConsonants(fp, string, disarray, trans)
    FILE *fp;
    char string[];
    int disarray[], trans;
{
    int j, k, m, isvowel;

    m = 0;
    for(j = 0; j < strlen(string); j++)
        {
        isvowel = FALSE;
        for(k = 0; k < 5; k++)
            if(toupper(string[j]) == vowels[k] ||
                isalpha(string[j]) == 0)
                isvowel = TRUE;
        if(isvowel != TRUE)
            {
            printf("%c ",string[j]);
            fprintf(fp, "%c ",string[j]);
            disarray[m++] = string[j] + trans;
            }
        }
}
/*********************************************************/
hasvowel(string)
    char string[];
{
    int j, k, isvowel;

    for(j = 0; j < strlen(string); j++)
        {
        isvowel = FALSE;
        for(k = 0; k < 5; k++)
            if(toupper(string[j]) == vowels[k] ||
                isalpha(string[j]) == 0)
                isvowel = TRUE;

        if(isvowel == TRUE)
                return(TRUE);
        }
    return(FALSE);
}
/* END OF TXTPARSE.C */
/*=====================================*/
```

# Program execution

```
TXTPARSE.EXE

Filename for input text ? test.txt

Filename for output data ? junk

Filename for Script score ? junk.sc
Do you want a global transposition value? (1) yes 1
Enter transposition value for the array -46
Keep the punctuation? (1) = yes 1

Original complete text:
So i went to a concert the other day.

They were playing a piece by you know who.

It was the same old thing - bash bash bash

clang clang clang

c'mon baby give it to me.
Current string:
So i went to a concert the other day.

It is 38 characters long (including spaces)
The string as integers:
 83 111 105 119 101 110 116 116 111  97  99 111 110  99 101 114
116 116 104 101 111 116 104 101 114 100  97 121  46

Max = 121 Min = 46

it has 11 vowels
it has 17 consonants
it has 1 punctuation
The vowels are:
o i e o a o e e o e a
P    F5   B4   G4   F5   D#4  F5   G4   G4   F5   G4   D#4

The consonants are:
S w n t t c n c r t t h t h r d y
P    C#3  C#6  E5   A#5  A#5  F4   E5   F4   G#5  A#5  A#5  A#4
P    A#5  A#4  G#5  F#4  D#6

The punctuations marks are:
P    C0

There are 9 words total
There are 9 words in this line

------------------------------------------------------

Current string:
They were playing a piece by you know who.


It is 43 characters long (including spaces)
The string as integers:
 84 104 101 121 119 101 114 101 112 108  97 121 105 110 103  97
```

```
     112 105 101  99 101  98 121 121 111 117 107 110 111 119 119 104
     111  46
```

Max = 121 Min = 46

it has 13 vowels
it has 20 consonants
it has 1 punctuation
The vowels are:
e e e a i a i e e o u o o
P   G4   G4   G4   D#4   B4   D#4   B4   G4   G4   F5   B5   F5
P   F5

The consonants are:
T h y w r p l y n g p c b y y k n w w h
P   D3   A#4   D#6   C#6   G#5   F#5   D5   D#6   E5   A4   F#5   F4
P   E4   D#6   D#6   C#5   E5   C#6   C#6   A#4

The punctuations marks are:
P   C0

There are 18 words total
There are 9 words in this line

-------------------------------------------------------

Current string:
It was the same old thing - bash bash bash


It is 43 characters long (including spaces)
The string as integers:
```
     73 116 119  97 115 116 104 101 115  97 109 101 111 108 100 116
    104 105 110 103  45  98  97 115 104  98  97 115 104  98  97 115
    104
```

Max = 119 Min = 45

it has 10 vowels
it has 22 consonants
it has 1 punctuation
The vowels are:
I a e a e o i a a a
P   D#2   D#4   G4   D#4   G4   F5   B4   D#4   D#4   D#4

The consonants are:
t w s t h s m l d t h n g b s h b s h b s h
P   A#5   C#6   A5   A#5   A#4   A5   D#5   D5   F#4   A#5   A#4   E5
P   A4   E4   A5   A#4   E4   A5   A#4   E4   A5   A#4

The punctuations marks are:
-
P   R

There are 28 words total
There are 10 words in this line

-------------------------------------------------------

Current string:
clang clang clang

It is 18 characters long (including spaces)
The string as integers:
 99 108  97 110 103  99 108  97 110 103  99 108  97 110 103

Max = 110 Min = 97

it has 3 vowels
it has 12 consonants
it has 0 punctuation

The vowels are:
a a a
P   D#4   D#4   D#4

The consonants are:
c l n g c l n g c l n g
P   F4    D5    E5    A4    F4    D5    E5    A4    F4    D5    E5    A4

The punctuations marks are:


There are 31 words total
There are 3 words in this line

------------------------------------------------------

Current string:
c'mon baby give it to me.


It is 26 characters long (including spaces)
The string as integers:
  99   39 109 111 110  98  97  98 121 103 105 118 101 105 116 116
111 109 101  46

Max = 121 Min = 39

it has 7 vowels
it has 11 consonants
it has 2 punctuation
The vowels are:
o a i e i o e
P   F5    D#4   B4    G4    B4    F5    G4

The consonants are:
c m n b b y g v t t m
P   F4    D#5   E5    E4    E4    D#6   A4    C6    A#5   A#5   D#5

The punctuations marks are:
'  .
P   R    C0

There are 37 words total
There are 6 words in this line

        *(text c.1987 Rodney Waschka II. Used by permission)

## FUNCTION GROUP: Drivel.c

1. WordSummary( )   MIC 6.30
2. MakeDrivel( )    MIC 6.31
3. ChopWords( )     MIC 6.40
4. ExtractWord( )   MIC 6.39

## Purpose

Reorder the words of an input text file.

## Notes

This program reads a text file a line at a time for input. Each line is "chopped" into words (delimited by white space) and stored. The words are then randomly selected to make "drivel."

## Programming ideas

1. Add functions to the program to randomly rearrange complete lines of text within the output paragraph.
2. Modify MakeDrivel( ) function to allow the program user to build a table containing occurrence probabilities for each of the constituent words in the text.
3. Convert the program to a pattern/process-oriented function group by providing the means for patterned rotation and repetition of words on the original lines of text using techniques similar to those found in Loopgen1( ) MIC 7.1 and Loopgen2( ) MIC 7.2.

## Program source code

```
DRIVEL.C
#include "text.h"
#include "fgetline.c"
main()
{
    int j;
    char string[80];
    FILE *fp;

    printf("\nFilename: ");
        gets(string);
    fp = fopen(string, "r");
    while(!feof(fp))
        {
        fgetline(fp, string, 80);
        puts(string);
        ChopWords(string);
        }
    WordSummary();
    fclose(fp);
```

```c
    fp = fopen("junk.txt", "w");
    MakeDrivel(fp);
    fclose(fp);
}
/*============== MIC 6.30 ==============*/
WordSummary()
{
    int j;
    for(j = 0; j < wct; j++)
        printf("%s\n", words[j]);
} /* end of WordSummary() function */
/*============== MIC 6.31 ==============*/
MakeDrivel(fp)
    FILE *fp;
{
    int j, num, howmany, prt;

    printf("\nHow many words do you want?\t");
    howmany = getnum();
    printf("\nWrite to file? (1) = yes\t");
    prt = getnum();
    randomize();
        for(j = 0; j < howmany; j++)
                {
                num = irand(0, wct - 1);
                printf("%s ", words[num]);
                if((j % 6) == 5)
                  printf("\n");
                if(prt == 1)
                    {
                    fprintf(fp, "%s ", words[num]);
                    if((j % 6) == 5)
                      fprintf(fp, "\n");
                    }
                }
} /* end of MakeDrivel() function */
/*============== MIC 6.39 ==============*/
ExtractWord(string, position)
    char string[];
    int position;
{
    int j = 0;
    char *word;

    word = (char *) malloc(80);
    while(!isspace(string[position]))
        word[j++] = string[position++];
    word[j++] = '\0';
    words[wct++] = word;
    return(position);
} /* end of ExtractWord() function */
/*============== MIC 6.40 ==============*/
ChopWords(string)
    char string[];
{
    int position = 0;
    while(position < strlen(string))
        {
        if(isspace(string[position]))
            position++;
        else
```

```
          position = ExtractWord(string, position);
     }
} /* end of ChopWords() function */
/* END OF DRIVEL.C */
```

# Program execution

```
Filename: test.txt

So i went to a concert the other day.

They were playing a piece by you know who.

It was the same old thing - bash bash bash

clang clang clang

c'mon baby give it to me.


So
i
went
to
a
concert
the
other
day.
They
were
playing
a
piece
by
you
know
who.
It
was
the
same
old
thing
-
bash
bash
bash
clang
clang
clang
c'mon
baby
give
it
to
me.

How many words do you want?    100
Write to file? (1) = yes        2
```

piece was clang who. i piece
the by day. They piece who.
was piece clang clang were other
a to to clang a me.
thing It thing concert know same
me. a piece - it bash
the who. same it bash to
piece the They bash playing me.
bash - to bash the the
a a bash - know clang
went went They bash give it
thing to same the know to
clang who. day. the It old
old the who. the you thing
clang clang the clang They -
thing thing bash They It a
So baby you baby

# 7
# *General composition*

---

## FUNCTION: Loopgen1( )   MIC 7.1

### Purpose

Provide two modes—additive and subtractive—of note loop alteration over a number of copies.

### Notes

This procedural function is oriented toward music in which repeated patterns are subjected to gradual change. It generates a given number of copies (loops) of a source integer sequence while altering loop length. In additive alteration mode, the loop copies begin with a predetermined melodic nucleus and grow longer over successive iterations. In subtractive mode, the first loop copy begins with the entire source sequence and subsequent copies grow shorter with each iteration. The variable "startnum" determines initial loop nucleus size, the variable "factor" controls the number of values added to the nucleus or subtracted from the entire sequence, and the variable "period" tells the subroutine when to advance to the next loop-size. Loop copies are printed out within the function, and are not passed back to the calling program.

### Programming ideas

Include Loopgen1( ) in a program that:

1. generates a sequence of random-order, registrated, 12-tone pitch series,
2. derives integers for the rhythm duration parameter from the first 12-tone series generated in step 1),

3. provides duration values to match the pitches by making length-altered copies of the rhythm integers in additive or subtractive mode,

4. maps the rhythm duration sequence, in retrograde order and properly scaled, to the volume parameter.

## Program source code

```c
/* LOOPGEN1.C  ( additive/subtractive loop alterations) */
#include <stdio.h>
main()
{
 int num[15];
 int j;
 int period = 2;      /*alter loop every other iteration*/
 int factor = 3;      /* alter loop by group of three elements*/
 int startnum = 15;   /* sequence nucleus */
 int notes = 15;      /*number of values in original sequence*/
 int many = 10;       /*number of loop copies to generate*/
 int mode = 0;        /*toggle subtractive mode*/
 void Loopgen1();

 printf("a array of ascending integers\n");
 for (j = 0;j < notes;j++)
     {
      num[j] = j + 1;
      printf("%d ",num[j]);
     }

 /* call loop generator in subtractive mode */
 Loopgen1(num,period,factor,startnum,notes,many,mode);

 mode = 1;                /* toggle additive mode */
 startnum = 1;            /* sequence nucleus */
 factor = 4;              /* change elements factor */

 /* call loop generator in additive mode */
 Loopgen1(num,period,factor,startnum,notes,many,mode);

} /* end of main */
/*=============== MIC 7.1 ===============*/
/* Loopgen1() function  (generates a given number of copies
             of an input sequence while processing it in
             one of two length-altering modes: additive,
             or subtractive */

void Loopgen1(num,period,factor,startnum,notes,many,mode)
int num[],period,factor,startnum,notes,many,mode;
{
 int alter;         /* stores current sequence length */
 int incr = factor;/* stores # of elements to add/subtract*/
 int iter = period;/* counts cycles, controls loop-length*/
 int copies;        /* loop index */
 int dup;           /* loop index */

 if (mode)
     {
      alter = startnum;
```

```
                  printf("\nadditive mode loop processing\n");
                }
            else
       {
        alter = notes;
        printf("\nsubtractive mode loop processing\n");
       }
  for (copies = 0;copies < many;copies++)
       {
        if (copies >= iter)
            {
             if (mode)
                 alter = startnum + incr;
             else
                 alter = notes - incr;
             if (alter > notes)
                 alter = notes;
            }
        for (dup = 0;dup < alter;dup++)
            printf("%d ",num[dup]);
        printf("\n");
        if (copies == many)
            break;
        if (copies < iter)
            continue;
        incr += factor;
        iter  += period;
       }
} /* end of Loopgen1() function */
/*=====================================*/
/* END OF LOOPGEN1.C */
```

## Program execution

LOOPGEN1.EXE

```
a array of ascending integers
1 2 3 4 5 6 7 8 9 10 11 12 13 14 15
subtractive mode loop processing
1 2 3 4 5 6 7 8 9 10 11 12 13 14 15
1 2 3 4 5 6 7 8 9 10 11 12 13 14 15
1 2 3 4 5 6 7 8 9 10 11 12
1 2 3 4 5 6 7 8 9 10 11 12
1 2 3 4 5 6 7 8 9
1 2 3 4 5 6 7 8 9
1 2 3 4 5 6
1 2 3 4 5 6
1 2 3
1 2 3

additive mode loop processing
1
1
1 2 3 4 5
1 2 3 4 5
1 2 3 4 5 6 7 8 9
1 2 3 4 5 6 7 8 9
1 2 3 4 5 6 7 8 9 10 11 12 13
1 2 3 4 5 6 7 8 9 10 11 12 13
1 2 3 4 5 6 7 8 9 10 11 12 13 14 15
1 2 3 4 5 6 7 8 9 10 11 12 13 14 15
```

# FUNCTION: Loopgen2( )   MIC 7.2

## Purpose

Provide systematic rotation of loop elements over a given number of copies; shifted elements may be placed in reverse order.

## Notes

This function is pattern/phase-music oriented. It generates a given number of copies (loops) of an integer sequence while rotating (in forward or reverse order) a predetermined number of loop elements. Control variables are: "many"—the number of altered loop copies to return; "factor"—the number of loop elements to shift from end-of-loop to front-of-loop; and "reverse"—a signal to place the shifted elements in reverse order.

When the procedure is used to produce music that emphasizes the phasing of several layers of pitch loops, it is helpful to add another control variable [as in MIC 7.1:Loopgen1( )] to govern rotation frequency over the total number of returned copies. For example, suppose you wish to subject each parameter of a melodic sequence to independent element rotation. The pitch parameter might shift 2 elements every other copy while the rhythm parameter shifts 3 elements with each copy—and so on. (Note that function array temp[ ] must be congruent with mainroutine array x[ ].)

## Programming ideas

Write an interactive program using Loopgen2( ) that:

1. allows the user to input values for all control variables.
2. provides options to independently rotate pitch, rhythm, articulation, and volume parameter elements of a melodic sequence,
3. formats and files a score consisting of multiple notelists to be played concurrently.

## Program source code

```
/* LOOPGEN2.C  (Loop-element rotation function) */
#include <stdio.h>
main()
{
  int x[16];            /* stores loops */
  int j;                /* loop index */
  int numvals=15;       /* sequence total */
  int factor=6;         /* number of values to shift */
  int many=6;           /* number of loops to return */
  int reverse=1;        /* toggles reverse order shift */
  void Loopgen2();
```

```
        printf("original integer sequence:\n\n");
        for (j = 1;j <= numvals;j++)
            {
            x[j] = j;
            printf("%d ",x[j]);
            }
        printf("\n\n%d %s %d %s %s",many,"copies, with", factor,
               "values shifted \n(reverse order)",
               "during each cycle:\n\n");

        Loopgen2(x,numvals,factor,many,reverse);

} /* end of main */
/*=============== MIC 7.2 ===============*/
/* Loopgen2() function (shifts a specific number of values
                   from the end of a sequence to the beginning
                   while generating a given number of loop copies;
                   shifted values can be placed in retrograde.)*/

void Loopgen2(x,numvals,factor,many,reverse)
int x[],numvals,factor,many,reverse;
{
  int temp[16];/* stores values to be shifted; it must be
                   the same size as main routine array x[].*/
  int copies;  /* loop index */
  int hold;    /* loop index, pointer to array temp[] */
  int group;   /* loop index */
  int shift;   /* loop index, pointer to array x[] */
  int replace; /* loop index, pointer to array x[] */
  int currloop;/* loop index, pointer to array x[] */

    for (copies = 1;copies <= many;copies++)
        {
        for (hold = 0;hold < factor;hold++)
            temp[hold + 1] = x[numvals - hold];
        for (group = 1;group <= factor;group++)
            {
             for (shift = numvals;shift >= 1;shift--)
                x[shift] = x[shift - 1];
            }
        for (replace = 1;replace <= factor;replace++)
            if (reverse)
                x[replace] = temp[replace];
            else
                x[replace] = temp[factor + 1 - replace];
        for (currloop = 1;currloop <= numvals;currloop++)
            printf("%d ",x[currloop]);
        printf("\n\n");
        }
} /* end of Loopgen2() function */
/*===================================*/
/* END OF LOOPGEN2.C */
```

# Program execution

```
LOOPGEN2.EXE

original integer sequence:

1 2 3 4 5 6 7 8 9 10 11 12 13 14 15

6 copies, with 6 values shifted
(reverse order) during each cycle:

15 14 13 12 11 10 1 2 3 4 5 6 7 8 9

9 8 7 6 5 4 15 14 13 12 11 10 1 2 3

3 2 1 10 11 12 9 8 7 6 5 4 15 14 13

13 14 15 4 5 6 3 2 1 10 11 12 9 8 7

7 8 9 12 11 10 13 14 15 4 5 6 3 2 1

1 2 3 6 5 4 7 8 9 12 11 10 13 14 15
```

# FUNCTION GROUP: Primops.c

1. Primintv( )    MIC 7.3
2. Primnum( )    MIC 7.4

## Purpose

Generates 2 arrays:

1. a range-limited prime number list;
2. a list of numeric intervals between the prime numbers.

## Notes

Function Primintv( ) invokes function Primnum( ) to check each ascending consecutive integer within a predetermined range to see if it is prime; if so, array X( ) receives it. Primintv then subtracts the previous prime number from the current one and places the remainder in array Y( ).

Interestingly, shifting the prime number testing range upward increases the interval size range at the high end while preserving the smallest interval size. In rhythmic applications you can harness this characteristic to create a gradual expansion or contraction of duration patterns by generating prime interval sequences derived from contiguous integer ranges.

## Programming ideas

1. Modify the main routine to sequentially generate prime number intervals in the following ranges: 1–300, 300–600, 600–900, 900–1200, 1200–1500. Observe the relative occurrence frequency shift of various numeric interval sizes.
2. Write an interactive program which:

    a. allows the user to input values for the variables "low" and "high"
    b. offers options to scale the returned prime interval array to the range requirements of any musical parameter,
    c. prepares a set of pointers to the requested element table.

## Program source code

```
/* PRIMOPS.C (prime number operations)*/
#include <stdio.h>
#include <math.h>
main()
{
  int x[1000]; /* list of prime numbers */
```

```c
int y[1000]; /* list of numeric intervals between primes */
int j;          /* loop index */
int low = 1; /* smallest integer within test range */
int high = 1000; /* largest integer within teast range */
int pcnt;       /* prime number counter, pointer to x[],y[] */
int Primintv();

printf("prime numbers within range %d to %d :\n",low,high);
pcnt = Primintv(x,y,low,high);
for (j = 0;j < pcnt;j++)
    {
     if (j % 10 == 0)
        printf("\n");
     printf("%d ",x[j]);
    }
printf("\n\nnumeric intervals between primes:\n");
for (j = 0;j < pcnt - 1;j++)
    {
     if (j % 10 == 0)
        printf("\n");
     printf("%d ",y[j]);
    }
printf("\n\n\n");

} /* end of main */
/*=============== MIC 7.3 ===============*/
/* Primintv() function  (creates an array of primes and
                and an array of numeric intervals separating
                the primes */

int Primintv(x,y,low,high)
int x[],y[],low,high;
{
 int pcnt = 0; /* prime number counter */
 int num;       /* number to be tested for prime */
 int prim;      /* flag indicating a prime number */
 int Primnum();

 for (num = low;num <= high;num++)
    {
     prim = Primnum(num);
     if (prim != 1)
        continue;
     x[pcnt] = num;
     if (pcnt >  0)
        y[pcnt - 1] = x[pcnt] - x[pcnt - 1];
     pcnt += 1;
    }
 return(pcnt);
} /* end of Primintv() function */
/*=============== MIC 7.4 ===============*/
/* Primnum() function (locates and returns prime numbers
                        from a stream of ascending integers*/

int Primnum(num)
int num;
{
 int prim = 1; /* prime number flag */
 int divisor;  /* loop index, divisor for prime test */
 int limit;     /* prime test limit */
 float sqrt();
```

```
       limit = sqrt(num * 1.0);
       for (divisor = 2;divisor <= limit;divisor++)
           if (num % divisor == 0)
               {
               prim = 0;
               break;
               }
       return(prim);
   } /* end of Primnum() function */
   /*=====================================*/
   /* END OF PRIMOPS.C */
```

## Program execution

PRIMOPS.EXE

prime numbers within range 1 to 1000 :

```
1 2 3 5 7 11 13 17 19 23
29 31 37 41 43 47 53 59 61 67
71 73 79 83 89 97 101 103 107 109
113 127 131 137 139 149 151 157 163 167
173 179 181 191 193 197 199 211 223 227
229 233 239 241 251 257 263 269 271 277
281 283 293 307 311 313 317 331 337 347
349 353 359 367 373 379 383 389 397 401
409 419 421 431 433 439 443 449 457 461
463 467 479 487 491 499 503 509 521 523
541 547 557 563 569 571 577 587 593 599
601 607 613 617 619 631 641 643 647 653
659 661 673 677 683 691 701 709 719 727
733 739 743 751 757 761 769 773 787 797
809 811 821 823 827 829 839 853 857 859
863 877 881 883 887 907 911 919 929 937
941 947 953 967 971 977 983 991 997
```

numeric intervals between primes:

```
1 1 2 2 4 2 4 2 4 6
2 6 4 2 4 6 6 2 6 4
2 6 4 6 8 4 2 4 2 4
14 4 6 2 10 2 6 6 4 6
6 2 10 2 4 2 12 12 4 2
4 6 2 10 6 6 6 2 6 4
2 10 14 4 2 4 14 6 10 2
4 6 8 6 6 4 6 8 4 8
10 2 10 2 6 4 6 8 4 2
4 12 8 4 8 4 6 12 2 18
6 10 6 6 2 6 10 6 6 2
6 6 4 2 12 10 2 4 6 6
2 12 4 6 8 10 8 10 8 6
6 4 8 6 4 8 4 14 10 12
2 10 2 4 2 10 14 4 2 4
14 4 2 4 20 4 8 10 8 4
6 6 14 4 6 6 8 6
```

# FUNCTION: Trantabl( )   MIC 7.5

## Purpose

Prepare a first-order table of transitional probabilities to determine melodic pitch class order.

## Notes

A two-dimensional matrix holds occurrence frequency probabilities that make the current note choice conditional on the previous choice. The appropriate probabilities are entered in the matrix P( ), either as program DATA statements, or via user INPUT statements.

For output data to be accurate, it is important that the sum of each column be 1.0. Moreover, the data table should be well thought out to prevent situations with no exit. For instance, if in TABLE 7-1 the probability that C follows F is changed to 0.0, the probability that F follows F is changed to 1.0, and the probability that G follows F is changed to 0.0—nothing but the pitch F will be generated once F is selected.

Table 7-1   Example of Concept.

|  |  | Last pitch | | | |
|---|---|---|---|---|---|
|  |  | **C** | **F** | **G** | **B** |
|  | **C** | 0.0 | 0.5 | 0.1 | 0.0 |
| Next | **F** | 0.1 | 0.2 | 0.5 | 0.1 |
| pitch | **G** | 0.6 | 0.3 | 0.1 | 0.5 |
|  | **B** | 0.3 | 0.0 | 0.3 | 0.4 |

Read columns for last pitch, rows for next pitch. For instance, if the last pitch returned was B (col 4), then the probability of the next pitch being B (row 4) is 0.1. This principle can be extended to three, four, or more dimensions, but quickly becomes difficult to comprehend.

## Programming ideas

Write an interactive program based on Trantabl( ) which allows the user to input data for the matrix and apply it to any musical parameter.

## Program source code

```
/* TRANTABL.C (table of 1st-order transitional probs) */
#include <stdio.h>
#include <math.h>
```

```
main()
{
  int startpitch = 2,total = 100;
  void Trantabl();

  Trantabl(startpitch,total);
} /* end of main */
/*=============== MIC 7.5 ================*/
/* Trantabl() function   (generates pitch sequences in
                 conformity with probabilities stored in
                 a 2-dimensional matrix; to change the probs,
                 edit the static float ptabl[][] array. */

void Trantabl(nextpitch,total)
int nextpitch;
{
int j9, k;      /* loop indices */
int seed = -3944;
double u;        /* random number > 0 & < 1.0 */
float t;         /* threshold test value */

/* probability table */
static float ptabl[4][4]=
     { 0.0,.5,0.0,.1,.2,.5,.1,.6,.3,.1,.5,.3,0.0,.3,.4};

/* pitch table */
 static char *pitch[] = {"C ","F ","G ","B "};

srand(seed);
printf("\ncurrent probability table:\n\n");
for (j9 = 0;j9 < 4;j9++)
    {
     for (k = 0;k < 4;k++)
         printf("%.1f    ",ptabl[j9][k]);
     printf("\n");
    }
printf("\n%s%s%s","pitch sequence beginning with ",
       pitch[nextpitch],":\n");
for (j9 = 0;j9 < total;j9++)
    {
     if (j9 % 10 == 0)
         printf("\n");
     printf("%s ",pitch[nextpitch]);
     u = rand() / 32767.;
     t = 0;
     for (k = 0;k < 4;k++)
         {
          t = ptabl[k][nextpitch] + t;
          if(u <= t)
             {
              nextpitch = k;
              break;
             }
         }
    }
} /* end of Trantabl() function */
/*====================================*/
/* END OF TRANTABL.C */
```

# Program execution

```
TRANTABL.C

current probability table:

0.0    0.5    0.0    0.1
0.2    0.5    0.1    0.6
0.3    0.1    0.5    0.3
0.0    0.3    0.4    0.0

pitch sequence beginning with G :

G   B   F   F   C   C   C   C   C   F
F   F   C   F   F   C   G   B   F   F
F   F   C   F   C   G   G   B   F   C
C   F   F   F   C   G   B   G   G   G
G   B   F   C   C   G   G   F   C   C
F   F   C   C   G   G   B   F   F   C
C   C   C   F   C   G   F   C   C   C
F   C   F   C   G   B   F   F   F   F
C   C   F   F   F   F   F   C   G   G
G   G   B   F   C   F   C   G   G   G
```

# FUNCTION GROUP: Valuprob.c

1. Probtabl( )    MIC 7.6
2. Probcalc( )    MIC 7.7

## Purpose

Generate an array of random-order integers distributed in accordance with weights contained in a cumulative probability table.

## Notes

Function Probtabl( ) establishes a table of occurrence frequency probabilities from weights contained in the static integer array wtabl[ ]. Because the weights are relative, the program user need not be concerned with their sum. (Function Probcalc( ) reconciles them with the random number generator range.)

Function Probcalc( ) returns random-order integers 1 – n over a run of n values in relative proportion to probability weights contained in wtabl[ ]. The output array x[ ] serves as a set of pointers to any musical parameter.

## Programming ideas

1. Write a program that:

    a. allows the user to enter values for variables "probs," "total," and array wtabl[ ],
    b. offers an option to read a probability weight disk file to fill wtabl[ ], and
    c. assigns the output set of pointers to any selected parameter element table.

2. Adapt MIC 2.23: Freqtabl( ) to record occurrence frequencies of alphabet letters in a source text. Enter a short poem in English, and use the occurrence frequencies as probability weights for the generation of an array of pitches. Repeat the frequency analysis and pitch generation for poems in French, Italian, and German; observe the respective effects on tonal characteristics.

## Program source code

```
/* VALUPROB.C (reads relative weights into a cumulative
              probability table, then generates an
              integer sequence with occurrence fre-
              quencies in relative proportion to table
              weights.)*/
#include <stdio.h>
main()
```

```
{
 int x[200];
 int j;
 int probs = 5;   /* number of probabilities */
 int total = 200; /* number of integers to return */
 int wsum;        /* sum of probabilities */
 int seed = 31231;
 int Probtabl();
 void Probcalc();
 static int wtabl[5] = {1,5,10,15,20};

 srand(seed);
 wsum = Probtabl(wtabl,probs);
 Probcalc(x,wtabl,probs,total,wsum);
 printf("\nhere is the sequence generated by the table:\n");
 for (j = 0;j < total;j++)
    {
     if (j % 20 == 0)
        printf("\n");
     printf("%d ",x[j]);
    }
} /* end of main */
/*=============== MIC 7.6 ===============*/
/* Probtabl() function  (converts probability table
                         weights to cumulative form) */
int Probtabl(wtabl,probs)
int wtabl[],probs;
{
 int wsum = 0; /* sum of probabilities */
 int k;        /* loop index */

 for (k = 0;k < probs;k++)
    {
     wtabl[k] = wtabl[k] + wsum;
     wsum = wtabl[k];
    }
 return(wsum);
} /* end of Probtabl() function */
/*=============== MIC 7.7 ===============*/
/* Probcalc() function  (generates integers in relative
                         proportion to weights contained
                         in a cumulative table. */
void Probcalc(array1,array2,probs,total,wsum)
int array1[],array2[],probs,total,wsum;
{
 int k,l;   /* loop indices */
 int u;     /* random integers */

 for (k = 0;k < total;k++)
    {
     u = rand() % wsum; /* get normalized random integer */
     for (l = 0;l < probs;l++)
         if (u < array2[l])
            {
             array1[k] = l + 1;
             break;
            }
    }
} /* end Probcalc() function */
/*=======================================*/
/* END OF VALUPROB.C */
```

# Program execution

`VALUPROB.EXE`

`here is the sequence generated by the table:`

```
5 4 4 3 5 4 5 3 5 4 3 3 2 4 5 2 3 4 3 4
3 5 3 5 3 2 5 5 4 4 5 5 5 2 2 4 3 5 4 5
4 5 5 5 3 5 5 5 5 5 1 4 2 1 3 4 2 3 5 5
4 4 5 5 5 4 4 4 5 3 4 3 3 5 5 5 5 4 5 3
5 4 1 4 3 4 4 3 3 5 4 3 5 4 5 5 2 4 4 5
3 2 5 4 5 3 5 3 5 5 5 2 5 4 3 4 4 2 5 2
5 5 2 4 4 4 5 4 4 3 4 3 5 3 3 4 5 5 5 4
5 2 5 2 4 4 5 4 2 3 5 5 2 4 5 4 5 4 3 2
5 3 3 2 5 2 4 4 4 5 5 2 5 4 3 4 5 5 4 4
5 5 3 4 2 3 4 4 5 2 4 5 4 4 4 4 5 4 5 5
```

# FUNCTION: Randwalk( )   MIC 7.8

## Purpose

Simulate a simple, bi-directional random walk which is restricted at upper and lower boundaries.

## Notes

This function tosses a coin to determine each step up or down the consecutive integer series from an input start point. It cannot step-in-place because each decision forces a move.

Repeated values can be obtained by filling an array with integers distributed according to compositional plan, then walking through the array using the output of Randwalk( ) as pointers.

## Programming ideas

1. Write a program that:

   a. reads a composed pitch sequence from a disk file,
   b. assigns the sequence to a program array,
   c. allows the user to select the random walk start location, then
   d. generates an output array consisting of a random walk of n values through the composed pitches,
   e. uses the integers in the output array as literal probability weights for the generation of other musical parameters (use Function Group: VALUPROB.C)

2. Adapt the above program to read a disk text file (add appropriate string handling functions from Chapter 6); allow the user to create an output disk file consisting of random walks through the words of the input file. How does the output of MIC 7.8: Randwalk( ) differ from the output of subroutines MIC 6.3: Randline( ) and MIC 6.7: Randword( )?

## Program source code

```
/* RANDWALK.C (simulates a simple, bi-directional,
                 random walk which is bounded at both ends)*/
#include <stdio.h>
main()
{
  int total = 200;    /* take 200 steps */
  int currloc = 7;    /* start at position seven */
  int seed = -8675;
  void Randwalk();

  srand(seed);
  printf("here is the random walk:\n");
```

```
  Randwalk(total,currloc);
  } /* end of main */
/*=============== MIC 7.8 ===============*/
/* Randwalk() function */
 void Randwalk(total,currloc)
 int total,currloc;
 {
  int dir;        /* step direction */
  int nextstep;   /* step location */
  int j;          /* loop index */
  float u;        /* random number > 0 & < 1.0 */

  for (j =0;j < total;j++)
      {
       if (j % 15 == 0)
         printf("\n");
       printf("%d ",currloc);
       dir = 1;
       u = rand() / 32767.;
       if (u < .5)
         dir = -1;
       nextstep = currloc + dir;
       if (nextstep > 15)
         nextstep = 14;
       else
         if (nextstep < 1)
           nextstep = 2;
       currloc = nextstep;
      }
 } /* end of Randwalk() function */
/*=====================================*/
/* END OF RANDWALK.C */
```

## Program execution

```
here is the random walk:

7 8 9 10 11 10 11 10 11 12 13 14 13 12 11
10 11 12 11 10 9 10 9 10 9 10 11 12 13 12
13 14 15 14 13 14 13 12 11 10 9 10 9 8 9
10 11 12 13 14 13 14 13 12 11 10 9 8 7 8
9 10 11 12 13 14 15 14 13 12 13 12 13 12 13
12 13 14 15 14 13 14 13 12 13 14 13 12 13 12
11 10 11 12 11 12 11 12 13 14 13 12 13 12 11
12 11 10 9 8 9 8 9 10 11 10 11 12 13 12
11 12 11 12 13 12 11 12 11 12 13 14 15 14 13
12 13 14 15 14 13 12 13 14 15 14 15 14 13 14
15 14 15 14 15 14 13 14 15 14 15 14 15 14 15
14 13 14 15 14 13 14 15 14 13 14 15 14 13 14
15 14 15 14 13 12 11 12 13 14 13 12 13 12 13
14 13 14 15 14
```

# FUNCTION: Matwalk( )  MIC 7.9

## Purpose

Simulate a multidirectional random walk within the boundaries of a two-dimensional matrix.

## Notes

This function differs from MIC 7.8: Randwalk( ) in that the walker is free to step up, down, sideways, diagonally, or in-place around a rectangular plane. Vertical/horizontal proportions of the matrix are determined and the walker's start position coordinates are set in the main routine; by reshaping the matrix in various proportions, the program user can influence the character of the number sequence produced by a random walk.

For example, when the values generated by the random walk are to be interpreted as pointers to a registrated pitch element table, the consequences of matrix reconfiguration are significant:

| 1 | 2 | 3 | 4 | 5 | 6 | 7 | 8 | 9 | 10 | 11 | 12 | 13 | 14 | 15 |
|----|----|----|----|----|----|----|----|----|----|----|----|----|----|----|
| 16 | 17 | 18 | 19 | 20 | 21 | 22 | 23 | 24 | 25 | 26 | 27 | 28 | 29 | 30 |
| 31 | 32 | 33 | 34 | 35 | 36 | 37 | 38 | 39 | 40 | 41 | 42 | 43 | 44 | 45 |
| 46 | 47 | 48 | 49 | 50 | 51 | 52 | 53 | 54 | 55 | 56 | 57 | 58 | 59 | 60 |
| 61 | 62 | 63 | 64 | 65 | 66 | 67 | 68 | 69 | 70 | 71 | 72 | 73 | 74 | 75 |
| 76 | 77 | 78 | 79 | 80 | 81 | 82 | 83 | 84 | 85 | 86 | 87 | 88 | 89 | 90 |

The 15 × 6 matrix produces melodic interval-sizes of magnitude (+ or –) 1, 14, 15, & 16 exclusively.

| 1 | 2 | 3 | 4 |
|----|----|----|----|
| 5 | 6 | 7 | 8 |
| 9 | 10 | 11 | 12 |
| 13 | 14 | 15 | 16 |
| 17 | 18 | 19 | 20 |
| 21 | 22 | 23 | 24 |
| 25 | 26 | 27 | 28 |
| 29 | 30 | 31 | 32 |
| 33 | 34 | 35 | 36 |

The 4 × 9 matrix produces melodic interval-sizes of magnitude (+ or –) 1, 3, 4, & 5 exclusively.

## Programming ideas

1. Modify the main routine to read contents of an integer data file into the two-dimensional matrix.
2. Assign the output resulting from variously configured matrices as pointers to rhythm, volume, and articulation element tables.

# Program source code

```
/* MATWALK.C (2-dimensional random walk around a matrix)*/
#include <stdio.h>

#define rows 10    /* (edit row and column sizes to try */
#define cols 10    /*  other matrix proportions) */
main()
{
 int w[rows][cols];      /* random walk matrix */
 int count = 0;          /* aids screen printing ot matrix*/
 int total = 200;        /* take 200 steps */
 int j,k;                /* loop indices */
 int xloc = 5,yloc = 5;  /* walk start coordinates */
 int seed = 19274;
 void Matwalk();

 srand(seed);
 printf("the matrix for this walk:\n");
 for (j = 0;j < rows;j++)
     {
     for (k = 0;k < cols;k++)
         {
         w[j][k] = (j * cols) + k + 1;
         count++;
         if (count % cols== 0)
             printf("%d\n",w[j][k]);
         else
             printf("%d  ", w[j][k]);
         if (count <= 9)
             printf(" ");
         }
     }
 printf("\nstart coordinates are: row %d; column %d;\n",
          xloc+1,yloc+1);
 Matwalk(w,total,xloc,yloc);
} /* end of main */
/*=============== MIC 7.9 ===============*/
/* Matwalk() function */
void Matwalk(w,total,xloc,yloc)
int w[rows][cols],total,xloc,yloc;
{
 int xstep; /* step direction random integer: -1,0,or +1 */
 int ystep; /* step direction random integer: -1,0,or +1 */
 int k;     /* loop index */

 for (k = 0;k <  total;k++)
     {
     if (k % 15 == 0)
         printf("\n");
     printf("%d ",w[xloc][yloc]);
     xstep = rand() % 3 - 1;
     ystep = rand() % 3 - 1;
     xloc += xstep;
     yloc += ystep;
     if (xloc < 0)
       xloc = 1;
     else
       if (xloc >= rows)
         xloc = rows-1;
     if(yloc < 0)
```

```
        yloc = 1;
      else
        if (yloc >= cols)
          yloc = cols-1;
    }
  printf("\n\n");
} /* end of Matwalk() function */
/*==================================*/
/* END OF MATWALK.C */
```

# Program execution

MATWALK.EXE

```
the matrix for this walk:
1    2    3    4    5    6    7    8    9    10
11   12   13   14   15   16   17   18   19   20
21   22   23   24   25   26   27   28   29   30
31   32   33   34   35   36   37   38   39   40
41   42   43   44   45   46   47   48   49   50
51   52   53   54   55   56   57   58   59   60
61   62   63   64   65   66   67   68   69   70
71   72   73   74   75   76   77   78   79   80
81   82   83   84   85   86   87   88   89   90
91   92   93   94   95   96   97   98   99   100

start coordinates are: row 6; column 6;

56 47 47 58 58 59 48 37 26 25 14 25 14 14 23
23 24 13 3 3 2 11 2 11 1 2 11 2 1 2
2 13 24 25 35 25 14 4 13 4 13 14 13 12 21
21 11 12 11 2 12 23 23 32 33 33 33 42 33 43
33 43 54 43 43 54 64 75 75 74 74 85 84 73 63
64 53 52 63 74 73 62 63 54 63 53 63 72 71 72
72 83 83 92 91 91 81 81 81 71 72 63 64 65 64
53 63 62 63 54 54 53 62 61 72 71 72 71 81 81
82 81 81 72 72 71 62 63 62 52 51 42 51 52 52
51 62 51 42 42 33 42 32 32 33 44 34 43 52 51
62 62 72 81 72 73 82 92 91 92 93 84 84 75 64
54 53 62 52 43 34 24 13 2 1 12 13 13 23 24
35 24 34 23 23 13 23 14 25 35 24 25 15 5 16
6 15 25 14 14
```

# FUNCTION: Voss( )   MIC 7.10

## Purpose

Generate an integer array that exhibits fractal ($1/f$ fractional noise) characteristics.

## Notes

This function generates sequential integer patterns which are self-similar in nature. Many composers consider fractal patterns to be more useful than other types of randomly generated sequences because they seem to closely resemble the patterns found in traditional music.

Subroutine output consistently reflects a high degree of microformal/macroformal relatedness, in that patterns on the large scale are similar to internal patterns. Moreover, a group of values selected from the end of a sequence will seem to be close variants of a group of integers selected from the beginning of the same sequence. (To test this out, compare the number and type of melodic interval-sizes present between the internal values of each sequence chunk.)

Each $1/f$ value returned by the function is conditional on the previous generated, and all constituent values correlate logarithmically with the past, which is why the process is said to have long-term memory.

## Programming ideas

1. Write an interactive program that allows the user to enter element tables and control variables, and provides options to generate and file the pitch, rhythm, volume, and articulation parameters of a fractal melodic line. Transcribe the melody for a solo instrument such as a clarinet.
2. Write an interactive program that builds and files a polyphonic musical texture using the fractal algorithm. Perform the score on a digital synthesizer.
3. Run the above programs using carefully thought out input to provide material for a composition for solo instrument and synthesizer.

## Program source code

```
/* VOSS.C (Fractals routine)*/
#include <stdio.h>
main()
{
  int x[200];
  int last = 24;    /* last value generated */
  int total = 200,seed = 3111;
  void Voss();
```

```
    srand(seed);
    printf("\nhere is the resulting fractal sequence:\n");
    Voss(x,total,last);
} /* end of main */
/*=============== MIC 7.10 ===============*/
/* Voss() fractals function   (generates 1/f fractional
                                noise patterns) */
void Voss(x,total,last)
int x[50],total,last;
{
 int fract;       /* current 1/f value */
 int halfvals;    /* 1/2 the number of possible values */
 int temp;        /* temporary computation storage */
 int k;           /* loop index */
 float prob;      /* 1/number of possible values */
 float u;         /* randum number > 0 & < 1.0 */

 for (k = 0;k < total;k++)
     {
      if (k % 15 == 0)
         printf("\n");
      fract = 0;
      halfvals = 16;
      prob = .03125;
      while (halfvals >= 1)
          {
           temp = last/halfvals;
           if (temp == 1)
              last=last - halfvals;
           u = rand() / 32767.;
           if (u < prob)
              temp = 1 - temp;
           fract = fract + temp * halfvals;
           halfvals /= 2;
           prob *= 2.;
          }
      x[k] = fract;
      printf("%d ",x[k]);
      last = fract;
     }
} /* end of Voss() fractals function */
/*====================================*/
/* END OF VOSS.C */
```

## Program execution

VOSS.EXE

here is the resulting fractal sequence:

```
27 30 29 28 29 29 30 30 31 31 30 28 28 30 29
31 25 28 31 30 25 26 26 26 27 30 26 26 26 26
27 27 24 26 27 26 25 25 8 12 12 13 12 13 13
12 31 25 26 8 0 21 21 20 23 23 23 22 23 21
23 21 22 23 18 17 16 21 22 20 23 31 30 29 29
31 30 31 28 28 30 30 30 30 30 22 31 30 31 31
31 31 29 30 30 28 24 26 26 24 24 25 25 8 15
14 14 12 13 15 15 13 12 12 12 10 8 10 9 9
9 8 9 9 11 15 15 15 15 14 15 30 28 24 25
```

```
29  25  25  25  24  25  26  28  28  31  30  31  30  28  28
29  31  28  20  20  25  24  25  25  24  24  25  24  24  25
28  31  29  28  29  31  30  31  29  30  30  21  21  22  22
23  23  30  31  29  28  29  14  14  12  12  15  15  12  28
29  29  25  29  28
```

# FUNCTION GROUP: Rdintchd.c

1. Rdintchd( )   MIC 7.11
2. Printpitch( )   MIC 3.1

## Purpose

Generate a group of variable-density chords built from constrained, random-order interval-sizes.

## Notes

Designed to provide a background chordfile from which melodic lines will be extracted, Rdintchd( ) builds varying length vertical structures from low pitch to high pitch via random interval selection from a circumscribed, continuous interval-size range. Chord root (C to B), starting octave (1 – 3), number of chord members (3 – 9), and interval range limits (1 – 12) are randomly chosen within the main routine. Final selection of each upward interval is made in conformity with values passed from the main routine.

To illustrate, if variable "small" is set to 4, and variable "large" is set to 7, then the resultant chords will be composed entirely of random-order major third, perfect fourth, augmented fourth and perfect fifth intervals.

## Programming ideas

1. Modify the main routine to accept user input for the primary control variables; don't forget to add prompts and error detection statements to alert the user when they have entered values that will cause program failure (too many wide intervals over a large number of chordtones will quickly go out of pitch table range).
2. Add a program routine to file the chords on disk; place flags in the file after each chord to signal chord articulation.
3. Add a program routine to randomly extract the chords from a file, display them on the CRT, and generate random-order melodic pitches based on the chord sequence.
4. Apply the integer values of the chordfile as pointers to other musical parameter tables.

## Program source code

```
/* RDINTCHD.C (generates a group of variable-density chords
                having in common a random-order interval
                aggregate. */
#include <stdio.h>
main()
{
  int j; /* loop index */
```

```
      int chordtotal = 15;
      int seed = 9121;
      void Rdintchd();
      int root;          /* lowest chordtone "C" - "B" */
      int octave;        /* chord root octave register */
      int chordmems;     /* number of tones in chord */
      int small;         /* smallest allowable interval in chord */
      int large;         /* largest allowable interval in chord */
      int intvalrange;  /* range of allowable interval-sizes */

      srand(seed);
      for (j = 0;j < chordtotal;j++)
         {
         printf("chord %d:",j+1);
         /* select random values   */
         /* for primary parameters */
         root = rand() % 12 + 1;
         octave = rand() % 3 + 1;
         chordmems = rand() % 7 + 3;
         small = rand() % 2 + 1;
         large = rand() % 6 + 5;
         intvalrange = large - small + 1;

         Rdintchd(root,octave,chordmems,small,intvalrange);
         printf("\n");
         }
   } /* end of main */
/*=============== MIC 7.11 ===============*/
/* Rdintchd() function */
void Rdintchd(root,octave,chordmems,small,intvalrange)
int root,octave,chordmems,small,intvalrange;
{
  int intval,chordtone,k;

  static char *pitch[] = {
     "C0 ","C#0","D0 ","D#0","E0 ","F0 ","F#0","G0 ","G#0",
     "A0 ","A#0","B0 ","C1 ","C#1","D1 ","D#1","E1 ","F1 ",
     "F#1","G1 ","G#1","A1 ","A#1","B1 ","C2 ","C#2","D2 ",
     "D#2","E2 ","F2 ","F#2","G2 ","G#2","A2 ","A#2","B2 ",
     "C3 ","C#3","D3 ","D#3","E3 ","F3 ","F#3","G3 ","G#3",
     "A3 ","A#3","B3 ","C4 ","C#4","D4 ","D#4","E4 ","F4 ",
     "F#4","G4 ","G#4","A4 ","A#4","B4 ","C5 ","C#5","D5 ",
     "D#5","E5 ","F5 ","F#5","G5 ","G#5","A5 ","A#5","B5 ",
     "C6 ","C#6","D6 ","D#6","E6 ","F6 ","F#6","G6 ","G#6",
     "A6 ","A#6","B6 ","C7 "   };
  chordtone = root;
  for (k = 0;k < chordmems;k++)
     {
     printf("%s ",pitch[chordtone + ((octave-1)*12)]);
     intval = rand() % intvalrange + small;
     chordtone = chordtone + intval;
     }
  printf("\n");
} /* end of Rdintchd() function */
/*====================================*/
/* END OF RDINTCHD.C */
```

# Program execution

```
RDINTCHD.EXE

chord 1:C#0 G#0 D1

chord 2:E0   F#0 B0

chord 3:A2   C3   E3   D4   A4   C5   A#5 D#6 F6

chord 4:A#2 C3   F3   A#3

chord 5:B1   D2   F#2 G2   B2   D3   E3   F3   A3

chord 6:G#1 C#2 D#2 G2   B2   D3

chord 7:F0   A#0 D#1 F1

chord 8:C3   F3   A#3 C4   F#4 B4   C5   F#5

chord 9:E1   A1   C2

chord 10:B0   D1   A1

chord 11:A0   B0   C#1 G1   A#1 F2   C3   F3

chord 12:C2   D2   F2   C3   D#3 F3   G#3 D#4

chord 13:F#2 C#3 F#3 B3   D#4 B4   D5

chord 14:D#1 F1   B1   C2   F#2 A2   A#2

chord 15:F0   G#0 D#1 F1   B1
```

# FUNCTION: Octscale( )   MIC 7.12

## Purpose

Generate registrated, octave-repeating, scale/gamut segments derived from an input interval array.

## Notes

Octscale( ) is similar to MIC 7.11: Rdintchd( ) in that it returns varying length pitch sequences arranged in low to high order; however, the intent here is to prepare scales/gamuts identical in interval content from octave-to-octave as a resource for an external melody generation procedure.

The function first selects scale start pitch (tonic) and start octave, then determines scale segment length before computing the gamut pitches (dictated by interval array gamints[ ]). The process continues until the number of segments required by "segtotal" is reached, whereupon the process repeats for each of the unique interval sets called for by "gamuts."

You can easily convert this subroutine group to interactive use, but statements must be added to prevent the user from requesting scales/gamuts that exceed pitch element table boundaries.

## Programming ideas

1. Modify the main routine to prompt user input for array gamints[ ] and variables "gamuts," "segtotal," and "intotal."
2. Modify MIC 7.12: Octscale( ) to prompt user input for variables "tonic," "startoctave," and "scalemens."
3. Write an interactive program that includes MIC 7.11: Rdintchd( ) and MIC 7.12: Octscale( ); provide additional code to file the output on disk.

## Program source code

```
/* OCTSCALE.C (generates octave-repeating scales/gamuts) */
#include <stdio.h>
main()
{
  int gamints[11]; /* array of interval sizes in 1/2 steps */
  int j, j1, k;    /* loop indices */
  int intotal = 6; /* current # of intervals in gamints[] */
  int gamuts = 3;  /* number of unique gamuts to generate */
  int segtotal = 3;/* scale segments to return per gamut */
  int highoctave;  /* upper octave-register limit */
  int exceed;      /* flags interval set octave over-run */
  int seed = 9132;
  void Octscale();

  srand(seed);
```

```
      for (j = 0;j < gamuts;j++)
          {
          printf("scale gamut %d interval set:\n",j+1);
          highoctave = 7;
          exceed = 0;
          do {
              exceed = 0;
              for (k = 0;k < intotal;k++)
                  {
                   gamints[k] = rand() % 3 + 1;
                   exceed += gamints[k];
                  }
              }
          while (exceed > 11);
          for (j1 = 0;j1 < intotal;j1++)
              printf("%d ",gamints[j1]);
          Octscale(gamints,highoctave,intotal,segtotal);
          }
} /* end of main */
/*=============== MIC 7.12 ===============*/
/* Octscale() function (generates octave-repeating scales
                    from a set of intervals) */
void Octscale(gamints,highoctave,intotal,segtotal)
int gamints[],highoctave,intotal,segtotal;
{
 int count;        /* tabulates chordtone generation */
 int tonic;        /* lowest scale/gamut tone */
 int scaletone;    /* next scale/gamut member */
 int startoctave;  /* scale segment tonic register */
 int scalemems;    /* number of tones in current segment */
 int k,l,m;        /* loop indices */
 static char *pitch[] = {
     "C0 ","C#0","D0 ","D#0","E0 ","F0 ","F#0","G0 ","G#0",
     "A0 ","A#0","B0 ","C1 ","C#1","D1 ","D#1","E1 ","F1 ",
     "F#1","G1 ","G#1","A1 ","A#1","B1 ","C2 ","C#2","D2 ",
     "D#2","E2 ","F2 ","F#2","G2 ","G#2","A2 ","A#2","B2 ",
     "C3 ","C#3","D3 ","D#3","E3 ","F3 ","F#3","G3 ","G#3",
     "A3 ","A#3","B3 ","C4 ","C#4","D4 ","D#4","E4 ","F4 ",
     "F#4","G4 ","G#4","A4 ","A#4","B4 ","C5 ","C#5","D5 ",
     "D#5","E5 ","F5 ","F#5","G5 ","G#5","A5 ","A#5","B5 ",
     "C6 ","C#6","D6 ","D#6","E6 ","F6 ","F#6","G6 ","G#6",
     "A6 ","A#6","B6 ","C7 "   };

   for (k = 0;k < segtotal;k++)
       {
       /* select random values for the control parameters */
       tonic = rand() % 12 + 1;
       startoctave = rand() % 3 + 1;
       scalemems = rand() % 12 + 4;
       printf("\nscale segment %d = %d notes\n",k+1,scalemems);
       count = 0;
       for (l = startoctave - 1;l < highoctave;l++)
           {
           scaletone = tonic;
           for (m = 0;m <= intotal;m++)
               {
               printf("%s ",pitch[scaletone +(l *12)]);
               count++;
               if (count == scalemems)
                   break;
               if (m >= intotal)
```

```
            break;
          scaletone=scaletone + gamints[m];
              }
        if (count == scalemems)
           break;
        }
    }
 printf("\n");
}/* end of Octscale() function */
/*=====================================*/
/* END OF OCTSCALE.C */
```

## Program execution

```
scale gamut 1 interval set:
3 1 3 2 1 1
scale segment 1 = 11 notes
B1   D2   D#2 F#2 G#2 A2   A#2 B2   D3   D#3 F#3
scale segment 2 = 5 notes
D2   F2   F#2 A2   B2
scale segment 3 = 6 notes
G0   A#0 B0   D1   E1   F1
scale gamut 2 interval set:
2 3 1 1 1 3
scale segment 1 = 13 notes
C#0 D#0 F#0 G0   G#0 A0   C1   C#1 D#1 F#1 G1   G#1 A1
scale segment 2 = 7 notes
D2   E2   G2   G#2 A2   A#2 C#3
scale segment 3 = 6 notes
D1   E1   G1   G#1 A1   A#1
scale gamut 3 interval set:
1 1 2 3 1 3
scale segment 1 = 13 notes
G1   G#1 A1   B1   D2   D#2 F#2 G2   G#2 A2   B2   D3   D#3
scale segment 2 = 5 notes
D1   D#1 E1   F#1 A1
scale segment 3 = 13 notes
B2   C3   C#3 D#3 F#3 G3   A#3 B3   C4   C#4 D#4 F#4 G4
```

# FUNCTION: Intgam( )   MIC 7.13

## Purpose

Generate a group of variable-density gamuts/chords from an input interval array.

## Notes

This function is a hybrid version of MIC 7.11: Rdintchd( ) and MIC 7.12: Octscale( ). It returns gamuts based on a fixed set of random-order intervals, but the group of intervals need not be octave-constrained. (The interval sequence will simply be reiteratively applied measuring current pitch outcome against the previous pitch.)

Although the main routine generates random values for "gamints[ ]," "root," "octave," and "chordmems," an interactive version of the function would optionally allow the user to determine these values.

## Programming ideas

1. Write an interactive program that:

   a. includes functions MIC 7.11: Rdintchd( ), MIC 7.12: Octscale( ), and MIC 7.13: Intgam( ),
   b. offers the program user three methods of generating scale/gamut/chord sequences, plus a fourth option to manually enter the individual pitches of each sequence,
   c. places end-of-segment flags in the output array,
   d. files on disk the complete set of scales/chords produced by a single program run.

2. Write a program that individually extracts the sequences from a file and passes them to a melody generation subroutine.

## Program source code

```
/* INTGAM.C (generates non-octave-repeating gamuts/chords
            derived from an interval set) */
#include <stdio.h>
main()
{
  int gamints[12]; /* array of interval-sizes in 1/2-steps */
  int j;           /* loop index */
  int intotal = 6; /* number of intervals in gamints[] */
  int chdtotal = 5;/* number of chord/gamuts to return */
  int root;        /* lowest chord/gamut member */
  int octave;      /* start octave register */
  int chordmems;   /* number of pitches in each chord/gamut*/
  int seed = 21;
  void Intgam();
```

```
      srand(seed);
      for (j = 0;j < intotal;j++)
          gamints[j] = rand() % 3 + 1; /* get intervals */
      for (j = 0;j < chdtotal;j++)
          {
           printf("chord %d\n",j+1);
           root = rand() %12 + 1;      /* get random start pitch */
           octave = rand() % 3 + 1; /* get random start octave */
           chordmems = rand() % 10 + 6; /* get gamut-length */
           Intgam(gamints,root,octave,chordmems,intotal);
           printf("\n");
          }
} /* end of main */
/*=============== MIC 7.13 ==============*/
/* Intgam() function */
void Intgam(gamints,root,octave,chordmems,intotal)
int gamints[],root,octave,chordmems,intotal;
{
 int count,chordtone,k,l;

 static char *pitch[] = {
     "C0 ","C#0","D0 ","D#0","E0 ","F0 ","F#0","G0 ","G#0",
     "A0 ","A#0","B0 ","C1 ","C#1","D1 ","D#1","E1 ","F1 ",
     "F#1","G1 ","G#1","A1 ","A#1","B1 ","C2 ","C#2","D2 ",
     "D#2","E2 ","F2 ","F#2","G2 ","G#2","A2 ","A#2","B2 ",
     "C3 ","C#3","D3 ","D#3","E3 ","F3 ","F#3","G3 ","G#3",
     "A3 ","A#3","B3 ","C4 ","C#4","D4 ","D#4","E4 ","F4 ",
     "F#4","G4 ","G#4","A4 ","A#4","B4 ","C5 ","C#5","D5 ",
     "D#5","E5 ","F5 ","F#5","G5 ","G#5","A5 ","A#5","B5 ",
     "C6 ","C#6","D6 ","D#6","E6 ","F6 ","F#6","G6 ","G#6",
     "A6 ","A#6","B6 ","C7 "   };

 count = 0;
 chordtone = root + ((octave-1) * 12);
   do
     {
      for (l = 0;l < intotal;l++)
          {
           printf("%s ",pitch[chordtone]);
           count++;
           if (count == chordmems)
               break;
           chordtone += gamints[l];
          }
     }
   while (count != chordmems);
}/* end of Intgam() function */
/*====================================*/
/* END OF INTGAM.C */
```

## Program execution

```
INTGAM.EXE

chord 1
G0  G#0 A#0 C1  C#1 D1  D#1 E1  F#1 G#1 A1  A#1 B1
chord 2
A#0 B0  C#1 D#1 E1  F1
```

```
chord 3
B0  C1   D1   E1   F1   F#1 G1   G#1 A#1 C2   C#2 D2   D#2 E2
chord 4
D1   D#1 F1   G1   G#1 A1   A#1 B1   C#2 D#2 E2   F2   F#2 G2
chord 5
A#2 B2   C#3 D#3 E3   F3   F#3 G3   A3   B3   C4   C#4 D4   D#4 F4
```

# FUNCTION GROUP: Rhyprops.c

1. Parstore( )    MIC 2.4
2. Parxtrct( )    MIC 2.5
3. Rhyprops( )   MIC 7.14

## Purpose

Convert rhythmic proportions into note durations.

## Notes

One important method of dealing with time articulation within a composition is to conceive a sequence of proportional rhythmic relationships to be translated into attack points or note durations. Although the serial timepoint system derives its values from details within a set of integers, the proportional method takes a more global approach: it first describes what the relationships will be among the rhythmic details, then computes the final note durations. Because serial procedures act upon proportional rhythmic flow, results are produced that differ from those of the timepoint system. (Refer to output which follows the program listing.)

Proportion information consists of three parts. For example, 1:4:8 means that there will be one duration that will occupy the amount of time taken by four one-eighth note durations. Inversely, 4:1:8 means that four notes will equally divide the amount of time taken by a one-eighth note. The output is expressed as fractions of a whole note. For example, $4/1$ represents a duration equal to four whole notes; $1/4$ means a duration equal to one quarter of a whole note.

To illustrate this concept, Parstore( ) function selects three rhythmic proportions for conversion to rhythm values; you can adapt it to accept a proportion series from the keyboard by adding an array to hold the input.

To prevent the return of overly complex fractions, the following guidelines should be observed:

When value 1 is larger than value 2 (e.g., 9:8), value 2 should conform to one of the following numbers:

$$1,2,4,8,16.$$

When value 2 is larger than value 1 (e.g., 4:9), value 1 should conform to one of the above numbers.

## Programming ideas

1. Modify the main routine to accept keyboard input of all control variables.
2. Add file-writing code to store the output.

# Program source code

```
/* RHYPROPS.C (rhythmic proportion conversion program */
#include <stdio.h>
main()
{
  double c[20];     /* list of rhythm proportions */
  int total = 3;    /* number of items in each proportion */
  int e = 0;        /****  loop  ********************/
  int f = total-1;  /********  control  **************/
  int i = 0;        /****************  parameters ****/
  int g = 1;        /********************************/
  void Parstore(),Parxtrct();

  Parstore(c,total);
  printf("\noriginal form:\n");
  Parxtrct(c,i,f,e,g);
  printf("\nretrograde form:\n");
  i = total-1;      /********   adjust    **********/
  f = 0;            /******** loop control **********/
  g = -1;           /******** parameters   **********/
  Parxtrct(c,i,f,e,g);
  printf("\ninverted form:\n");
  e = 1;            /********   adjust    **********/
  i = 0;            /******** loop control **********/
  f = total-1;      /******** parameters   **********/
  g = 1;            /********              **********/
  Parxtrct(c,i,f,e,g);
  printf("\nretrograde inverted form:\n");
  i = total-1;      /********   adjust    **********/
  f = 0;            /******** loop control **********/
  g = -1;           /******** parameters   **********/
  Parxtrct(c,i,f,e,g);
} /* end of main */
/*=============== MIC 2.4 ================*/
/* Parstore() function (adapted to program specs) */
void Parstore(array,total)
double array[20];
int total;
{
  int k,base;
  double r1 = 0,r2 = 0;  /* part1 & part 2 of proportion */
  for (k = 0;k < total;k++)
    {
      r1 = (k+1) * (k+1);  /* load arbitrary proportion*/
      r2 = (k+1) + 3.0; /* load arbitrary proportion*/
      base = 8;          /*load metrical base*/
      printf("selected proportion -  %.0f:",r1);
      printf("%.0f\n",r2);
      printf("metrical base = %d\n",base);
      r1 = r1 * 1000000.;
      r2 = r2 * 1000.;
      array[k] = r1 + r2 + base;
    }
  } /* end of Parstore() function */
/*=============== MIC 2.5 ================*/
/* Parxtrct() function (adapted to program specs) */
void Parxtrct(c,i,f,e,g)
double c[];
int i,f,e,g;

{
```

```c
      double d;
      int r1,r2,base,k,Rhyprops();

      for (k = i;;k +=g)
        {
          d = c[k];
          d = d / 1000000.;
          r1 = d;
          r2 = (d - r1) * 1000;
          d = d * 1000.;
          base = (d - (int)d) * 1000. + .5;
          Rhyprops(r1,r2,base,e);
          if (k == f)
              break;
        }
}  /* end of Parxtrct() function */
/*=============== MIC 7.14 ==============*/
/* Rhyprops() function (convert rhythm proportions to
                        note duration values expressed
                        as fractions of a whole note) */
int Rhyprops(r1,r2,base,e)
int r1,r2,base,e;
{
int num;      /* converted duration fraction numerator */
int temp;     /* temporary computation storage */
int l;        /* loop index */
float den;    /*  converted duration fraction denominator */

if (e == 1)
    {
     temp = r1;
     r1 = r2;
     r2 = temp;
    }
if (r1 < r2)
    {
     den = (float)r2 / r1;
     while ((int)den != den)
           {
            den = den * 2.;
            base = base * 2;
           }
     for (l = 1;l <= r1;l++)
         printf("%.0f/%d ",den,base);
     printf("\n");
     return;
    }
 num = 1;
 den = r1 * base / r2;
 while ((int)den != den)
     {
      num = num * 2;
      den = den * 2.;
     }
 for (l = 1;l <= r1;l++)
     printf("%d/%.0f ",num,den);
 printf("\n");
 return;
}  /* end of Rhyprops() function */
/*====================================*/
/* END OF RHYPROS.C */
```

# Program execution

```
RHYPROPS.EXE

selected proportion -   1:4
metrical base = 8
selected proportion -   4:5
metrical base = 8
selected proportion -   9:6
metrical base = 8

original form:
4/8
5/32 5/32 5/32 5/32
1/12 1/12 1/12 1/12 1/12 1/12 1/12 1/12 1/12

retrograde form:
1/12 1/12 1/12 1/12 1/12 1/12 1/12 1/12 1/12
5/32 5/32 5/32 5/32
4/8

inverted form:
1/32 1/32 1/32 1/32
1/10 1/10 1/10 1/10 1/10
3/16 3/16 3/16 3/16 3/16 3/16

retrograde inverted form:
3/16 3/16 3/16 3/16 3/16 3/16
1/10 1/10 1/10 1/10 1/10
1/32 1/32 1/32 1/32
```

## FUNCTION GROUP: Polyrhy.c

1. Polyrhy( )   MIC 7.15
2. Durred( )    MIC 2.10

## Purpose

Generate multiple, polyrhythmic/metric, random-order, synchronously terminating, rhythm duration sequences on four selectable complexity levels.

## Notes

The operation of Polyrhy( ) is inversely similar to the method musicians use to figure out how to count a particular rhythm pattern. It computes the requested number of durations by subdividing and randomly regrouping the number of metrical pulse values required to fill the specific number of whole notes indicated by the variable "timescale." The variable "level" selects the degree of pulse subdivision required to produce a particular complexity level. (Smaller pulse subdivisions and subsequent random micropulse regroupings produce patterns that are more aperiodic in nature.) The variable "m1" is the median—the metric/rhythmic base value of the duration sequence; for example, 4 = one-quarter whole note, 5 = one-fifth whole note, 7 = one-seventh whole note, etc. Computed rhythm durations are reduced to lowest terms (consistent with the metrical base) by Function Durred( ).

The main routine is set up to output four layers of rhythm durations, each of a different meter, length, and complexity level. Variables "total," "median," and "level" grow larger with each loop iteration, but "timescale" remains constant to ensure that multiple length duration sequences will end synchronously.

## Programming ideas

1. Modify the main routine to be interactive, and add a function to file the output sequences on disk.
2. Write a program that invokes MIC 7.15: Polyrhy( ) and MIC 7.2: Loopgen2( ) to process duration sequences, then assigns them to pitch sequences generated by another function such as MIC 7.5: Trantabl( ).

## Program source code

```
/* POLYRHY.C (Polyrhythmic/metric duration
              sequence generator)*/
#include <stdio.h>
main()
{
```

```c
int j;              /* loop index */
int total = 10;     /* number of durations to return */
int m1 = 3;         /* metrical base value */
int level = 1;      /* rhythm complexity level (1-2-4-8) */
int timescale = 10; /* arbitrary time frame */
int seed = 4544;
void Polyrhy();

srand(seed);
for (j = 0;j < 4;j++)
    {
    printf("\npass %d\n",j+1);
    printf("number of durations in rhythm sequence =%d\n",
          total);
    printf("median = %d\n",m1);
    printf("timescale = %d (scale = 1 - 10)\n",timescale);
    printf("level = %d (from a choice of 1-2-4-8)\n",level);
    Polyrhy(total,timescale,m1,level);
    level += level;
    total += 10;
    m1++;
    }
} /* end of main */
/*=============== MIC 7.15 ===============*/
/* Polyrhy() function */
void Polyrhy(total,timescale,m1,level)
int total,timescale,m1,level;
{
int dur[200];       /* stores duration numerators */
int newmed;         /* reduced duration fraction denominator */
int k,l;            /* loop indices */
int odd;            /* flag for odd number of values in sequ.*/
int sum;            /* total micropulses in raw sequence */
int base;           /* number of micropulses to distribute */
int median;         /* metrical base value (3,4,5,7,9,etc.)*/
int factor;         /* determinant of random integer range */
int range;          /* span of random integers */
int wedge;          /* low limit of random integers */
int rcomp;          /* stores computation over- or under-run*/
int u1, u2, u3;     /* random integers */
int Durred();

odd = 0;
sum = 0;
median = m1;
base = median * timescale;
if (total == 1)
    {
    printf("%d\n",timescale);
    return;
    }
if (timescale - total > 0)
    {
    if (base / 2.0 != base / 2)
        {
        base = base - 1;
        odd = m1;
        }
    for (k = 0;k < 100;k++)
        {
```

```c
            if (base/2.0 != base/2 || median/2.0 != median/2)
                break;
            if (total <= base / 2)
                {
                 median /= 2;
                 base /= 2;
                }
            else
                break;
            }
        }
    else
        {
        for (k = 1;k <= 30;k++)
            {
            if (total > base)
                {
                median *= 2;
                base *= 2;
                }
            else
                break;
            }
        }
    base *= level;
    median *= level;
    if (level == 4) factor = 3;
    else if (level == 8) factor = 4;
    else factor = level;
    wedge = factor;
    range = (factor + level) + base / total;
    for (k = 1;k <= total;k++)
        {
        u1 = rand() % range + wedge;
        dur[k] = u1;
        sum += u1;
        }
    rcomp = base - sum;
    while (rcomp !=0)
        {
        for (l = 1;l <= total;l++)
            {
            if (rcomp < 0)
                {
                if (dur[l] > 1)
                    {
                    dur[l] = dur[l]-1;
                    rcomp = rcomp + 1;
                    }
                continue;
                }
            if (rcomp == 0)
                break;
            else
                {
                dur[l] = dur[l]+1;
                rcomp = rcomp - 1;
                break;
                }
            }
```

```
        }
  if (odd == 1)
     {
        u2 = rand() % total + 1;
        do
           u3 = rand() % total + 1;
        while (total > 1 && u3 == u2);
        dur[u2] = dur[u2] + dur[u3];
        dur[u3] = -1;
     }
  for (k = 1;k <= total;k++)
        {
        if (k % 10 == 0)
           printf("\n");
        newmed = median;
        if (dur[k] / 2.0 == dur[k]/2 && newmed/2.0 == newmed/2)
        newmed = Durred(dur,newmed,k);
        if (dur[k] < 0)
           printf("1/%d ",odd);
        else
           printf("%d/%d ",dur[k],newmed);
        }
  printf("\n");
  } /* end of Polyrhy() function */
  /*=============== MIC 2.10 ===============*/
  /* Durred() function (adapted to program specs) */
  int Durred(dur,median,k)
  int dur[],median,k;
  {
   do
     {
        dur[k] = dur[k]/2;
        median = median / 2;
     }
   while (dur[k]/2.0 == dur[k]/2 && median/2.0 == median/2);
   return(median);
  } /* end of Durred() function */
  /*====================================*/
  /* END OF POLYRHY.C */
```

## Program execution

```
pass 1
number of durations in rhythm sequence =10
median = 3
timescale = 10 (scale = 1 - 10)
level = 1 (from a choice of 1-2-4-8)
3/3 1/3 1/3 4/3 5/3 2/3 2/3 5/3 2/3
5/3

pass 2
number of durations in rhythm sequence =20
median = 4
timescale = 10 (scale = 1 - 10)
level = 2 (from a choice of 1-2-4-8)
3/8 1/1 1/2 1/2 3/4 3/8 1/8 1/2 5/8
1/2 1/4 3/8 5/8 1/4 1/8 1/1 1/2 1/2 7/8
1/4
```

```
pass 3
number of durations in rhythm sequence =30
median = 5
timescale = 10 (scale = 1 - 10)
level = 4 (from a choice of 1-2-4-8)
11/20 1/20 11/20 1/20 5/10 11/20 3/5 3/10 1/20
3/5 7/20 3/10 1/20 9/20 3/5 5/20 5/10 5/10 1/20
3/10 1/10 7/20 1/20 11/20 3/20 1/20 5/20 11/20 3/5
1/5

pass 4
number of durations in rhythm sequence =40
median = 6
timescale = 10 (scale = 1 - 10)
level = 8 (from a choice of 1-2-4-8)
1/3 3/24 13/48 17/48 9/48 1/24 19/48 1/48 9/48
3/48 3/24 3/48 17/48 21/48 15/48 19/48 17/48 21/48 11/48
17/48 9/24 11/48 17/48 9/48 13/48 7/48 1/6 3/24 1/48
3/48 11/48 1/48 9/48 15/48 7/24 9/24 11/24 9/24 9/24
19/48
```

# FUNCTION GROUP: Meline.c

1. Rdmelint( )     MIC 7.16
2. Rest( )          MIC 7.17
3. Printpitch( )    MIC 3.1

## Purpose

Generate a random-order, interval-constrained, melodic pitch sequence containing a percentage of rest values.

## Notes

The core of the group is Rdmelint( ), similar in concept to Rdintchd( ), but differing in two areas. Firstly, it returns a bidirectional melodic line rather than unidirectional harmonic chord sequence. Secondly, the probability that overall line direction will drift upward or downward is influenced by the value entered for variable "up."

Function Rest( ) allows the user to provide a rest occurrence probability (in %) to articulate the melodic line; uniform random integers smaller than a threshold value trigger the insertion of rests.

## Programming ideas

Write a program based on Function Group: MELINE.C which:

1. contains control variables for increasing or decreasing the interval-size range over the course of program execution,
2. allows the user to generate a number of disparate-range melodic sequences within a single run,
3. files the melodies on disk along with keys to facilitate extraction of individual sequences,
4. individually retrieves the melodic sequences for application of variation procedures,
5. prints out the original melodies in alternation with their variations in ABACADAE form (Rondo).

## Program source code

```
/* MELINE.C (generates a randon-order,interval-constrained,
             melodic line containing a percentage of
             rest values) */
#include <stdio.h>
main()
{
  int j,k;            /* loop indices */
  int total = 20;     /* length of sequence */
  int small = 1;      /* smallest allowable interval-size */
  int large = 3;      /* largest allowable interval-size */
```

```
int up = 80;        /* prob. (in %) of ascending intervals */
int rest = 10;      /* prob. (in %) of rest interpolation */
int start = 48;     /* sequence start value */
int seed = 3923;
void Rdmelint();

srand(seed);
for (j = 0;j < 4;j++)
    {
    printf("pass %d\n",j+1);
    printf("total=%d small=%d large=%d\n",total,small,large);
    printf("up=%d rest=%d start=%d\n",up,rest,start);
    Rdmelint(start,small,large,up,rest,total);
    total += 10;
    small += 1;
    large += 2;
    up -= 20;
    rest += 20;;
    }
} /* end of main */
/*=============== MIC 7.16 ===============*/
/* Rdmelint() function (computes an interval-constrained
                          pitch sequence ) */
void Rdmelint(note,small,large,up,restprob,total)
int note,small,large,up,restprob,total;
{
 int j;                 /* loop index */
 int flag;              /* rest note indicator */
 int intvalrange;       /* span of allowable interval-sizes */
 int u;                 /* random integers */
 int Restgen();
 static char *pitch[] = {
 "C0 ","C#0","D0 ","D#0","E0 ","F0 ","F#0","G0 ","G#0",
 "A0 ","A#0","B0 ","C1 ","C#1","D1 ","D#1","E1 ","F1 ",
 "F#1","G1 ","G#1","A1 ","A#1","B1 ","C2 ","C#2","D2 ",
 "D#2","E2 ","F2 ","F#2","G2 ","G#2","A2 ","A#2","B2 ",
 "C3 ","C#3","D3 ","D#3","E3 ","F3 ","F#3","G3 ","G#3",
 "A3 ","A#3","B3 ","C4 ","C#4","D4 ","D#4","E4 ","F4 ",
 "F#4","G4 ","G#4","A4 ","A#4","B4 ","C5 ","C#5","D5 ",
 "D#5","E5 ","F5 ","F#5","G5 ","G#5","A5 ","A#5","B5 ",
 "C6 ","C#6","D6 ","D#6","E6 ","F6 ","F#6","G6 ","G#6",
 "A6 ","A#6","B6 ","C7 ","R " };
 intvalrange = large - small + 1;
 printf("%s ",pitch[note]);
 for (j = 0;j < total-1;j++)
    {
    if (j % 12 == 0)
       printf("\n");
    flag = Restgen(restprob);
    if (flag)
       {
       printf("%s ",pitch[85]);
       continue;
       }
    u = rand() % intvalrange + small;
    if (rand() % 100  < up)
       note = note + u;
    else
       note = note - u;
    if (note > 85)
       note -= 12;
```

```
          else if (note < 1)
              note += 12;
          printf("%s ",pitch[note]);
          }
  printf("\n\n");
} /* end of Rdmelint function */
/*=============== MIC 7.17 ===============*/
/* Restgen() function */
int Restgen(restprob)
int restprob;
{
  int flag;

  flag = 0;
  if (rand() % 100 < restprob)
     flag = 1;
  return(flag);
} /* end of Restgen() function */
/*==================================*/
/* END OF MELINE.C */
```

# Program execution

MELINE.EXE

```
pass 1
total=20 small=1 large=3
up=80 rest=10 start=48
C4  A#3 B3  D4   F4  G#4 G4   A4   C5  D5  E5   D#5
F#5 R   A5  B5   C6  D6  D#6 F6

pass 2
total=30 small=2 large=5
up=60 rest=30 start=48
C4  R   D4  E4   A4  F4  C#4 R    G#3 A#3 R    C4
F4  A#4 R   C5   R   D#5 F#5 E5   F#5 G#5 C#6 G#5
E5  A5  R   R    C6  R

pass 3
total=40 small=3 large=7
up=40 rest=50 start=48
C4  F3  A#2 F#2 B1  F1  R   R   A1  R   R   R
F1  A#0 E1  B0  R   R   R   G0  R   R   R   C#0
F#0 R   A#0 R   R   R   R   R   R   F1  R   R
A#0 R   F#0 B0

pass 4
total=50 small=4 large=9
up=20 rest=70 start=48
C4  R   R   R   R   R   R   R   R   R   R   R
D#3 R   F#2 R   R   R   C2  E1  R   R   R   G#0
R   R   C#1 R   R   G#0 R   R   R   R   R   R
B0  R   R   R   R   F0  R   R   R   R   R   R
R   R
```

# FUNCTION: Partspan( )   MIC 7.18

## Purpose

Compute instrumental voice ranges from a common pitch aggregate in one of three modes: stratified, interlocking, or common.

## Notes

In circumstances requiring coordinated generation of melodic lines from a source element table (such as ascendingly sorted scale or chord pitch gamuts), control over the range/register segment occupied by each voice might be desirable. Partspan( ) accomplishes this task by dividing the total pitch gamut into equal subranges, or by distributing overlapping range/register assignments to all parts, or making the entire gamut range available to each part.

The main routine is configured to generate random pitches selected from within the range of each part. Simple modification will allow the substitution of function calls to other melody-generation algorithms.

By extension, MIC 7.18 can be applied to any sequence of values— ascending, descending, or random-order—to determine the details of selected parameters by interpreting subroutine output as a set of pointer ranges for extraction of element table segments.

## Programming ideas

Write an interactive program that generates a chord file using MIC 7.13: Intgam( ), extracts part ranges for four instruments, serializes pitch parameter note selections for each voice, then generates durations for the rhythm parameter of each voice using Function Group POLYRHY.C.

Transcribe the output to conventional music for performance by four acoustic instruments.

## Program source code

```
/* PARTSPAN.C (Computes instrumental part ranges from a
              common pitch aggregate in one of 2 modes:
              stratified or interlocking.) */
#include <stdio.h>
main()
{
  int note[40];        /* stores source pitchbank */
  int part[4];         /* list of part ranges */
  int adjust[4];       /* list of part lower limits */
  int u;               /* random integer */
  int chordlength = 40; /* # of notes in source pitchbank */
  int voices = 4;      /* number of score parts to return */
  int melength=  80; /* length of melody to generate */
  int interlock;       /* part range relationship indicator */
```

```c
int seed = 2113;
int j,k,l;               /* loop indices */
void Partspan();
static char *pitch[] = {
"C0 ","C#0","D0 ","D#0","E0 ","F0 ","F#0","G0 ","G#0",
"A0 ","A#0","B0 ","C1 ","C#1","D1 ","D#1","E1 ","F1 ",
"F#1","G1 ","G#1","A1 ","A#1","B1 ","C2 ","C#2","D2 ",
"D#2","E2 ","F2 ","F#2","G2 ","G#2","A2 ","A#2","B2 ",
"C3 ","C#3","D3 ","D#3","E3 ","F3 ","F#3","G3 ","G#3",
"A3 ","A#3","B3 ","C4 ","C#4","D4 ","D#4","E4 ","F4 ",
"F#4","G4 ","G#4","A4 ","A#4","B4 ","C5 ","C#5","D5 ",
"D#5","E5 ","F5 ","F#5","G5 ","G#5","A5 ","A#5","B5 ",
"C6 ","C#6","D6 ","D#6","E6 ","F6 ","F#6","G6 ","G#6",
"A6 ","A#6","B6 ","C7 "  };

srand(seed);
printf("%s %s %s","pitchbank (chord or scale) from which",
        "random-order\nmelodies will be derived to test",
        "the distribution:\n");
for (j = 0;j < chordlength;j++)
/* load and display example scale/chord structure */
    {
     if (j % 11 == 0)
        printf("\n");
     note[j] = (j+1) * 2;
     printf("%s ",pitch[note[j]]);
    }
for (j = 0;j < 2;j++)
    {
     if (j >0)
        {
         printf("\nPASS 2, INTERLOCKING:\n");
         interlock = 1;
        }
     else
        {
         printf("\n\nPASS 1, STRATIFIED:\n");
         interlock = 0;
        }
     Partspan(part,adjust,voices,chordlength,interlock);
     for (k = 0;k < voices;k++)
        {
         printf("\nvoice %d melody:\n",k+1);
         printf("range = %s to ",pitch[note[adjust[k]]]);
         printf("%s \n",pitch[note[adjust[k]+part[k]-1]]);
         for (l = 0;l < melength;l++)
            {
             if (l % 11 == 0)
                printf("\n");
             u = (rand() % part[k]) + adjust[k];
             printf("%s ",pitch[note[u]]);
            }
         printf("\n");
        }
 printf("\n");
    }
} /* end of main */
/*=============== MIC 7.18 ===============*/
/* Partspan() function */
void Partspan(part,adjust,voices,chordlength,interlock)
int part[],adjust[],voices,chordlength,interlock;
```

```
{
  int span;     /* subdivision of total pitch bank range */
  int extra;    /* any remainder from subdivision */
  int comp;     /* compensatory value added to parts */
  int j;        /* loop index */

  span = chordlength / voices;
  extra = chordlength - voices * span;
  for (j = 0;j < voices;j++)
      {
        if (extra <= 0)
          comp = 0;
        else
          comp = 1;
        part[j] = span + comp;
        extra -= 1;
        adjust[0] = 0;
        if (j < voices-1)
          adjust[j+1] = adjust[j] + part[j];
      }
  if (interlock < 1)
     return;
  for (j = 0;j < voices-1;j++)
      part[j] = part[j] + part[j] * .5;
} /* end of Partspan() function */
/*=====================================*/
/* END OF PARTSPAN.C */
```

## Program execution

PARTSPAN.EXE

pitchbank (chord or scale) from which random-order
melodies will be derived to test the distribution:

```
D0   E0   F#0  G#0  A#0  C1   D1   E1   F#1  G#1  A#1
C2   D2   E2   F#2  G#2  A#2  C3   D3   E3   F#3  G#3
A#3  C4   D4   E4   F#4  G#4  A#4  C5   D5   E5   F#5
G#5  A#5  C6   D6   E6   F#6  G#6
```

PASS 1, STRATIFIED:

voice 1 melody:
range = D0  to G#1

```
E1   F#1  D1   G#0  G#1  E0   G#1  G#1  D0   C1   G#1
D1   D1   E1   G#1  D0   E1   D0   E1   A#0  D0   E1
E0   C1   G#0  A#0  G#0  G#1  E0   C1   E0   G#0  E1
C1   F#1  G#0  A#0  E1   C1   F#1  G#0  C1   G#1  G#1
E1   C1   E0   C1   G#0  C1   E0   E1   E1   A#0  G#0
E0   C1   D0   D0   E0   F#1  E1   D1   F#1  G#0  D0
E0   C1   F#0  A#0  C1   F#1  A#0  D1   D1   D0   E1
F#1  C1   E1
```

voice 2 melody:
range = A#1 to E3

```
D2   A#1  A#1  C3   F#2  G#2  A#2  G#2  G#2  C2   C3
A#1  E3   A#2  E2   D2   D3   G#2  D2   A#1  D3   F#2
```

```
E2   C3   A#2  C2   A#1  E3   F#2  A#1  E2   D2   G#2
E3   A#2  D3   C3   D3   D2   D3   D3   C2   D2   D2
A#1  E2   F#2  C3   C3   G#2  A#1  G#2  E3   D2   D2
A#1  A#1  G#2  E3   D2   A#1  D2   C2   A#2  E2   E3
E3   D3   C2   C3   E2   D2   D2   E2   D2   G#2  E3
G#2  D2   G#2
```

voice 3 melody:
range = F#3 to C5

```
G#3  G#3  C5   A#3  A#4  A#4  E4   G#4  F#3  F#4  A#3
G#4  C5   F#4  D4   G#3  F#3  F#4  D4   G#4  G#4  D4
C4   A#3  G#3  C5   C4   G#3  C5   G#3  C5   A#4  F#4
F#4  C4   E4   G#4  C5   E4   C5   C5   D4   F#3  F#3
E4   D4   A#4  G#3  E4   C5   D4   G#4  G#4  F#4  A#3
A#4  A#4  F#4  E4   F#3  C5   D4   C5   D4   A#3  C4
F#4  A#4  F#4  F#3  C5   A#4  A#3  A#3  G#3  G#3  A#4
D4   G#4  C4
```

voice 4 melody:
range = D5  to G#6

```
E6   A#5  E5   D5   F#6  A#5  C6   A#5  F#5  C6   E6
A#5  F#5  E5   C6   D5   A#5  E5   G#6  C6   D5   D6
D5   E6   G#6  F#6  C6   F#5  F#5  G#5  D5   D6   F#5
A#5  E5   F#6  E6   C6   E6   D5   E5   C6   G#5  F#6
D5   C6   E5   D6   E5   G#6  F#6  C6   D6   F#5  E5
A#5  G#5  E5   A#5  F#6  G#6  C6   F#6  F#6  C6   D6
F#6  D5   F#6  G#5  D5   D5   F#5  G#5  G#6  D5   G#6
F#5  E5   E6
```


PASS 2, INTERLOCKING:

voice 1 melody:
range = D0  to F#2

```
D2   D2   D0   C2   E1   F#2  F#0  E0   F#2  E2   G#0
E1   E0   D2   C1   C1   A#1  D2   C1   D0   G#0  G#0
G#0  E1   F#1  C1   G#0  F#1  C1   E0   D1   C2   E0
D0   G#1  A#1  C2   G#0  D2   E1   C1   C2   F#1  D2
C1   A#1  C2   E0   F#0  E0   E2   C2   F#2  E1   D1
C2   F#2  F#1  C1   D2   D2   G#1  E2   A#0  D2   F#0
A#0  E0   E2   A#0  F#0  E1   E0   D1   F#1  C1   F#2
C1   C1   C1
```

voice 2 melody:
range = A#1 to D4

```
A#1  E2   A#2  E2   C3   D2   F#3  F#3  A#2  D4   D3
E2   D2   D3   C4   F#3  F#2  C4   C3   A#1  F#2  E2
A#3  D4   D2   A#3  C3   F#2  C3   C2   D2   C2   D4
A#2  C2   A#3  E2   D4   F#2  A#1  C2   C4   D2   E3
C2   A#3  F#2  E2   A#1  E2   C4   E2   C4   C2   E2
C4   D2   D2   C3   A#2  A#3  C3   A#3  F#2  E3   E3
A#3  F#3  D4   C3   A#1  C4   E2   E3   D3   C2   D4
A#1  A#1  E3
```

```
voice 3 melody:
range = F#3 to A#5

D4   G#5  A#3  E5   D5   F#5  A#3  D5   A#5  D5   F#3
A#3  G#3  D4   G#3  C4   C5   F#3  E5   C5   F#4  A#5
F#3  F#5  A#4  G#5  E5   E5   F#3  C4   C4   A#5  A#3
E4   G#4  E5   C5   F#3  D4   D4   F#4  F#5  F#5  A#4
F#4  G#4  F#5  C5   C5   D4   G#3  E4   F#4  E4   G#3
E5   C5   G#3  G#5  G#4  G#3  D4   E4   F#4  D5   F#4
F#5  D5   D4   C4   G#4  G#5  G#5  E4   A#4  F#3  E4
G#4  G#5  G#4

voice 4 melody:
range = D5  to G#6

G#5  A#5  E5   A#5  E5   G#5  E6   E6   G#6  G#5  E6
D5   E6   F#6  D6   G#6  D6   G#5  E6   D6   E5   C6
F#5  G#6  A#5  G#5  C6   G#6  E5   E5   G#5  A#5  D6
A#5  G#5  G#6  E6   G#5  F#5  D6   F#6  E5   C6   F#6
C6   D6   F#6  E5   F#5  E6   G#6  E5   F#6  C6   D6
G#6  A#5  F#6  F#5  D6   E5   E5   A#5  F#6  F#5  G#5
F#5  G#6  E5   G#5  F#5  E6   C6   F#5  C6   G#6  E6
A#5  E5   F#5
```

# FUNCTION GROUP: Ornament.c

1. Ornselec( )    MIC 7.19
2. Addorn( )     MIC 7.20

## Purpose

Generate a random-order pitch sequence, then add embellishments to selected notes in accordance with probability weights for four ornament types.

## Notes

The main routine spins-up a temporary array of random-order pitches. The array is then passed to Function Ornselec( ), which loads a probability table with weights for each of four ornament patterns, then calls Function Addorn( ) to expand the pitch array by inserting the selected embellishments.

The four standard ornament types (-,-,,--,,--,) may be augmented to include any number and type of pattern desired by the program user; simply dimension larger arrays embtable[ ], dec[ ], and orn[ ], and enter the appropriate patterns.

## Programming ideas

1. Modify the main routine to allow user-input melodic sequences for embellishment.
2. Modify the main routine to read a pitch data file for embellishment of melodies.
3. Add a function to the program to introduce and apply rest note probabilities.
4. Write an interactive program that:

   a. generates melodies using MIC 7.5: Trantabl( ),
   b. includes Function Group: ORNAMENT.C,
   c. includes MIC 7.2: Loopgen2( ), and
   d. writes multiple, processed loop melodies to disk.

## Program source code

```
/* ORNAMENT.C (Generates a random-order pitch sequence,
               then adds embellishments to a percentage
               of notes in accordance with probability
               weights assigned to each of four ornament
               types.)*/
#include <stdio.h>
main()
{
  int temp[200];      /* sequence prior to decoration */
```

```
int final[500];    /* final embelished pitch seq.  */
int embseq;        /* number of pitches in final sequence */
int deco = 70;     /* prob. (in %) of note decoration */
int melength = 30; /* length of original pitch sequence */
int j;             /* loop index */
int seed = -18763;
int Ornselec();

static char *pitch[] = {
"C0 ","C#0","D0 ","D#0","E0 ","F0 ","F#0","G0 ","G#0",
"A0 ","A#0","B0 ","C1 ","C#1","D1 ","D#1","E1 ","F1 ",
"F#1","G1 ","G#1","A1 ","A#1","B1 ","C2 ","C#2","D2 ",
"D#2","E2 ","F2 ","F#2","G2 ","G#2","A2 ","A#2","B2 ",
"C3 ","C#3","D3 ","D#3","E3 ","F3 ","F#3","G3 ","G#3",
"A3 ","A#3","B3 ","C4 ","C#4","D4 ","D#4","E4 ","F4 ",
"F#4","G4 ","G#4","A4 ","A#4","B4 ","C5 ","C#5","D5 ",
"D#5","E5 ","F5 ","F#5","G5 ","G#5","A5 ","A#5","B5 ",
"C6 ","C#6","D6 ","D#6","E6 ","F6 ","F#6","G6 ","G#6",
"A6 ","A#6","B6 ","C7 " };

srand(seed);
printf("%s%d%s","unembellished pitch sequence = ",
       melength," notes\n");
for (j = 0;j < melength;j++)
   {
   if (j % 10 == 0)
      printf("\n");
   temp[j] = rand() % 80 + 2;
   printf("%s ",pitch[temp[j]]);
   }
embseq = Ornselec(temp,final,melength,deco);
printf("%s%d%s%s","\n\nembellished pitch sequence:\n(",
       deco,"% of original melody notes",
       " have been ornamented)\n");
for (j = 0;j < embseq;j++)
   {
   if (j % 10 == 0)
      printf("\n");
   printf("%s ",pitch[final[j]]);
   }
} /* end of main */
/*=============== MIC 7.19 ==============*/
/* Ornselec() function (computes ornament-type probabilities
                        and invokes Addorn() function to add
                        selected ornaments */

int Ornselec(temp,final,melength,deco)
int temp[],final[],melength,deco;
{
 int j;            /* loop index */
 int wsum = 0;    /* sum of ornament prob. weights */
 int embseq = 0; /* pointer to array final[] */

 int orn[] =       /* ornament patterns */
     {1002,2003,2004,4006};
 int dec[] =       /* values for pattern reference */
     {-1,0,-1,0,1,0};
 int embtable[] = /* ornament pattern probabilities */
     {4,3,2,1};
 int rand(),Addorn();
```

```
if (deco == 0)
  {
   printf("\nfinished\n");
   return(0);
  }
printf("%s%s","\n\nornaments being added",
       " (prob. weights 4,3,2,1):\n");
printf("1) _ - 2) - _ 3) -_- 4) _-_");
for (j = 0;j < 4;j++)
    {
     embtable[j] += wsum;
     wsum = embtable[j];
    }
for (j = 0;j < melength;j++)
    {
     if (rand() % 100 < deco)
         embseq = Addorn(temp,final,embtable,orn,
                         dec,wsum,j,embseq);
     else
        {
         final[embseq] = temp[j];
         embseq += 1;
        }
    }
 return(embseq);
} /* end of Ornselec() function */
/*=============== MIC 7.20 ===============*/
/* Addorn() function (interpolates selected ornament
                      patterns into original pitch
                      sequence) */

int Addorn(temp,final,embtable,orn,dec,wsum,j,embseq)
int temp[],final[],embtable[],orn[],dec[],wsum,j,embseq;
{
 int k,l,m,n;   /* loop indices */
 float b;       /* loop index computation */

 for (m = 0;m < 4;m++)
    {
     if (rand() % wsum >= embtable[m])
       continue;
     else
        {
         k = orn[m] / 1000.;
         b = orn[m] / 1000.;
         l = (b - k) * 1000. + .5;
        }
     for (n = k-1;n <= l-1;n++)
        {
         final[embseq] = temp[j] + dec[n];
         embseq += 1;
        }
     return(embseq);
    }
 return(embseq);
 } /* end of Addorn() function */
/*========================================*/
/* END OF ORNAMENT.C */
```

# Program execution

`ORNAMENT.EXE`

unembellished pitch sequence = 30 notes

```
C3   F#4 B3   B5    C#1 G#5 E3    A#4 D3    B1
B5   D1  B3   G3    A1  A3  A#1   C#3 D#5 F3
D3   F#6 D#4 F#0   B3  C4  C#1   D3  F#0 F5
```

ornaments being added (prob. weights 4,3,2,1):
1) _ - 2) - _ 3) -_- 4) _-_

embellished pitch sequence:
(70% of original melody notes have been ornamented)

```
C3   B2   F4   F#4 B3   A#3 A#5 B5   C#1 D1
C#1 G#5 G5   G#5 E3   D#3 A#4 D3   C#3 B1
A#1 B5   A#5 D1   C#1 B3   F#3 G3   G#1 A1
A3   G#3 A#1 C#3 C3   C#3 D#5 E3   F3   C#3
D3   F#6 D#4 F0   F#0 B3   B3   C4   C#1 C1
D3   C#3 F#0 F5   E5
```

# FUNCTION GROUP: Seqstore.c

1. Seqstore( )   MIC 7.21
2. Seqxtrct( )   MIC 7.22

## Purpose

Provide means for storing and retrieving an articulated group of integer sequences.

## Notes

Function Seqstore( ) generates and stores an array of integer sequences, together with keys to the length of each constituent sequence. (Function calls to other data-generating algorithms can be substituted.) Array x[ ] is then available to the calling routine for further processing.

Function Seqxtrct( ) retrieves a multi-sequence array that contains sequence-lengths keys, and displays array contents.

## Programming ideas

Write an interactive program using Function Group SEQSTORE.C which

1. invokes MIC 7.11: Rdintchd( ) to generate an extensive chord array,
2. retrieves the chords from the array and makes them individually available to a melody generation function, then
3. derives interval-constrained, random-order melodic sequences from the chords.

## Program source code

```
/* SEQSTORE.C (store and retrieve an articulated group
               of integer sequences.)*/
#include <stdio.h>
main()
{
  int x[200];      /* stores sequence-group with keys */
  int seqtotal=5; /* number of sequences in group to store */
  int notetotal;   /* number of values in sequence-group */
  int seed = -912;
  int Seqstore();
  void Seqxtrct();

  srand(seed);
  printf("a group of random-integer sequences are now being stored.\n");
  printf("here is how they are represented in the array:\n");
  notetotal = Seqstore(x,seqtotal);
  printf("\n\nextracted sequence-group looks like this:");
  Seqxtrct(x,notetotal);
} /* end of main */
```

```
/*=============== MIC 7.21 =============*/
/* Seqstore() function */
int Seqstore(x,seqtotal)
int x[],seqtotal;
{
  int j,k,notecount,seqlen,storeval;

  notecount = 0;
  for (j = 0;j < seqtotal;j++)
      {
       seqlen = rand() % 10 + 5;
       for (k = 0;k < seqlen;k++)
           {
            storeval = (k+1) * (j+1);
            if (k == 0)
               {
                x[k+notecount] = storeval * 1000 + seqlen;
                printf("%d ",x[k+notecount]);
               }
            else
               {
                x[k+notecount] = storeval;
                printf("%d ",x[k+notecount]);
               }
           }
       notecount = notecount + seqlen;
       printf("\n");
      }
  return(notecount);
 } /* end of Seqstore() function */
 /*=============== MIC 7.22 =============*/
void Seqxtrct(x,notetotal)
int x[],notetotal;
{
  int j,seqcounter;
  seqcounter = 0;
  for (j = 0;j < notetotal;j++)
      {
       if (x[j] < 1000)
          printf("%d ",x[j]);
       else
          {
           seqcounter +=1;
           printf("\nsequence %d \n",seqcounter);
           printf("%d ",x[j]/1000);
          }
      }
  printf("\n");
 } /* end of Seqxtrct() function */
 /*===================================*/
 /* END OF SEQSTORE.C */
```

## Program execution

SEQSTORE.EXE

a group of random-integer sequences are now being stored.
here is how they are represented in the array:
1005 2 3 4 5

```
2010  4  6  8  10  12  14  16  18  20
3014  6  9  12  15  18  21  24  27  30  33  36  39  42
4012  8  12  16  20  24  28  32  36  40  44  48
5008  10  15  20  25  30  35  40


extracted sequence-group looks like this:
sequence 1
1  2  3  4  5
sequence 2
2  4  6  8  10  12  14  16  18  20
sequence 3
3  6  9  12  15  18  21  24  27  30  33  36  39  42
sequence 4
4  8  12  16  20  24  28  32  36  40  44  48
sequence 5
5  10  15  20  25  30  35  40
```

## FUNCTION GROUP: Scorform.c

1. IntegerToPitch( )   MIC 7.23
2. PutPitch( )          MIC 7.24
3. ScriptArray( )       MIC 7.25

## Purpose

Compile data for separate musical parameters into a comprehensive notelist score for a single instrument.

## Notes

To demonstrate SCORFORM.C, the main routine places ascending integers in a note-attribute array. It then performs any necessary data-type conversion and writes parameter values as a block of note-names or integers to the screen. Each line is appropriately flagged with a P,R,A, V, or T to represent Pitch, Rhythm, Articulation, Volume, or Timbre parameters. Pitch is output as an alphabetic pitch-class with numeric octave register.

Rhythm is specified (herein) as the denominator of a whole-note fraction ($22 = \frac{1}{22}$ of a whole note, etc.); Articulation, Volume, and Timbre parameters are all scaled in percentages of maximum value—that is, a 50 in the V parameter represents a half-maximum loudness. This form of representation lends itself neatly to performance by some digital synthesizers. However, if the output is to serve as a score for an acoustic instrument, then transcription to conventional notation is necessary. If this is the case, a scale of standard symbols should be adopted to convert the data output in percentages, and to meaningfully apply Timbre parameter data.

## Programming ideas

1. Write an interactive program that makes various data generation algorithms available to the user for application to any selected parameter.
2. Add file-writing functions to the interactive program to store the finished notelist on disk for future reference.
3. Modify the interactive program to allow creation of a score for multiple channels (voices, parts, etc.).

## Source code listing

```
/* SCORFORM.C  (compile a notelist score of data for 5
               musical parameters for output to the screen
               or printer) */
#include <ctype.h>
main()
{
    int j, datarray[87];
```

```
      for(j = 0; j < 87; j++)
         datarray[j] = j;          /* generate some integers for
                                       parameter data;substitute
                                       your own algorithm . */
      printf("Notelist using R 1-1\n");
      ScriptArray(datarray, 'P', j);
      ScriptArray(datarray, 'R', j);
      ScriptArray(datarray, 'A', j);
      ScriptArray(datarray, 'V', j);
      ScriptArray(datarray, 'T', j);
} /* end of main() */
/*=========================================*/
/* This module incorporates a recent C language addition:
   FUNCTION PROTOTYPES; delete this module if your C
   compiler doesn't support prototyping. */

char *IntegerToPitch(int num);
PutPitch(int num);
ScriptArray(int datarray[], char lnhead, int size);
/*=============== MIC 7.23 ==============*/
/* IntegerToPitch() function (an adaptation of
          MIC 2.3 Pitchtab(), which converts numbers
          to pitches */
#define MAXPIT 84
char *IntegerToPitch(num)
int num;
{
        static char pitch[4];
        static char *names[] ={ "C","C#","D","D#","E","F","F#",
                                "G","G#","A","A#","B" };
        static char *rest = {"R"};
        int pc,oct;

        if (num < 0 || num > MAXPIT)
           return (rest);
        else {
           pc = num % 12;
           oct = (num/12);
           sprintf(pitch,"%s%d", names[pc], oct);
           return (pitch);
           }
} /* end of IntegerToPitch() function */
/*=============== MIC 7.24 ==============*/
/* PutPitch() function */
PutPitch(num)
   int num;
{
   printf("%-4s", IntegerToPitch(num));
} /* end of PutPitch() function */
/*=============== MIC 7.25 ==============*/
/* ScriptArray() function */
ScriptArray(datarray, lnhead, size)
   int datarray[];
   char lnhead;
   int size;
{
   int k;
   int j = 0;
   int offset = 0;

      while(j + offset < size)
```

```c
        {
        printf("\n%c   ", lnhead);
        while(j < 10 && j + offset < size)
            switch(lnhead)
                {
                case 'P' :
                        printf("  ");
                        PutPitch(datarray[j++ + offset]);
                        break;
                case 'R' :
                        printf("  ");
                        printf("%-4d", datarray[j++ + offset]);
                        break;
                case 'A' :
                        printf("  ");
                        printf("%-4d", datarray[j++ + offset]);
                        break;
                case 'V' :
                        printf("  ");
                        printf("%-4d", datarray[j++ + offset]);
                        break;
                case 'T' :
                        printf("  ");
                        printf("%-4d", datarray[j++ + offset]);
                        break;
                case ' ' :
                        PutPitch(datarray[j++ + offset]);
                        break;
                }
        offset += j;
        j = 0;
        }
    printf("\n");
} /* end of ScriptArray() function */
/*=====================================*/
/* END OF SCORFORM.C */
```

## Program execution

SCORFORM.EXE

Notelist using R 1-1

| P | C0 | C#0 | D0 | D#0 | E0 | F0 | F#0 | G0 | G#0 | A0 |
|---|----|-----|----|----|----|----|-----|----|-----|----|
| P | A#0 | B0 | C1 | C#1 | D1 | D#1 | E1 | F1 | F#1 | G1 |
| P | G#1 | A1 | A#1 | B1 | C2 | C#2 | D2 | D#2 | E2 | F2 |
| P | F#2 | G2 | G#2 | A2 | A#2 | B2 | C3 | C#3 | D3 | D#3 |
| P | E3 | F3 | F#3 | G3 | G#3 | A3 | A#3 | B3 | C4 | C#4 |
| P | D4 | D#4 | E4 | F4 | F#4 | G4 | G#4 | A4 | A#4 | B4 |
| P | C5 | C#5 | D5 | D#5 | E5 | F5 | F#5 | G5 | G#5 | A5 |
| P | A#5 | B5 | C6 | C#6 | D6 | D#6 | E6 | F6 | F#6 | G6 |
| P | G#6 | A6 | A#6 | B6 | C7 | R | R | | | |
| | | | | | | | | | | |
| R | 0 | 1 | 2 | 3 | 4 | 5 | 6 | | 8 | 9 |
| R | 10 | 11 | 12 | 13 | 14 | 15 | 16 | 1 | 18 | 19 |
| R | 20 | 21 | 22 | 23 | 24 | 25 | 26 | 27 | 28 | 29 |
| R | 30 | 31 | 32 | 33 | 34 | 35 | 36 | 37 | 38 | 39 |
| R | 40 | 41 | 42 | 43 | 44 | 45 | 46 | 47 | 48 | 49 |
| R | 50 | 51 | 52 | 53 | 54 | 55 | 56 | 57 | 58 | 59 |
| R | 60 | 61 | 62 | 63 | 64 | 65 | 66 | 67 | 68 | 69 |

| R | 70 | 71 | 72 | 73 | 74 | 75 | 76 | 77 | 78 | 79 |
|---|----|----|----|----|----|----|----|----|----|----|
| R | 80 | 81 | 82 | 83 | 84 | 85 | 86 |    |    |    |
|   |    |    |    |    |    |    |    |    |    |    |
| A | 0  | 1  | 2  | 3  | 4  | 5  | 6  | 7  | 8  | 9  |
| A | 10 | 11 | 12 | 13 | 14 | 15 | 16 | 17 | 18 | 19 |
| A | 20 | 21 | 22 | 23 | 24 | 25 | 26 | 27 | 28 | 29 |
| A | 30 | 31 | 32 | 33 | 34 | 35 | 36 | 37 | 38 | 39 |
| A | 40 | 41 | 42 | 43 | 44 | 45 | 46 | 47 | 48 | 49 |
| A | 50 | 51 | 52 | 53 | 54 | 55 | 56 | 57 | 58 | 59 |
| A | 60 | 61 | 62 | 63 | 64 | 65 | 66 | 67 | 68 | 69 |
| A | 70 | 71 | 72 | 73 | 74 | 75 | 76 | 77 | 78 | 79 |
| A | 80 | 81 | 82 | 83 | 84 | 85 | 86 |    |    |    |
|   |    |    |    |    |    |    |    |    |    |    |
| V | 0  | 1  | 2  | 3  | 4  | 5  | 6  | 7  | 8  | 9  |
| V | 10 | 11 | 12 | 13 | 14 | 15 | 16 | 17 | 18 | 19 |
| V | 20 | 21 | 22 | 23 | 24 | 25 | 26 | 27 | 28 | 29 |
| V | 30 | 31 | 32 | 33 | 34 | 35 | 36 | 37 | 38 | 39 |
| V | 40 | 41 | 42 | 43 | 44 | 45 | 46 | 47 | 48 | 49 |
| V | 50 | 51 | 52 | 53 | 54 | 55 | 56 | 57 | 58 | 59 |
| V | 60 | 61 | 62 | 63 | 64 | 65 | 66 | 67 | 68 | 69 |
| V | 70 | 71 | 72 | 73 | 74 | 75 | 76 | 77 | 78 | 79 |
| V | 80 | 81 | 82 | 83 | 84 | 85 | 86 |    |    |    |
|   |    |    |    |    |    |    |    |    |    |    |
| T | 0  | 1  | 2  | 3  | 4  | 5  | 6  | 7  | 8  | 9  |
| T | 10 | 11 | 12 | 13 | 14 | 15 | 16 | 17 | 18 | 19 |
| T | 20 | 21 | 22 | 23 | 24 | 25 | 26 | 27 | 28 | 29 |
| T | 30 | 31 | 32 | 33 | 34 | 35 | 36 | 37 | 38 | 39 |
| T | 40 | 41 | 42 | 43 | 44 | 45 | 46 | 47 | 48 | 49 |
| T | 50 | 51 | 52 | 53 | 54 | 55 | 56 | 57 | 58 | 59 |
| T | 60 | 61 | 62 | 63 | 64 | 65 | 66 | 67 | 68 | 69 |
| T | 70 | 71 | 72 | 73 | 74 | 75 | 76 | 77 | 78 | 79 |
| T | 80 | 81 | 82 | 83 | 84 | 85 | 86 |    |    |    |

## Procedure for creating MIDI-format output score files

The simplest way to play the output of a BASIC program on MIDI synthesizers is to choose commercial sequencing software that will accept a properly formatted ASCII file and convert it to a compatible sequence. We use the Promidi Studio System, manufactured by Systems Design Associates, 5068 Plano Parkway, Suite 121, Plano, Texas 75075. The system is supplied in the form of a MIDI-interface card that fits into one of the (IBM-compatible) personal computer expansion slots. Two cables, input and output, connect the interface to the synthesizer. The Promidi Studio System includes complete recording, playback, and editing software as well as the TOPM.EXE program for converting the BASIC program ASCII output files to compiled musical sequence form for immediate playback on the synthesizer. A program, PCV.EXE, is also available to allow direct conversion of program output to standard music notation. The converted information can then be printed in sheet music form by the IBM-compatible software package "PERSONAL COMPOSER" which is commercially available from music stores.

## Adaptation of programs to MIDI format

The steps to be followed in creating an output file, converting it to MIDI-format, and playing it on the synthesizer are:

1. Add ASCII file-writing instructions to the BASIC program,
2. send the ASCII output file through a sequence-conversion program,
3. enter the commercial sequencing software environment,
4. and play the sequence on the MIDI synthesizer.

Step (1) involves the addition of statements at strategic points in the program to print the note-event data records to a disk file. This file can be thought of as the music score, because it will contain complete information for the performance of the sequence, first note to last.

A disk file is created and opened by the statement:

```
f1 = fopen("mididata","w");
```

Next, values must be assigned to a number of variables required by each note-event record. If you are only interested in listening to the pitch result of an algorithm, then fixed values can be assigned for the Volume (Velocity), Rhythm, and Articulation parameters, and for the channel assignment of the note as follows:

```
int j,notes,seed;
unsigned long int start_time = 0; /* noteon start time in clock
                                ticks */
unsigned int channel = 0; /* MIDI channels can be 0 - 15 */
unsigned port = 0;/* for PROMIDI ASCII file, port must be
```

```
                    set to 0 */
unsigned int pitch; /* MIDI note number (0-127) */
unsigned int velocity; /* MIDI "loudness" (0-127) */
unsigned int artdur; /* articulated note-duration */
float duration; /* total time in clock ticks allowed for note */
float articulation;/* factor to shorten (articulate) the note */
```

Then, at the point in the program where you would normally print the Pitch parameter to the CRT screen, add statements to get the current pitch, volume, duration, articulation, and channel assignment values, advance the note-on (event start-time), and print one record to the ASCII disk file:

```
pitch = rand() % 65 +30; /* lowest pitch will be 30 */
channel = rand() % 15; /* randomly assign MIDI channel */
velocity = rand() % 50 + 75; /* randomly assign volume */
duration = 192/(rand() % 9 + 2); /* 192 clock ticks per
                                    quarter-note */
artdur = duration * articulation; /* shorten the time

fprintf(f1,"%lu %u %u %u %u %u\n",start_time,pitch,velocity,
       artdur,channel,port);
 start_time += duration;  /* advance noteon time */
```

Notice that the variable "duration" is not part of filed information in this case; it is added to the original start-time (in clock ticks) to calculate the start time of the next note-event. The variable artdur holds the shortened (articulated-duration) duration value; this is to provide adequate synthesizer gate time in situations where each voice of an eight-voice polyphonic synthesizer is assigned to a separate part. If the synthesizer is set to allow the playing of chords, then the note start times can be allowed to overlap in time.

Function Midifile( ), MIC 7.26, demonstrates the aforementioned MIDI-format ASCII file writing principles. Study it to be sure you understand the function of all the variables, then execute it a number of times using different pitch ranges.

## FUNCTION: Midifile( )   MIC 7.27

## Purpose

Compile a notelist score of data for four musical parameters (Pitch, Duration, Velocity, Articulation) and write it to a file in Promidi Studio System ASCII format.

## Notes

File must then be converted to a sequence file using TOPM.EXE, provided as part of sequencing software by Systems Design Associates, 5068 Plano Parkway, Suite 121, Plano, Texas 75075.

## Programming ideas

1. Write an interactive program that makes various data generation algorithms available to the user for application to any selected parameter.
2. Modify FUNCTION: Midifile( ) to allow creation of a score for multiple channels (voices, parts, etc.).

## Source code listing

```
/* MIDIFILE.C  (compiles a notelist score of data for 4 musical
parameters and writes it to a file in PROMIDI STUDIO SYSTEM ASCII
format).

NOTE:  File must then be converted to a sequence file using
TOPM.EXE, provided  as part of sequencing software by Systems
Design Associates, 5068 Plano Parkway, Suite 121, Plano, Texas
75075 */

#include <stdio.h>
#include <stdlib.h>
main()
{
 void Midifile();
 Midifile();
} /* end of main */
/*================ MIC 7.26 ===============*/
/* Midifile() function */
void Midifile()
{
 FILE *f1, *fopen();
 int j,notes,seed;
 unsigned int pitch,velocity,channel,port,artdur;
 float duration,articulation;
 unsigned long int start_time = 0;
 channel = 0; /* assign notelist to MIDI Channel 1 */
 port = 0; /* for PROMIDI ASCII file port must be set to 0 */
```

```
f1 = fopen("mididata","w");
printf("enter an integer seed for the random generator\n");
scanf("%d",&seed);
printf("how many events in your notelist?\n");
scanf("%d",&notes);
printf("enter articulation as a real > 0 & <= .85\n");
scanf("%f",&articulation);
srand(seed);
for(j = 0;j < notes;j++)
    {
        pitch = rand() % 65 +30; /* lowest pitch will be 30 */
        channel = rand() % 15; /* randomly assign MIDI channel */
        velocity = rand() % 50 + 75; /* randomly assign volume */
        duration = 192/(rand() % 9 + 2); /* 768 clock ticks per
                                          whole-note */
        artdur = duration * articulation; /* shorten the time
                                           note sounds */
        printf("%lu %u %u %u %u %u\n",start_time,pitch,velocity,
               artdur,channel,port);
       fprintf(f1,"%lu %u %u %u %u %u\n",start_time,pitch,velocity,
               artdur,channel,port);
        start_time += duration;  /* advance noteon time */
    }
fclose(f1);
} /* end of Midifile() function */
```

## Program execution

MIDIFILE.EXE

enter an integer seed for the random generator    301
how many events in your notelist? 45
enter articulation as a real > 0 & <= .85    .50

```
0 83 87 130 2 0
153 77 84 92 12 0
262 70 78 81 4 0
358 36 93 326 5 0
742 60 108 81 6 0
838 42 103 108 5 0
966 93 103 217 2 0
1222 82 115 326 6 0
1606 84 121 81 11 0
1702 57 77 163 4 0
1894 44 92 92 6 0
2003 59 96 130 1 0
2156 94 88 163 10 0
2348 62 96 326 9 0
2732 52 100 130 5 0
2885 88 108 92 11 0
2994 54 75 326 9 0
3378 85 114 81 13 0
3474 33 75 326 9 0
3858 43 103 81 5 0
3954 83 93 72 12 0
4039 62 121 130 14 0
4192 92 109 108 13 0
4320 37 78 64 2 0
4396 44 117 81 6 0
```

```
4492 52 97 81 6 0
4588 43 123 108 8 0
4716 33 114 64 8 0
4792 91 121 108 6 0
4920 40 84 217 11 0
5176 90 78 92 13 0
5285 71 96 72 7 0
5370 74 117 72 13 0
5455 33 85 108 0 0
5583 33 112 326 13 0
5967 45 119 217 13 0
6223 48 81 81 7 0
6319 35 76 326 3 0
6703 49 118 163 1 0
6895 92 85 326 4 0
7279 87 100 108 12 0
7407 39 104 92 4 0
7516 88 77 163 5 0
7708 42 122 217 5 0
8599 45 102 108 1 0
```

# A
# *Program header (.h) files*

```
/*==================== MIC_H3 ====================*/
/* FILENAME:  SCRPTPRSR.H */
#include <stdio.h>
#include <ctype.h>
#include "fgetline.c"
#ifndef SYNCLAVIE_C
#include "synclavi.c"
#endif
#include "getfnam.c"
#include "stoi.c"
#ifndef MAXDATA
#define MAXDATA 1000
#endif
#define MAXSIZE 80;
int parray[MAXDATA];
int rarray[MAXDATA];
int aarray[MAXDATA];
int varray[MAXDATA];
int tarray[MAXDATA];
int psize, rsize, asize, vsize, tsize;
#ifndef inputfile
FILE *inputfile;
#endif
FILE *getfnam();

/*==================== MIC_H4 ====================*/
/* TEXT.H */
#include <stdio.h>
#include <ctype.h>
#include <alloc.h>
#include "randmain.c"
#define MAXDATA 100
#define MAXVOCAB 100
#define MAXWORDSIZE 80
#define TRUE 1
#define FALSE -1
static char vowels[6] = {"AEIOU"};
static char punctuation[10] = {".,;:'!-/?"};
char *phones[MAXVOCAB];
char *dipth[MAXVOCAB];
char *words[MAXVOCAB];
```

```
char *verbs[MAXVOCAB];
char *adjectives[MAXVOCAB];
char *nouns[MAXVOCAB];
char *articles[3] = {"a", "the", "an"};
int wct = 0;
int dip = 0;
int ph = 0;                    /* size of arrays */
int vbct = 0;
int adct = 0;
int nct = 0;
int act = 3;
```

# B
# *Subprogram (.c) library*

```c
/****************************************************************/
/* MIC_SP1.0    ARRAY.C
                purpose: function-group to handle array
                         processing (retro,invert,rotate,etc.) */
#include "array.pro"
/*============= MIC_SP1.1 ===============*/
invshape(shape, inv, size)
   int shape[], inv[], size;

{
int j;
for(j = 0; j < size; j++)
   {
   if(shape[j] > 0)
      inv[j] = shape[j] - abs(shape[j] * 2);
   else
      inv[j] = shape[j] + abs(shape[j] * 2);
   }
}
/*============= MIC_SP1.2 ===============*/
getshape(datarray, shapearray, size)
   int datarray[];
   int shapearray[];
   int size;

{
int a ,b, j;
    for (j = 0; j < size - 1 ; j++)
        {
            a = datarray[j];
            b = datarray[j + 1];
            shapearray[j] = b - a;
        }
}
/*============= MIC_SP1.3 ===============*/
FputArray(fp, datarray, size)
    FILE *fp;
    int datarray[];
    int size;
{
   int k;
   int j = 0;
   int offset = 0;
```

```
        while(j + offset < size)
            {
                while(j < 18 && j + offset < size)
                    fprintf(fp, "%3d ", datarray[j++ + offset]);

                offset += j;
                j = 0;
                fprintf(fp,"\n");
            }
}
/*============= MIC_SP1.4 ===============*/
PutArray(datarray, size)
    int datarray[];
    int size;
{
    int j;= 0;
    int offset = 0;

    while(j + offset < size)
        {
            while(j < 18 && j + offset < size)
                printf("%3d ", datarray[j++ + offset]);

            offset += j;
            j = 0;
            printf("\n");
        }
}
/*============= MIC_SP1.5 ===============*/
PutLn()
{
    int j;
    printf("\n/*");
    for(j = 0; j < 68; j++)
        printf("%c", '-');
    printf("*/\n");
}
/*============= MIC_SP1.6 ===============*/
FputLn(fp)
    FILE *fp;
{
    int j;
    fprintf(fp, "\n/*");
    for(j = 0; j < 68; j++)
        fprintf(fp, "%c", '-');
    fprintf(fp, "*/\n");
}
/*============= MIC_SP1.7 ===============*/
RetroArray(datarray, size)
    int datarray[];
    int size;
{
    int retrograde[MAXDATA];
    int ask;
    int j, k;

    for(j = size-1, k = 0; j >= 0; j--, k++)
        {
        PutPitch(datarray[j]);
        retrograde[k] = datarray[j];
        }
```

```c
    printf("\n");
    printf("\nDo you want to store it in the data array? yes (1) no (2) ");
    scanf("%d", &ask);
    if( ask == 1)
      {
      for(j = 0; j < size; j++)
        datarray[j] = retrograde[j];
      }
/*============= MIC_SP1.8 ================*/
getmax(datarray, size)
   int datarray[];
   int size;
{
    int j, max;
     for(max = datarray[0], j = 1; j < size; j++)
        if(datarray[j] > max)
                    max = datarray[j];
       return max;
}
/*============= MIC_SP1.9 ================*/
getmin(datarray, size)
   int datarray[], size;
{
    int j, min;
     for(min = datarray[0], j = 1; j < size; j++)
        if(datarray[j] < min)
                    min = datarray[j];
       return min;
}
/*============= MIC_SP1.10 ================*/
float getmaxf(datarray, size)
   float datarray[];
   int size;
{
    int j;
        float max;
     for(max = datarray[0], j = 1; j < size; j++)
        if(datarray[j] > max)
                    max = datarray[j];
       return max;
}
/*============= MIC_SP1.11 ================*/
float getminf(datarray, size)
   float datarray[];
   int size;
{
    int j;
        float min;
     for(min = datarray[0], j = 1; j < size; j++)
        if(datarray[j] < min)
                    min = datarray[j];
       return min;
}
/*============= MIC_SP1.12 ================*/
FrotateArray(fp, size, datarray)
    FILE *fp;
    int size;
    int datarray[];
    {
    register int rotation, j, k, m, tran, ask;
```

```
        int disarray[MAXDATA];
        tran = 0;
printf("ROTATIONS");
        for(rotation=0; rotation < size; rotation++)
            {
            printf("\nArray rotation no %d\n", rotation);
            fprintf(fp, "\n/* Array rotation no %d */\n", rotation);
            for(j=0; j < size - rotation; j++)
                disarray[j] = datarray[j + rotation] + tran;

                for(k=0; k < rotation; k++)
                    disarray[j + k] = datarray[k] + tran;

                    ScriptArray(disarray, 'P', size);
                    FscriptArray(fp, disarray, 'P', size);
            }
}
/*============= MIC_SP1.13 ================*/
RotateArray(datarray, disarray, size, rotation)
        int datarray[];
        int disarray[];
        int size, rotation;
        {
        register int j, k;
        int temp[MAXDATA];
            for(j = 0; j < size - rotation; j++)
                temp[j] = datarray[j + rotation];

            for(k = 0; k < rotation; k++)
                temp[j + k] = datarray[k];

            for(j = 0; j < size; j++)
                disarray[j] = temp[j];
}
/*============= MIC_SP1.14 ================*/
imbricate(darray, imarray, start, imsize, imbeg)
    int darray[], imarray[];
    int start, imsize, imbeg;
{
    int j;
    for(j= start; j < start + imsize; j++)
        imarray[imbeg++] = darray[j];
}
/*============= MIC_SP1.15 ================*/
sumarray(arry, size)
    int arry[];
    int size;
{
    int j;
    int sum = 0;

    for (j = 0; j < size; j++)
        sum += abs(arry[j]);
     return (sum);
}
/*****************************************************/
/* MIC_SP2.0   INPUTYOU.C
                purpose: user input of data to array */
/*=============== MIC_SP2.1 ================*/
InputYourOwn(datarray)
    int datarray[];
```

```
{
    int j, k, size;
#ifdef debug
printf("\n\t\t\t\t\tentering inputyourown\n");
#endif

    printf("\nHow many numbers do you want to input? ");
    scanf("%d", &size);
     for(j = 0; j < size; j++)
        {
          printf("Input integer # %d \t-\b", j+1);
           scanf("%d", &k);
           if(k >= 0 && k < 85)
             datarray[j] = k;
           else
             {
             do{
             printf("\nBetween 0 and 84, remember?\n");
             printf("Input integer # %d \t-\b", j+1);
             scanf("%d", &k);
             datarray[j] = k;
             } while ( k < 0 || k > 84);
             }
        }
    printf("\nHere is what you typed in\n");
     for(j = 0; j < size; j++)
       printf("%d ", datarray[j]);
    printf("\n\n");
    return (size);
}
/***********************************************************/
/* MIC_SP4.0   GETFNAM.C
                 purpose: obtain filename from console for
                           reading,writing, or appending */
/*================ MIC_SP4.1 =====================*/
FILE *getfnam(use,mode)

    char *use,*mode;
{
    FILE *fp,*fopen();
    char name[80],c;
    int ask;

        printf("\n\nFilename for %s ? ",use);
        scanf("%s",name);

        if (name[0] == '='){
            c = *mode;
            switch(c){
                case 'r': return (stdin);
                case 'w':
                case 'a': return (stdout);
            }
        }

        if ((fp = fopen(name,mode)) == NULL){
            printf("Error opening %s for %s.",name,use);
            printf("\nEnter 1 to try again; any other key to abort.");
            scanf("%d", &ask);
            if(ask ==  1)
                fp = getfnam(use,mode);
```

```
            else exit(0);
        }
        return (fp);
}
/*=============================================---======-*/

/*******************************************************/
/* MIC_SP6.0        SCORFORM.C
                    purpose: to convert integer data to score
                             (notelist) format for use by
                             synthesizers.
#include <ctype.h>
#include "scorform.pro"
/*================= MIC_SP6.1 =============*/
ValidPitch(pitch)
        char *pitch;
{
        int j, valid;

        for(j = 0; j < 3; j++)
            {
            if(pitch[j] <= 'G' || pitch[j] >= 'A' || pitch[j] >='0' ||
                pitch[j] <= '9' || pitch[j] == '#' || pitch[j] == '-')
                valid = 1;
            else
                return(0);
            }
            return(valid);
}
/*================= MIC_SP6.2 =============*/
#define REST 85
#define INVALID 86
int PitchToInteger(pitch)
        char *pitch;
{
        int PitchNumber = 24, oct = 3, accidental = 0, i, isvalid;
        static int letternums[] = {9,11,0,2,4,5,7};
                                /* A B C D E F G */
        char c;

            isvalid = ValidPitch(pitch);
            if(isvalid == 0)
                return(INVALID);
            if(pitch[1] == 'F')         /* convert all flats to - */
                {
                pitch[1] = '-';
                if(pitch[0] == 'C')
                    pitch[2] -= 1;
                }

            while( (c = *pitch++) != '\0')
            {
                if(iscntrl(c))
                    return (INVALID);
                if(c == '\0')
                    return (INVALID);
                if (c == 'R')
                    return REST;

                else if (c >= 'A' && c <= 'G')
                    {
```

```
                         i = c - 'A';
                         PitchNumber = letternums[i];
                  }
              else if (c >= '0' && c <= '9')
                  oct = c - '0';
              else switch(c)
              {
                  case '#': accidental += 1; break;
                  case '+': accidental += 1; break;
                  case 'b': accidental -= 1; break;
                  case '-': accidental -= 1; break;
                  case 'x': accidental += 2; break;
                  default: printf("\ninvalid %c", c);
                              return (INVALID);
              }

          }
          PitchNumber = ((PitchNumber + 12 + accidental) % 12) +
                          (oct * 12);
          return (PitchNumber);
}
/*=============== MIC_SP6.3 =============*/
#define MAXPIT 84
char *IntegerToPitch(num)
int num;
{
        static char pitch[4];
        static char *names[] ={ "C","C#","D","D#","E","F","F#",
                                        "G","G#","A","A#","B" };
        static char *rest = {"R"};
        int pc,oct;

        if (num < 0 || num > MAXPIT)
           return (rest);
        else {
            pc = num % 12;
            oct = (num/12);
            sprintf(pitch,"%s%d", names[pc], oct);
            return (pitch);
            }
}
/*=============== MIC_SP6.4 =============*/
PutPitch(num)
   int num;
{
   printf("%-4s", IntegerToPitch(num));
}
/*=============== MIC_SP6.5 =============*/
ScriptArray(datarray, lnhead, size)
   int datarray[];
   char lnhead;
   int size;
{
   int k;
   int j = 0;
   int offset = 0;

       while(j + offset < size)
        {
        printf("\n%c  ", lnhead);
        while(j < 15 && j + offset < size)
```

```
        switch(lnhead)
            {
             case 'P' :
                    printf(" ");
                    PutPitch(datarray[j++ + offset]);
                    break;
             case 'R' :
                    printf(" ");
                    printf("%-4d", datarray[j++ + offset]);
                    break;
             case 'A' :
                    printf(" ");
                    printf("%-4d", datarray[j++ + offset]);
                    break;
             case 'V' :
                    printf("%-4d", datarray[j++ + offset]);
                    break;
             case 'T' :
                    printf(" ");
                    printf("%-4d", datarray[j++ + offset]);
                    break;
             case ' ' :
                    PutPitch(datarray[j++ + offset]);
                    break;
            }
        offset += j;
        j = 0;
        }
    printf("\n");
}
/***********************************************************/
/* MIC_SP7.0   SYNCLAVI.C
        purpose:   provide screen output and data filing
                   in computer music notelist format; an
                   expansion of SCORFORM.C      */

#include "synclavi.pro"
#include <stdio.h>
#include <ctype.h>
/*================= MIC_SP6.1 ==============*/
ValidPitch(pitch)
    char *pitch;
{
    int j, valid;

    for(j = 0; j < 3; j++)
        {
        if(pitch[j] <= 'G' || pitch[j] >= 'A' || pitch[j] >='0' ||
           pitch[j] <= '9' || pitch[j] == '#' || pitch[j] == '-')
           valid = 1;
        else
           return(0);
        }
        return(valid);
}

/*================= MIC_SP6.2 ==============*/
#define REST 85
#define INVALID 86
/*
 * PitchToInteger:      convert a pitch string to an integer value
```

```
 */
int PitchToInteger(pitch)
     char *pitch;
{
     int PitchNumber = 24, oct = 3, accidental = 0, i, isvalid;
     static int letternums[] = {9,11,0,2,4,5,7}; /* A B C D E F G */
     char c;

        isvalid = ValidPitch(pitch);
        if(isvalid == 0)
           return(INVALID);
         if(pitch[1] == 'F')          /* convert all flats to - */
            {
            pitch[1] = '-';
            if(pitch[0] == 'C')
              pitch[2] -= 1;
            }

        while( (c = *pitch++) != '\0')
           {
            if(iscntrl(c))
             return (INVALID);
            if(c == '\0')
             return (INVALID);
            if (c == 'R')
             return REST;

            else if (c >= 'A' && c <= 'G')
               {
                   i = c - 'A';
                   PitchNumber = letternums[i];
               }
            else if (c >= '0' && c <= '9')
                   oct = c - '0';
            else switch(c)
               {
                   case '#': accidental += 1; break;
                   case '+': accidental += 1; break;
                   case 'b': accidental -= 1; break;
                   case '-': accidental -= 1; break;
                   case 'x': accidental += 2; break;
                   default: printf("\ninvalid %c", c);
                            return (INVALID);
               }

           }
        PitchNumber = ((PitchNumber + 12 + accidental) % 12) + (oct * 12
        return (PitchNumber);
}
/*=============== MIC_SP6.3 ==============*/
#define MAXPIT 84
char *IntegerToPitch(num)
int num;
{
        static char pitch[4];
        static char *names[] ={ "C","C#","D","D#","E","F","F#",
                                        "G","G#","A","A#","B" };
        static char *rest = {"R"};
        int pc,oct;

        if (num < 0 || num > MAXPIT)
```

```
                 return (rest);
            else {
                pc = num % 12;
                oct = (num/12);
                sprintf(pitch,"%s%d", names[pc], oct);
                return (pitch);
                }
}
/*================ MIC_SP6.4 ==============*/
PutPitch(num)
    int num;
{
    printf("%-4s", IntegerToPitch(num));
}
/*================ MIC_SP7.1 ==============*/
FputPitch(fp,num)
    FILE *fp;
    int num;
{
    fprintf(fp,"%-4s", IntegerToPitch(num));
}
/*================ MIC_SP6.5 ==============*/
ScriptArray(datarray, lnhead, size)
    int datarray[];
    char lnhead;
    int size;
{
    int k;
    int j = 0;
    int offset = 0;

        while(j + offset < size)
          {
          printf("\n%c  ", lnhead);
          while(j < 15 && j + offset < size)
            switch(lnhead)
                {
                case 'P' :
                      printf(" ");
                      PutPitch(datarray[j++ + offset]);
                      break;
                case 'R' :
                      printf(" ");
                      printf("%-4d", datarray[j++ + offset]);
                      break;
                case 'A' :
                      printf(" ");
                      printf("%-4d", datarray[j++ + offset]);
                      break;
                case 'V' :
                      printf(" ");
                      printf("%-4d", datarray[j++ + offset]);
                      break;
                case 'T' :
                      printf(" ");
                      printf("%-4d", datarray[j++ + offset]);
                      break;
                case ' ' :
                      PutPitch(datarray[j++ + offset]);
                      break;
                }
```

```
            offset += j;
            j = 0;
            }
    printf("\n");
}
/*================= MIC_SP7.2 ==============*/
FscriptArray(fp, datarray, lnhead, size)
    FILE *fp;
    int datarray[];
    char lnhead;
    int size;
{
    int k;
    int j = 0;
    int offset = 0;

        while(j + offset < size)
          {
          fprintf(fp, "\n%c  ", lnhead);
          while(j < 15 && j + offset < size)
              switch(lnhead)
                  {
                    case 'P' :
                        fprintf(fp, " ");
                        FputPitch(fp, datarray[j++ + offset]);
                        break;
                    case 'R' :
                        fprintf(fp, " ");
                        fprintf(fp, "%-4d", datarray[j++ + offset]);
                        break;
                    case 'A' :
                        fprintf(fp, " ");
                        fprintf(fp, "%-4d", datarray[j++ + offset]);
                        break;
                    case 'V' :
                        fprintf(fp, " ");
                        fprintf(fp, "%-4d", datarray[j++ + offset]);
                        break;
                    case 'T' :
                        fprintf(fp, " ");
                        fprintf(fp, "%-4d", datarray[j++ + offset]);
                        break;
                    case ' ' :
                        FputPitch(fp, datarray[j++ + offset]);
                        break;
                  }
          offset += j;
          j = 0;
          }
    fprintf(fp, "\n");
}
/************************************************************/
/* MIC_SP8.0  SCREEN.C
              purpose: ansi screen escape characters */

#include "screen.pro"
#define BOLD        "\033[1m"
#define UNDER       "\033[4m"
#define BLINK       "\033[5m"
#define REVERSE     "\033[7m"
```

```
#define NOBOLD        "\033[2;2m"
#define NOUNDER       "\033[2;[4m"
#define NOBLINK       "\033[2;[5m"
#define NOREVERSE     "\033[2;[7m"
#define NORM          "\033[0m"         /* cancels special modes */
#define CURSUP        "\033[A"
#define CURDN         "\033[B"
#define CURR          "\033[C"
#define CURL          "\033[D"
#define HOME          "\033[H"
#define BIGTOP        "\033#3"
#define BIGBOT        "\033#4"
#define NORMAL        "\033#5"
#define WIDE          "\033#6"
int vt;
/*=============== MIC_SP8.1 ===============*/
/* centerf        centers string              */
centerf(string)
char *string;
{
     int l;
     l = (80 - strlen(string)) / 2;
     while (l-- > 0) putchar(' ');
     printf("%s\n",string);
}
/*=============== MIC_SP8.2 ===============*/
centerwidef(string)
char *string;
{
     int l;
     l = (40 - strlen(string)) / 2;
     while (l-- > 0) putchar(' ');
     printf("%s%s%s\n",WIDE, string, NORM);
}
/*=============== MIC_SP8.3 ===============*/
centerbigf(string)
char *string;
{
     int l;
     l = (40 - strlen(string)) / 2;
     while (l-- > 0) putchar(' ');
     printf("%s%s%s\n",BIGTOP, string, NORM);
     l = (40 - strlen(string)) / 2;
     while (l-- > 0) putchar(' ');
     printf("%s%s%s\n",BIGBOT, string, NORM);
}
/*=============== MIC_SP8.4 ===============*/
Cls()
{
   if (vt == 1)
      vt52cls();
   else
      vt100cls();
}
/*=============== MIC_SP8.5 ===============*/
ScrCurs(row, col)
   int row, col;
{
   if (vt == 1)
      vt52scrCurs(row, col);
   else
```

```c
        vt100scrCurs(row, col);
}
/*================ MIC_SP8.6 ===============*/
vt52cls()
{
    printf("\033H\033J");
}
/*================ MIC_SP8.7 ===============*/
vt52scrCurs(row, col)
int row, col;
{
    printf("\033Y%c%c",row + 31, col + 31);
}
/*================ MIC_SP8.8 ===============*/
vt100cls()
{
    printf("\033[H\033[2J");
}
/*================ MIC_SP8.9 ===============*/
vt100scrCurs(row, col)
    int row, col;
{
    printf("\033[%d;%dH", (row) + 1, (col) + 1);
}
/*================ MIC_SP8.10 ===============*/
getvt()
{
    vt = 1; /* for ibm pc with ansi driver installed */
}
/************************************************************/


/************************************************************/
/* MIC_SP9.0     GETNUM.C */
getnum()
{
    int j;
    char string[10];

    gets(string);
    j = atoi(string);
    return(j);
}


/************************************************************/
/* MIC_SP10.0    FUSARRAY.C  */

#include "fusarray.pro"
/*================ MIC_SP10.1 ===============*/
FusePair(fp, dat, fusarray, size)
    FILE *fp;
    int dat[];
    int fusarray[][2];
    int size;
{
    int j, row, col;
    printf("\n\tFUSIONS\n");
    fprintf(fp, "\n\tFUSIONS\n");
    printf("\n\n\tIntervals to be fused : \n\t");
    fprintf(fp, "\n\n\tIntervals to be fused : \n\t");
    PutArray(dat, size);
    FputArray(fp, dat, size);
```

```
          row = 0;
          for(j=0; j < size - 1; j++)
             {
             col = 0;
             fusarray[row][col++] = dat[j];
             fusarray[row++][col] = dat[ j + 1];
             }
}
/*=============== MIC_SP10.2 ===============*/
fusion(dat, fusarray, size, limit)
     int dat[];
     int fusarray[][2];
     int size;
     int limit;
{
     int x, j, k, col;
     int row = 0;
     int m = 0;
     int n = 0;


     for(x = 2; x <= size - 1; x++)
        {
        for(j = 0, k = size - 1; j <= size - x, k >= x; j++, k--)
           {
           m = summation(dat, j, x);   /* sum dat from j to x */
           n = negsum(dat, k, x);      /* sum dat from k down to x */
           if(m <= limit)
              {
              col = 0;
              fusarray[row][col++] = dat[j];
              fusarray[row++][col] = m;
              }
           if(n <= limit)
              {
              col = 0;
              fusarray[row][col++] = dat[k];
              fusarray[row++][col] = n;
              }
           }
        }
     return(row);

}
/*=============== MIC_SP10.3 ===============*/
fusion2(dat, fusarray, size)
     int dat[];
     int fusarray[][2];
     int size;
{
     int j, k, m, n, row, col;

     row = 0;
     for(j=0; j < size - 3; j++)
        {
        k = dat[j] + dat[j + 1];
        m = dat[j + 2] + dat[j + 3];
           col = 0;
           fusarray[row][col++] = k;
           fusarray[row++][col] = m;
        }
     return(row);
```

```
    }
    fusion3(dat, fusarray, size)
        int dat[];
        int fusarray[][2];
        int size;
    {
        int j, k, m, n, row, col;

        row = 0;
        for(j=0; j < size - 4; j++)
            {
            k = dat[j] + dat[j + 1] + dat[j + 2];
            m = dat[j + 1] + dat[j + 2] + dat[j + 3];

                col = 0;
                fusarray[row][col++] = k;
                fusarray[row++][col] = dat[j + 3];

                col = 0;
                fusarray[row][col++] = dat[j];
                fusarray[row++][col] = m;
            }
        return(row);
    }
    /*================ MIC_SP10.4 ==============*/
    summation(darray, start, num)
        int darray[];
        int start;
        int num;
        {
        int j;
        int k = 0;
        for(j = 1; j <= num; j++)
          k += darray[start + j];
        return(k);
    }
    /*================ MIC_SP10.5 ==============*/
    negsum(darray, start, num)
        int darray[];
        int start;
        int num;
    {
        int j = 0;
        int k;
        for(k = 1; k <= num; k++)
          j += darray[start - k];
        return(j);
    }


    /***********************************************************/
    /* MIC_SP11.1    MATRIX.C  */

    #include "quicksort.c"
    #include "matrix.pro"
    /*================ MIC_SP11.1 ==============*/
    /* should be sorted first */
    PutMatrixFq(matrix, fq, rsize, csize)
        int matrix[][2];
        int fq[];
```

```
        int rsize;
        int csize;
{

        int j, k;
        printf("\n fusion\t\t\tfrequency");
        printf("\n ------\t\t\t---------\n");
        for(j = 0; j < rsize; j+=fq[j])
            {
            for(k = 0; k < csize; k++)
                printf("%d\t", matrix[j][k]);
            printf("\t     %d\n", fq[j]);
            }
}
/*================ MIC_SP11.2 ==============*/
FputMatrixFq(fp, matrix, fq, rsize, csize)
        FILE *fp;
        int matrix[][2];
        int fq[];
        int rsize;
        int csize;
{

        int j, k;
        fprintf(fp, "\n fusion\t\t\tfrequency");
        fprintf(fp, "\n ------\t\t\t---------\n");

        for(j = 0; j < rsize; j+=fq[j])
            {
            for(k = 0; k < csize; k++)
                fprintf(fp, "%d\t", matrix[j][k]);
            fprintf(fp, "\t     %d\n", fq[j]);
            }
}
/*================ MIC_SP11.3 ==============*/
FindMatrixFreq(matrix, fq, size)
        int matrix[][2];
        int fq[];
        int size;

{
        int j, k, key, key2;
printf("\nFinding matrix frequency\nPlease be patient\n");
for(j = 0; j< size; j++)
        fq[j] = 0;

for(j = 0; j< size; j++)
        {
        key = matrix[j][0];
        key2 = matrix[j][1];
        for(k = 0; k< size; k++)
            {
            if(key == matrix[k][0] && key2 == matrix[k][1])
                fq[k] += 1;
            }
        }
}
/*================ MIC_SP11.4 ==============*/
MatrixSort(matrix, rsize, csize)
        int matrix[][2];
        int rsize;
        int csize;
```

```
{
    int i, j, k, temp, temp2;
printf("\nSorting matrix\nPlease be patient\n");
/* sort rows */
    for(i = 0; i < rsize-1; ++i)
      for(j = i + 1; j < rsize; ++j)
          if(matrix[i][0] > matrix[j][0])
              {
              temp = matrix[i][0];
              temp2 = matrix[i][1];
              matrix[i][0] = matrix[j][0];
              matrix[i][1] = matrix[j][1];
              matrix[j][0] = temp;
              matrix[j][1] = temp2;
              }
/* sort cols */
    for(i = 0; i < rsize-1; ++i)
      for(j = i + 1; j < rsize; ++j)
          if(matrix[i][1] > matrix[j][1] && matrix[i][0]
                            == matrix[j][0])
              {
              temp = matrix[i][1];
              matrix[i][1] = matrix[j][1];
              matrix[j][1] = temp;
              }


}
/*================ MIC_SP11.5 ==============*/
MatrixQuickSort(matrix, rsize, csize)
    int matrix[][2];
    int rsize;
    int csize;
{
    int i, j, tmp;
int temp[5000];
int temp2[5000];
printf("\nSorting matrix\nqs\n");
/* sort rows */
    for(i = 0; i < rsize; i++)
        temp[i] = matrix[i][0];
    QuickSort(temp, 0, rsize-1);

/* sort cols */

    for(i = 0; i < rsize-1; ++i)
      for(j = i + 1; j < rsize; ++j)
          if(matrix[i][1] > matrix[j][1] && matrix[i][0]
                                == matrix[j][0])
              {
              tmp = matrix[i][1];
              matrix[i][1] = matrix[j][1];
              matrix[j][1] = tmp;
              }

    for(i = 0; i < rsize-1; ++i)
        matrix[i][0] = temp[i];


}
/*================ MIC_SP11.6 ==============*/
```

```
    PutMatrix(matrix, nrow, ncol)
        int matrix[][2];
        int nrow;
        int ncol;
    {
        int j, k;
        for(j = 0; j < nrow; j++)
            {
            for(k = 0; k < ncol; k++)
                printf("%d\t", matrix[j][ k]);
            printf("\n");
            }
    }
    /*================ MIC_SP11.7 ==============*/
    FputMatrix(fp, matrix, nrow, ncol)
        FILE *fp;
        int matrix[][2];
        int nrow;
        int ncol;
    {
        int j, k;
        for(j = 0; j < nrow; j++)
            {
            for(k = 0; k < ncol; k++)
                fprintf(fp, "%d\t", matrix[j][ k]);
            fprintf(fp, "\n");
            }
    }
    /*================ MIC_SP11.8 ==============*/
    ZeroMatrix(matrix, rowsize, colsize)
        int matrix[];
        int rowsize;
        int colsize;
    {
        int j, k;
        for (j = 0; j < rowsize; j++)
            {
            for(k = 0; k < colsize; k++)
                matrix[j, k] = 0;
            }
    }
    /******************************************************************/
    /* MIC_SP12.0    QUICKSOR.C    */

    /*================ MIC_SP12.0 ==============*/
    /* call : quicksort(sorted, 0, size - 1);    */
    /* sorted = int array, size =length of array */
    QuickSort(item,left,right)
        int item[], left, right;
    {
    register int i, j;
    char x,y;

        i= left;
        j = right;
        x = item[(left + right)/2];
        do {
            while(item[i] < x && i < right) i++;
            while(x < item[j] && j > left) j--;

            if(i <= j)
```

```
            {
            y = item[i];
            item[i] = item[j];
            item[j] = y;
            i++; j--;
            }
      } while(i <= j);
      if(left< j) QuickSort(item, left, j);
      if(i < right) QuickSort(item, i, right);
}
/*=============== MIC_SP11.9 ==============*/
quick(item, count)
    int item[];
    int count;
{
    QuickSort(item, 0, count-1);
}

/************************************************************/
/* MIC_SP12.0    STATFUNC.C    */

/*  calls:
                    a = mean(data, num);
                    std = StdDev(data, num);
                    m = median(data, num);
                    md = FindMode(data, num);
                    regress(data, num);
*/
/*=============== MIC_SP12.1 ==============*/
#define MAX 1000
float mean(), StdDev();


float
mean(data, num)
    int data[];
    int num;
{
    int t, sum = 0;
    float avg;

    for(t = 0; t < num; ++t)
        sum += data[t];
    avg = sum/num;
     return avg;
}
/*=============== MIC_SP12.2 ==============*/
float
StdDev(data, num)
    int data[];
    int num;
{
    register int t;
    float std, avg;
    double temp, sqrt();
    avg = mean(data, num);
    std = 0;
    for(t = 0; t < num; ++t)
        {
        std += ((data[t] - avg) * (data[t] - avg));
        }
```

```
        std /= num;
        temp = std;
        temp = sqrt(temp);
        std = temp;
        return std;
}
/*================= MIC_SP12.3 ==============*/
median(data, num)
    int data[];
    int num;
{
    register int t;
    int dtemp[MAX];

    for(t = 0; t < num; ++t)
        dtemp[t] = data[t];
     quick(dtemp, num);
     return dtemp[num/2];

}
/*================= MIC_SP12.4 ==============*/
FindMode(data, num)
    int data[];
    int num;
{
    register int t, w;
    int oldmode;
    int count, oldcount, md;

    oldmode = 0;
    oldcount = 0;
    for(t = 0; t < num; ++t)
        {
        md = data[t];
        count = 1;
    for(w = t + 1; w < num; ++w)
        if(md == data[w]) count++;
        if(count > oldcount)
            {
            oldmode = md;
            oldcount = count;
            }
        }
    return oldmode;
}
/*================= MIC_SP12.5 ==============*/
regress(data, num)
    int data[];
    int num;
{
    float a, b, x, x_avg, y_avg, temp, temp2;
    float cor;
    int data2[580];
    float StdDev();
     int t, min, max;
    char s[80];

y_avg = 0;
    for(t = 0; t < num; ++t)
        y_avg += data[t];
     y_avg /= num;
```

```
    x_avg = 0;
       for(t = 0; t <= num; ++t)
           x_avg += t;
        x_avg /= num;

    temp=0;
    temp2=0;
       for(t = 0; t <= num; ++t)
          {
          temp += (data[t-1]- y_avg) * (t-x_avg);
          temp2 += (t-x_avg) * (t-x_avg);
          }
    b = temp/temp2;
    a = y_avg - (b * x_avg);
       for(t = 0; t < num; ++t)
           data2[t] = t + 1;
           cor = temp/(num);
           cor=cor/(StdDev(data, num) * StdDev(data2, num));

    printf("\nRegression equation is Y = %f + %f * X\n",a,b);
    printf("Correlation coefficient: %f\n",cor);
    /*printf("\nPlot data points and regression line? (y/n)");
    gets(s);
    if(toupper(*s) == 'N') return;
       for(t = 0; t < num * 2; ++t)
           data2[t] = a+(b*(t+1));
    min = getmin(data, num) * 2;
    max = getmax(data, num) * 2;
    scatterplot(data,num, min, max, num*2);
    scatterplot(data2, num*2, min, max, num*2);
    gets(s);*/
    }
/*================ MIC_SP12.6 ==============*/
get_num()
{
    char s[80];
    gets(s);
    return(atoi(s));
}
/**********************************************************/
/* MIC_SP13.0    SCRPTPRS.C */

/*================ MIC_SP13.1 ==============*/
#include "scrptprs.h"

GetLines(fp)
    FILE *fp;
{
    char *line;
    int lnsize, j;

    line = (char *) malloc(80);
    printf("\nReading file:\n");

    while (!feof(fp))
    {
    lnsize = fgetline(fp, line, 80);
    printf("%s",line);
    getlnhead(line, lnsize);
    }
```

```c
        printf("File read complete");
}
/*================ MIC_SP13.2 ==============*/
PutData()
{
    int j;
    printf("\n\nHere is the pitch array size= %d\n",psize);
    for(j = 0; j < psize; j++)
        printf("%d ", parray[j]);
    printf("\n\nHere is the rhythm array size= %d\n",rsize);
    for(j = 0; j < rsize; j++)
        printf("%d ", rarray[j]);
    printf("\n\nHere is the articulation array size= %d\n",
            asize);
    for(j = 0; j < asize; j++)
        printf("%d ", aarray[j]);
    printf("\n\nHere is the volume array size= %d\n",vsize);
    for(j = 0; j < vsize; j++)
        printf("%d ", varray[j]);
    printf("\n\nHere is the rte array size= %d\n",tsize);
    for(j = 0; j < tsize; j++)
        printf("%d ", tarray[j]);
}
/*================ MIC_SP13.3 ==============*/
getlnhead(line, lnsize)
    char line[];
    int lnsize;
{
    int j, size;
    char lnhead;

    size = 0;
    j = 0;
    while (line[j] == ' ')
        j++;
    lnhead = toupper(line[j]);
#ifdef DEBUG
    printf("\nlnhead %c ", lnhead);
#endif
    switch(lnhead)
      {
        case 'P' : size = getparray(line, lnsize, parray, psize);
                   psize = size;
                   break;
        case 'R' : size = getnarray(line, lnsize, rarray, rsize);
                   rsize = size;
                   break;
        case 'A' : size = getnarray(line, lnsize, aarray, asize);
                   asize = size;
                   break;
        case 'V' : size = getnarray(line, lnsize, varray, vsize);
                   vsize = size;
                   break;
        case 'T' : size = getnarray(line, lnsize, tarray, tsize);
                   tsize = size;
                   break;
        case '/' : j = SkipComment(line, j, lnsize);
                   break;
        case 'D' : printf("\nDefines not yet supported");
                   break;
      }
```

```
}
/*================ MIC_SP13.4 ==============*/
SkipComment(line, offset, lnsize)
     char *line;
     int offset;
     int lnsize;
{
     do {
     switch(line[offset])
         {
         case '*' :  if(line[offset+1] == '/')
                     return(offset + 2);
                     break;
         case '\n':  lnsize = fgetline(inputfile, line, 80);
                     printf("line read:\n");
                     puts(line);
                     getlnhead(line, lnsize);
                     break;
         default :   offset++;
                     break;

         }
       } while(--lnsize > 0);
       return(offset);
}
/*================ MIC_SP13.5 ==============*/
getparray(line, lnsize, datarray, xsize)
     char line[];
     int lnsize;
     int datarray[];
     int xsize;
{
     int i, j, k, pc, isp;
     char pitch[4];

     i = j = k = 0;
#ifdef DEBUG
     printf("\ngetparray size=%d \n",xsize);
     puts(line);
#endif
     do {
         j = 0;
         for(i = 0; i < 4; i++)
            pitch[i]=' ';
         isp = 0;
         pc = 86;
         while(line[k] != ' ' && j < 3 && line[k] != 'P')
             {
             pitch[j++] = line[k++];
             --lnsize;
             isp = 1;
             }
         if(isp == 1)
             {
             pitch[j] = '\0';
             pc = PitchToInteger(pitch);
             }
         k++;
         if(pc != 86)
             {
             datarray[xsize++] = pc;
#ifdef DEBUG
```

```
                printf("\nparray[%d] = %d pc=%d " ,xsize-1,
                        datarray[xsize-1],pc);
                PutPitch(datarray[xsize-1]);
#endif
                }
            } while (line[k] != '\n' && --lnsize > 0);
        return(xsize);
}
/*================ MIC_SP13.6 ==============*/
getnarray(line, lnsize, datarray, xsize)
        char *line;
        int lnsize;
        int datarray[];
        int xsize;
{
        int i, j, k;
        char num[4];

          j = k = 0;
        do{
          j = 0;
          for(i = 0; i < 4; i++)
              num[i]= ' ';
          while(line[k] != ' ' && j < 3)
              {
              num[j++] = line[k++];
              --lnsize;
              }
              num[3] = '\0';
              k++;
           if(isdigit(num[0]) && (!isspace(num[0])) )
              {
              datarray[xsize++] = stoi(num);
#ifdef DEBUG
              printf("\ndatarray[%d]=%d num = %s ",xsize-1,
                      datarray[xsize-1],num);
#endif
              }
            } while (line[k] != '\n' && --lnsize > 0);

        return(xsize);
}


/****************************************************************/
/* MIC_SP15.0   FGETLINE.C */

fgetline(fp, line, MaxSize)
    FILE *fp;
    char *line;
    int  MaxSize;
{
    int  ch;
    int  ReturnSize = 0;

    if ( MaxSize == 0 )
        {
        *line = '\0';
        return( 0 );
        }

    while (( --MaxSize > 0 ) && ((ch = getc(fp)) != EOF )
```

```
                            && ( ch != '\n' ))
        line[ReturnSize++] = ch;
    if (ch == '\n')
        line[ReturnSize++] = ch;

    line[ReturnSize] = '\0';
    return(ReturnSize);
}
/***********************************************************/

/* MIC_SP16.0  STOI.C */

stoi(string)
    char string[];
{
    int j, ival, retval;
    retval = 0;

    for(j = 0; string[j] >= '0' && string[j] <='9'; ++j)
        {
        ival = string[j] - '0';
        retval *= 10;
        retval += ival;
        }
    return(retval);
}
/***********************************************************/

/* MIC_SP19.0  RANDMAIN.C */
#include <time.h>
#include <stdio.h>
#include <stdlib.h>
#include "getnum.c"
/*=============== MIC_SP19.1 ==============*/
RandMain(datarray)
    int datarray[];
{
    int i, hi, lo;
    int size = 0;

    printf("\nHow many random numbers do you want?\t");
    size = getnum();
    printf("Enter lowest number in gamut\t");
    lo = getnum();
    printf("Enter highest number in gamut\t");
    hi = getnum();

        randomize();
    for(i = 0; i < size; i++)
        {
        datarray[i] = irand(lo, hi);
            printf("%d ", datarray[i]);
        }
    return(size);
}
/*=============== MIC_SP19.2 ==============*/
irand(l, h)
    int l,h;
{
        int range,min;
        long tm;
```

```
                min = (1 <= h) ? 1 : h;
                range = abs(h - 1) + 1;
                return (rand() % range + min);
        }
        /****************************************************************/


        /*================ MIC_SP20.0 ===============*/
        /* GPRINTF: Used like PRINTF except the output is sent to the   */
        /* screen in graphics mode at the specified co-ordinate.        */
        /*                                                              */

        int gprintf( int *xloc, int *yloc, char *fmt, ... )
        {
          va_list  argptr;                  /* Argument list pointer         */
          char str[140];                    /* Buffer to build sting into    */
          int cnt;                          /* Result of SPRINTF for return  */

          va_start( argptr, format );       /* Initialize va_ functions      */
          cnt = vsprintf( str, fmt, argptr );/* prints string to buffer */
          outtextxy( *xloc, *yloc, str );/* Send string in graphics mode */
          *yloc += textheight( "H" ) + 2;/* Advance to next line */

          va_end( argptr );                         /* Close va_ functions*/

          return( cnt );                    /* Return the conversion count*/

        }
        /*================ MIC_SP21.0 ===============*/
        #include <ctype.h>
        fgetword( Word, WordLength, fp )
           char *Word;
           int  WordLength;
           FILE *fp;

        {
           int  ch;

           if ( WordLength <= 0 )
               {
                   *Word = '\0';
                   return;
               };
           ch = *Word++ = getc( fp );
           if ( isspace( ch ) )
               while ( --WordLength > 0 )            /* skip  white space    */
                   {
                       ch = *Word++ = getc( fp );
                       if ( !isspace( ch ) )
                           {
                               ungetc( ch, fp );
                               break;
                           }
                   }
           else
               while ( --WordLength > 0 )
                   {
                       ch = *Word++ = getc( fp );
                       if ( isspace( ch ) )
                           {
                               ungetc( ch, fp );
                               break;
```

```
                        }
                }
    if ( WordLength == 0 )
        ungetc( *( Word - 1 ), fp );
    *( Word - 1 ) = '\0';
}

/*******************************************************/

/*================= MIC_SP23.0 ==============*/
/* TEXTLIB.C */
#include "text.h"
SoundSummary()
{
    int j;

        printf("\nSounds\n");
        for(j = 0; j < ph; j++)
                printf("phones %d = %s\n", j, phones[j]);
        printf("%d phones\n", ph);
        for(j = 0; j < dip; j++)
                printf("dipthongs %d = %s\n", j, dipth[j]);
        printf("%d dipthongs\n", dip);
}
/************************************************************/
WordSummary()
{
    int j;
    for(j = 0; j < wct; j++)
        printf("%s\n", words[j]);
}
/************************************************************/
MakeDrivel(fp)
    FILE *fp;
{
    int j, num, howmany, prt;

    printf("\nHow many words do you want?\t");
    howmany = getnum();
    printf("\nWrite to file? (1) = yes\t");
    prt = getnum();
        for(j = 0; j < howmany; j++)
                {
                num = irand(0, wct - 1);
                printf("%s ", words[num]);
                if((j % 6) == 5)
                    printf("\n");
                if(prt == 1)
                    {
                    fprintf(fp, "%s ", words[num]);
                    if((j % 6) == 5)
                        fprintf(fp, "\n");
                }
                }
}
/************************************************************/
MakeText(fp)
    FILE *fp;
{
    int j, num, howmany, prt;
```

```
        printf("\nHow many words do you want?\t");
        howmany = getnum();
        printf("\nWrite to file? (1) = yes\t");
        prt = getnum();

               for(j = 0; j < howmany; j++)
                       {
                       num = irand(0, ph - 1);
                       printf("%s", phones[num]);
                       if(prt == 1)
                           fprintf(fp, "%s", phones[num]);
                       num = irand(0, dip - 1);
                       printf("%s", dipth[num]);
                       if(prt == 1)
                           fprintf(fp, "%s", dipth[num]);
                       }
}
/***************************************************************/
getphone(string, position)
    char string[];
    int position;
{
    char *cstr;
    int j = 0;

        cstr = (char *) malloc(80);
        while(isvowel(string[position]) == FALSE)
                       {
                             if(!isspace(string[position]))
                 cstr[j++] = string[position++];
                             else
                                 position++;
                             if(ispunct(cstr[j]))
                               {
                               cstr[j+1] = ' ';
                               j++;
                               }
                       }
             cstr[j] = '\0';
             if(strlen(cstr) > 0)
                 phones[ph++] = cstr;          /* ph is global counter *
          return(position);
}
/***************************************************************/
getdipth(string, position)
    char string[];
    int position;
{
    char *vstr;
    int j = 0;

    vstr = (char *) malloc(80);
               while(isvowel(string[position]) == TRUE)
                       {
                             if(!isspace(string[position]))
                 vstr[j++] = string[position++];
                             else
                                 position++;
                       }
                 vstr[j] = '\0';
                   if(strlen(vstr) > 0)
```

```
                        dipth[dip++] = vstr;          /* dip is global counter
                return(position);
}
/************************************************************/
chop(string)
    char string[];
{
    int position = 0;

    while(position < strlen(string))
        {
            if(isvowel(string[position]) == FALSE)
                    position = getphonews(string, position);
            else if(isvowel(string[position])  == TRUE)
                    position = getdipthws(string, position);
            else
                position++;
        }
}
/************************************************************/
isvowel(ch)
    char ch;
{
    int j;

    for(j = 0; j < 5; j++)
        if(toupper(ch) == vowels[j])
            return(TRUE);
        return(FALSE);
}
/*************************************************************/
getdipthws(string, position)    /* keep the spaces */
    char string[];
    int position;
{
    char *vstr;
    int j = 0;

    vstr = (char *) malloc(80);
            while(isvowel(string[position]) == TRUE)
              vstr[j++] = string[position++];
              vstr[j] = '\0';
                if(strlen(vstr) > 0)
                dipth[dip++] = vstr;        /* dip is global counter */
        return(position);
}
/************************************************************/
getphonews(string, position)
    char string[];
    int position;
{
    char *cstr;
    int j = 0;

        cstr = (char *) malloc(80);
        while(isvowel(string[position]) == FALSE)
                {
            cstr[j++] = string[position++];
                    if(ispunct(cstr[j - 1]))
                        cstr[j++] = ' ';
                    }
```

Subprogram (.c) library    355

```
                cstr[j] = '\0';
                if(strlen(cstr) > 0)
                    phones[ph++] = cstr;          /* ph is global counter */
                return(position);
}
/*************************************************************/
ExtractWord(string, position)
    char string[];
    int position;

{
    int j = 0;
    char *word;

    word = (char *) malloc(80);
    while(!isspace(string[position]))
        word[j++] = string[position++];
    word[j++] = '\0';
    words[wct++] = word;
    return(position);
}
/*************************************************************/
ChopWords(string)
    char string[];

{
    int position = 0;
    while(position < strlen(string))
        {
        if(isspace(string[position]))
            position++;
          else
              position = ExtractWord(string, position);
          }

}
/*************************************************************/
/*================= MIC_SP24.0 ==============*/
/*FGETWORD.C*/
#include <ctype.h>
fgetword( Word, WordLength, fp )
    char *Word;
    int  WordLength;
    FILE *fp;


{
    int  ch;

    if ( WordLength <= 0 )
        {
        *Word = '\0';
        return;
        };
    ch = *Word++ = getc( fp );
    if ( isspace( ch ) )
        while ( --WordLength > 0 )          /* skip  white space    */
            {
                ch = *Word++ = getc( fp );
                if ( !isspace( ch ) )
                    {
                        ungetc( ch, fp );
                        break;
                    }
            }
```

```
        else
            while ( --WordLength > 0 )
                    {
                    ch = *Word++ = getc( fp );
                    if ( isspace( ch ) )
                        {
                            ungetc( ch, fp );
                            break;
                        }
                    }
        if ( WordLength == 0 )
            ungetc( *( Word - 1 ), fp );
        *( Word - 1 ) = '\0';
}
/*================ MIC_SP25.0 ==============*/
/*GETFNAM.C*/
FILE *getfnam(use,mode)
    char *use,*mode;
{
    FILE *fp,*fopen();
    char name[80],c;
    int ask;

        printf("\n\nFilename for %s ? ",use);
        scanf("%s",name);

        if (name[0] == '='){
            c = *mode;
            switch(c){
                case 'r': return (stdin);
                case 'w':
                case 'a': return (stdout);
            }
        }

        if ((fp = fopen(name,mode)) == NULL){
            printf("Error opening %s for %s.",name,use);
            printf("\nEnter 1 to try again; any other key to abort.");
            scanf("%d", &ask);
            if(ask ==   1)
                fp = getfnam(use,mode);
            else exit(0);
        }
        return (fp);
}
```

# C
# *Function prototype (.pro) files*

```
/*=================== MIC_P1 ===================*/
/* MIRROR.PRO   */

/* Source file: mirror.c */
/* function prototypes */
main(void);
PutPeform(FILE *fp, int ShapeSize,  char motname[]);
WriteComment(FILE *fp,int data[], int size, char comment[]);
loop(FILE *fp, int shape[], int ShapeSize, int num, int center,
     char motname[]);
PutChord(FILE *fp, int chord[], int ChordSize);
GetChord(int up[], int down[], int chord[], int size);
GetPatterns(int disarray[], int up[], int down[], int size);
OpenChord(FILE *fp);
EndChord(FILE *fp);
GetCenter(int up[], int down[], int center);
PutRhythm(FILE *fp, int chord[], int ChordSize);


/*=================== MIC_P2 ===================*/
/*   SETS.PRO */

/* Source file: sets.c */
/* function protypes */

GetIndex( int imsize, int size, int setsize);
GetSetSize(void);
GetImsize(void);
Order( int test[], int ordered[], int vector[], int setnumber[],
      int setsize, int k);
ShowOriginal( FILE *fp, int original[], int test[], int setsize);
GetTestSets( int test[], int pcarray[], int datarray[],
   int original[], int imarray[],int setsize, int imsize, int k);
GetSetnumber( int ordered[], int setsize);
NotSetError( FILE *fp, int setsize);
PutSetData( FILE *fp, int test[], int setsize, int ordered[],
            int setnumber, int setfq[]);
```

```
PutSetSummary( FILE *fp, int setfq[], int setsize);
PutTable( FILE *fp);
GetData( int datarray[], int setfq[], int pcarray[]);
WhichArray(void);
showdata( FILE *fp, int datarray[], int pcarray[], int size);
ShowImbricated( FILE *fp, int pcarray[],int imarray[],
                int imsize, int size);
NormalOrder( int pcarray[], int ordered[], int setsize);
endvector( int vector[], int size);
rotate( int datarray[], int disarray[], int size);
set3cmp( int test[]);
set4cmp( int test[]);
set5cmp( int test[]);
set6cmp( int test[]);
PrintSetTable( struct sets set[], int setsize);
FprintSetTable( FILE *fp, struct sets set[], int setsize);
PutSubset( int setnumber, int setsize);
FputSubset( FILE *fp, int setnumber, int setsize);
PutSetArray( int SetArray[], int setsize);
PutSetInversion( int SetInversion[], int setsize);
PutSetArrayPitches( int SetArray[], int setsize);
PutSetInversionPitches( int SetInversion[], int setsize);
FputSetArrayPitches( FILE *fp, int SetArray[], int setsize);
FputSetInversionPitches( FILE *fp, int SetInversion[],
                         int setsize);
PutSetVector( int SetVector[]);
FputSetArray( FILE *fp, int SetArray[], int setsize);
FputSetInversion( FILE *fp, int SetInversion[], int setsize);
FputSetVector( FILE *fp, int SetVector[]);
PrintSetInfo( struct sets set[], int setnumber, int setsize);
FprintSetInfo( FILE *fp, struct sets set[], int setnumber,
               int setsize);
PutContains( int setnumber, int setsize);
PutSimilar( int setnumber, int setsize);
FputContains( FILE *fp, int setnumber, int setsize);
FputSimilar( FILE *fp, int setnumber, int setsize);

/*================= MIC_P3 =================*/
/* FILENAME: ARRAY.PRO
        purpose: function protypes
*/
invshape(int shape[], int inv[], int size);
getshape(int datarray[], int shapearray[], int size);
FputArray(FILE *fp, int datarray[], int size);
PutArray(int datarray[], int size);
PutLn();
FputLn(FILE *fp);
RetroArray(int datarray[],int size);
getmax(int datarray[],int size);
getmin(int datarray[], int size);
float getmaxf(float datarray[],int size);
float getminf(float datarray[], int size);
FrotateArray(FILE *fp, int size, int datarray[]);
RotateArray(int datarray[], int disarray[], int size,
            int rotation);
imbricate(int darray[], int imarray[], int start, int imsize,
          int imbeg);
sumarray(int arry[], int size);
```

```
/*================== MIC_P4 ==================*/
/* FILENAME: POEM.PRO */
/* Source file: poem.c */
/* function prototypes */
int GetVocab(void);
void MakePoem(void);
void VocabSummary(void);
main(void);
GetVocab(FILE *fp,char *part[]);
assign(FILE *fp, char *part[],int position);
void VocabSummary(void);
void MakePoem(FILE *fp);
SelectWord(FILE *fp,char *part[], int ct, int flag);


/*================== MIC_P5 ==================*/
/*FILENAME PHONE.PRO*/
/* Source file: phone.c */
/* function prototypes */
SoundSummary(void);
WordSummary(void);
MakeDrivel(FILE *fp);
MakeText(FILE *fp);
getphone(char string[], int position);
getdipth(char string[],int position);
chop(char string[]);
isvowel(char ch);
getdipthws(char string[], int position);
getphonews(char string[], int position);
ExtractWord(char string[], int position);
ChopWords(char string[]);


/*================== MIC_P8 ==================*/
/*FILENAME MIRROR.PRO*/
/* Source file: mirror.c */
/* function prototypes */
main(void);
PutPeform(FILE *fp, int ShapeSize,  char motname[]);
WriteComment(FILE *fp,int data[], int size, char comment[]);
loop(FILE *fp, int shape[], int ShapeSize, int num, int center,
     char motname[]);
PutChord(FILE *fp, int chord[], int ChordSize);
GetChord(int up[], int down[], int chord[], int size);
GetPatterns(int disarray[], int up[], int down[], int size);
OpenChord(FILE *fp);
EndChord(FILE *fp);
GetCenter(int up[], int down[], int center);
PutRhythm(FILE *fp, int chord[], int ChordSize);

/*================== MIC_P9 ==================*/
/*FILENAME MATRIX.PRO*/
/* file: matrix.pro */
/* function prototypes */
PutMatrixFq(int matrix[][2], int fq[], int rsize, int csize);
FputMatrixFq(FILE *fp, int matrix[][2], int fq[], int rsize,
             int csize);
FindMatrixFreq(int matrix[][2], int fq[], int size);
MatrixSort(int matrix[][2], int rsize,int csize);
```

```
MatrixQuickSort(int matrix[][2], int rsize, int csize);
PutMatrix(int matrix[][2], int nrow, int ncol);
FputMatrix(FILE *fp, int matrix[][2], int nrow, int ncol);
ZeroMatrix(int matrix[], int rowsize, int colsize);


/*================== MIC_P12 ==================*/
/* FILENAME CONSTEL.PRO */
/* Source file: constel.c */
/* function prototypes */
main(void);
con(void);
FindFreq(struct pitchrec pit[], int size);
GetPitchStats(FILE *outputfile, int statarray[], int size);
FusionMain(void);
PutFusPitch(FILE *fp, int fusarray[][2], int size);


/*================== MIC_P13 ==================*/
/* FILENAME FUSARRAY.PRO */
/* Source file: fusarray.c */
/* function prototypes */
FusePair(FILE *fp, int dat[], int fusarray[][2], int size);
fusion(int dat[], int fusarray[][2], int size, int limit);
fusion2(int dat[], int fusarray[][2], int size);
fusion3(int dat[], int fusarray[][2], int size);
summation(int darray[],int start, int num);
negsum(int darray[], int start, int num);

/*================== MIC_P14 ==================*/

/* FILENAME SCRPTPRS.PRO */
/* function prototypes */
GetLines(FILE *fp);
PutData(void);
getlnhead(char line[], int lnsize);
SkipComment(char *line, int offset, int lnsize);
getparray(char line[], int lnsize, int datarray[], int xsize);
getnarray(char *line, int lnsize, int datarray[], int xsize);


/*================== MIC_P15 ==================*/
/*FILENAME SETS.PRO */
/* source file sets.c */

GetIndex( int imsize, int size, int setsize);
GetSetSize(void);
GetImsize(void);
Order( int test[], int ordered[], int vector[], int setnumber[],
       int setsize, int k);
ShowOriginal( FILE *fp, int original[], int test[], int setsize);
GetTestSets( int test[], int pcarray[], int datarray[],
    int original[], int imarray[],int setsize, int imsize, int k);
GetSetnumber( int ordered[], int setsize);
NotSetError( FILE *fp, int setsize);
PutSetData( FILE *fp, int test[], int setsize, int ordered[],
            int setnumber, int setfq[]);
PutSetSummary( FILE *fp, int setfq[], int setsize);
PutTable( FILE *fp);
GetData( int datarray[], int setfq[], int pcarray[]);
WhichArray(void);
showdata( FILE *fp, int datarray[], int pcarray[], int size);
```

```
ShowImbricated( FILE *fp,int pcarray[],int imarray[], int imsize,
                int size);
NormalOrder( int pcarray[], int ordered[], int setsize);
endvector( int vector[], int size);
rotate( int datarray[], int disarray[], int size);
set3cmp( int test[]);
set4cmp( int test[]);
set5cmp( int test[]);
set6cmp( int test[]);
PrintSetTable( struct sets set[], int setsize);
FprintSetTable( FILE *fp, struct sets set[], int setsize);
PutSubset( int setnumber, int setsize);
FputSubset( FILE *fp, int setnumber, int setsize);
PutSetArray( int SetArray[], int setsize);
PutSetInversion( int SetInversion[], int setsize);
PutSetArrayPitches( int SetArray[], int setsize);
PutSetInversionPitches( int SetInversion[], int setsize);
FputSetArrayPitches( FILE *fp, int SetArray[], int setsize);
FputSetInversionPitches( FILE *fp, int SetInversion[], int setsize);
PutSetVector( int SetVector[]);
FputSetArray( FILE *fp, int SetArray[], int setsize);
FputSetInversion( FILE *fp, int SetInversion[], int setsize);
FputSetVector( FILE *fp, int SetVector[]);
PrintSetInfo( struct sets set[], int setnumber, int setsize);
FprintSetInfo( FILE *fp, struct sets set[], int setnumber,
                int setsize);
PutContains( int setnumber, int setsize);
PutSimilar( int setnumber, int setsize);
FputContains( FILE *fp, int setnumber, int setsize);
FputSimilar( FILE *fp, int setnumber, int setsize);
/*==============================================*/
```

# Index

dhop( ), 355
digital sampling, 9
discrete random variables, 177
displace( ), xx, 83-85, 95, 218, 221
displace.c, 83-85
double precision floating point, xv
drivel.c, xxiv, 233, 254-257
durred( ), xix, 46-48, 295, 365

**E**

ecological acoustics, 3, 7
encoding data, computer music, 14-17
EndChord( ), 136-143
EndMot( ), 136-143
Endvector( ), 152
enumerated data type, xv
environments, xii
escape characters, ANSI screen, 337-339
esthetics, 7
eucreduc( ), xix, 48-49, 365
Eulerian Beta Distribution, xxii
event vectors, 15, 26
    extraction function, 38-40
    storage function, 38-40
expansion, intervallic, 86-88
expcurve( ), 41-43
expert systems, 2, 5, 11
expon( ), xxii, 186-187
exponential probability distributions, 186-187, 200
ExtractWords( ), 239-242, 254-257, 356

**F**

fgetline( ), 350
Fgetline.c, 350-351
fgetword( ), 352, 356
fgetword.c, 356-357
Fibonacci series, 129
filename, obtain from console, 331-332
filtering, 177
Finale, 31
FindFreq( ), 167-176
FindMatrixFreq( ), 342
FindMode( ), 346
float getmaxf( ), 329
float getminf( ), 329
floating point, xv
For statement, xvi
formative music notation representation, 12
fpower( ), xii, 33-35, 202-203
FprintSetInfo( ), 159
FprintSetTable( ), 154
FputArray( ), 327

FputContains( ), 161
FputLn( ), 328
FputMatrix( ), 344
FputMatrixFq( ), 342
FputPitch( ), 336
FputSetArray( ), 158
FputSetArrayPitches( ), 158
FputSetInversion( ), 158
FputSetInversionPitches( ), 158
FputSetVector( ), 159
FputSimilar( ), 162
FputSubset( ), 156
fracdec( ), xix, 56-57
fractab( ), xix, 44-45, 50, 365
fractals, 279-281
fractsum.c, xix, 44, 50-52, 365
freqtab2( ), 129-132
freqtabl( ), 70-72, 271
FrotateArray( ), 329
FscriptArray( ), 337
function calls, xiii-xiv
function declaration, xiii
function prototypes, 359-363
functions, xii-xiii, xvii
Fusarray.c, 339-341
fusarray.pro, 362
FusePair( ), 339
fusion( ), 340
fusion2( ), 340
fusion3( ), 341
FusionMain( ), 167-176
future research and development, 8-9

**G**

gamma probability distributions, 188-189
gamma( ), xxii, 188-189
gamuts/chords, variable-density, 288-290
gauss( ), xxii, 190-191
Gaussian distributions, 179-181, 184, 188, 190-191
general systems theory, 3
getarray( ), 243-253
GetCenter( ), 136-143
GetChord( ), 136-143
GetData( ), 149
getdipth( ), 354
getdipthws( ), 239-242, 355
getfnam( ), 331, 357
getfnam.c, 137
getImsize( ), 146
getIndex( ), 145
GetLines( ), 347
getInhead( ), 348
getmax( ), 329
getmin( ), 329
getnarray( ), 350

getnum( ), 339
getparray( ), 349
getpart.c, 137
GetPatterns( ), 136-143
getphone( ), 354
getphonews( ), 239-242, 355
GetPitchStats( ), 167-176
GetSetnumber( ), 146
getSetSize( ), 145
getshape( ), 327
getstring( ), 243-253
GetTestSets( ), 146
gettrans( ), 243-253
GetVocab( ), 234-238
getvt( ), 339
get_num( ), 347
Good Sound Foundation, 6
gprintf( ), 352
grammatical music notation representation, 11-12
greatestCommonDivisor( ), 110-113

**H**

hardware, 18-21
harmony, 8
hasvowel( ), 243-253
header files, 137, 325-326
Hiller, Lejaren A., 4
histograms, 178
hypcos( ), xxii, 192-193
hyperbolic cosine probability distributions, 192-193

**I**

imbricate( ), 330
include filename, 136-137
information theory, 3, 7
information transmission, 21-25
inputyou.c, 137, 144
InputYourOwn( ), 330
insertion sorting and searching, 218-220
insertst( ), xxiii, 218-221
integers, xv-xvi
IntegerToPitch( ), 315-320, 333, 335
interlocking voice ranges, 303-307
intermedia explorations, 3
interpolation search, 230
intgam( ), xxv, 288-290, 303
intlink( ), 123-125
intlink.c, xxi, 123-125
inverse( ), 73-78
inversion, intervallic, 79-82
inversion tone rows, 95-97
InvertShape( ), 136-143
invshape( ), 327
irand( ), 351
isvowel( ), 239-242, 355

# Computer Music In C

If you are intrigued with the possibilities of the programs included in *Computer Music in C* (TAB Book No. 3637), you should definitely consider having the ready-to-compile disk containing the examples. These files are guaranteed free of manufacturer's defects. (If you have any problems, return the disk within 30 days, and we'll send you a new one.) Not only will you save the time and effort of typing the data, but also the disk eliminates the possibility of errors in the data. Interested?

Available on either 5¼″ or 3½″ disk requiring Turbo C and 512K at $24.95, plus $2.50 shipping and handling.

YES, I'm interested. Please send me:

_____ copies 5¼″ disk for Turbo C (#6755S), $24.95 each . . . . . . . . . . . . . . . . . $ _____

_____ copies 3½″ disk for Turbo C (#6756S), $24.95 each . . . . . . . . . . . . . . . . . $ _____

_____ TAB BOOKS catalog (free with purchase; otherwise send $1.00
in check or money order and receive coupon worth $1.00 off your next
purchase) . . . . . . . . . . . . . . . . . . . . . . . . . . . . . . . . . . . . . . . . . . . . $ _____

Shipping & Handling: $2.50 per disk in U.S.
($5.00 per disk outside U.S.) $ _____

Please add applicable state and local sales tax. $ _____

TOTAL $ _____

☐ Check or money order enclosed made payable to TAB BOOKS

Charge my ☐ VISA ☐ MasterCard ☐ American Express

Acct No. _____ Exp. Date _____

Signature _____

Name _____

Address _____

City _____ State _____ Zip _____

**TOLL-FREE ORDERING: 1-800-822-8158**
(in PA, AK, and Canada call 1-717-794-2191)
or write to TAB BOOKS, Blue Ridge Summit, PA 17294-0840

Prices subject to change. Orders outside the U.S. must be paid in international money order in U.S. dollars.